Corporate Power, Oligopolies, and the Crisis of the State

Corporate Power, Oligopolies, and the Crisis of the State

LUIS SUAREZ-VILLA

Published by State University of New York Press, Albany

For information, contact State University of New York Press, Albany, NY
www.sunypress.edu

Production, Ryan Morris
Marketing, Michael Campochiaro

Library of Congress Cataloging-in-Publication Data

Suarez-Villa, Luis.
   Corporate power, oligopolies, and the crisis of the state / Luis Suarez-Villa.
      pages cm
   Includes bibliographical references and index.
   ISBN 978-1-4384-5485-6 (hc : alk. paper)—978-1-4384-5486-3 (pb : alk. paper)
   ISBN 978-1-4384-5487-0 (ebook)
   1. Corporate governance.   2. Oligopolies.   3. State, The.   I. Title.

   HD2741.S843 2015
   306.3—dc23   2014008966

10 9 8 7 6 5 4 3 2 1

Contents

Introduction

Five hundred years from now, our society may likely be seen as one where corporate behemoths became the most powerful entities. Politically, economically, culturally, and in almost every aspect of daily life, large corporations have gained immense influence over us. Before the cradle and even after the grave, and for almost everything in between, we depend on corporations as never before. How we are governed, what we consume, how we care for our health, our nutrition, what we know or believe, how we manage our finances, how we communicate or transport ourselves, and how we deal with each other and with nature, are now subject to the priorities and interests of large corporations.

At the same time, the state seems more incapable of providing fair governance and justice, securing the public's well-being, and managing its fiscal resources. The welfare of future generations seems seriously compromised, for the short-term benefit of a very small but also very powerful segment of society. Massive bailouts for the most powerful corporations, along with tax breaks and loopholes, guarantees, subsidies, giveaways, and numerous forms of corporate welfare, drain the state's coffers while some of the most fundamental needs of the population are ignored. At the same time, the vast accumulation of debt incurred by the state to pay for corporate well-being seems unsustainable, and is likely setting the stage for major future crises. Credit downgrades promise greater fiscal stress over the long term, and will likely require substantial cuts in services and benefits for the vast majority of the population. Meanwhile, a lack of public trust in the state has become a hallmark of our time, as inequalities and social injustice deepen while corporate wealth sets historical records.

Critical discourse on this difficult reality remains muted. Voices of dissent are few, and all too often fail to take into account the larger panorama of social distress. The real causes of distress also seem impossible, or at least very difficult, to grasp by the vast majority of the public. Many people's identification with

1

the interests of corporations seems unwavering, even when it damages their own individual or family well-being. Censorship—self-imposed or tacitly induced by circumstance and vested interests—has become part of our reality, as incisive critiques garner indifference or a deaf reception, even by those most negatively affected by the status quo. The educational system seems incapable of addressing the long-term problems facing us, as conformity or expediency trump critical depth and action. Academia and academics, meanwhile, have joined the status quo, with apologies—if not support—becoming the accepted attitude among those who set agendas.

American business schools and economics departments have become inspirational beacons for expanding corporate control, while critical perspectives on corporate power are tacitly censored. Critical views on corporate capitalism today seem as far removed from business and economics curricula as bald eagles are from deep ocean life. Tacit discrimination against those who raise critical or radical arguments on corporate power is all too customary, as higher education becomes another target for corporate control. Such discrimination has now penetrated most fields in the social sciences, turning them into apologists for the status quo—aided by reductionist approaches that prevent consideration of the larger social panorama. Perhaps this can explain why academic publishing on corporations seems almost exclusively targeted at making corporate power stronger, more efficient, or more exploitive. The vast number of how-to books published every year with these objectives—and publishers' unwillingness to fit critical work on corporate capitalism in their programs—is testimony of how much academia has become subservient to the corporate domain.

The media, for their part, now largely owned—or controlled—by corporate power have increasingly turned away from critical perspectives, becoming cheerleaders of corporate hegemony—and of almost any action that leads to greater corporate "competitiveness," no matter the cost. Voices critical of corporate power are all too frequently branded as enemies of "freedom" and of "free" markets, when in fact what is at stake is not freedom but rather the expanding social, political, and economic control by a privileged few over the rest of society—along with deepening social injustice, greater inequality, and the destruction of fair governance. Trivia and disguised pro-corporate propaganda rule the established channels of news and information, while the most egregious social injustices of our time go unnoticed. Reporting on corporate crimes and abuses, in particular, revolves around technicalities and minutia and seldom takes into account the broader panorama of corporate hegemony over society—or the corruption of the political system that it entails.

Politicians have largely become servants of corporate power—most of all, the oligopolies—while politics has turned into a game targeting money. Almost any political candidate can be made to seem appropriate, if large amounts of corporate money are available to fuel propaganda spins and image engineering. Politicians exclude the public from democratic decision making, as they conduct their dealings behind closed doors—all too often on the basis of their own personal interest and that of their corporate patrons. The lack of any national political referenda on the most important issues of our time—such as corporate power and corruption, bailouts, inequality, taxes, wars—attests to the lack of democratic consultation in our governance. Politicians thus disrespect us and our rights, and then tax us to pay for the abuses and crimes of corporate power. Think tanks funded by vast amounts of corporate money "orient" politicians on the "right" policies to pursue—which are typically those favored by corporate interests—their views enjoying wide diffusion in the corporate-owned media that now control almost every bit of information we receive, directly or indirectly.

How successful the tacit censorship of critical perspectives has been can be seen in the dearth of awareness among the public. Showered with corporate propaganda and advertising, exhorted to consume more and incur greater debt, mined for personal data, and prompted to elect politicians who either perpetuate the status quo or expand corporate power, the public seems to have lost sight of its own interest. Many therefore identify themselves with corporate power, especially the oligopolies, even when doing so counters their own welfare. Many vote for politicians with agendas that harm their interest as a class, or individually as members of society. Among those who object to our current reality there seems to be a general lack of understanding of the larger social panorama, and of the overwhelming influence of corporate power in it—most of all, the oligopolies. Apathy or resignation—or despair—seem to pervade the attitudes of many among the young, with abuse (of self or others) becoming a frequent outlet. Antisocial attitudes, existential emptiness and fragility, and destructive behavior seem to characterize the lives of much of the population. These features, coupled with the individual treadmill of economic insecurity, underemployment, stagnant wages, debt, and downward mobility, seem to make everyone too busy to understand the larger panorama of distress.

Meanwhile, Wall Street finance has turned almost every aspect of life and nature with a probabilistic dimension into a betting proposition. A casino culture has emerged, with paper profits taking a primordial place in the minds and motivation of many—a social phenomenon that reflects how deeply finance has been severed from production. A few financial oligopolies now control the vast majority of transactions—directly or indirectly—generating immense wealth, power, and political influence for the very small elite associated with them. So large and important have the financial oligopolies become that they pose a "systemic risk" to the entire American economy, and also the world's, when some of their bets go wrong. Their sheer size, market power, and links around the globe required bailouts of unprecedented magnitude by the state in the most recent crisis—an egregious instance of corporate welfare that will likely be repeated. A state subservient to the financial oligopolies means that, following the bailouts, the political will was absent to pursue little more than cosmetic measures— intended primarily to refloat the status quo—likely guaranteeing that the next crisis may be worse than the last one.

The disengagement of finance from production has helped increase the frequency of financial crises in recent decades. This phenomenon has been accompanied by a split of reproduction from commodification within production—largely due to the overwhelming importance of intangibles in both manufacturing and services production. Evidence of this second disengagement is all around, in the importance of societal networks for intangibles—networks that are external to, and largely out of the control of, the corporate domain. Although new technology sectors are most impacted, this phenomenon now affects practically all industrial and service sectors. The split of reproduction from commodification has thus complicated production greatly in the context of advanced capitalism—making the casino culture more appealing, and contributing further to the disengagement of finance from production. These two disengagements—within processes fundamental to capitalism—augur more crises as the twenty-first century advances, with negative consequences for the vast majority of the population. The two disengagements have oligopolistic corporate power at their core—in finance and in the rest of the economy—and are likely to make the state's dysfunction more visible, if not also more intractable.

The hegemony of oligopolistic corporate power in our society is largely responsible for another phenomenon—one that is typically ignored by mainstream economists and policymakers. This is long-term stagnation, defined as slow growth, due to the overaccumulation of capital—a problem created by excessive oligopolistic power and control. Such control goes beyond tacit price fixing, and involves fencing in entire sectors by establishing entry barriers, acquiring new or potential competitors, merging with other oligopolies and large companies, or imposing standards that keep potential entrants out. As a result, oligopolistic profits set historical records and vast amounts of capital accumulate that find limited investment possibilities. High monetary liquidity by central banks, most of all the Federal Reserve, has also compounded the overaccumulation dynamic. Thus, capital overaccumulation has become endemic to advanced capitalism. The result is long-term stagnation, involving very slow growth that fosters long-term underemployment and limits aggregate demand. This problem affects consumers greatly over the long term, reducing or limiting the purchasing power of the vast majority of the population—while pricing becomes ever more subject to oligopolistic control.

Associated with the oligopolies and their hegemony is the emergence of an extremely wealthy and politically powerful elite. This privileged, very small, but very powerful elite can be considered a new form of oligarchy, given its reach into almost every aspect of society and its vast influence over politics and the state. Unlike the conventional oligarchies, however, it is fragmented, dynamic, and often exhibits contradictory interests within its ranks. It also tends to be rootless, multifaceted, and difficult to define. By far the richest element within this privileged group derives its wealth and power from Wall Street and the financial oligopolies. Some of the more powerful members of the new oligarchy also derive their wealth from the technology oligopolies that emerged in recent decades. Whether in finance, technology, or any other sector, they exercise their influence over politics and the state through immense amounts of money contributed to political organizations, campaigns, and the lobbying apparatus. It is therefore almost impossible today for any politician to be elected to major office without their money and support—campaign rhetoric and propaganda spins notwithstanding.

This book seeks to raise our awareness of oligopolistic corporate power and the fundamental role it plays in the crisis of the state in contemporary advanced capitalism. Its systemic outlook—and the vast number of examples and references—provide a broad, multidisciplinary perspective on what is possibly the most difficult social phenomenon of our time. A phenomenon that is bound to affect the trajectory of entire societies over the twenty-first century, and that raises serious questions about the legitimacy of the state. A phenomenon that negates core notions of fairness, as safeguarding the interests of a privileged few becomes the main priority of the state. *It is a central premise of this book that any consideration of this phenomenon must take into account the need for social justice and fairness as a fundamental objective of public governance.* That premise must serve as a guiding principle if the state is to serve the interests of the people. To the extent that corporate power and its influence over the state negate this premise, governance becomes dysfunctional and illegitimate.

Today, the United States provides the prime example of oligopolistic hegemony over society. Nonetheless, the discussions in this book also apply in varying degrees to the case of other advanced capitalist nations. Western Europe and Japan have long been participants in the trajectory toward oligopolistic hegemony. Within specific nations in Western Europe, oligopolistic power is already very important and seems likely to strengthen, as internal and cross-border consolidations increase. National governments, meanwhile, seem incapable of stopping this trend—as the international rules of trade and state intervention are rewritten to favor oligopolistic expansion. The projection of oligopolistic power over the entire planet already seems attainable within a relatively short time, as almost every nation finds itself enlisted to support oligopolistic priorities in one way or another. The contents of this book may serve as a warning to less developed countries, for which the situation in advanced capitalist nations is often presented as a model of what they should become—or, alternatively, the nations they should become more dependent on—if they are to advance their well-being. Needless to say, the model of "development" presented to the less developed countries is one fundamentally ruled by oligopolistic corporations—all of which tend to be based in advanced capitalist nations.

The elaboration of this book faced considerable difficulties since its beginnings. Among them was the hostility of fellow academics and their unwillingness to acknowledge a phenomenon that is all around—and that manifests itself through numerous social pathologies in our daily existence. Veiled forms of prejudice and thinly disguised personal attacks also became evident at times, with ideological and in some cases also ethnic undertones, as the contents of this work made it clear that an apologetic perspective was not part of its agenda. It may be difficult for those not in academia today to understand how difficult exposing social injustice has become, in an environment where many administrators and faculty have embraced corporate values as their own. Through the attitudes and behavior of such individuals, it became obvious that works that adopt the kind of critical perspective this book provides can only deserve indifference, at best, but more commonly disdain and rejection. So much have corporate values and practices been taken to heart (and minds) in American academia, that any critical contradiction of those cherished values evokes much the same attitude one could expect from corporate executives. The latter, knowing all too well what they do, are in fact often more candid and forthcoming than their academic counterparts.

Most sincerely, this book is dedicated to all authors who have faced similar difficulties in their work, for exposing injustice and for refusing to become apologists for the status quo. Few people seem to understand the high personal cost of rejection and intellectual discrimination that we must endure from those who support or take up apologetic positions toward the status quo. Many have lost their careers or been crippled financially and intellectually by such discrimination. Many more stand to be crippled, unless this form of injustice is exposed and made known to all who care to listen, or who can maintain an open mind in the midst of the confusion that characterizes our time. To my spouse, I owe special gratitude for her support and patience, especially during times when it seemed nearly impossible to continue or make any progress. Her advice and fortitude, despite her longstanding illness and its effects on her well-being, deserve to be noted here. She, more than anyone else, knows the tribulations that writing this work entailed and the kind of discouragement that had to be overcome to complete it.

Many scholars have contributed insights over the years, and as the contents of this book developed. They are far too numerous to name here, but they all know that I remain deeply grateful for their time and consideration. To Dr. Michael Rinella, my editor at the State University of New York Press, I owe special gratitude for his efforts to have this work reviewed fairly and constructively, for his understanding of what I tried to accomplish, and for his counsel to improve it. To the anonymous reviewers of this work I must express my deep appreciation for their toil in reading and criticizing its contents. This book has benefited substantially from their views, and I wholeheartedly sought to address their concerns in the revisions. The efforts of the editorial and production staff at the State University of New York Press, and especially Senior Production Editor Ryan Morris, are also much appreciated. I am very grateful for their consideration and their dedication to the details of publishing and production. To all the readers of this work, I hope that its contents can help make all of us better and wiser human beings as we face the challenges of our time.

Oligopolies

The crisis of the state is a product of the overwhelming power of corporate interests over governance and society—a condition that will be referred to as *corporatocracy* in this book. Corporatocracy therefore involves public governance that serves corporate interests first and foremost, above those of the public and of society at large.[1] Corporate interests that have much influence over the kind of government we have, and over decisions that affect our well-being, how we live and work, how we manage our existence, what we know or believe, and how we deal with each other and with nature. But, how did those corporate interests obtain so much power? The answer to this question is all around us, if we care to look, in the form of *oligopolies*.[2]

Corporatocracy is as important to oligopolies as water is to marine life—one cannot exist without the other. Through their oligopolistic

---

1. The earliest formulation of the general condition encompassed by the term *corporatocracy* can be traced to political economist Rudolf Hilferding's *Finance Capital: A Study of the Latest Phase of Capitalist Development* (London: Routledge and Kegan Paul, 1981), translated from his *Das Finanzkapital: eine Studie über die jüngste Entwicklung des Kapitalismus* (Vienna: Brand, 1910). Although Hilferding did not use the term *corporatocracy* (literally), his analyses of capitalism revealed how the early consolidation of industrial, mercantile, and financial capital searched for—and tried to structure—a state subservient to their interests. Other political economists, writing after Hilferding's time, also referred to this general condition without using the term in their work; see, for example, James O'Connor, *The Corporations and the State: Essays in the Theory of Capitalism and Imperialism* (New York: Harper and Row, 1974). John Perkins, in his *Confessions of an Economic Hit Man* (San Francisco: Berrett-Koehler, 2004), provided a personal account of his experiences as an international consultant working for the U.S. government, and used the term *corporatocracy* to refer to the combination of multinational corporate interests and financial institutions that collude to manipulate, corrupt, and influence governments around the world.

2. The term *corporation* (or *corporate*) will be used to refer to profit-seeking entities that have rights and liabilities that are legally differentiated from those of owners, shareholders, and employees—for practical purposes, the terms corporation, corporate, company, and firm (including partnerships) will be considered synonymous. An *oligopolistic corporation* is defined

9

control over key sectors of the economy, corporate interests have amassed the immense power they exercise, collectively, over public governance and society. The word *oligopoly* has, however, become insignificant in mainstream political and economic discourse. Thus, the relations of power that oligopolies represent are largely ignored by the public today—lost in an avalanche of reports that are largely pro-corporate, and that view corporate interests as beneficial to most everyone. Neoliberal arguments favoring the predominance of markets above everything are also part of this propaganda and, together with pro-corporate publicity, have practically taken over contemporary public discourse. Lost in this avalanche of propaganda is the fact that those markets that neoliberal ideologues have fervently advocated for are mostly dominated by corporate oligopolies. *Oligopolies that wield immense power over most everything we do, in most sectors of the economy, and that influence most every aspect of public governance.*

---

in this book as a company (or the subsidiary of a company) that can control or manipulate pricing in any given sector or market niche. Control over pricing can be a product of tacit collusion and a range of strategies that may involve follow-the-leader price setting, product differentiation, market entry barriers, controlled obsolescence, or the imposition of technical standards that lock in a given sector or market niche, for example. While in case studies of a specific sector or market niche the setting of a rigid benchmark for oligopolistic influence might be warranted, the broad scope of this book makes it unwise to specify such a threshold. Oligopolistic control can vary greatly between sectors or market niches. In semiconductor equipment manufacturing, for example, the five most important global corporations had slightly more than 52 percent of market share (measured by value of sales) in 2012. Two of the five corporations had market shares of 6 and 7 percent—a relatively low level—yet both (along with the other three) engaged in what can be considered oligopolistic practices. A merger of the two largest corporations in this sector in 2013 provided the merged entity with control of slightly over 25 percent of the market—not a substantial proportion but nonetheless significant enough to provide oligopolistic power in terms of pricing and other aspects; see Don Clark, Daisuke Wakabayashi, and Kana Inagaki, "Merger Makes a Chip Giant," *Wall Street Journal*, September 25, 2013, B1 (based on data from Gartner Research); "Semiconductor Equipment: Applied Economics," *The Economist*, September 28, 2013, 62. In another sector, toilet equipment manufacturing, the four most important corporations in the United States controlled 59 percent of the market (measured by share of revenues) in 2012. One of the four corporations accounted for only 8 percent, but it can nonetheless be considered part of the oligopolistic group that dominates this sector because of its pricing practices and other market features; see James R. Hagerty, "America's Toilet Turnaround," *Wall Street Journal*, September 25, 2013, B1 (based partly on data from The Freedonia Group). The definition of the oligopolistic corporation used in this book is flexible enough to accommodate the evolution of corporate forms and entities, such as the emergence of the master limited partnership (MLP)—also known as "distorporation"; see, for example, "The New American Capitalism: Rise of the Distorporation," *The Economist*, October 26, 2013, 29–31.

This chapter will provide a broad overview of the power of oligopolistic corporations in contemporary American society—a phenomenon that will likely become one of the most important features of the twenty-first century. Numerous examples of sectors and market niches that are largely under oligopolistic control will be considered, along with their effects on public governance and societal well-being. The most important political vehicles of oligopolistic influence, the factors behind oligopoly formation and sustenance, and the conceptual premises that have shaped policymaking will also be addressed.

Evidence on the rising power of oligopolistic corporations is everywhere around us. Since the early 1980s, a rising concentration of power in the hands of a few corporations became a reality in most sectors of the American economy—a phenomenon that spread to almost every rich nation and many developing nations around the world. Sectors that were previously competitive were taken over by oligopolistic corporate behemoths. Mergers, acquisitions, and takeovers, fueled by deregulation and the growing importance of finance capital, generated an unprecedented consolidation of corporate firms in most every economic sector. Despite the predominance of neoliberal policies, and the fact that neoliberal ideologues typically assumed that deregulation would lead to greater competition, the opposite actually occurred.

In retail commerce, for example, concentration in the four largest American corporations engaged in computer-related sales increased from barely 26 percent in 1992, to almost 75 percent by 2007.[3] In the case of general merchandise stores, concentration increased from less than 50 percent to over 73 percent during the same period. In retail banking, waves of mergers and acquisitions made possible by financial deregulation reduced the number of very large American retail banks from twenty to four between 1982 and 2009.[4] Concentration also occurred in investment banking, with

---

3. Measured as percentage of total sales, based on data provided by the U.S. Bureau of the Census, *Economic Census* for 1992 and 2007 (Washington, DC: U.S. Department of Commerce, 1994, 2009). See also John Bellamy Foster, Robert W. McChesney, and R. Jamil Jonna, "Monopoly and Competition in Twenty-First Century Capitalism," *Monthly Review* (April 2011): 1–39.

4. Consolidation increased after 2009, due to the failure of many small and medium-size banks. As of June 2013, the number of banks had sunk to the lowest level since the Great Depression; see Ryan Tracy, "Tally of US Banks Sinks to Record Low," *Wall Street Journal*, December 3, 2013, A1. The consolidation of retail banking was a major aspect of a phenomenon that has been defined as *financialization* in the literature; see, for example, John Bellamy Foster and Harry Magdoff, *The Great Financial Crisis* (New York: Monthly Review Press, 2008); Randy Martin, *The Financialization of Daily Life* (Philadelphia: Temple University Press, 2002).

a handful of Wall Street behemoths controlling most transactions directly or indirectly. In 1995, for example, the total assets of the six largest bank holding corporations in the United States amounted to 17 percent of gross domestic product (GDP). By the end of 2006, they were at 55 percent, and by 2010—well into the deepest crisis since the Great Depression—they were at 64 percent of GDP.[5] Compounding this level of concentration is the fact that the largest banks—all of them oligopolists—now overwhelmingly control the full range of banking services—retail, commercial, investment, insurance underwriting, and derivatives financing. According to the U.S. Comptroller of the Currency, for example, the five largest banks together control 96 percent of all outstanding derivatives in the United States.[6] Worldwide, concentration in the banking sector is also overwhelming—the ten largest megabanks in the planet control 70 percent of all assets, an unprecedented level. Government bailouts of these corporate behemoths around the world were estimated to cost about $17 trillion between 2008 and 2010 alone, adding up to a magnitude of corporate welfare that had no precedent in financial history.

Oligopoly power has reached education, a sector that is fundamentally important for society and human well-being. Online education—in some ways a continuation of the massification of higher education that started in the late 1940s with the creation of large public university systems—has been taken over by for-profit corporate behemoths. Six for-profit corporations— Apollo, Education Management, DeVry, Career Education, Kaplan Higher Education, and ITT Educational Services—have more than a million students (or "customers") in the United States alone.[7] These corporations

---

5. On October 13, 2008—with the financial system on the verge of collapse—the combined assets of the nine most important financial corporations (JP Morgan Chase, Bank of America, Citigroup, Wells Fargo, Goldman Sachs, Morgan Stanley, Merrill Lynch, Bank of New York, State Street) accounted for 70 per cent ($9 trillion) of total assets in the U.S. financial system, according to the then chairperson of the Federal Deposit Insurance Corp. See Sheila Bair, *Bull by the Horns: Fighting to Save Main Street From Wall Street and Wall Street From Itself* (New York: Free Press, 2012).

6. U.S. Comptroller of the Currency, Administrator of National Banks, *OCC's Quarterly Report on Bank Trading and Derivatives Activity,* http://www.occ.treas.gov/topics/capital-markets/financial-markets/trading/derivatives/dq111.pdf (accessed April 28, 2012); Tyler Durden, "Five Banks Account for 96% of the $250 Trillion in Outstanding US Derivative Exposure; Is Morgan Stanley Sitting on an FX Derivative Time Bomb?" *Zero Hedge,* September 24, 2011, http://www.zerohedge.com/news/.

7. U.S. Senate Committee on Health, Education, Labor, and Pension (HELP), *Emerging Risk: An Overview of Growth, Spending, Student Debt, and Unanswered Questions in For-Profit Higher Education,* June 24, 2010; http://help.senate.gov (accessed May 13, 2011). See also Tom Harkin, "The For-Profit College Bubble," *Los Angeles Times,* July 13, 2010, A13.

operate mostly online, but some also have on-campus degree programs—one of them, Kaplan, for example, has seventy-five "campuses" in addition to its vast array of online programs.[8] These for-profit corporations now enroll the majority of students seeking an online diploma. Federal funds—in the form of government-guaranteed student loans—account for almost all of their revenue, in what amounts to a new type of taxpayer-supported corporate welfare.[9]

American taxpayers are, of course, responsible for all unpaid student loans. Defaults in the for-profit educational corporate sector have been as high as two-thirds of all loans issued, an unprecedented rate for any government-guaranteed loan program. Potentially, students enrolled in degree programs run by these for-profit corporations could default on as much as $275 billion of government-guaranteed loans. This form of corporate welfare generates hundreds of millions of dollars in average annual profits for the online diploma corporations.[10] One of the largest corporations in this sector was estimated to have a 40 percent profit margin, larger than that of most Fortune 500 corporations, including some highly profitable tech companies.[11] Their executives typically earn millions of dollars in individual annual compensation—and walk away with tens of millions of dollars in additional income and lump-sum pensions through "golden farewell" arrangements—that are practically funded by taxpayers. This immensely profitable and increasingly oligopolistic sector is thus almost completely supported one way or another by the public treasury. Also, a

---

8. The "campuses" are often single buildings or parts of a building shared with other (non-educational) businesses.

9. See, for example, "For-Profit Colleges: Monsters in the Making?" *The Economist,* July 24, 2010, 36; Julia Love, "For-Profit Colleges May Be a Bust for Taxpayers," *Los Angeles Times,* July 25, 2010, A20; Don Lee, "College Debt a Looming 'Time Bomb,'" *Los Angeles Times,* March 6, 2012, B1. Former high-level federal officials often serve in the boards of online diploma corporations—and receive substantial monetary rewards for their advice and influential contacts; see, for example, Michael Hiltzik, "What's Behind This Odd Alliance?" *Los Angeles Times,* June 2, 2013, B1.

10. See Harkin, "For-Profit College Bubble." An attempt by the federal government to limit its—and taxpayers'—liability for defaulted loans failed, after being successfully challenged in court by an association representing the interests of the online, for-profit education oligopolies; see, for example, Douglas Belkin, "For-Profit Colleges Score a Victory," *Wall Street Journal,* July 3, 2012, A3.

11. See U.S. Senate Committee (HELP), *Emerging Risk*; "For-Profit Higher Education: Schools of Hard Knocks," *The Economist,* September 11, 2010, 73. The high profits of online diploma corporations has attracted some established universities and business schools to become their "partners"; see, for example, "Honours Without Profits?: A Business School's Link-up with a Private Firm Is an Interesting Case Study," *The Economist,* June 29, 2013, 60.

commission-driven approach to student recruitment has virtually ensured that "customers" (students) will always be found, especially among the least academically qualified who are desperate to possess a diploma.

The poor quality of the degrees awarded by these highly profitable corporations virtually ensures that high loan default rates will occur, all at taxpayers' expense. Their degree programs are typically not accredited, and their students usually find themselves with low-paying menial or dead-end jobs after graduation, if not unemployed.[12] Clever propaganda and advertising typically conceal these facts from unsuspecting potential students, and the corporations can use their enormous profits and capital to sue anyone who reveals the reality of their business to the people they target. Their political influence in the U.S. Congress is considerable, and their lobbying power is usually referred to as the "Teflon lobby" due to its untouchable character, mostly because of the large amounts of money they contribute to politics.[13] Their political lobby is therefore accustomed to getting its way in Washington, despite the fact that the U.S. Department of Education has repeatedly found many of the corporations in this sector to be guilty of falsifying student data in order to obtain more federal funding.[14]

The oligopolistic, for-profit educational corporations spend as much as half of all their revenues in marketing and recruitment of students— non-educational expenses, therefore—leading an experienced Wall Street financial specialist to characterize them as "marketing machines masquerading as universities," adding that "the government, the students and the taxpayer bear all the risk, and the for-profit [educational] industry reaps all the rewards."[15] In contrast with their vast marketing and recruitment budgets, these corporations were found to spend only 17 percent of their revenues on instruction, according to a 2012 U.S. Senate committee report, pointing up a link between their high dropout rates and the lack of resources spent on instruction.[16] Their high profitability and political clout has not been lost on

---

12. U.S. Senate Committee (HELP), *Emerging Risk*; Harkin, "For-Profit College Bubble."

13. Walter Hamilton, "For-Profit Colleges Face a Difficult Test," *Los Angeles Times,* February 6, 2011, B1.

14. Harkin, "For-Profit College Bubble."

15. See Love, "For-Profit Colleges."

16. U.S. Senate Committee on Health, Education, Labor, and Pensions, *Executive Summary, Report on For-Profit Colleges*; http://www.help.senate.gov/imo/media/for_profit_report/ ExecutiveSummary.pdf (accessed July 31, 2012); Jamie Goldberg, "Report Slams Colleges Run for a Profit: A Democratic Senate Staff Investigation Finds They Fail Students and Burden Taxpayers," *Los Angeles Times,* July 31, 2012, AA2. The thirty largest for-profit colleges in the

Wall Street speculators and hedge funds, which have been taking them over or establishing large stakes. One such speculator was found to have amassed a $700 million stake in Career Education Corporation and in ITT Educational Services—two very large for-profit corporations in this sector—while serving as chair of the University of California Board of Regents.[17] The fact that this person's spouse is one of the most influential senators in the U.S. Congress raised some questions about the connection of online diploma corporations with political power and Wall Street finance. The potential conflict of interest posed by this individual's chairmanship of the governing body of the largest and best-recognized public university system in the United States, and his immense stake in corporations that are often referred to as "diploma mill" companies, also struck a note of concern among some observers.

One of the largest online diploma corporations, Kaplan Higher Education, is owned by the holding company that controls the *Washington Post* newspaper, providing some insight on how some large and powerful media corporations are being consolidated with the oligopolists in this sector. Kaplan's vast profits and oligopolistic power over its market niche help offset substantial losses made by the *Washington Post*. In 2008 and 2009, for example, Kaplan made an operating profit of $450 million, while the *Washington Post* and other newspapers of the Post Company (owner of Kaplan) lost a combined $356 million.[18] Its for-profit online diploma business thus more than offset the losses incurred by the newspapers owned by this powerful corporation. Kaplan, originally a test preparation company before its acquisition by the Post Company, expanded its business to online diplomas and also acquired numerous small, campus-based colleges that were either bankrupt or had closed down. One of its most important acquisitions was Quest Education, a corporation that had built a large clientele of online

---

United States employed 35,202 recruiters in 2010, compared with 3,512 career service staff, according to the Senate report, and they accounted for 13 percent of all college enrollment in the United States but had 47 per cent of all federal student loan defaults.

17. Michael Hiltzik, "Is UC Regent's Vision Clouded?" *Los Angeles Times,* July 14, 2010), B1—Richard Blum, spouse of U.S. Senator Dianne Feinstein, owns the Blum Capital hedge fund.

18. See Russell Adams and Melissa Korn, "For-Profit Kaplan U. Hears Its Fight Song: Washington Post, Parent of Education Chain, Defends Profit Generator Against Planned Regulations," *Wall Street Journal,* August 30, 2010, B1. Partly because of its losses with the newspaper—and to diversify—the Washington Post Co. launched itself into health care, laying the ground for what may become a conglomerate with an oligopolistic reach into various sectors; see Keach Hagey, "From Newspaper to Hospice: Washington Post Branches Out from Core Businesses with Stake in Health Firm," *Wall Street Journal,* October 2, 2012, B2.

diploma customers. The fact that it is owned by the company that also controls the highly influential *Washington Post* has provided Kaplan with political clout over the years.

Health care provides another example of how oligopoly capitalism has reached into key sectors of American society and the economy. A hospital oligopoly has long been emerging, with very large corporations such as Community Health Systems, Tenet, and HCA controlling almost two-thirds of all hospital services in the United States.[19] In contrast, during the late 1970s large corporations controlled little more than one-quarter of all hospitals. Related to this oligopolization trend is the lack of disclosure on hospital performance and pricing practices to the public—a situation denounced by some well-known physicians as the result of a corporate-imposed code of silence—which means that, for example, error-prone hospitals go unnoticed and unreported.[20] The longwinded consolidation trend among hospital corporations is in part driven by their objective of amassing greater power when negotiating with health insurers—and also by their keen search for ever higher profits and greater political power.

Political power has become very important for hospital corporations, since almost one-half of all health care spending in the United States goes to hospitals. It should not surprise, therefore, that one of the most important (yet little known) aspects of the health care reforms passed in 2010 was to perpetually guarantee profits to health care corporations—especially the hospital oligopolies—even though most such profits will likely end up being paid by American taxpayers and the insured.[21] A publicly run health care system would have eliminated this form of corporate welfare, along

---

19. See, for example, "American Hospital Companies," *The Economist*, April 30, 2011, 68.

20. Marty Makary, *Unaccountable: What Hospitals Won't Tell You and How Transparency can Revolutionize Health Care* (New York: Bloomsbury, 2012). Dr. Makary notes how the effort to contain costs and increase revenues leads hospital corporations to put pressure on doctors to increase volume, resulting in an overuse of numerous treatments and surgical procedures.

21. Lynn Sweet, "Obama on Why He Is Not for Single Payer Health Insurance; New Mexico Town Hall Transcript," *Chicago Sun Times,* May14, 2009, http://blogs.suntimes.com (accessed June 1, 2009). As health care reforms neared implementation, corporations in this sector sharply reduced the number of hospitals and doctors that would provide services to the insured—to reduce costs and improve profitability; see, for example, Chad Terhune, "Narrow Networks: Insurers Hold Down Premiums by Making Fewer Doctors Available, Raising Concerns about Patients' Access to Care," *Los Angeles Times,* September 15, 2013, A1; Timothy W. Martin, "Shrinking Hospital Networks Greet Health-Care Shoppers," *Wall Street Journal,* December 14, 2013, A4. Another result involves employers' greater shift of insurance costs to employees; see Theo Francis, "Companies Prepare to Pass More Health Costs to Workers," *Wall Street Journal,* November 25, 2013, A1.

with the substantial administrative costs of processing payments and other support for the oligopolistic corporations in this sector. Largely because of the oligopolization of hospitals and other elements of health care, the average daily cost of hospital services in the United States has been estimated to be over four times more than in other rich nations with highly developed health care systems.[22] These examples point to the political importance of oligopolies, as public governance becomes the servant—and provider—of profits to corporate power. In health care, as in education and in most every other key sector of American society, corporations and corporate elites gain substantial influence through oligopolistic power.

The drive to build up oligopolistic power in the health care sector became all too obvious when one of the largest corporations, Community Health Systems, attempted a hostile takeover of another very large hospital corporation, Tenet Healthcare, in 2011. To try to fend off the unwanted takeover, Tenet filed lawsuits accusing Community Health of overbilling government and private health programs hundreds of millions of dollars, in what became one of the most rancorous takeover disputes in the history of this sector.[23] Despite such efforts, hostile takeovers of one oligopolist by another are usually successful, given the added clout of the combined companies, and the fact that stock market sentiment tends to be favorable toward such mergers. When combined, these two corporations were estimated to be able to reap at least $22 billion in revenue annually, becoming the second largest oligopolist in this sector after HCA.

Health insurance oligopolists have also been building up their power, extending into related health-care sectors through takeovers and acquisitions. The targets are companies that manufacture health care products—such as prescription pharmaceuticals—along with hospital operators, physicians' groups, and providers of diverse health services.[24] The purpose is to create "closed loops" that are under an oligopolistic corporation's power, and that

---

22. International Federation of Health Plans, *2012 Comparative Price Report: Variation in Medical and Hospital Prices by Country,* http://www.ifhp.com/documents/; Chad Terhune, "US Medical Costs Top Other Nations': An Annual Report by a Health Plan Trade Group Compares Prices in 12 Countries," *Los Angeles Times,* March 27, 2013, B6.

23. Susan Kelly, "Tenet Sues Community Health for Medicare Abuse," *Reuters,* April 11, 2011: http://www.reuters.com/article/2011/04/11/us-tenet-lawsuit-idUSTRE73A4FR20110411.

24. In the case of physician practices, for example, when they are purchased by hospital oligopolies the rates charged to health insurance companies typically surge—in many cases by 400 percent or higher; see Anna Wilde Matthews, "Same Doctor Visit, Double the Cost: Insurers Say Rates Can Surge after Hospitals Buy Physician Practices; Medicare Spending Rises, Too," *Wall Street Journal,* August 27, 2012, B1.

allow it to control or dictate patient care in a comprehensive way—with the prime objective of increasing profits. WellPoint, the health insurance oligopolist that owns Anthem Blue Cross, for example, purchased the world's largest contact lens retailer (1-800-Contacts Inc.). Through this acquisition, WellPoint gained the power to prevent entry to new companies in this sector—or to drive other contact lens providers out of business by excluding them from its "loop."[25] At the same time, this purchase allows it to control eye care for patients, setting terms of service, pricing, and technical requirements that are closely associated with profitability and costs.

The closed loop strategy is part of an effort to offset regulations—passed in 2010—that prohibit a refusal of coverage to unhealthy people (or those with expensive illnesses). Creating a closed loop therefore enables the oligopolist to control patients' treatments completely—setting up what will likely become the oligopoly-controlled, *corporate-medical-industrial complex* of the future. Everything a patient needs is determined by the oligopolistic corporation that insures the individual, with the insurance oligopolist controlling all aspects of health care provision. Arbitration clauses built into all health insurance contracts make it impossible for patients to sue their health insurer, and also practically guarantee that the vast majority of disputes will be decided in favor of the insurance oligopolist—since arbitration judges tend to be hired by the insurance provider.[26] As for doctors, those who breach a health insurance oligopolist's closed loop—by referring patients for treatments outside—run the risk of having their network contracts cancelled. Also, their patients may be refused partial or full coverage, or will end up having to pay very high bills for treatment received outside the loop. In a case that attracted some media attention, for example, a twenty-minute outpatient procedure performed on one individual—a teacher with very limited resources—outside the loop was billed at $87,500 to the patient, while another simple procedure costing $7,612 within the oligopolist's closed loop, was billed at $73,536 because it was performed outside the loop.[27] When payments are denied to physicians

25. David Lazarus, "Healthcare Buyouts May Add Up to Trouble," *Los Angeles Times,* June 12, 2012, B1.

26. The vast majority of cases brought to arbitration by corporations are won by them; see, for example, Searle Civil Justice Institute, *Consumer Arbitration Before the American Arbitration Association* (Chicago: Northwestern University School of Law, March 2009); David Lazarus, "Aiming to Restore Our Right to Sue," *Los Angeles Times,* October 18, 2011, B1, and his "Giving Up Your Right to Sue," *Los Angeles Times,* May 3, 2009, B1.

27. Chad Terhune, "Small Surgery, Huge Markup: $87,500 for a 20-Minute Procedure? It's Just an Extreme Example of Overbilling by Out-of-Network Outpatient Centers, Experts Say," *Los Angeles Times,* January 13, 2013, B1.

and other medical practitioners, the only recourse left is to sue the insurance oligopolist that denies payment, requiring costly and uncertain litigation. In one case, for example, a large health insurance oligopolist—with eighteen million clients in the United States and millions more around the world—was sued by a physicians' group when contracts for treatment were cancelled and payments for services rendered were denied.[28] In keeping with the nature of corporatocracy, no laws restrict these practices—or the closed loop strategy—and the prospects are for further oligopolistic concentration in this vital sector for human well-being.[29]

Difficult as it may seem, the health insurance oligopolists have also been offshoring jobs from the United States, which involves not just data processing related to billing and patient records, but also such vital technical functions as diagnosing—interpreting X-rays and test results for numerous conditions, for example. Preservice nursing positions, which help assess patient needs and determine treatment methods, are also being offshored. UnitedHealth Group, Aetna, WellPoint, and Health Net are all engaged in this practice, in some cases creating subsidiaries—such as WellPoint's Radiant Services—to specialize in offshoring and outsourcing nursing positions.[30] The main objective of this strategy is to increase profits by lowering costs—a major aspect of oligopolistic concentration in most every sector—despite already very high profit levels. WellPoint, for example, made a profit of $2.65 billion in 2011, while reducing total employment—partly through offshoring—by 7 percent during the previous two years.[31] Rising profits allow oligopolists in the health insurance sector to devote increasing resources to lobby politicians and fund political organizations, so that their interests—as a group—are well served.

The pharmaceutical sector, another vital component of health care and human well-being, has also witnessed an unprecedented consolidation

28. Chad Terhune, "Aetna Is Sued by Doctors in State: The Suit Is Part of a Growing Legal Battle over Referrals Outside an Insurer's Network," *Los Angeles Times,* July 4, 2012, B1, and his "Aetna Is Retaliating, Doctors Say," *Los Angeles Times,* August 30, 2012, B1.

29. A most troubling aspect is that placing profits over health care provision is at the core of rising oligopolistic concentration in this sector. See, for example, William H. Wiist, *The Bottom Line or Public Health: Tactics Corporations Use to Influence Health and Health Policy, and What We Can Do to Counter Them* (New York: Oxford University Press, 2010).

30. Don Lee, "Worries Grow as Health Jobs Go Offshore: The Outsourcing of Nursing Functions May Be the Most Risky of the Positions Being Shifted to Save Costs," *Los Angeles Times,* July 25, 2012, A1. At the same time that they increase their job-offshoring efforts, some of these corporations are expanding their operations into other markets, with the aim of becoming global oligopolies in their sectors; see, for example, Chad Terhune, "UnitedHealth Is Expanding into Brazil," *Los Angeles Times,* October 9, 2012, B2.

31. Lee, "Worries Grow," A11.

of corporate power. A small group of very large corporations controls most pharmaceutical production in the United States. Corporations such as Pfizer, Johnson and Johnson, Merck, Eli Lilly, and Allergan have long been acquiring other pharmaceutical and many biotechnology companies— building up empires that tacitly fix prices and exercise substantial influence over research funding, regulation, and tax credits.[32] These oligopolists are now setting the future agenda for pharmaceutical biotechnology, by dictating the norms that will govern how this new sector is developed and regulated.[33] Although large foreign pharmaceutical companies, such as Novartis and GlaxoSmithKline also market their products in the United States, the power of the few very large domestic pharmaceuticals seems greater than ever.

Pharmaceutical oligopolists exercise considerable influence over government, having spent almost three billion dollars on political lobbying during the past decade. One major target of their formidable lobbying apparatus has been to allegedly mislead politicians and the public about the cost of research, in order to seek faster new drug approvals, larger tax breaks, and stronger protection from generic drug producers.[34] Their most commonly diffused disinformation has apparently involved the research costs of bringing a new drug to market, which the corporations have pegged at values that range from one to several billion dollars, depending on the type of medication.[35] Such figures have apparently been part of a pervasive political lobbying campaign which claims pharmaceutical corporations require huge profits in order to fund their research—and thus deserve

---

32. In the four-year period following 2009, Johnson and Johnson completed 51 acquisition or merger deals, Pfizer 34, Merck 23, Bristol-Myers 13, and Eli Lilly (itself acquired by King Pharmaceuticals in 2011) 13—among the largest foreign-owned corporations in this sector, Novartis completed 48 such deals, GlaxoSmithKline 39, Roche 29, and AstraZeneca 21—see Peter Loftus and Jonathan D. Rockoff, "Merck's Labs Get Makeover," *Wall Street Journal*, December 28, 2013, A1 (based on data from Dealogic, www.dealogic.com).

33. See Wiist, *Bottom Line*; Brenda Inouye, *Unpacking the Pharma Biotech Engines: How the Leading Pharmaceutical Corporations Are Driving the Biotech Agenda* (Ottawa: Polaris Institute, 2002); Tony Clarke and Brenda Inouye, *Galloping Gene Giants: How Big Corporations are Re-Organizing Their Push for a Biotech Future and What Can Be Done to Challenge This Agenda* (Ottawa: Polaris Institute, 2002).

34. See, for example, Michael Hiltzik, "How Big Pharma Distorts Costs of Developing Drugs," *Los Angeles Times*, April 3, 2011, B1; Marcia Angell, *The Truth About the Drug Companies: How They Deceive Us and What to Do About It* (New York: Random House, 2004).

35. According to data and reports published by the Pharmaceutical Research and Manufacturers of America (PhRMA), www.phrma.org; Hiltzik, "How Big Pharma Distorts."

more tax breaks, faster approval of new drugs, and less regulation. The success of this propaganda campaign may partly account for the fact that profit margins for pharmaceutical companies have reached as high as 49 percent—one of the highest corporate profit rates of any sector in the American economy.

A recent study by two prominent analysts found the real average cost of research to bring a new medication to market to be as much as 94 percent lower than the cost advertised by pharmaceutical corporations in their propaganda.[36] The vast difference in those estimates—and the fact that the figures long diffused by pharmaceutical corporations were typically accepted at face value by politicians and the public—point to the considerable power and success that oligopolistic corporations have in making others believe what they say. Another disturbing aspect is that the corporations often backed up their claims on research costs with "studies" that used data provided by the companies themselves, using "samples" where the specific drugs involved were kept secret, applying dubious assumptions about "opportunity cost" multipliers to inflate expenses, and failing to reveal exactly what was measured—or provide a way for outsiders to verify the "findings."[37]

Another aspect of corporate pharmaceutical research is that negative findings in clinical trials are often ignored, while only results that show a benefit are published or publicized.[38] Thus, physicians, regulators, and the public are left ignorant about the clinical trials and products that fail—knowledge that might help other researchers avoid the same mistakes or prevent mishaps. A very well-known physician and science writer who has researched this aspect noted that pharmaceutical trials are often run on unrepresentative samples of patients, with statistical results being spun to provide as favorable a view as possible.[39] Also, many clinical trials tend to

---

36. Donald W. Light and Rebecca Warburton, "Demythologizing the High Costs of Pharmaceutical Research," *BioSocieties* 6 (2011): 34–50.

37. See, for example, Hiltzik, "How Big Pharma Distorts."

38. See, for example, Robert L. Hotz, "What You Don't Know about a Drug Can Hurt You: Untold Numbers of Clinical-Trial Results Go Unpublished; Those That Are Made Public Can't Always Be Believed," *Wall Street Journal,* December 12, 2008, A16; "Drug Maker Buried Antipsychotic Study: AstraZeneca Knew Long Ago That the Pricey Seroquel Caused Significant Weight Gain, Documents Show," *Washington Post,* reprinted in *Los Angeles Times,* March 18, 2009, A18; "Absence of Evidence: Do Drug Firms Suppress Unfavourable Information About New Products?" *The Economist,* November 29, 2008, 82.

39. Ben Goldacre, *Bad Pharma: How Drug Companies Mislead Doctors and Harm Patients* (London: Fourth Estate, 2012).

be run not as scientific experiments but as promotional campaigns designed to sway physicians to prescribe a corporation's product. Medical journals, for their part, frequently fail to verify or check on the articles they accept and print—leading to the suspicion that many significant mistakes in published studies are never corrected.[40] Also, increasing numbers of articles in medical journals have had to be retracted when either errors or falsifications are found—often by independent researchers who happen to be working on related projects. Pharmaceutical oligopolists are often involved indirectly in such cases, by funding the research or by providing researchers with professional support in the form of consulting arrangements, conference travel funds, payments for advertising endorsements, and the like.[41] Many published studies have been found to have been written not by the academic authors whose names appear on the article, but by ghostwriters hired by the pharmaceutical corporations that funded the research—leading to scandals in some of the most prestigious medical journals.[42] All of these problems are derived from the immense power that the pharmaceutical oligopolists have over research, and over the careers of those involved.

The pharmaceutical oligopolists' influence over regulation is now also a well-established fact, which has led to numerous scandals. Changes in U.S. Food and Drug Administration (FDA) regulatory policy to favor corporate priorities, for example, have led to deaths and injuries due to insufficient testing. Criticisms by FDA scientists of the agency's practices have met with reprisals, while consumer lawsuits against pharmaceutical corporations have been blocked by the agency, despite objections from its own scientists.[43] In many cases, advisers who are supposed to provide the FDA

40. See David Armstrong, "How the New England Journal Missed Warning Signs on Vioxx: Medical Journal Waited Years to Report Flaws in Article that Praised Pain Drug," *Wall Street Journal,* May 15, 2006, A1; "Scientific Journals: Publish and Be Wrong; One Group of Researchers Thinks Headline-Grabbing Scientific Reports Are the Most Likely to Turn Out to Be Wrong," *The Economist,* October 11, 2008, 109; "The Undisclosed Background of a Paper on Depression Treatment," *Science,* August 4, 2006, 598.

41. See, for example, Denise Gellene, "Financial Ties Found among Clinical Trials," *Los Angeles Times,* November 30, 2006, A22; Goldacre, *Bad Pharma.*

42. Anna Wilde Mathews, "At Medical Journals, Writers Paid by Industry Play Big Role," *Wall Street Journal,* December 13, 2005, A1. See also David Armstrong, "Medical Group Seeks Probe of Its Journal," *Wall Street Journal,* March 28, 2009, A4; Ron Winslow and Rachel Zimmerman, "High Blood Pressure: A Medical Journal, Doctors Sever Ties," *Wall Street Journal,* July 29, 2005, B1; Goldacre, *Bad Pharma.*

43. See Ricardo Alonso-Zaldivar, "FDA Scientist Says He Faces Retaliation: Star Witness Who Criticizes His Agency's Drug Safety Record Contends He's Under Pressure to be 'Exiled' to

with independent judgments on medications have simultaneously served pharmaceutical oligopolists as consultants, researchers, and promotional speakers.[44] Independent monitoring groups, such as the Institute for Safe Medication Practices (ISMP), typically report tens of thousands of deaths and injuries from medications every year due to poor regulation and insufficient testing.[45] Over a period of four months in 2008, for example, the ISMP reported 21,000 injuries and 4,825 deaths from harmful medications—this involved a 38 percent increase in injuries from the previous year's quarterly average, and a 300 percent increase in deaths from the previous four-month period. Because the reporting of adverse medication cases is solely voluntary, however, the number of recorded cases may be considerably higher—reported events are thought to account for less than 10 percent of the total. These effects can be correlated with pharmaceutical corporations' pressure to get new drugs to market faster and to increase profits by any and all possible means. On the FDA's side, stock market insider trading by its own scientists, using their knowledge of drug approval prospects and their impact on pharmaceutical corporations' stock, is another symptom of this regulatory agency's entwined relationship with corporate priorities.[46]

Another example of the close relationship between government agencies and corporate power involved the U.S. Department of Health and Human Services' (HHS) approval, without any competitive bidding, of a contract worth $433 million to supply an experimental treatment for an illness—smallpox—that was practically eradicated worldwide more than thirty-five years ago. Using terrorism as a justification, the pharmaceutical

---

a Different Job," *Los Angeles Times,* November 25, 2004, A26; Alicia Mundy, "FDA Memos Undercut Stance on Pre-Empting Drug Suits," *Los Angeles Times,* October 30, 2008, A3, and her "Political Lobbying Drove FDA Process," *Wall Street Journal,* March 6, 2009, A1; David Willman, "How a New Policy Led to Seven Deadly Drugs," *Los Angeles Times,* December 20, 2000, A1.

44. See, for example, Thomas Burton, "FDA Advisers Had Ties to Bayer," *Wall Street Journal,* January 11, 2012, B1.

45. See Institute for Safe Medication Practices, "Adverse Drug Events," www.ismp.org; Thomas H. Maugh II, "Side Effects of Prescribed Drugs Reach Record," *Los Angeles Times,* October 23, 2008, A12. Reports on these problems in the press are scarce and infrequent, despite their importance for human well-being. See Mundy, "FDA Memos"; David Willman, "Drug Trials with a Dose of Doubt," *Los Angeles Times,* July 16, 2006, A1; Ricardo Alonso-Zaldivar, "Drug Linked to Traffic Mishaps," *Los Angeles Times,* May 25, 2008, A20.

46. Alicia Mundy, "Probe Deepens of Alleged Inside Trades at FDA," *Wall Street Journal,* June 3, 2011, C1; Brent Kendall, "Former FDA Chemist Admits Fraud," *Wall Street Journal,* October 19, 2011, A2.

corporation in question fiercely lobbied the federal government to provide the contract to produce its treatment, despite the fact that no evidence whatsoever could be found of any terrorists possessing or planning to use smallpox as a weapon. During its lobbying efforts, the corporation's chief executive served on the U.S. National Biodefense Science Board, which advises HHS on how to respond to potential health emergencies. Siga Technologies, practically owned by a billionaire shareholder—one of the world's richest individuals, and a longtime and very generous donor to political organizations and campaigns—thus received a very large, "sole source" federal contract that would provide an estimated profit of at least 180 percent.[47] The price of $255 per dose was substantially above what government specialists in the HHS had estimated was reasonable. It was, moreover, considered very uncertain whether the medication will work at all since it cannot be tested in humans—and tests on animals could not be considered sufficiently reliable to prove it would work. Uncertainty over the FDA's approval to use the medication on humans—and that agency's own substantial skepticism of the proposed product—were overruled along with evaluations by well-known scientists, who concluded that it would be a waste of public funds and time.[48]

The harmful effects of many medications, partly due to aggressive marketing by oligopolistic pharmaceutical corporations, have risen considerably in recent decades. One such case was the marketing by Allergan—one of the largest biopharmaceutical corporations—of Botox, a cosmetic product approved for temporarily smoothing wrinkles, with inflated claims that categorized it as a "miracle drug" comparable to penicillin, while failing to warn about its dangers.[49] Botox became an

---

47. David Willman, "Costly Drug for Smallpox Questioned: How a Company Got a No-bid $433-million Contract to Supply an Experimental Treatment for a Threat That May Not Exist," *Los Angeles Times,* November 13, 2011, A1; James Love, "How the US Government Subsidized Ron Perelman's Smallpox Drug: ST-246 (Tecovirimat)," *Knowledge Ecology International,* November 13, 2011, http://keionline. org/node/1314. Other cases related to potential bioterrorism remedies have generated large sums for individuals with strong political connections (or former high-level government officials); see, for example, David Willman, "Raising an Alarm and His Income: Biowarfare Consultant Urged the Government to Stockpile a Type of Anthrax Remedy. But He Had a Stake in One Such Drug's Success," *Los Angeles Times,* May 19, 2013, A1.

48. Among the scientists who offered opinions, one was a renowned international epidemiologist with a long history advising the FDA; see Willman, "Costly Drug," A28.

49. Lisa Girion, "Lawsuit Targets Botox Maker: Allergan is Alleged to Have Failed to Warn about the Dangers of the Anti-Wrinkle Drug," *Los Angeles Times,* July 10, 2008, C1.

extremely profitable product, generating as much as one-third of Allergan's net sales in 2009—revenues and profits that, to the company, apparently more than justified any unintended side effects. Another case involved the marketing of the antipsychotic drug Risperdal, one of the best selling products of pharmaceutical oligopolist Johnson and Johnson, for uses that the FDA determined to be unsafe and ineffective.[50] Partly because of the flood of aggressive, unregulated marketing by oligopolistic pharmaceutical corporations, the use of powerful psychiatric medications—such as Risperdal, Seroquel, Ritalin, Zoloft, and many others—has spread widely, causing the overmedication not only of adults, but also of many children, while generating enormous profits for the corporations that produce them, despite their often strong, negative, and unadvertised side effects.[51]

Aggressive marketing by pharmaceutical oligopolists is also partly responsible for the kind of overprescription that leads to serious long-term negative effects for the public at large, such as the emergence of antibiotic-resistant strains of bacteria that results from overconsumption of antibiotics.[52] Direct, forceful marketing to consumers has, moreover, practically turned science enterprises into consumer goods companies, despite the fact that most consumers lack the expertise to judge the value, safety, and adequacy of the

---

50. Jonathan D. Rockoff and Joann S. Lublin, "US is Seeking $1 Billion over J&J's Marketing," *Wall Street Journal,* May 13, 2011, B1. A fierce lobbying drive to end the FDA's ban on off-label (unintended and unapproved usage of medications) marketing has become a major objective for pharmaceutical oligopolists; see, for example, Thomas M. Burton, "The Free Speech Pill: Drug Firms See Opening to Push for End to Off-Label Marketing Ban," *Wall Street Journal,* November 3, 2011, B1.

51. See, for example, Shirley S. Wang, "Psychiatric Drug Use Spreads: Pharmacy Data Show a Big Rise in Antipsychotic and Adult ADHD Treatments," *Wall Street Journal,* November 16, 2011, A3; U.S. Government Accountability Office, *Foster Children: HHS Guidance Could Help States Improve Oversight of Psychotropic Prescriptions,* Testimony GAO-12-27OT (December 1, 2011):http://www.gaogov/new.items/d12270t.pdf; Thomas M. Burton, "Foster Kids Are Overly Medicated, Report Says," *Wall Street Journal,* December 2, 2011, A4; "Drug Maker Buried Antipsychotic Study: AstraZeneca Knew Long Ago That the Pricey Seroquel Caused Significant Weight Gain, Documents Show," *Washington Post,* reprinted in *Los Angeles Times,* March 18, 2009, A18.

52. See Mary Engel, "Deadly Bacteria Defy Antibiotics: Hospitals Are Vulnerable to New Drug-Resistant Strains, and Experts Fear the Toll Could Rise," *Los Angeles Times,* February 17, 2009, A10. The overuse of antibiotics for meats and poultry, to increase animal weight and raise profitability, has also been linked to the emergence of antibiotic-resistant bacteria; see "Food and Health: The Overuse of Antibiotics in the Meat and Poultry Industries May Help Spawn Superbugs," *Los Angeles Times,* May 1, 2008, A22.

products advertised to them.[53] Marketing to consumers thus seeks to convince individuals who lack the necessary expertise to pressure their physicians to prescribe a medication based on advertising text, slogans, pictures, or talk from telegenic individuals who claim to have been helped by the products (but who in fact may have never taken them). Such marketing is typically aimed at emotionally vulnerable populations and fails to fully disclose the risks involved, but it dovetails well with corporate profit motives—as can be readily seen in Allergan's promotion of its Lap-Band product to reduce obesity, which requires major surgery and carries substantial risks.[54] This flood of aggressive marketing to consumers by pharmaceutical oligopolists partly accounts for the fact that pharmaceutical products have already surpassed traffic accidents in the United States as a cause of death.[55] Oligopolistic power over pharmaceutical production and markets is at the core of these marketing strategies, with companies diverting part of their enormous profits to finance multibillion-dollar advertising and propaganda campaigns.

Conflicts of interest involving the co-optation of doctors by pharmaceutical oligopolists, through payments and perks for prescribing their products, have also increased in recent decades—as noted by a prominent physician and medical professor.[56] Similarly, co-optation of

---

53. See Christopher Lane, "Sick of Drug Ads," *Los Angeles Times,* July 22, 2009, A25; Greg Critser, "What's Ailing Big Pharma," *Los Angeles Times,* March 25, 2009, A31; Daniel Costello, "Healthcare: Two Drugs Might Have No Benefit," *Los Angeles Times,* March 31, 2008, C1; Katherine Eban, "Painful Medicine: What the Strange Saga of Purdue Pharma—and Its $3 Billion Drug, OxyContin—Tells Us about Our National Dependence on Painkillers," *Fortune,* November 21, 2011, 143–52.

54. Michael Hiltzik, "Lap-Band Maker Wants It Both Ways," *Los Angeles Times,* January 23, 2011, B1, and his "Inaction as Weight Surgery Toll Rises," *Los Angeles Times,* January 22, 2012, B1; Stuart Pfeifer, "Lap-Band Maker Targets Teenagers," *Los Angeles Times,* May 24, 2011, A1, and his "Lap-Band Patient Dies: Fifth Person Since 2009 Succumbs after Surgery at Clinics Tied to 1-800-GET-THIN," *Los Angeles Times,* September 24, 2011,A1.

55. See Lisa Girion, Scott Glover, and Doug Smith, "Drugs Now Deadlier than Autos: Fuelled by Highly Addictive Prescription Pain Medications, Fatal Overdoses Have Surpassed Traffic Deaths Nationwide," *Los Angeles Times,* September 18, 2011, A1.

56. See Jerome P. Kassirer, *On the Take: How America's Complicity with Big Business Can Endanger Your Health* (New York: Oxford University Press, 2005), and his "Tainted Medicine," *Los Angeles Times,* April 6, 2008, M6; Angell, *Truth about the Drug Companies*; Alicia Mundy, "Senate Panel Hits Sanofi Payments," *Wall Street Journal,* May 25, 2011, B3. In one case, a medical device corporation paid more than $15 million over a three-month period to 227 orthopedic specialists, surgeons, and doctor groups; see Thomas M. Burton, "Medtronic Discloses Pay to Doctors," *Wall Street Journal,* June 1, 2010, B3.

researchers to report positive results or overlook negative ones has risen substantially.[57] Many studies of medications' effectiveness have often been financed by the same medications' manufacturers, raising suspicions of favoritism and corruption about their findings.[58] In one case, for example, a very well-known researcher reportedly fabricated data for twenty-one studies that were published by internationally well-known anesthesiology journals.[59] In the U.S. government's top agency for medical research—the National Institutes of Health (NIH)—it was estimated that more than half of all the agency's researchers had violated the agency's policies on conflicts of interest involving corporate links, according to one internal survey.[60] In one case, a NIH researcher served as consultant and witness for one of the largest pharmaceutical corporations, testifying in favor of approval of its products, despite rules that ban federal employees from representing nongovernmental entities before government agencies—the medication in question then went on to generate revenues of $859 million during the first five years of sales.[61] Exposing these ethical problems carries a high personal cost that often induces self-censorship in those who find them—as individual researchers end up being sidelined by the government agencies that employ them or are tacitly blacklisted by the corporations involved, making it practically impossible to obtain funding for their research or pass peer reviews conducted by individuals with links to the corporations.[62]

---

57. See "Absence of Evidence: Do Drug Firms Suppress Unfavourable Information About New Products?" *The Economist*, November 29, 2008, 82; *Washington Post*, "Drug Maker"; Hotz, "What You Don't Know about a Drug Can Hurt You."

58. See, for example, Denise Gellene, "Financial Ties Found among Clinical Trials," *Los Angeles Times*, November 30, 2006, A22; Matthews, "At Medical Journals, Writers Paid by Industry Play Big Role"; "The Undisclosed Background of a Paper on Depression Treatment," *Science* (August 4, 2006): 598; Armstrong, "How the New England Journal Missed Warning Signs on Vioxx."

59. See Keith J. Weinstein and David Armstrong, "Top Pain Scientist Fabricated Data in Studies, Hospital Says," *Wall Street Journal*, March 11, 2009, A12.

60. David Willman, "NIH Inquiry Shows Widespread Lapses, Lawmaker Says," *Los Angeles Times*, July 14, 2005, A23.

61. David Willman, "NIH Scientist Charged with Conflict," *Los Angeles Times*, December 5, 2006, A11, and his "NIH Audit Criticizes Scientist's Dealings," *Los Angeles Times*, September 10, 2006, A1.

62. See, for example, Cynthia Crossen, "A Medical Researcher Pays for Challenging Drug-Industry Funding," *Wall Street Journal*, January 3, 2001, A1; Alonso-Zaldivar, "FDA Scientist."

Supporting and increasing the power of corporate oligopolies in the health care sector is the changing of diagnostic standards to increase treatments and sell more medications. The adjustment of diagnostic standards has therefore become a powerful vehicle for corporations to reap more profits out of health care. As a result more diagnoses that require treatment—and costly medications—are being provided to millions of individuals in the United States who would not have been considered ill in the past, or in need of any treatment or medication.[63] Lower thresholds for diagnoses have become a reality in American health care, as pharmaceutical corporations, hospitals, and other health care oligopolies seek to turn more people into patients in order to increase profits. Thus, millions more people are being treated for a diverse range of supposed problems, such as high blood pressure, osteoporosis, heart disease, diabetes, and many others, that would not have been required to be treated in the past.

One of the unfortunate outcomes of this diagnosis-driven frenzy for corporate profit and power is the higher incidence of negative side effects and damage that result from lowered diagnostic thresholds. A prominent physician and medical professor with decades of experience, for example, noted the common and unnecessary treatment of osteopenia (lower than normal bone density) that often leads to ulcers in the esophagus and makes bones more brittle over the long term.[64] Similarly, the unnecessary treatment of the prostate gland leads to serious bladder and bowel damage that often requires surgery and more medications. In this way, the lowering of diagnostic thresholds also creates new problems through negative side effects and damage—that in turn require further treatment and medications—thus increasing sales and profit for the oligopolistic corporations that now control American health care.

In mental health care, an area that has been a growing source of profits for the pharmaceutical oligopolists, overdiagnosing and widespread prescribing have also taken root. Today, more than three-quarters of all antidepressants dispensed in the United States are prescribed by nonpsychiatrists, with a growing proportion being given to individuals who are not diagnosed with a mental illness.[65] Aggressive marketing by pharmaceutical oligopolists with large stakes in the production of psychotropic drugs has had much to do

---

63. H. Gilbert Welch, Lisa Schwartz, and Steven Woloshin, *Overdiagnosed: Making People Sick in the Pursuit of Health* (Boston: Beacon Press, 2011); H. Gilbert Welch, "Diagnosis as Disease," *Wall Street Journal*, May 6, 2011, A29.

64. Welch, "Diagnosis as Disease."

65. See Shirley S. Wang, "Antidepressants Given More Widely," *Wall Street Journal*, August 4, 2011, A5; Wang, "Psychiatric Drug Use"; Burton, "Foster Kids."

with this trend. The spread of these drugs is such that mass culture and behaviors are now thought to be increasingly influenced by them, with academic researchers being co-opted by the pharmaceutical oligopolies to help create an ever larger market—one that now even includes small children and pets.[66] Oligopolists' influence in this important area of health also encompasses standards setting, as in so many other fields. Revisions of the *Diagnostic and Statistical Manual of Mental Disorders,* psychiatry's encyclopedia of mental illnesses, for example, has often been criticized for redefining common personality quirks as pathologies. This manual is today the most important diagnostic guide for psychiatric conditions, and it defines problems for which pharmaceutical corporations manufacture almost all of their mental health products. One unfortunate aspect is that past revisions to this manual were performed in great secrecy and away from any public scrutiny, by panels that included individuals who received significant financial support from pharmaceutical oligopolists.[67]

Efforts by pharmaceutical oligopolists to avoid price competition by any means possible often leads to attempts to co-opt generic drug producers into delaying the introduction of their cheaper products. This is very important for pharmaceutical corporations with soon-to-expire patents, because of the drastic reduction in profits that occurs whenever the monopoly power provided by patent protection evaporates.[68] Securing additional time by co-opting generics producers can provide very substantial benefits, especially when the medication losing patent protection is a high-selling one. The high profits obtained by pharmaceutical oligopolists—through their control over pricing—also guarantees that they can pay off generic drug producers to prevent their medications from being marketed, as noted in a report by the U.S. Federal Trade Commission, which stated that "the continuing stream of monopoly profits is large enough to pay the generic competitors more than they could hope to earn if they entered the market at competitive

---

66. See David Healy, *The Creation of Psychopharmacology* (Cambridge: Harvard University Press, 2002).

67. See, for example, Ron Grossman, "Psychiatry Manual's Secrecy Criticized," *Los Angeles Times,* December 29, 2008, A19; Shari Roan, "Psychiatric Diagnoses Get a Rethinking," *Los Angeles Times,* May 22, 2011, A27; "Psychiatric Diagnosis: That Way, Madness Lies; A New Manual for Diagnosing Diseases of the Psyche Is about to Be Unveiled," *The Economist,* February 6, 2010, 88.

68. See "The Pharmaceutical Industry: The Bitterest Pill," *The Economist,* January 26, 2009, 62–63, and "Cliffhanger: Big Pharma Struggles to Protect Its Blockbusters as They Lose Patent Protection," *The Economist,* December 3, 2011, 76.

prices."[69] In one case, for example, a large pharmaceutical oligopolist struck a deal with a generics manufacturer to delay the introduction of a cheaper medication by twenty months, reaping an additional $22 billion from the medication whose patent was expiring.[70] In another case, a large European pharmaceutical oligopolist doing substantial business in the United States paid $90 million to an American generics manufacturer to delay the introduction of a lower-priced rival to its best-selling heart medication.[71] For patients and consumers, such co-optation and collusion can be quite damaging, because of the higher prices they must pay and the resulting loss of purchasing power.[72] A European Union study, for example, found that medication prices typically drop an average of 25 percent when a generic substitute enters the market, and then drop an additional 40 percent after two years.[73]

When attempts to co-opt generics manufacturers fail, pressure tactics such as lawsuits can be brought into play by a pharmaceutical oligopolist. Practically every lawsuit in this area tends to be settled out of court in the United States, with settlement conditions that typically require a generics manufacturer to delay the introduction of its lower-priced product. Agreeing to that condition can save significant amounts of money to a generics manufacturer in litigation costs, particularly when the amount of revenue to be generated by its product is uncertain or low—due, for example, to its lower projected price, insufficient marketing clout, limited production capacity, or to the likely entry of other manufacturers with a similar product. In many cases, agreeing to a delay can also help prevent other lawsuits from the same pharmaceutical oligopolist, if the generics manufacturer plans to launch production of other medications with expiring patent protection. For the pharmaceutical corporation losing patent protection, a delay by a generics manufacturer can help pile up substantial additional revenue

69. David Lazarus, "Insider Sheds Light on Murky Business: Counting the Many Ways Drug Prices Are Jacked Up," *Los Angeles Times*, March 26,2013, B6; U.S. Federal Trade Commission, *Overview of FTC Antitrust Actions in Health Care Services and Products* (Washington: FTC, 2013), http://www.ftc.gov/.

70. Avery Johnson, "Pfizer Buys More Time for Lipitor," *Wall Street Journal*, June 29, 2008, B1.

71. "Prescription Drugs: Protection Racket," *The Economist*, May 19, 2009, 58.

72. "Pharmaceuticals," *The Economist*; Jonathan Rockoff, "How a Drug Maker Tries to Outwit Generics," *Wall Street Journal*, November 18, 2008, B1.

73. "Pharmaceuticals: Patently Absurd," *The Economist*, December 6, 2008, 82.

through the higher prices that patients and consumers must pay. A delay of seven months in one case, for example, generated almost $4 billion in revenue for the pharmaceutical corporation that owned a soon-to-expire patent on a high-selling medication.[74] Unfortunately, the public and the vast majority of patients and consumers are typically unaware of these collusion games and power plays, despite the harm they cause to their economic well-being and to society's ability to provide affordable health care.

The news media, a vital component of democracy, provide another example of oligopolistic concentration. Starting in the 1970s, ownership of media modes—such as newspapers, radio, and television—became increasingly concentrated through mergers and acquisitions. The large corporations that emerged out of this three-decades-long process of consolidation were out to enhance their profits and political power above everything else, and journalism was simply a means to achieve those ends.[75] This process of consolidation took on a new dimension when media multibillionaire Rupert Murdoch—one of the richest men in the world—established a foothold for his global media empire in the United States and acquired the most important national daily newspaper, *The Wall Street Journal*, along with other important newspapers and television networks. The arrival of Murdoch's oligopolistic media empire was not the only example of how immense personal wealth is tied to control over media, however. The richest man in the world—multibillionaire Carlos Slim Helú—who controls most of Mexico's telecommunication networks (along with other Mexican billionaires in the media sector) has also been extending his business empire into the United States.[76] The attractiveness of the nation for these and other individuals is no doubt driven by the supportive political environment for corporate oligopolies—a major outcome of the three-decades-old neoliberal era.

The result is a proliferation of oligopolized media modes that subtly—although sometimes quite overtly as in the case of Murdoch's Fox television network—promote corporate propaganda, diffuse values favorable to

74. Ibid.; Rockoff, "How a Drug Maker."

75. See Robert W. McChesney and John Nichols, *The Death and Life of American Journalism* (New York: Nation Books, 2010).

76. See, for example, Tracy Wilkinson, "Mexican Titans Wage Telecom War," *Los Angeles Times,* May 17, 2011, B1; "Monopolies in Mexico," *The Economist,* May 7, 2011, 41; "Carlos Slim: Let Mexico's Moguls Battle," *The Economist,* February 4, 2012, 67–68; Nathaniel Parish Flannery, "Televisa vs. the People: Mexico's Broadcast Monopoly Helped a Candidate Win the Election," *Fortune,* September 24, 2012, 24.

oligopolistic corporate power, and otherwise vituperate or ignore those who question the immense power of corporate oligopolies. Buying up politicians through contributions to political organizations and campaigns, lobbying, funding political action committees, providing favorable coverage of campaigns and performance in office, employing favored politicians' relatives, friends, and supporters as consultants or staff, and exercising influence to get away with unethical or illegal practices, has been part of these billionaire-controlled media oligopolies. During the past decade, for example, Murdoch's British media oligopoly—News International—was found to have mined personal data, eavesdropped on telephones, and hacked the e-mail communications of hundreds of individuals who were targeted as potential sources of sensitive information that might have resulted in newsworthy stories, scandals, damage to its political foes, promotion of allies, or otherwise served as tools to spin news in terms favorable to that corporation's interests.[77]

In another case, the chief executive for the European edition of Murdoch's most influential newspaper—*The Wall Street Journal*—pressured reporters into writing published articles favorable to a corporation that had been contracted by the newspaper's circulation department.[78] The

---

77. See Tim Rutten, "America's Murdoch Problem," *Los Angeles Times*, July 16, 2011, A17; Joe Flint, "General Counsel of News Corp. Is Leaving," *Los Angeles Times*, June 9, 2011, B3. Investigations of Murdoch's newspapers in London, in particular, revealed the extent to which corporate-owned media can concoct strategies to manipulate public officials. See, for example, Janet Stobart, "News Corp. Papers Tied to Bribery: A Police Official Says the London Tabloids Regularly Paid Police for News Tips on Celebrities and Others," *Los Angeles Times*, February 28, 2012, A3; Cassell Bryan-Low, "Phone-Hacking Suits against News Corp. Rise," *Wall Street Journal*, October 8, 2011, B3; Meg James and Dawn C. Chmielewski, "News Corp. Exec to Step Down: Human Resources Chief Beryl Cook Was Seen as a Key Member of James Murdoch's 'Shadow Government,'" *Los Angeles Times*, November 4, 2011, B3; Janet Stobart, "4 Journalists Arrested in Phone Hacking Case," *Los Angeles Times*, January 29, 2012, A6; Henry Chu, "6 More Arrested in British Scandal," *Los Angeles Times*, March 14, 2012, A5; Jenny Gross and Jeanne Whalen, "Guilty Pleas Disclosed in UK Trial: Opening Arguments Begin in Phone-Hacking Case; Prosecutor Also Alleges Tabloids Bribed Officials," *Wall Street Journal*, October 31, 2013, B6; Jenny Gross and Cassell Bryan-Low, "Ex-Editor Accused of Coverup," *Wall Street Journal*, November 5, 2013, B4. These articles reveal facets of a major scandal that was largely discovered by accident. Because of coverups implemented by executives, and the fact that important public officials were involved, it became impossible to see the full extent of wrongdoing involved early on—only very limited bits of information and details could be learned, as investigations unfolded.

78. Paul Sonne and Bruce Orwall, "WSJE Publisher Quits After Ethics Inquiry," *Wall Street Journal*, October 12, 2011, B2, and their "WSJ Europe Faces Scrutiny," *Wall Street Journal*, October 13, 2011, B2; "WSJE Sales Under Spotlight," *Wall Street Journal*, October 14, 2011, B2.

corporation in question had a contract to promote the newspaper and to artificially boost its circulation numbers, by providing thousands of free or heavily discounted copies. This company was also surreptitiously enlisted to sponsor and organize pro-corporate propaganda events—such as the Future Leadership Institute, an initiative set up by *The Wall Street Journal Europe*'s circulation department—or to host and organize events in ways that would not link the newspaper directly to them, such as the launching of new books with pro-corporate content. The wording of the contract between that company and the newspaper even included a promise that favorable coverage would be provided, thus violating a fundamental ethical principle of journalism. In this case, therefore, the generic (unspecific) pro-corporate propaganda routinely published by *The Wall Street Journal* in its Opinion and Editorial pages was complemented by favorable published coverage of a specific corporation that the newspaper had a contractual relationship with. This ethical problem, and the conflict of interest it represented, was only found out because a former employee of the newspaper's parent company (Dow Jones and Co., owned by Murdoch's News Corp.) lodged a complaint that gained public attention through another newspaper's investigation—meaning that the case could no longer be covered up and kept as an internal matter by *The Wall Street Journal* or by Murdoch's Dow Jones and Co.

Domestic news media corporations in the United States—such as Gannett, McClatchy, and Tribune—emerged as nationally powerful vehicles by acquiring what were previously independent city-based newspapers and television and radio networks. Most of the newspapers those corporations own are now local monopolies in many American metropolises—as rivals disappeared or were taken over by them. In this way, a collection of local monopolies and oligopolies have developed under the control of a single newspaper holding corporation. The newspaper monopolies and oligopolies—and the corporations that own them—exercise considerable influence over local politics and government, since they decide the local news that will be given prominence or reported, the editorial opinions and political campaign endorsements that will be provided to the public, and even the letters to be published. In many cases, a political endorsement from one of those local monopolies has made the difference between victory and defeat for many a politician running for local office.

One corporation with control over numerous local news monopolies is Tribune Co.—owner of *The Chicago Tribune* newspaper. Its acquisition of many local or regional monopolies—such as *The Los Angeles Times* and numerous other news, television, and media-related enterprises around the

United States—provided it with substantial local control over its sector.[79] Tribune was taken over by multimillionaire speculator Sam Zell—who piled the immense debts he incurred to finance the takeover on the company. The resulting high debt load eventually drove Tribune into bankruptcy protection. A misleading aspect of the takeover was to disguise it as an employee-owned stock ownership plan, which in fact never existed, and was ruled by a federal judge to be a fraudulent scheme.[80] Shortly after the takeover and bankruptcy filing, much of the news-gathering capabilities of the newspapers owned by Tribune were curtailed in order to cut costs. Cost cutting as a result of bankruptcy—a product of the high debts piled on the company by its new speculator-owner—thus resulted in extensive layoffs of journalists and other employees. Two of the consequences of these layoffs were cuts in reporting and an increasing dependence on advertising—to the point that more than 90 percent of all printed space in the newspaper is often taken up by advertisements, with corporate-paid ads and propaganda accounting for most revenue. Reporting of issues with negative implications for corporate influence over government then declined substantially, in what may be considered a collateral effect.[81]

Company stripping by hedge funds that take over news media corporations is also part of the oligopolization dynamic. Clear Channel Communications, an oligopolistic media conglomerate that owns various subsidiaries involved in broadcasting, advertising, and events promotion, for example, was taken over by two major Wall Street hedge funds in 2009—a buyout that incurred massive amounts of debt, all of it loaded onto the acquired company.[82] After another hedge fund took over one of the subsidiaries (Clear Channel Outdoor Holdings), it found that large amounts ($656 million in 2011 alone) had been siphoned by the debt-laden parent

79. Among Tribune's acquisitions were nineteen television stations for $2.7 billion, and entertainment data provider Gracenote Inc. for $170 million; see Meg James, "Tribune to Purchase 19 TV Stations," *Los Angeles Times*, July 2, 2013, B1; Keach Hagey and Mike Spector, "Tribune to Split Newspaper, TV Businesses," *Wall Street Journal*, July 11, 2013, B3; Don Clark, "Tribune Buying Gracenote from Sony," *Wall Street Journal*, December 24, 2013, B7.

80. Laura Webber Sadovi, "Sam Zell Turns Selective," *Wall Street Journal*, June 15, 2011, C6; Holman W. Jenkins Jr., "Sam Zell's Nightmare Continues," *Wall Street Journal*, May 21, 2011, A15.

81. See, for example, Robert W. McChesney, *Corporate Media and the Threat to Democracy* (New York: Seven Stories Press, 1997); McChesney and Nichols, *Death and Life*.

82. Gregory Zuckerman, "Transfers at Clear Channel in Dispute," *Wall Street Journal*, March 7, 2012, C1.

corporation from the subsidiary—to cover some of the debts incurred in the parent corporation's buyout by the two hedge funds that took it over. The $656 million transfer represented a fivefold increase from the $123 million already siphoned by the parent company two years earlier. Major conflicts of interest were part of this case of company stripping, since four members of the subsidiary's board were also members of the parent company's governing board. Interest rates paid by the parent corporation to the subsidiary for "loans" it received, moreover, were far below market rates (9.25 versus 17.5 percent at the time) for companies with similar credit ratings. Also, the parent company's ratings sank to subprime ("junk") level after the two hedge funds loaded their buyout debt on it.[83]

The high amounts of debt loaded onto taken-over news media corporations also made them targets for "distressed debt" hedge funds such as Angelo, Gordon and Company, Alden Global Capital, Ariel Investments, Platinum Equity, and Oaktree Capital Management.[84] Distressed debt speculators, commonly referred to as "vultures" in finance, typically look for highly indebted companies to acquire at low prices, subsequently seeking bankruptcy protection in order to wring concessions from creditors, to reduce debt, and to restructure operations—all of which usually lead to substantial layoffs and reduced news-gathering and reporting capabilities. News media corporations thus started to become property of powerful Wall Street speculators, with implications for reporting and editorial control that may be at odds with the ethics and practice of journalism. Businesses in other sectors taken over by hedge funds have, for example, found that the operating regimes introduced by their new owners often diverted them substantially from their prior mission, creating conflicts of interest and disrupting the notions of service and social responsibility that had been at the core of their operations.

The strategy of those speculative funds—often in partnership with oligopolistic megabanks such as JPMorgan Chase—can also involve buying up much of the targeted companies' debt and transforming it into vast amounts of company stock. This provides them with a controlling interest in, if not outright ownership of, the companies whose debt they purchased. In case of bankruptcy—due to the resulting high debt loaded on the taken-over companies—the megabanks that financed the debt would *also* be at the

---

83. Zuckerman, "Transfers," C2.

84. Michael Oneal, "Newspaper Industry's New Masters: Hedge Funds Seek to Profit from Investments in Bankrupt Publishers Such as Tribune," *Los Angeles Times,* June 6, 2010, B1.

head of the line to collect as creditors, thus making considerable profits on the takeovers regardless of the outcome. As a result, the megabanks behind the deals win no matter how the takeovers by the vulture funds turn out. A small number of hedge funds and megabanks are therefore acquiring immense power over an increasingly oligopolistic news media sector.

The prime interest of the financial speculators that are taking over America's news media is not with journalism but with increasing profits by any means possible, along with their political power. Further consolidation involving takeovers and mergers—and most of all, greater control over the news media sector—can therefore be expected since it seems to be the only means for increasing profits. A vehicle supporting this emerging reality is the takeover—by the hedge funds—of the governing boards of the various news media corporations they acquire. Thus, a single hedge fund often ends up taking over the boards of several of its acquired news media corporations, further consolidating its oligopolistic control—along with the potential for tacit censorship of any reporting that casts a negative light on corporate power. When profitability is less than expected, mergers and acquisitions between the controlling hedge funds can provide a way out—and most likely lead to additional staff layoffs and reduced news-gathering capabilities in the taken-over media corporations. Consolidation among the hedge funds themselves can therefore also be expected as a means to raise profits, monetize their investments, and consolidate their power in this sector.

One of the consequences of this dynamic is the decline of journalism. Starting in the 1980s, the number of employed journalists per capita began to decline in the United States, even though corporate profits in this sector were high and increasing during the last two decades of the twentieth century. As profits declined during the first decade of the current century, the reduction in the number of employed journalists accelerated. One of the striking indicators of this trend is the ratio of public relations specialists to journalists employed by news media corporations. This ratio increased from roughly one to one in the early 1960s to about four to one five decades later—indicating the growing power of public relations and propaganda diffusion in the news media.[85] One of the outcomes of this trend seems to be the growing emphasis on trivia or pro-corporate spins in reporting

---

85. See Robert W. McChesney, *The Political Economy of Media: Enduring Issues, Emerging Dilemmas* (New York: Monthly Review Press, 2008); John Bellamy Foster and Robert W. McChesney, "The Internet's Unholy Marriage to Capitalism," *Monthly Review*, March 2011, 18.

and editorial writing, along with the increasing neglect of topics that cast a negative light on corporate influence.

Oligopoly power has also reached into another area of publishing—one highly connected with learning, professional practice, and the diffusion of knowledge—academic journal publishing. Unlike news publishing, this sector caters to an erudite audience, comprising researchers, academics, professionals, and advanced students in practically all fields. The six largest corporations publishing academic journals now own close to half of this sector, with annual profit margins as high as 40 percent or more being fairly common. One of the largest oligopolists—Elsevier—for example, had a profit margin of 37 percent in 2011, on revenues of over $3.2 billion.[86] The fifth largest oligopolist in this sector—Sage—controls about 650 journals alone, and owns practically all the most important journals in some fields, such as sociology.[87] All of the oligopolists in this sector operate as multinational corporations, with staffs in the thousands and worldwide distribution networks. Control over pricing—the prime characteristic of oligopolistic corporate power—is at the core of their high profit margins. Over nearly three decades, for example, prices for corporate-controlled academic journals rose thirty-fold, at an average of almost 14 percent annually, far outstripping inflation in the United States and any increases in distribution, production, paper, printing, or computer system costs. Compared to academic society–owned journals, which are typically nonprofit, prices for corporate-owned academic journals are between three and nine times more expensive per page today—an astounding difference that reflects the top priority of the oligopolists in this sector—a key one for the advancement of knowledge and future human well-being.[88]

A peculiar aspect is that journals' content—the most important element of what the corporations in academic journal publishing sell—is provided virtually *free* by authors and editors. The extremely profitable corporate oligopolies in this sector, and the high compensation packages they pay their top executives, thus fundamentally rest on intangibles—knowledge,

---

86. "Scientific Publishing: Brought to Book; Academic Journals Face a Radical Shake-Up," *The Economist,* July 21, 2012, http://www.economist.com/node/21559317.

87. "Notes from the Editors," *Monthly Review,* October 2012), http://monthlyreview.org/2012/10/01/ mr-064-05-2012-09.

88. Armin Beverungen, Steffen Böhm, and Christopher Land, "The Poverty of Journal Publishing," *Organization,* August 8, 2012, http://org.sagepub.com/content/early/2012/07/05/1350508412448858; "Notes," *Monthly Review.*

creativity—that are generated and provided at practically no cost to them. The oligopolists' only costs are, technically, those incurred in distribution and any layout work needed on the freely contributed product. One consequence of oligopolistic corporate control over this sector, beyond the high prices charged, is that the corporations in charge sometimes tend to orient journals' content—despite their assurances of editorial independence—toward areas that are more likely to provide higher revenue, due to a larger subscription market—and thus be more supportive of their profit objective.[89] Another consequence is that academic institutions—the places that generate the intangibles that are provided for free—have to pay very high sums for subscriptions, in order to have access to the knowledge that they had a fundamental role creating. Also, because in many cases taxpayer funds are used to generate such knowledge—as occurs when public universities and government research grants are involved—the oligopolists' revenues and profits are supported by taxpayers.[90] The oligopolization and corporatization of the diffusion of such fundamentally important knowledge is a troubling aspect—one that may have major negative ramifications for future social well-being.

Related to academic journal publishing, book publishing has also become increasingly oligopolistic, as mergers create global corporations with substantial power over pricing and distribution. In one case, for example, the merger of two major publishing corporations—Bertelsmann and Pearson— will likely provide the merged entity with control over about one-quarter of all English-language book sales.[91] This kind of merger would also allow more power in negotiating distribution deals, and higher prices to consumers. Such mergers allow the publishing oligopolies to more effectively exploit authors, by cutting advance payments and eliminating "midlist" authors— those that do not bring in very large sales volumes—knowing that authors will have fewer doors to knock on whenever they seek publication of their work. Greater emphasis on publishing authors with the largest sales volumes can therefore be expected from such mergers. Media oligopolies

89. "Notes," *Monthly Review*; Scott Jaschik, "Who Controls Journals?," *Inside Higher Ed*, July 7, 2009), http://www.insidehighered.com/.

90. See "Academic Publishing: Open Sesame; When Research Is Funded by the Taxpayer or by Charities, the Results Should Be Available to All Without Charge," *The Economist*, April 14, 2012, http://www.economist.com/node/21552574.

91. "Waddling Forward: The Merger of Two Big Publishers Shows the Book Business's Challenges," *The Economist*, November 3, 2012, 66.

are also interested in this sector, as they seek greater power over all forms of publishing, news, and entertainment. Thus, for example, a potential merger of book publisher HarperCollins—owned by Rupert Murdoch's News Corporation—with either Bertelsmann's Random House or Pearson's Penguin brands, or both—would provide a formidable advantage to the merged entity, to increase book prices, exploit authors more effectively, and eventually set the stage for launching a takeover of major distributors, such as Amazon.[92]

The oligopolization of telephone service is now a fact of life in the United States. The evolution toward oligopolistic power in this sector, however, occurred through a process of mergers and acquisitions after the end of regulatory control. An old telephone service corporation—AT&T— was run as a public utility until the early 1980s, when deregulation started. AT&T was then broken up into seven regional corporations in 1984. One of those corporations—SBC Communications—led a merger effort after deregulation, and eventually re-consolidated four of the regional companies into AT&T by 2006. Through this consolidation, the largest telephone oligopoly was created—in what became a dramatic contradiction of deregulatory efforts aimed at fostering competition. Before deregulation, AT&T had exercised considerable influence over its regulators through political lobbying, since its profitability depended greatly on their decisions. After deregulation, AT&T and the other regional companies continued their lobbying efforts—and were joined by the new companies that emerged in this sector—to ensure that mergers and acquisitions would continue unobstructed. Important in this effort was their belief that mergers—and the resulting consolidation—would allow them to profit more, through the pricing power gained over consumers.[93]

---

92. See ibid.

93. See, for example, Alan Stone, *Wrong Number: The Breakup of AT&T* (New York: Basic, 1989); Richard H. K. Vietor, *Contrived Competition: Regulation and Deregulation in America* (Cambridge, MA: Belknap, 1994); Timothy Wu, *The Master Switch: The Rise and Fall of Information Empires* (New York: Knopf, 2010). Monopoly and oligopolies in the communications sector have a long history—the first nationwide monopoly in the United States was held by telegraph service provider Western Union, considered to be AT&T's predecessor; see Joshua D. Wolff, *Western Union and the Creation of the American Corporate Order, 1845–1893* (New York: Cambridge University Press, 2013). This sector also saw the formation of the first duopoly when Western Union made a pact with the Postal Telegraph and Cable Co. in 1888 to divide up the market and set prices.

Thus, contrary to the public's expectations, the market power of the telephone corporations that emerged after deregulation grew substantially. Mergers became a major outcome of deregulation, and were justified under the flawed assumption that they would allow the consolidated corporations to prepare for a new era of competition. Therefore, what was initially billed by neoliberals and by the corporations themselves as a new epoch of competition actually turned out to be the opposite. Through the deregulation dynamic, AT&T became an extremely powerful oligopolist, raising prices at will. Its rates for basic telephone service—the one most commonly used by working people and the poor—went up considerably, far outpacing inflation. Charges for other services also increased substantially—fees for direct telephone assistance, for example, went up by 226 percent over the three years following AT&T's deregulation, while charges for keeping a telephone number unlisted went up by 614 percent.[94] AT&T was not alone in pursuing this strategy, however. Another telephone oligopolist that emerged after deregulation—Verizon—followed AT&T's practices in what became a follow-the-leader mode of price fixing.

The arrival of wireless telephony then provided these oligopolists with another opportunity to raise prices with more frequency.[95] Additional practices were also concocted, such as digital locking, that would provide more opportunities to raise prices while keeping consumers fenced in. Thus, perpetual digital locking of customers' mobile phones to the oligopolists' networks became the norm, thanks to corporate lobbying efforts, political contributions, and the 1998 U.S. Digital Millenium Copyright Act—a law intended to regulate access to copyrighted works, but out of which perpetual locking became a reality.[96] The behemoths in the telephony sector also amassed enough oligopolistic power to either acquire new entrants or ensure that no significant new competitors emerged. As a result, 70 percent of wireless telephony in the United States was under the control of AT&T

---

94. California Senate Office of Oversight and Outcomes, *Gaps Emerge in Consumer Protections After Phone Deregulation* (Sacramento: California Senate, 2012), www3.sen.ca.gov/oversight.

95. See, for example, Anton Troianovski and Thomas Gryta, "New Front Opens in Wireless Battle: Verizon Overhauls Plans to Shift Bulk of Bill to Data Use; AT&T Ready to Follow," *Wall Street Journal,* June 13, 2012, B1.

96. "Locked into Your Phone," *Los Angeles Times,* January 29, 2013, A10; U.S. Copyright Office, *The Digital Millennium Copyright Act of 1998* (Washington: U.S. Copyright Office, December 1998), http:// www.copyright.gov/legislation/dmca.pdf.

and Verizon Wireless by 2013.[97] Three other companies that practically controlled the rest of the wireless market—Sprint Nextel, T-Mobile, and MetroPCS—vied to merge with each other or with the two main oligopolists, while also acquiring the smaller service providers that remained.

When the Internet spread after the mid-1990s—mainly because of the World Wide Web—AT&T and Verizon started to seize the new technology by using the telephone wire networks to provide service. New companies aiming to provide such service were then taken over, in what became a big fish-eat-small fish buyout dynamic. Both Internet and telephone service could, however, also be provided by television cable corporations, and therein emerged a new set of oligopolists. Broadband Internet service provision thus came under the control of corporations with oligopolistic power over combined access to cable television and telephone service. These corporations effectively prevented other companies from using their land-wire networks, thus exercising a monopoly over the geographical areas they controlled. A process of mergers and acquisitions then reduced the number of companies providing these combined services—cable television, Internet access, telephone—to six very large corporations over a relatively short period of time.[98]

By these means, oligopoly capitalism began to make inroads into the Internet. Long considered a wondrous new technology that would democratize communications and promote transparency, this vital service is now being taken over by a few large corporations.[99] According to Robert McChesney, the best-known scholar on the political economy of communications, deregulation led to the worst possible outcome for the Internet—an oligopolistic market with few restraints, while the corporations

---

97. This kind of market power allowed the telephone oligopolists to sell massive amounts of customers' data to other corporations—especially telemarketers; see Anton Troianovski, "Phone Firms Sell Data on Customers," *Wall Street Journal,* May 22, 2013, B1.

98. See, for example, "DISHing Out the Dosh: Mega-Bids Are Set to Transform America's Wireless Industry," *The Economist,* April 20, 2013, 67–68; McChesney, *Political Economy of Media.*

99. The Internet's promise for democracy was overestimated from the start. Among recent authors who have shed light on the fallacies that accompanied early expectations are Matthew Hindman, *The Myth of Digital Democracy* (Princeton: Princeton University Press, 2009); Evgeny Morozov, *The Net Delusion: The Dark Side of Internet Freedom* (New York: Public Affairs, 2011); Robert W. McChesney, *Communication Revolution* (New York: New Press, 2007).

that took over this vital service increased their political power substantially.[100] McChesney points out that the oligopolization of service provision has been disastrous for the development of broadband Internet communications in the United States. The oligopolists that control broadband access are not required to allow competitors access to their networks, thus practically eliminating competition. The result, according to the U.S. Federal Communications Commission (FCC), is that almost 80 percent of American households today have no more than two broadband Internet service providers to choose from, while nearly 20 percent have no more than one provider.[101]

Political lobbying by the powerful oligopolistic corporations in this sector was a major factor for this outcome. Hefty political contributions, arranged directly by the corporations or through employees and friends—and through political action organizations sometimes quietly set up by the corporations themselves—were at the core of their lobbying and political strategies. The hiring of federal employees who are in charge of regulation, after they leave their positions, also became an increasingly important strategy in the corporate lobbying game. Service in federal regulatory agencies became a "revolving door," whereby individuals in charge of regulation gained lucrative employment as lobbyists for the corporations—after leaving their federal posts.[102] In one case, for example, a FCC official was hired by Comcast Corporation—one of the largest cable television, telephone, and Internet broadband service providers—immediately after leaving her federal position, and only four months after she voted to approve Comcast's own acquisition of NBCUniversal, one of the largest broadcasting networks.[103] Her vote as a federal official helped this corporation secure a formidable

100. Foster and McChesney, "Internet's Unholy Marriage," 6–7. See also Susan Crawford, *Captive Audience: The Telecom Industry and Monopoly Power in the New Gilded Age* (New Haven: Yale University Press, 2013).

101. U.S. Federal Communications Commission, *Connecting America: The National Broadcast Plan* (Washington, DC: FCC, 2010), 37–38. Television cable providers that also provide Internet service enjoy a monopoly in many local markets, and are considered a major obstacle to the spread of broadband in the United States; see, for example, Michael Hiltzik, "Why the US Has to Settle for Low-Speed Data," *Los Angeles Times,* August 25, 2013, B1.

102. See, for example, Tom McGinty, "Revolving Door at the SEC: Staffer One Day, Opponent the Next," *Wall Street Journal,* April 5, 2010, C1. Thomas Frank, in his "The Gulf Spill and the Revolving Door," *Wall Street Journal,* May 12, 2010, A17, notes how the "revolving door" has long been customary in other sectors.

103. Michael Hiltzik, "Door Revolves Quickly at FCC," *Los Angeles Times,* May 22, 2011, B1; Amy Schatz, "Comcast Queried on FCC Hire," *Wall Street Journal,* May 21, 2011, B3.

increase in its oligopolistic power through that merger. Mergers of this sort usually end up promoting higher fees and tolls for consumers, and become a major obstacle for independent content production.

High-level executives of corporations being regulated also take a leave of absence and join regulatory agencies for a period of time, only to return later once their federal service ends—in what amounts to a two-way version of the "revolving door" scheme. In this way, regulatory agencies get direct influence from individuals with executive experience in the corporations being regulated, while inside knowledge of the regulatory process gets transferred back to the corporations being regulated. Executives also sometimes join the staffs of powerful politicians when they leave their corporate employer, as a way to gain direct experience with the political process—and to later use such experience to benefit corporate interests. Reviews of financial disclosure forms, for example, revealed that about 250 staff members of politicians in the U.S. Congress received $13 million in a single year—from former corporate employers or from companies they themselves owned.[104] One case involved a former Comcast Corporation executive, who received $1.2 million from that corporation after he started to work as a top aide for one of the most powerful senators in the U.S. Congress.

In the American wireless telecommunications sector, four corporations dominate, with the two largest covering more than one hundred million subscribers each.[105] That oligopolistic control is partly to blame for the United States' lag in broadband development, as it discourages those companies from upgrading their networks. Thus, even though the United States was at the forefront of broadband Internet access in the late 1990s, it is now far behind most other rich nations in practically every measure of broadband connectivity, low cost, and service quality.[106] As technological convergence between broadband Internet, wireless communications, and cable television advances, those four corporations are likely to expand their oligopolistic power. One vehicle, beyond tacit price fixing, is to ration broadband

---

104. Brody Mullins and Danny Yadron, "Government Jobs, Outside Income," *Wall Street Journal,* June 22, 2011, A1.

105. The two largest corporations in this sector are AT&T and Verizon (as of January 2011). See Foster and McChesney, "Internet's Unholy Marriage," 7; Crawford, *Captive Audience.*

106. See, for example, James Losey and Chiehyu Li, *Price of the Pipe: Comparing the Price of Broadband Service around the Globe* (Washington, DC: New America Foundation, 2010); Hiltzik, "Why the US Has to Settle."

Internet access by charging differential rates to customers, based on access speed, amount of data downloaded, number of sites visited, or time used.[107] Some Internet service providers—such as oligopolist Cox Communications, originally a provider of cable television but now a combined television, Internet, and telephone service corporation—are already charging differential rates based on speed, thereby implementing what is essentially a toll charge that rations usage.[108] Such charges—and the tacit price fixing that often occurs among oligopolists—will most likely increase the power of the few corporations that control Internet access, while deepening the digital divide as households unable to afford the tolls and higher prices curtail their usage, or are forced to drop it altogether.

Technological convergence has also driven cable television oligopolists—most of which now also provide Internet and conventional telephone service—to expand into the domains conquered by the wireless telecommunication oligopolies. Comcast is, for example, overhauling its technology to make it possible to provide live television to any device that can connect to the Internet, most of all, the wireless ones.[109] To do so, Comcast is utilizing the same standard used to deliver data over the Internet—a protocol that has long been employed by companies that challenge its traditional for-pay cable television business model. Its acquisition of film and television oligopolist NBCUniversal in 2013 also allowed Comcast to turn itself into a diversified media oligopoly, expanding its control to a sector where it did not previously operate.[110] As a result, Comcast became the world's largest media corporation—and the most powerful one in the United States—with control over a vast range of content through broadcast and cable television networks, in addition to a

---

107. See Christopher Rhoads and Niraj Sheth, "Carriers Eye Pay-As-You-Go Internet," *Wall Street Journal,* October 21, 2009, B5.

108. Cox Communications provides four levels of residential broadband Internet access, based on speed; see http://ww2.cox.com/residential/internet.cox (accessed November 27, 2011).

109. Jessica E. Vascellaro, "Comcast Tests Tech Overhaul," *Wall Street Journal,* May 26, 2011, B1.

110. Martin Peers, John Jannarone, and Kate Linebaugh, "Comcast Buys Rest of NBC's Parent," *Wall Street Journal,* February 13, 2013, A1; "Comcast's Future: Thinking Outside the Set-Top Box—America's Largest Cable Company Is Becoming More Like the Firms It Is Battling Against for the Attention of Couch Potatoes," *The Economist,* December 14, 2013, 69–70. Further consolidation among other cable television oligopolists seems likely, as they try to imitate Comcast and expand their power over related media sectors; see Shalini Ramachandran, Dana Cimilluca, and Brent Kendall, "Rivals Eye Deal for No. 2 Cable Company," *Wall Street Journal,* November 23, 2011, A1.

major Hollywood studio and even a theme park. A projected outcome of convergence and concentration in this area is a rapid rise in charges—cable television service charges alone, for example, are projected to rise by 43 percent between 2011 and 2015, and 132 percent between 2015 and 2020, for the average American household.[111] Another result of oligopolistic convergence in the cable television and wireless telecom sectors is likely to be more mergers and even larger oligopolies—leading to the emergence of fully integrated, television-telecommunications-Internet access mega-oligopolies.

Looking beyond service provision, the Internet itself has become a medium for oligopoly creation. One corporation—Google—controls almost three-quarters of the search engine sector, and seems set to increase its power.[112] Large Internet-related corporations—such as Intel, Microsoft, Amazon, Cisco, Facebook, and eBay—have substantial oligopolistic power over specific sectors and are set to expand their control to related service niches.[113] Any new market

---

111. NDP Group, "Average Monthly Pay-TV Subscription Bills May Top $200 by 2020" (April 10, 2012), https://www.npd.com/wps/portal/npd/us/news/pressreleases/pr_120410. Over a sixteen-year period (1996–2012), the average price for basic cable TV increased by three times the annual inflation rate, on an annual basis—a result of oligopolistic concentration in that sector; see John McCain, "Cable TV, the Right Way," *Los Angeles Times,* May 23, 2013, A23.

112. See Siva Vaidhyanathan, *The Googlization of Everything (And Why We Should Worry)* (Berkeley: University of California Press, 2011); André Schiffrin, *Words and Money* (London: Verso, 2011); Jeffrey Katz, "Google's Monopoly and Internet Freedom," *Wall Street Journal,* June 8, 2012, A15; Jia Lynn Yang, "Google: A 'Natural' Monopoly?" *Fortune,* May 10, 2009, http://money.cnn.com; Beth Kowitt, "One Hundred Million Android Fans Can't Be Wrong: The Inside Story of How Google Conquered the Smartphone World," *Fortune,* July 4, 2011, 93–97. The U.S. Federal Trade Commission in 2013 dropped its antitrust case against Google, in what became another example of regulatory inaction on oligopoly formation; see, for example, Edward Wyatt, "A Victory for Google as FTC Takes No Formal Steps," *New York Times,* January 3, 2013, http://www.nytimes.com/2013/01/04, and his "Critics of Google Antitrust Ruling Fault the Focus," *New York Times,* January 6, 2013, http://www. nytimes.com/2013/01/07.

113. See, for example, Shira Ovide, "Microsoft to Buy Nokia's Mobile Business," *Wall Street Journal,* September 3, 2013, A1. Expansion of control includes owning much of the world's Internet backbone, by the oligopolists that supply online content. Google, for example, controlled more than 100,000 miles of fiber-optic cable routes around the world as of late 2013, and was set to expand its reach rapidly. Both Google and Facebook had invested heavily in new Asian submarine fiber optic cable routes in years prior to 2013. In Europe, Facebook had also started (in June 2013) to use dormant wireline (known as "dark fiber") to extend its reach, while Amazon and Microsoft had long been investing in cable network infrastructure to boost growth in their cloud-computing businesses. See Drew Fitzgerald and Spencer E. Ante, "Firms Aim to Control Internet's Backbone," *Wall Street Journal,* December 17, 2013, A1.

that can increase revenues significantly attracts their attention, as in the case of eBay and its plan to target minors for its business—part of an increasing effort by many Internet-based oligopolies to enlist children as customers.[114] In wireless Internet, two corporations control more than two-thirds of this sector, despite its relatively young age. Similar or greater concentrations of market power are developing in most other areas of Internet-based commerce. Music sales, for example, a competitive sector in pre-Internet days, is now one of the most oligopolized, with one corporation controlling close to 90 percent of music downloads.[115] The oligopolistic power of these corporations, and the ongoing convergence of Internet-based commerce, telecommunications, and entertainment, also pose serious threats to individual privacy. Personal data are being collected and mined by these corporations to an unprecedented extent, making it possible to spy on individuals' transactions, preferences, and communications in order to find ways to profit from them.[116]

Corporate oligopolies are also setting and appropriating standards for Internet-based services, such as online video. An essential standard in this area already serves almost three-quarters of the online video market, and is licensed to a small group of large and very powerful corporations that

---

114. Greg Bensinger, "Ebay to Target Under-18 Set," *Wall Street Journal,* July 26, 2012, B1. Children are increasingly being targeted as a major new source of revenue by oligopolists in diverse sectors; see Joel Bakan, *Childhood Under Siege: How Big Business Targets Children* (New York: Free Press, 2011). Food producer oligopolies, for example, target children through games in touch-screen telephones and tablets, using specially designed apps; see Anton Troianovski, "Child's Play: Food Makers Hook Kids on Mobile Games," *Wall Street Journal,* September 18, 2012, A1.

115. See Adam L. Penenberg, "The Evolution of Amazon," *Fast Company,* July 2009, 66–74; Sascha D. Meinrath, James W. Losey, and Victor Pickard, "Digital Feudalism: Enclosures and Erasures from Digital Rights Management to the Digital Divide," *CommLaw Conspectus* 19 (2011): 1–12.

116. See, for example, David Sarno, "Watching a Screen? It Watches You Too," *Los Angeles Times,* October 2, 2011, A1; Michael Hiltzik, "Online, They've Got My Number," *Los Angeles Times,* June 6, 2010, B1; Jessica E. Vascellaro, "TV's Next Wave: Tuning In To You," *Wall Street Journal,* March 7, 2011, A11; "Facebook's Face Problem," *Los Angeles Times,* June 11, 2011, A16; Julie Wernau, "Groupon Changes Privacy Policy to Collect More Info," *Los Angeles Times,* July 12, 2011, B5; Julia Angwin and Jennifer Valentino-DeVries, "Google's iPhone Tracking: Web Giant, Others Bypassed Apple Browser Settings for Guarding Privacy," *Wall Street Journal,* February 17, 2012, A1; "Microsoft and Privacy: Change of Track; Data on People's Online Behaviour Are Worth Both Paying For and Arguing Over," *The Economist,* June 9, 2012, 70. The fact that over 90 percent of the world's personal computers (desktops) run on a version of Microsoft's Windows provides a formidable opportunity in this regard; see "Microsoft Blues," *The Economist,* May 11, 2013, 72.

include Microsoft and Apple.[117] Through their license and the vast portion of the market the standard serves, this small group of powerful corporations can charge tolls for viewing selected online video content. Thus, for example, videos extracted from popular films or concerts would incur toll charges for those who want to access them, simply because they are in high demand and are deemed toll-worthy by the oligopolistic corporations that control the standard.

Computer operating systems provide another example of oligopolistic control, and of the staying power of oligopolies once they are established. Despite the free availability and higher quality of Open Source (Linux) software, Microsoft has managed to maintain its longstanding control over the desktop operating software sector. Microsoft's strategy was to turn its operating software into a "platform" upon which many others could build applications—specialized software products commonly known as "apps" that required Microsoft's basic operating system in order to work.[118] This "apps platform" strategy created a formidable entry barrier for any competitor seeking to build a rival operating system, since it locked in Microsoft's business users and apps producers. As a result, companies that built their business models on Microsoft's platform became totally dependent on its oligopolistic control over the underlying operating software. Their dependence provided increasing revenue streams to Microsoft, because of its pricing power and technical control—over a resource that became fundamental to sustain their business models. It has therefore proven very difficult for the Linux Open Source software to reduce Microsoft's oligopolistic power, despite its higher quality and free availability—given Microsoft's vast, locked-in customer base, the diversity of apps that its software platform supports, and its early, overwhelming control over its sector.

A similar strategy is now being pursued by companies with substantial power over some Internet-based markets, such as portable wireless computing and search engines. Apple Computer's strategy for its wireless devices, in particular, is to lock in customers by providing Internet-based applications that are specific to its products, and that will not work with any other

---

117. See Foster and McChesney, "Internet's Unholy Marriage," 9; Meinrath, Losey, and Pickard, "Digital Feudalism."

118. See, for example, Jennifer Edstrom and Martin Eller, *Barbarians Led by Bill Gates: Microsoft from the Inside, How the World's Richest Corporation Wields Its Power* (New York: Holt, 1998); James Wallace, *Overdrive: Bill Gates and the Race to Control Cyberspace* (New York: Wiley, 1997).

company's devices.[119] Apple's App Store, an online shop that sells the company's apps, for example, now stocks many hundreds of thousands of them.[120] Its constellations of apps are so vast and interrelated that they are often referred to as a digital ecosystem—a strategy that has helped this oligopolist gain control over much of the cybercommunications market. Google is also developing apps based on its dominance of the search engine market, providing a platform to launch tailored software tools that must use its engine and other services.[121] Once a significant number of users are locked into the apps, the usual practice for an oligopolist is to increase prices, thus building revenue streams on its control over the apps and the technology that sustains them.

Another disturbing aspect is that corporations that have oligopolistic power in the area of informatics and computing are drawing many of their innovations from Open Source networks. Open Source, once considered a revolutionary force for democratization, for collaborative research, and for creativity, is thus being turned into a corporate tool.[122] Taking or modifying what Open Source networks generate saves vast amounts in corporate Research and Development (R&D)—the most important single function of a tech corporation today, and often also the most expensive one to sustain. Large global corporations in computing and communications—such as IBM—now introduce Open Source–generated software in the hardware

---

119. See Jeffrey S. Young and William L. Simon, *iCon: Steve Jobs, the Greatest Second Act in the History of Business* (Hoboken: Wiley, 2005); Jeffrey L. Cruikshank, *The Apple Way* (New York: McGraw-Hill, 2006). Acquiring Internet-based companies that can expand Apple's locked-in market niche is also part of this strategy; see Daisuke Wakabayashi and Douglas MacMillan, "Apple Buys Twitter Data Tool," *Wall Street Journal,* December 3, 2013, B1.

120. See, for example, "Another Digital Gold Rush," *The Economist,* May 14, 2011, 85–87.

121. Mike Swift, "Google Apps Store Is a Launch Pad for Start-Ups," *Los Angeles Times,* May 26, 2011, B5.

122. It escaped the attention of many researchers of Open Source software that what the network produced might be used by for-profit corporations in their products. In this way, far from being a noncapitalist vehicle for creativity and research, Open Source becomes a tool of large oligopolistic corporations, and of corporate power in general. Most of the Fortune 500 corporations—all of them oligopolists in their respective sectors—for example, are now powered by Linux; see Roger Parloff, "How Linux Conquered the 500: Once Dismissed, It Now Powers Most of the Fortune 500," *Fortune,* May 20, 2013, 82. See also Johan Söderberg, *Hacking Capitalism: The Free and Open Source Software Movement* (New York: Routledge, 2007); "Born Free: Open-Source Software Firms Are Flourishing, But Are Also Becoming Less Distinctive," *The Economist,* May 30, 2009, 69.

they manufacture, thereby enhancing their oligopolistic power. In this way, Open Source creativity and products that are generated free of charge, through the work of thousands of volunteers around the world, are being tacitly appropriated to support oligopolistic corporate power.

The new reality threatening Open Source networks is compounded by the fact that inventions and new technologies are not leading to greater competition. If they do so it is often only temporarily, until a powerful corporation appropriates the new technology or takes over the firm that came up with it. Thus, when new technologies create new sectors or market niches that are not taken over by preexisting oligopolists, it can be expected that a new oligopolist will emerge. This was the case with Microsoft and its control over desktop computer operating software starting in the late 1970s, when IBM decided not to enter that market niche. Much the same happened with Facebook and its control over online social networks, a market segment that Google and other Internet-based corporations failed to identify early on and take over.[123] In this way, inventions and new technologies lead to fenced-in markets, through which oligopolists amass their power over consumers and society.

The corporate oligopolization of the Internet is also aided by a peculiar characteristic of networks. Unlike every other resource, the value of a network increases with greater connectivity rather than with its scarcity. This means that instead of scarcity driving up value for a wanted resource (in this case network access)—as mainstream economics has assumed for more than two centuries—abundance of connectivity is the real driver of value in networks.[124] Thus, once a corporation builds up connectivity, as in the case of Google in the search engine market, for example, a winner-takes-all condition develops that practically prevents any competitor from becoming established.[125] A winner-takes-all situation in the search engine market can also erect digital divides that favor specific languages, ethnicities, and political systems—as some peoples and nations have been

---

123. A phenomenon that is also occurring with other Internet social networking corporations; see "Tweeting All the Way to the Bank," *The Economist*, July 25, 2009, 61–62.

124. See the chapter "Networks as Mediators," in Luis Suarez-Villa, *Technocapitalism: A Critical Perspective on Technological Innovation and Corporatism* (Philadelphia: Temple University Press, 2009), for an extensive discussion of this aspect.

125. See, for example, Vaidhyanathan, *Googlization*; Steven Levy, *In the Plex: How Google Thinks, Works, and Shapes our Lives* (New York: Simon and Schuster, 2011).

finding out.[126] In the area of social networks, similarly, Facebook's early start in amassing connectivity provided it with a winner-take-all advantage that allows it to prevent potential competitors from emerging. Its purchase of a small but promising company involved in photo-sharing—Instagram—for one billion dollars (despite the fact that it had no revenues) is one such instance.[127] As a corporation achieves oligopolistic power, this value-connectivity feature of networks virtually ensures that it will amass more market power, effectively setting up barriers to entry that prevent potential competitors from establishing a foothold.

Those barriers to entry also allow oligopolists to amass considerable amounts of capital, turning them into the richest companies in the sectors they control. The large amounts of capital at their disposal, in turn, make it harder for any potential competitors to challenge their power, as the capital they have is deployed to take over companies that might become rivals. Such large amounts of capital may also be used to expand into other fields and extend their oligopolistic power, thus conquering emerging market niches and erecting new barriers to entry. This situation is most noticeable in high tech and Internet-based sectors, where corporations such as Google, Apple, and Microsoft have amassed tens of billions of dollars that they use to acquire other companies.

Microsoft, for example, acquired Internet telephone service provider Skype for $8.5 billion in 2011—the most expensive acquisition in Microsoft's history—and Nokia's mobile telephony business for $7 billion in 2013.[128] Microsoft's unsolicited bid for Skype, the substantial amount it paid, and its rush to acquire it (Skype had no other suitors) points to the takeover frenzy that has seized Internet-based oligopolists as they seek to expand their power and control. Over a nine-month period, Google alone acquired forty companies, setting a record for acquisitions as it extended its search engine empire to any area of the Internet that showed promise.[129] Other tech

---

126. See Elad Segev, *Google and the Digital Divide: The Bias of Online Knowledge* (Oxford: Chandos, 2010).

127. See "Facestagram's Photo Opportunity," *The Economist,* April 14, 2012, 71.

128. See, for example, Nick Wingfield, "Microsoft Dials Up Change: CEO Ballmer Defends Hefty $8.5 Billion Price Tag for Internet-Phone Firm Skype," *Wall Street Journal,* May 11, 2011, A1; Ovide, "Microsoft to Buy Nokia's Mobile Business."

129. See Michael Hiltzik, "Google Too Big for Own Good," *Los Angeles Times,* May 13, 2012, B1. The takeover of Web-based services by a few large corporations—and the consequent elimination of competition—are part of our contemporary online reality. See, for example, Foster and McChesney, "Internet's Unholy Marriage," 11; Michael Wolff, "The Web is Dead; Long Live the Internet. Who's to Blame: Them," *Wired,* September 2010, 166.

companies closely followed this strategy, striving to amass oligopolistic power in their respective sectors. Facebook, for example, acquired twelve companies in the first three months of 2012—in addition to the twelve other companies it had purchased in 2011.[130] Zynga acquired twenty-two companies in 2010 and 2011, while Groupon bought twenty-three companies between 2010 and early 2012.[131] Such acquisitions have also become common in other oligopolized sectors, and they account for the rising concentration of market power in the hands of a few large corporations almost everywhere we look.

In the oil industry, for example, another sector of vital importance, three giant corporations—Exxon Mobil, Chevron, and Conoco-Phillips—are consistently among the richest American companies by revenue, year after year.[132] These and a few other oligopolists not only control most oil distribution in the United States, but are also among the largest beneficiaries of corporate welfare, despite their enormous profits and the federal government's deficits.[133] It should not surprise, therefore, that these and other powerful corporations in this sector make substantial contributions to political organizations, particularly those that sponsor conservative politicians—most of all, those who serve on energy-related panels in the U.S. Congress.[134] The returns on these practices can be quite substantial—it has been estimated, for example, that oil companies receive $59 back for every dollar they spend on political donations and lobbying.[135] As a consequence, more than $40 billion per year in taxpayer-funded subsidies are provided to the oil oligopolies—especially the five largest (Exxon Mobil, Chevron, Conoco-Phillips, BP, Royal Dutch Shell)—a privilege that has

---

130. Shayndi Raice, "New Tech Spenders in Feeding Frenzy: Facebook, Groupon, and Zynga Snapped Up 21 Firms in First Quarter, Looking to Gain a Mobile Edge," *Wall Street Journal,* May 14, 2012, B1.

131. Ibid., B2.

132. These three corporations ranked second, third, and fourth, respectively, in total revenues for 2010 in the Fortune 500 annual ranking; see "Largest U.S. Corporations, Fortune 500," *Fortune,* May 23, 2011, F1–F10. The three companies' combined profits amounted to $61 billion in 2010, with Exxon Mobil and Chevron ranking as the first and third most profitable corporations in the United States.

133. See, for example, Kim Geiger and Tom Hamburger, "Oil's Rich History of Federal Subsidies," *Los Angeles Times,* May 25, 2010, A1.

134. "Big Breaks for Big Oil," editorial, *Los Angeles Times,* January 28, 2011, A26; Richard Simon, "GOP Halts Bid to Cut Oil Tax Breaks," *Los Angeles Times,* May 18, 2011, A10. See also the data compiled by the Center for Responsive Politics, www.opensecrets.org.

135. Steve Katzmann, "One Dollar In, Fifty-Nine Out," *Oil Change International* (January 26, 2012), http://priceofoil.org/2012/01/26/one-dollar-in-fifty-nine-out/.

become virtually impossible to reverse.[136] Their enormous profits also allow these oligopolists to mount pervasive and very costly propaganda campaigns, paying large sums to advertise their views and influence the public.[137]

The second largest privately held (unlisted in stock markets) corporation in the world, the conglomerate Koch Industries (property of Charles and David Koch, two of the richest individuals in the United States)—an oligopoly that owns numerous refineries, oil pipelines, and chemical and other energy-related businesses—is one of the largest political contributors. Koch Industries was the top oil and gas corporate donor to federal candidates, political parties, and outside groups during the 2010 election cycle. It supports conservative politicians' campaigns and has also created a web of wealthy donors and organizations to influence candidates.[138] Their main target is government and its regulatory role, advocating for the elimination of business regulation—and for a drastic reduction of government itself—apparently forgetting the massive amounts of corporate welfare that companies such as Koch receive from taxpayers. In general, political contributions from the oil sector have become a significant support for oligopolistic power—involving vast sums that politicians find impossible to ignore.

Another sector vital to the public and the economy, electricity generation, is now heavily influenced by Wall Street financial oligopolies engaged in wholesale energy speculation—such as JPMorgan's Ventures Energy Corp., Deutsche Bank, and Citigroup. One oligopolist in this sector, for example, was accused of manipulating bids in a case that was estimated to cost the rate-paying public as much as $200 million over a two-year period.[139] When asked by the federal agency that regulates energy to provide data, the corporation in this case evaded it for months and then furnished

---

136. See Lisa Mascaro and Christi Parsons, "Effort to End Oil Tax Breaks Fails," *Los Angeles Times*, March 30, 2012, B1; Bill McKibben, "Big Oil Needs Subsidies?" *Los Angeles Times*, April 5, 2012, A17.

137. See, for example, David Lazarus, "Chevron's Feel-Good, Misleading Ad Campaign," *Los Angeles Times*, May 13, 2011, B1.

138. Tom Hamburger, Kathleen Hennessey, and Neela Banerjee, "Conservative Duo Reach Seat of Power," *Los Angeles Times*, February 6, 2011, A11; Matea Gold and Joseph Tanfani, "Silent Money Speaks Volumes: More than $55 Million for the Conservative Agenda, But Where Did It All Come From?" *Los Angeles Times*, May 28, 2012, A1.

139. Michael Hiltzik, "Energy Trading Battles Persist," *Los Angeles Times*, September 30, 2012, B1; U.S. Federal Energy Regulatory Commission, "Order to Show Cause," (September 20, 2012), http://www.ferc.gov/whats-new/comm-meet/2012/092012/E-24.pdf.

what was determined to be incomplete and misleading information. In another case during the previous year, the same oligopolist had exploited a loophole to manipulate trading that was estimated to cost rate payers $5.3 million over a period of five days.[140] The corporation in question—a division of one of the largest Wall Street megabanks—had annual revenues of as much as $14 billion from its speculation with electricity generation at that time. Manipulation of trading involving this basic utility seems to be a chronic problem across the United States—since the oligopolistic corporations in charge own trading rights for many electricity-generating plants, which essentially places them in control of what the public will have to pay. Loopholes in regulation also abound, making it possible for speculative manipulations to go unnoticed. According to one writer who extensively researched this case, for example, "tens of millions of dollars can be won by squeezing through a single loophole before anyone notices."[141]

Air transportation, a basic necessity for long-distance travel in the United States, is also becoming oligopolized. The deregulation of this sector, which started in the late 1970s—long showcased as an example of how it can benefit consumers—has been imitated by many nations around the world. Today, however, after waves of mergers and takeovers, a small number of mega-carriers dominates most routes.[142] Three mega-airlines alone had more than 58 percent of the domestic market share for air travel in the United States in 2012—a proportion that rose to 83 percent after the merger of US Airways with American Airlines.[143] Air fares, although lower in real (deflated) terms than in pre-deregulation days, have become increasingly restrictive, becoming nonreimbursable or incurring penalties and high fees

---

140. Ibid.

141. Ibid., B8.

142. See, for example, David Lazarus, "Fewer Carriers, Higher Prices," *Los Angeles Times,* February 15, 2013, B1.

143. "The Last Great American Airline Merger," *The Economist,* January 12, 2013, 59 (based on data from the U.S. Department of Transportation and the Official Airline Guide [OAG] for September 2012). The merger of US Airways with American Airlines was approved by the U.S. Department of Justice after minimal concessions—prompting one highly experienced antitrust specialist to note that the government "settled for a mere slap on the wrist"; see Jack Nicas and Brent Kendall, "Big Air Merger Cleared to Fly: AMR, US Airways Yield Modestly to Appease US," *Wall Street Journal,* November 13, 2013, A1, A6. See also Susan Carey, Jack Nicas, and Mike Spector, "Fewer Airlines, More Profits: After Decades of Troubles and Restructurings, Four Airlines Dominate US," *Wall Street Journal,* February 12, 2013, B1; Susan Carey and Mike Spector, "Taking Flight," *Wall Street Journal,* February 14, 2013, B1.

for itinerary or travel time changes—and for food, baggage, and even the location of economy-class seats. Onboard and ground services quality has deteriorated compared to pre-deregulation days, an aspect that is usually lost on the public as memories fade. Tacit fare fixing has become fairly common in the airline sector, as carriers imitate one another and a follow-the-leader dynamic usually results in higher fares—whenever one oligopolistic airline raises prices, reduces capacity, or cuts flight frequencies.[144] As a result, air fare increases of 100 percent or more over the annual rate of inflation, on many routes, have been the norm in the United States for many years.[145] On routes where oligopolistic mergers occur, sudden (postmerger) air fare increases as high as 98 percent have occurred.[146] Fares of the so-called "discount" airlines—which do not have the oligopolistic pricing power of the large carriers—have also risen substantially over time, as price differences between carriers evaporate and follow-the-leader price-raising cycles become the norm.[147]

Most medium-size cities are typically served by three or fewer carriers that effectively have oligopolistic control over routes and fares. For many

---

144. See, for example, Doug Cameron and Jack Nicas, "Carriers Keep Capacity in Check: Airline Stocks Rise as United, Delta, and Southwest Extend Domestic Cuts," *Wall Street Journal,* September 14, 2011, B3.

145. See Hugo Martín, "Airlines Get an Early Jump on Fare Hikes in 2013," *Los Angeles Times,* February 25, 2013, A8, and his "US Airline Industry Sees Rise in Ticket Prices, Fees, Profits in 2012," *Los Angeles Times,* May 15, 2013, B5.

146. Scott McCartney, "Where Airfares Are Taking Off: For Travelers, the Math Points to Substantial Price Hikes Where Carriers Merge and Dominate," *Wall Street Journal,* April 11, 2013, D1. In one case, for example, a round-trip fare for a route with substantial traffic (Los Angeles-Houston) rose from $359 to $664 (between August 2012 and 2013) after the merger of United and Continental airlines—the routing to which this fare rise applied increased travel time from eight to twelve hours; see *Wall Street Journal,* Letters to the Editor, "DOJ Isn't Addressing Air Travel Industry's Real Issue" and letter by Robert Pisapia, August 23, 2013, A12.

147. See Scott McCartney, "Can't Call Southwest a Discount Airline These Days," *Wall Street Journal,* June 2, 2011, D1. Follow-the-leader fare increases are usually initiated by one of the large, oligopolistic carriers, but are also followed by the so-called discount airlines; see, for example, Hugo Martín, "Delta Sparks Airline Fare Hike," *Los Angeles Times,* January 13, 2012, B4. The very low fares that are sometimes advertised by the "discount" airlines are thought to be mostly useless to customers, since they are only available for very short periods, apply to very few seats, are usually offered on only one route or flight, and carry myriad restrictions; see Hugo Martín, "Ultra-Low Fares Fairly Useless? Not to Airlines," *Los Angeles Times,* October 7, 2013, A11.

small and medium-size cities served by only one carrier, fares are typically very high, depending on the route and time of travel. Regional carriers—the ones that usually serve those cities—tend to have lower standards for crew training, maintenance and operations, much higher relative accident rates than conventional airlines, and tend to operate as geo-oligopolists in the territories they serve.[148] Because of cuts in service to small and medium-size cities by the conventional airline oligopolists, regional carriers now account for more than half of all domestic airline departures in the United States. Most regional carriers also operate as subcontractors for the airline oligopolists, thus helping extend their power almost everywhere they fly. The airline oligopolists often acquire substantial stakes in the regional carriers, to ensure that they will serve their interests exclusively. Many small cities and towns lost airline service completely with airline deregulation, having to depend on regional rail or bus transportation geo-monopolies for travel. High public expenditures on airport facilities that are largely vacant, have thus become a financial drain for communities with scarce resources and limited tax revenues.[149] The lack of airline service also creates a formidable handicap for these communities' economic development, since businesses that can be a significant local source of employment are least likely to locate in places with limited or no airline access.

Since the late 1990s, the formation of three global airline alliances—all of which are dominated by a few mega-carriers—has exacerbated the trend toward oligopoly by engaging in tacit fare fixing, within each alliance and even between alliances, and by erecting formidable entry barriers to independent airlines in any of the markets they dominate. A growing number of cities in the United States are now entirely dependent on airline alliance members for domestic or international travel, in what has become a case of alliance geo-oligopoly. In international travel this trend has also gained as,

---

148. William J. McGee, *Attention All Passengers: The Airlines' Dangerous Descent—And How to Reclaim Our Skies* (New York: Harper, 2012).

149. Between 2007 and 2012, for example, two dozen small airports in the United States lost all commercial flights; see Michael D. Wittman and William S. Swelbar, *Trends and Market Forces Shaping Small Community Air Service in the United States* (Cambridge: MIT International Center for Air Transportation, 2013); Susan Carey and Jack Nicas, "Leaner Airlines, Meaner Routes," *Wall Street Journal*, May 8, 2013, B1. See also Susan Carey, "Small Airports Struggle to Get Off the Ground: Facilities Across US Go Largely Unused as Air Traffic Veers toward Big Players," *Wall Street Journal*, August 8, 2011, A9; Doug Cameron and Mia Lamar, "Delta Pulls Back from Small Cities," *Wall Street Journal*, July 16, 2011, B3.

for example, about two-thirds of all traffic across the Atlantic is now carried by the three global airline alliances that practically operate as oligopolistic flying-combines.[150] Passenger loyalty programs have helped this trend, by locking in millions of passengers who hope to accumulate miles for awards, while the carriers make it increasingly difficult to redeem such awards.[151] In this way, "fenced-in" markets have been created by the mega-carriers—not unlike those of the Internet-based corporations with their platforms and apps, mentioned earlier. The fact that regulators have supported—or done practically nothing to prevent—the oligopolization of airline travel, shows the growing collusion of government and corporate power in this sector.[152]

Meanwhile, working conditions and wages in the airline sector have steadily deteriorated, as airlines gained oligopolistic pricing power through mergers, alliances, and code-sharing agreements.[153] Pilots, airline mechanics, and flight attendants are working more hours than ever on a single shift—for lower (inflation-adjusted) salaries than in pre-deregulation days—in a sector where mandatory age-based retirement typically curtails careers. Increases in working hours have become particularly taxing for individuals who must operate highly complex technologies, and who must often make split-second decisions that can mean the difference between life and death for many people. Aircraft maintenance is thought to be not as closely overseen as before deregulation, while outsourcing of heavy maintenance and repairs to lower-cost nations is on the rise—where American inspectors are less able to evaluate them.[154] Labor grievances have become practically impossible to negotiate with management, as the setting of work standards becomes almost totally one-sided in favor of corporate power. A highly skilled segment of the American labor force has thus been practically relegated to the status of unskilled labor, as deregulation and corporate-friendly rules

---

150. "Climbing through the Clouds," *The Economist*, July 9, 2011, 68, and "The Air Miles-High Clubs: Three Airline Alliances Cover Most of the World—Where Do They Go Next?" *The Economist*, November 12, 2011, 76.

151. See, for example, Scott McCartney, "For Frequent Fliers, A Ranking of the Stingiest Airlines," *Wall Street Journal*, May 26, 2011, D1, and his "Frequent-Flier Award Inflation Is About to Get Worse," *Wall Street Journal*, November 21, 2013, D1. Mega-carriers are typically the most difficult for mileage award redemptions.

152. "Airline Alliances: Open the Skies," *The Economist*, November 12, 2011, 14–15.

153. See Scott McCartney, "The Parking Lot Where Pilots Sleep," *Wall Street Journal*, April 15, 2010, D1; Dan Weikel, "Beyond Their Limits?" *Los Angeles Times*, January 17, 2010, B1.

154. McGee, *Attention All Passengers*.

eliminated unions' capacity to secure better working conditions and higher compensation.

Another, often unmentioned effect of airline deregulation and of the growing oligopolization of this sector is the use of bankruptcy laws to eliminate pension obligations and union agreements. Before filing for bankruptcy reorganization, airlines typically underfund their pension plans so that a federal agency—the U.S. Pension Benefit Guarantee Corporation (PBGC)—ends up carrying those obligations at taxpayers' and workers' expense, but with substantial reductions in pension benefits for both current and future retirees. Bankruptcy judges typically load these obligations on the PBGC in order to make an airline more attractive to suitors—which often tend to be other oligopolistic airlines or speculative hedge funds. In one case, for example, AMR Corporation (the parent company of American Airlines), underfunded its pension plan by $10.2 billion before declaring bankruptcy.[155] Union agreements, which usually play an important role in determining pension benefits, are typically also vacated by judges in order to make it easier for an airline to emerge out of bankruptcy—under pressure from creditors and potential suitors.[156] The judicial system thereby colludes frequently with powerful corporate and financial interests in the case of airline bankruptcies—particularly when oligopolies are involved.

Meanwhile, the combination of tacit fare fixing, lower real wages, diminished benefits and pensions, increases in working hours, the neutralization of unions, the rising power of alliances, and the shift of pension obligations to taxpayers made it possible for airlines in the United States to take in record profits. Thus, the three-year period 2009–2011— which coincided with the worst economic crisis since the Great Depression— was among the most profitable one in U.S. airline history. The year 2010, in particular, set a historical record of $10.5 billion in operating profits for this sector—according to the U.S. Bureau of Transportation Statistics.[157] At

---

155. Susan Carey, Gina Chon, and Mike Spector, "AMR in Pension-Plan Spat: US Agency Presses in Bankruptcy Court for Disclosure as Possible Suitors Huddle," *Wall Street Journal,* January 14, 2012, B3.

156. Even in the rare occasion when a judge rules to uphold a labor contract in bankruptcy, the decision is usually overturned through appeals, refilings, and other legal maneuvers; see, for example, Jack Nicas and Doug Cameron, "AMR Continues Effort to Scrap Pilots' Contract," *Wall Street Journal,* August 18, 2012, B3.

157. U.S. Bureau of Transportation Statistics, *4ᵗʰ-Quarter 2010 Airline Financial Data,* May 2011, http://www.bts.gov/press_releases/; see also other quarterly data for the period 2009–2011.

the same time, executive compensation in the airline sector was higher than ever—as salaries, stock options, and bonuses increased substantially, partly because of the record profits. The widely diffused neoliberal notion that airline deregulation would translate into greater competition thus became a fantasy, as deregulation in this sector engendered formidable oligopolies. Oligopolies that are now also in control of what little regulation remains— exerting much influence on politicians and on legislation related to any aspect of air transportation.

As with the airlines, freight rail transportation provides another example of oligopolistic power in a vital sector. Four corporations now control 90 percent of all U.S. freight rail—Burlington Northern Santa Fe (BNSF), Norfolk Southern, CSX, and Union Pacific.[158] Before the start of freight rail deregulation in 1980—and the waves of mergers it triggered—there were about forty major freight railroad corporations in the United States, with significant competition on many routes. Now, the four oligopolists have divided up the United States into their own territorial monopolies, each with enormous pricing power.[159] Some business customers, for example, have experienced rate increases as high as 500 percent or more above the oligopolists' variable operational costs (which include such inputs as fuel and labor). The Surface Transportation Board (STB)—the federal agency with oversight over this sector—has a history of rulings that favor the four oligopolists, yet it is the only vehicle for customers with grievances. As with many other regulatory agencies, the STB has turned into a "revolving door" through which regulator-executives pass on the way to becoming highly paid rail executives and consultants. The STB chairman during 2002–06, for example, became BNSF's chief attorney after leaving his federal position. His predecessor became a highly paid outside attorney for another freight rail oligopolist, Union Pacific.[160]

Also in shipping, two oligopolists have taken over most express and package shipments in the United States. Federal Express (FedEx) and UPS now practically control almost all time-sensitive shipping—using their

---

158. See, for example, Mina Kimes, "Showdown on the Railroad," *Fortune,* September 26, 2011, 161–66.

159. Curiously, the oligopolization of this sector and its negative consequences seem to be completely ignored by some of the most important corporate-owned media—which provide much praise for the oligopolists' increases in productivity, operating revenue, and freight volumes; see "Back on Track: The Quiet Success of America's Freight Railways," *The Economist,* April 13, 2013, 65.

160. Kimes, "Showdown," 166.

own airlines and trucking fleets. Their combined fleets now operate more aircraft than those of the largest passenger airlines in the world, and also the air cargo carriers'. The rapid increase in e-commerce since the late 1990s boosted their oligopolistic power immensely, as regulators simply looked the other way, and politicians—benefiting from their lobbying and political contributions—avoided raising concerns. These two formidable oligopolies engage in tacit price collusion as a result, and have built insurmountable barriers to entry in their sector.[161] It is practically impossible today for any new or existing company to try to start operations in their sector, given the way they have fenced it in—with their acquisition strategies, the very high cost of building up airline and trucking fleets, the need to set up hubs that require substantial ground space, and the special relations these two oligopolists enjoy with customs authorities in the United States and around the world. Those authorities, for example, let them clear shipments while still airborne, thus saving considerable time. To expand their control in the United States and elsewhere, FedEx and UPS have acquired competing companies over the years, thus setting the stage for this sector to be largely dominated by three worldwide oligopolies—Germany-based DHL being the third one.[162]

Agriculture and food production have also seen rapid oligopolistic concentration, as global corporations—such as agro-biotech giant Monsanto, or the agribusiness behemoths Cargill (the largest privately held corporation in the United States) and Archer Daniels Midland (ADM)—exercise greater market control over crop production.[163] Monsanto, for example, provides almost three-quarters of all genetically engineered seeds for field corn—and four-fifths of all cotton and soybeans harvested in the United States have at least one of its patented genes.[164] This oligopolistic corporation's acquisitions—more than twenty in the 2000s decade alone—helped it

---

161. "Global Express-Package Companies: And Then There Were Three?" *The Economist,* September 1, 2012, 65.

162. Ibid.

163. See, for example, Byeong-Seon Yoon, "Who is Threatening Our Dinner Table? The Power of Transnational Agribusiness," *Monthly Review,* November 2006, 56–64, and the documentaries by Marie-Monique Robin, "The World According to Monsanto" (Ottawa: National Film Board of Canada, 2008), and Marianne Kaplan "Deconstructing Supper" (Oley, PA: Bullfrog Films, 2002). See also James B. Lieber, *Rats in the Grain: The Dirty Tricks and Trials of Archer Daniels Midland* (New York: Four Walls Eight Windows, 2000); Daniel Charles, *Lords of the Harvest: Biotech, Big Money, and the Future of Food* (Cambridge, MA: Perseus, 2002).

164. Roger Parloff, "Seeds of Discord," *Fortune,* May 24, 2010, 94–106.

create a horizontally and vertically integrated structure to support its genetic engineering platforms in soybeans, cotton, and corn.[165] Monsanto's control over genetically engineered seeds, and the associated pesticides it sells, has led to much controversy over their long-term ecological impacts—and their potential effects on human health.[166] Its political clout and its influence over regulation led to the adoption of testing standards for genetically engineered seeds that assumed their long-term effects to be similar to the natural ones they replace—to allow faster regulatory approval, rapid marketing, and to increase Monsanto's own profitability.[167] Farmers who use Monsanto's engineered seeds are required to buy fresh seeds every year, and its "Violator Exclusion Policy" denies access to its technology forever—to those who break any of its licensing terms.[168] Farmers who have refused to purchase its genetically engineered seeds have been sued by Monsanto if wind or water happen to carry any of them into their crops from adjacent farms.[169]

Harmful ecological impacts have also accompanied the power of the agro-biotech oligopolies. Certain weeds, for example, have evolved and become immune to Monsanto's best-known pesticide (Roundup)—used in as many as 90 percent of all soybean and corn crops—forcing farmers to use more toxic pesticides that will be yet more harmful, ecologically and environmentally.[170] Sensing a great opportunity to expand their power and profits, agro-chemical and biotech oligopolists such as Dow Chemical, DuPont, BASF, Syngenta, and Bayer came up with both new and long-ago

165. "The Parable of the Sower," *The Economist,* November 21, 2009, 71–73.

166. See, for example, Dennis Love, *My City Was Gone: One American Town's Toxic Secret, Its Angry Band of Locals, and a $700 Million Day in Court* (New York: Morrow, 2006); Robin, "World According to Monsanto"; Susan Gordon, ed., *Critical Perspectives on Genetically Modified Crops and Food* (New York: Rosen, 2006); John W. Miller, "Monsanto Loses Case in Europe Over Seeds," *Wall Street Journal,* July 7, 2010, B1.

167. Robin, "World According to Monsanto"; Dominic Clover, *Monsanto and Small Holder Farmers: A Case Study on Corporate Accountability,* IDS Working Paper (Brighton, UK: Institute for Development Studies, University of Sussex, 2007); Charles, *Lords of the Harvest*; Clive James, *Global Status of Commercialized Biotech/GM Crops* (Ithaca, NY: ISAAA SE Asia Center, 2006); Miller, "Monsanto Loses"; Doug Cameron, "Monsanto Says New Seeds are on Track as Sales Drop," *Wall Street Journal,* January 7, 2010, B7.

168. "Parable," *The Economist,* 73.

169. See Michael Perelman, *Steal This Idea: Intellectual Property Rights and the Corporate Confiscation of Creativity* (New York: Palgrave Macmillan, 2004), 123.

170. Scott Kilman, "Superweeds Hit Farm Belt, Triggering New Arms Race," *Wall Street Journal,* June 4, 2010, A1. See also Ian Berry, "Pesticides Make a Comeback: Many Corn Farmers Go Back to Using Chemicals as Mother Nature Outwits Genetically Modified Seeds," *Wall Street Journal,* May 22, 2013, B1.

discarded, more toxic pesticides to combat the evolved weeds—in what has essentially become a race to destroy entire ecologies, with potentially serious long-term impacts on human health and the environment. Among the long-term effects of these pesticides, for example, is their disruption of hormones in numerous species, such as sheep, trout, and rodents, and their genetic modification of many plants.[171] The new and more toxic pesticides introduced by these oligopolists also spread more easily through wind and precipitation than the ones they replace, and have had lethal effects on crops other than those they were intended for. Thus, for example, grapes and soybeans grown in proximity to fields where some of the pesticides are sprayed are decimated. In response, the agro-biotech oligopolists developed new, genetically engineered seeds for the affected crops—in what has become a cycle of yet more genetically modified crops that lead to yet more toxic pesticides, which in turn lead to more genetic crop modifications, and eventually to still stronger pesticides. This dynamic has been accompanied by efforts to keep the public from knowing how much of our food supply is now genetically modified—by preventing labeling, for example—which seems to have become a major objective of agribusiness, biotech, and processed foods oligopolists.[172] The high profitability, and the immense political power of oligopolistic corporations in this sector ensures that this dynamic will continue, even as entire ecologies are destroyed. More disturbing is that the agendas—and the interests—of these oligopolistic corporations are now being institutionalized, by incorporating them in the rules and standards that govern food production worldwide.[173]

---

171. Kilman, "Superweeds," A16. See also Brad Balukjian, "Pesticides Found in Frogs Far from Crops: Researchers Are Concerned that the Chemicals Made Their Way to Distant Sites," *Los Angeles Times,* July 29, 2013, AA3. Opinion articles favoring genetically modified foods in the corporate-controlled media typically ignore these and many other negative ramifications; see, for example, Marc Van Montagu, "The Irrational Fear of GM Food," *Wall Street Journal,* October 23, 2013, A15—written by the co-recipient of the 2013 World Food Prize (which also included two individuals employed by Monsanto and Syngenta). International awards usually given to individuals connected to the agro-biotech oligopolists are part of the effort to legitimize genetically modified foods and the corporate interests that profit from them.

172. In one campaign to prevent such labeling, for example, a combine of agribusiness, biotech, and food manufacturing oligopolists in California spent tens of millions of dollars to successfully defeat a ballot initiative; see Marc Lifsher, "Prop. 37 Foes Lead Money List: Big Food Growers Line Up Against Measure Requiring Genetic Modification Labeling," *Los Angeles Times,* August 22, 2012, B1.

173. See, for example, Jennifer Clapp and Doris A. Fuchs, *Corporate Power in Global Agrifood Governance* (Cambridge: MIT Press, 2009); Helena Paul and Ricarda Steinbrecher, *Hungry Corporations: How Transnational Biotech Companies Colonise the Food Chain* (London: Zed, 2003).

Important crop sectors in agriculture that are now largely oligopolistic also draw substantial subsidies from federal agencies. Granulated sugar production from beets and sugar cane, for example, is practically dominated by a few large and politically powerful corporations—such as American Crystal Sugar, Amalgamated Sugar, and U.S. Sugar.[174] Subsidies in this sector partly occur through the government's price-support program, which allows producers to artificially boost the price that consumers must pay—not only for sugar, but also indirectly for a vast range of products that contain this fundamentally important ingredient. Subsidies also involve substantial loans made by the federal government—such as the $862 million in loans that drew attention when a wave of defaults seemed likely in 2013.[175] At the same time, sugar imports are restricted by the price-support program, thereby practically eliminating price competition in this sector. Although initially intended to operate without any cost to taxpayers, the sugar support program was estimated to have cost American consumers as much as $14 billion during 2008–2012—as a result of new farm support legislation passed by the U.S. Congress (in 2008), which was preceded by considerable lobbying and political contributions by the sugar production oligopolists.[176] One consequence of this form of corporate welfare is that the public is harmed economically—most of all, the poor, working people and the middle class—in order to sustain profits for the oligopolistic corporations in this sector.

Food distribution and sales have also become largely oligopolistic. Supermarket chains have gained substantial power over local and national markets, with five large corporations controlling almost 50 percent of all supermarket food sales.[177] Institutional food service has also become largely oligopolistic—one corporation, for example, enjoys a monopoly on food services (cafeterias, restaurants, vending machines) in more than six hundred

---

174. See Alfred S. Eichner, *The Emergence of Oligopoly: Sugar Refining as a Case Study* (Baltimore: John Hopkins University Press, 1969).

175. Alexandra Wexler, "Big Sugar Is Set for a Sweet Bailout," *Wall Street Journal*, March 13, 2013, C1, and her "3 Firms Got Most Sugar Aid," *Wall Street Journal*, June 27, 2013, C1. Sugar processors defaulted on $171.5 million in 2013—despite the $106.7 million that the U.S. Department of Agriculture spent to support sugar prices during that year. In addition, unpaid loans from sugar producers cost American taxpayers $280 million; see Alexandra Wexler, "Despite Defaults, USDA Sweetens the Pot," *Wall Street Journal*, November 19, 2013, C1, and her "Sugar Loans Turn Sour," *Wall Street Journal*, October 23, 2013, C4.

176. Wexler, "Big Sugar," C4.

177. Aman Singh, "Choice at the Supermarket: Is Our Food System the Perfect Oligopoly?" *Forbes*, August 6, 2012, www.forbes.com/sites/csr/2012/08/06/.

college campuses, and also controls all food services at a vast number of prisons, hospitals, and sports arenas.[178] High concentration can be found at the level of food distributors or wholesalers. Only four corporations provide 57 percent of all poultry, 65 percent of all pork, and 79 percent of all beef sold in the United States, while the merger of the two largest food distributors—Sysco and U.S. Foods—virtually guaranteed that further consolidation among (or with) other large corporations in this sector will follow.[179] This dynamic is underlain by the demise of small farmers—since 1980, for example, 40 percent of all American cattle farmers and 90 percent of all hog farmers have gone out of business. In the 2000s decade alone, gross income for small and medium-size hog and cattle farmers declined by 32 percent, while 71 percent of all chicken farmers were estimated to be earning less annually than the federally set poverty income level.[180]

Most other important sectors of the economy have, in a longer time frame, also moved toward oligopoly. In automotive production, for example, only two domestic corporations remain, General Motors and Ford. A third, Chrysler, was briefly returned to American ownership when Wall Street hedge fund Cerberus acquired it from Germany's Daimler, but became bankrupt and was a beneficiary of substantial corporate welfare and a bailout from the U.S. federal government—before it was taken over by Italy's Fiat. Fiat thus became a beneficiary of Chrysler's bailout and of its corporate welfare, when it took a substantial stake in the company without investing any financial capital. Although the market power of all these giant automotive corporations is diluted through imports, they nonetheless have substantial political power, as could be seen from the multibillion dollar federal bailouts of General Motors and of its financial subsidiary GMAC—

---

178. Lauren Silva Laughlin, "The Fight for the Freshman 15: How Aramark Is Silently Taking Over Student Dining," *Fortune,* September 2, 2013, 16.

179. Singh, "Choice at the Supermarket"; Donald D. Stull and Michael J. Broadway, *Slaughterhouse Blues: The Meat and Poultry Industry in North America* (Belmont, CA: Wadworth Cengage, 2013); Annie Gasparro, Sarah E. Needleman, and Ryan Dezember, "Giant Food Distributors Merge," *Wall Street Journal,* December 10, 2013, B1; Technomic Inc., *Industry Reports* (accessed December 10, 2013), https://www.technomic.com/. Consolidation in food processing and distribution follows the oligopolistic trajectories of other related sectors. In soft drinks processing and distribution, for example, three oligopolistic corporations—Coca-Cola, PepsiCo, Dr Pepper Snapple Group—have long been dominant; see, for example, Tristan Donovan, *Fizz: How Soda Shook Up the World* (Chicago: Review Press, 2013); Michael Blanding, *The Coke Machine: The Dirty Truth Behind the World's Favorite Soft Drink* (New York: Avery, 2010).

180. Stull and Broadway, *Slaughterhouse Blues*; Singh, "Choice at the Supermarket."

along with Chrysler—in 2008–09.[181] General Motors' bailout alone was estimated to amount to $50 billion, and was said to be the largest ever in American industrial history.

The oligopolization of the American automobile industry was a drawn-out process, which involved numerous mergers and acquisitions over time. During the first half of the twentieth century, there were as many as twenty domestic automotive companies in the United States, supplying almost the entire domestic market. Some of those companies were taken over by General Motors, Ford, and Chrysler, and were turned into subsidiary brands—as in the case of Chevrolet, Oldsmobile, and Cadillac by GM—in what became the first major wave of consolidation in the American automotive industry.[182] Through takeovers and mergers, this sector gradually became concentrated, and the bargaining power of labor unions declined, setting the stage for the widespread automation of production, the curtailing of workers' benefits, greater job insecurity, and the eventual outsourcing of jobs and production capacity to lower-cost nations.

Those consolidation waves would be reenacted later in other heavy industry sectors, such as aircraft production, steel, shipbuilding, and rail vehicle manufacturing. In passenger aircraft production, for example, only one domestic corporation remains, Boeing. Around the middle of the twentieth century, in contrast, there were as many as seven companies (Douglas, Lockheed, Convair, Martin, Grumman, and Curtis, along with Boeing) producing aircraft of various sizes for the airlines. In most heavy industry sectors, such as steel and shipbuilding, the emergence of low-cost nations as producers in the second half of the twentieth century reduced or eliminated production in the United States, as American companies moved production abroad or acquired foreign competitors. The corporations that survived became larger and took up a multinational oligopolistic projection, retaining substantial market power in the United States while expanding in other nations.[183]

---

181. See Sharon Terlep and Josh Mitchell, "GM Revs Up Its Lobbying," *Wall Street Journal,* May 2, 2011, B1.

182. See, for example, Robert F. Freeland, *The Struggle for Control of the Modern Corporation: Organizational Change at General Motors, 1924–1970* (Cambridge: Cambridge University Press, 2001).

183. A trajectory that attracted much attention in the 1960s and became the central concern of Richard J. Barnet and Ronald E. Müller's *Global Reach: The Power of the Multinational Corporations* (New York: Simon and Schuster, 1974), and of Stephen Hymer's *The International Operations of National Firms: A Study of Direct Foreign Investment* (Cambridge: MIT Press, 1976).

Three important vehicles contribute to the immense political power of oligopolistic corporations in American society. These vehicles have helped establish and consolidate the corporatocratic state. *One of them involves massive corporate contributions to political agendas.* A very substantial pipeline of funds flows to political organizations—and, indirectly, to candidates—who support corporate power. Political action committees that in most cases operate as fronts for corporate interests are a major channel. A new breed of political action committees known as the "super-PACs"—brought into being by a U.S. Supreme Court ruling in 2010—can funnel *unlimited* amounts of money from corporations and from the corporate elites to political candidates, so long as they do not formally coordinate their activities with those of any politician's official campaign organization.[184] Those unlimited contributions can also be used to attack specific candidates, such as those considered unfavorable to corporate interests. Donors to the super-PACs can, moreover, remain anonymous—if political party primaries for the candidates they support are held before the federal deadlines for PAC financial disclosure—thus keeping the identities of specific donors secret to the voting public.[185] Early state-level political party primaries often decide—or at least have substantial influence on—the fate of individual candidates in elections, since they can be decisive in shaping voters' opinions—a feature that can become a formidable advantage for corporate-supported candidates with unlimited funding.[186]

---

184. Although coordination with super-PACs does occur, by means of clues and signals provided by candidates or their campaign organizations through the media; see, for example, Patrick O'Connor, "Campaigns Drop Clues to PACs: Barred from Direct Planning with Groups, Candidates Send Signals to Keep Them on Message," *Wall Street Journal,* July 7, 2012, A4. Perhaps more disturbing is the secrecy involving super PAC donors, and the vast amounts of money provided by the wealthiest and most privileged contributors; see Tom Hamburger, Matea Gold, and Melanie Mason, "Big Spenders to Stay Secret for a While: Several Primaries and Caucuses Take Place Before 'Super PAC' Donors Are Named," *Los Angeles Times,* October 6, 2011, A8; "A PACket of Money: Cash in Hand Is Not the Only Advantage Rich Candidates Have," *The Economist,* October 22, 2011, 34; Tom Hamburger and Melanie Mason, " 'Super PACs' Show Power: The Committees Outspend Candidates in the First Presidential Contest Since Donation Limits Were Ended," *Los Angeles Times,* January 1, 2012, A1; Matea Gold, Tom Hamburger, and Maloy Moore, "The 'Super PAC' Millionaires' Club," *Los Angeles Times,* February 2, 2012, A6; Melanie Mason and Matea Gold, "Operatives for 'Super PACs' Profit from Lack of Oversight," *Los Angeles Times,* February 23, 2012, A1, and their "Billionaires Keep Filling Up 'Super PACs,' " *Los Angeles Times,* March 21, 2012, AA2.

185. Dan Eggen, "The Influence Industry: Revised Primary Schedule Could Shield Super PAC Donors," *Washington Post,* October 5, 2011, http://www.washingtonpost.com/politics/; Hamburger, Gold, and Mason, "Big Spenders"; Gold and Tanfani, "Silent Money Speaks."

186. See, for example, Mark Mellman, "Early Primaries—It's Win One or Fail," *Los Angeles Times,* January 5, 2012, A15.

Oligopolistic corporations are typically the largest contributors to political agendas, and will very likely become much more important after the U.S. Supreme Court's 2010 ruling. Through this ruling, corporations are essentially treated the same way as individual human beings, thus making the law blind to corporate power over politics—a development that has increased substantially the amount of money contributed to political campaigns.[187] Powerful corporations and the corporate elites thereby obtain free rein to influence the outcomes of elections, through their funding of political agendas and organizations.[188] It has been estimated, for example, that if Exxon—a powerful oligopolist in the oil and petrochemicals sector—contributes only 2 percent of its 2008 profits—a year of mediocre profitability—to political organizations, the absolute amount involved would be far greater than the total amount expended by the Obama presidential campaign during that year—the most expensive political campaign in history.[189]

A ramification of the U.S. Supreme Court's 2010 decision involves contributions by federal corporate contractors—corporations that perform work for the federal government in any activity—to political organizations. A thirty-six-year-old ban on such contributions was practically voided when the Supreme Court's ruling determined that political expenditures could not be regulated based on who provided them.[190] As a result, super-PACs became

---

187. See Melanie Mason and Joseph Tanfani, "Obama, Romney Raised a Record $2 Billion-Plus," *Los Angeles Times,* December 7, 2012, AA2; Matea Gold and Christi Parsons, "Obama Hasn't Reined in Big Money," *Los Angeles Times,* January 10, 2013, A1.

188. Corporate elites—extremely wealthy individuals who made fortunes through their corporate activities, capital, or ownership—can also have a substantial effect on political campaign funding, even when they contribute independently from the corporations they own. See, for example, Jennifer Reingold and Doris Burke, "The New Billionaire Political Activist: After Amassing Great Wealth Building TD Ameritrade, Joe Ricketts Bought the Chicago Cubs for His Family; Now He Is Spending Millions to Promote His Political Vision and Unseat the President—Meet a Big Behind-the-Scenes Player in the Newly Deregulated Electoral System," *Fortune,* October 8, 2012, 100–107; Michelle Celarier, "Mitt Romney's Hedge Fund Kingmaker: Elite Money Manager Paul Singer Is a Passionate Defender of the 1% and a Rising Republican Power Broker—He's Determined to Put a Candidate Who Shares His Views Back in the White House," *Fortune,* April 9, 2012, 101–107.

189. Doug Kendall, "Elections for Sale? If the Supreme Court Lifts Restrictions on Corporate Campaign Contributions, Watch Out," *Los Angeles Times,* September 8, 2009, A21; Deborah Tedford, "Supreme Court Rips Up Campaign Finance Laws," National Public Radio, January 21, 2010, http://www.npr.org/templates/story/story.php?storyId=122805666.

190. Ian Duncan and Matea Gold, "Romney Backers Test a Ban on Donors: Federal Contractors Give to a 'Super PAC' Despite a Law Barring Such Activity," *Los Angeles Times,* March 19, 2012, A1.

a very important channel for those contributions—particularly for corporate oligopolists that have contracts with the federal government—in what is one more example of how potential conflicts of interest can arise in public governance. The Federal Elections Commission (FEC)—the most important regulatory body on elections—was practically neutralized by the Supreme Court's ruling, moreover, making it practically impossible to regulate this important aspect of electoral fairness and political accountability.[191] Many longstanding FEC regulations were thus rendered either ineffective or unconstitutional overnight, opening up many new potential opportunities for oligopolistic corporate power to influence elections.

Another important (and legal) conduit for political contributions by oligopolistic corporations is a type of nonprofit—and tax-exempt—organization known as the "501(c)4." These organizations are not required to disclose the identities of their donors, and they typically enable corporations to involve themselves in politics behind the scenes.[192] The law that created these organizations does not in any way prevent them from being political—in the broad sense of the term—or from aggressively backing candidates, although campaign activity cannot be their primary purpose. In practice, the sole purpose of these organizations is to provide a vehicle to conceal the identity of campaign donors and their donations, in what has become one of the most obvious evasions of accountability and democracy—and a hallmark of contemporary American politics.

The importance of 501(c)4 organizations is reflected in the vast, and rapidly rising, amounts of money they gather to finance political campaigns. Of the $300 million in outside political spending in the 2006 election cycle, for example, about 0.3 percent came from these organizations. In the 2008 cycle, they accounted for 13 percent of the total $585 million spent—a forty-two-fold increase in only two years. By 2010, these organizations accounted for 27 percent of all outside contributions in that election cycle—more than double the proportion of the previous one.[193] One 501(c)4 organization—Crossroads GPS—raised almost $77 million in nineteen months from a small group of secret donors—87 percent of this sum came from just two dozen donors who wrote checks of $1 million or more. This organization's president, a former general counsel of the U.S. Chamber

---

191. Ibid., A7.

192. Michael Hiltzik, "Artfully Dodging Donor Scrutiny," *Los Angeles Times,* March 4, 2012, B1, and his "501(c)4s Are the Real IRS Scandal," *Los Angeles Times,* May 15, 2013, B1.

193. Center for Responsive Politics, *Influence and Lobbying,* http://www.opensecrets.org/lobby/index.php (accessed March 13, 2012).

of Commerce and onetime deputy secretary of the U.S. Department of Labor—who also presides over its sister super-PAC organization American Crossroads—was paid $1.09 million in salary and bonuses during that nineteen-month period.[194] In another case, the top executive of a 501(c)4 super-PAC backing a presidential candidate was paid $3 million in fundraising fees over a fifteen-month period.[195] Sixteen anonymous donors contributed more than $1 million each to that organization during that period of time.

The coupling of 501(c)4 organizations with super-PACs also provides immense power to oligopolistic corporations to influence political campaigns—practically neutralizing the restrictions stipulated by campaign finance laws. This means, for example, that a corporate donor can contribute to a 501(c)4-type organization vast sums of money. That organization can then provide the contributed money to a super-PAC run by a friend of the favored political candidate—whose campaign the corporate donor wants to finance. The corporate donor thus ensures that the money contributed goes to the super-PAC, and because that organization is run by a friend of the candidate, the candidate also knows who provided the money—but voters will never know, since the 501(c)4 organization (through which the money was funneled) is not required to identify the donor at all.

Oligopolistic corporations in most every sector also contribute large amounts of money to politically active trade associations, such as the U.S. Chamber of Commerce. Information about these contributions is usually kept confidential, and is not disclosed by contributors even to their own shareholders. Recipients also typically do not disclose the contributions or identify the donors specifically. A survey by a major newspaper, for example,

---

194. Matea Gold, "Anti-Obama Group Nets $77 Million: Crossroads GPS, a 'Social Welfare' Nonprofit, Gets Most of Its Funding from Two Dozen Secret Donors," *Los Angeles Times*, April 18, 2012, A5.

195. Brody Mullins and Mark Maremont, "Romney PAC Fundraiser's Fee: $3 Million," *Los Angeles Times*, May 22, 2012, A1. Fundraisers are particularly important in securing personal access to a candidate; see, for example, Sara Murray and Neil King Jr., "Romney Gives Donors Added Access," *Wall Street Journal*, June 21, 2012, A4. Fundraisers are often considered "investment" brokers by political campaigns—thus, recruiting "investors" who will donate money turns into a fundamental objective, and becomes as important as securing an election victory. A close advisor for one presidential candidate, for example, referred to prominent donors invited to a weekend retreat with the candidate as "our major investors"; see Seema Mehta and Matea Gold, "Top Romney Donors Are Rewarded at Leader Retreat: They Spend Three Days at Posh Utah Resort Mingling with Other Republicans," *Los Angeles Times*, June 24, 2012, A19.

found that only 18 percent of the largest seventy-five corporations in the health care, energy, and financial sectors reported any such payments at all—and that among those that reported them, the figures were below the actual amounts paid, or the donors provided practically no details.[196] Oligopolistic corporations—such as ExxonMobil and ConocoPhillips in the oil sector, and JPMorgan Chase and Citigroup in the financial sector—have repeatedly fought shareholder initiatives that requested disclosure of those payments, arguing that they are "unnecessary"—despite the fact that these kinds of contributions are often much larger than those provided directly to political organizations and campaigns. In one case, for example, contributions to politically oriented trade associations by a large financial corporation were almost 3,000 per cent greater than the total amounts provided to political campaigns.[197]

A second vehicle involves corporate political lobbying. Such lobbying has become an established way of influencing the legislative agendas of politicians, particularly on regulation and taxes. Oligopolistic corporations in sectors that come under direct regulation, such as pharmaceuticals, food, medical care, chemicals, or communications, for example, have been among the highest spenders on lobbying. High returns on corporate lobbying, made possible by the nature of the corporatocratic state and its political system, make this activity a very worthwhile endeavor for any wealthy corporation. Such returns, for example, can be as high as $220 for every dollar spent on lobbying annually, making it one of the most rewarding investments a corporation can make.[198] There are presently no corporate investments that can provide this level of return over time, even in sectors over which substantial oligopolistic power exists.

The combination of corporate political lobbying with substantial campaign contributions can also provide valuable intelligence to corporate executives on legislative agendas. This form of political intelligence can be

196. Noam N. Levey and Kim Geiger, "Big Business Keeps Spending to Itself: Few Major Financial, Energy, and Healthcare Companies Disclose All the Cash They Lay Out, a Times Review Finds," *Los Angeles Times,* April 24, 2011, A15.

197. Levey and Geiger, "Big Business"; Paul DeNicola, Bruce F. Freed, Stefan C. Passantino, and Karl J. Sandstrom, *Handbook on Corporate Political Activity: Emerging Corporate Governance Issues,* Research Report R-1472-10-RR (Washington, DC: Conference Board, 2010).

198. "Investment and Lobbying: Money and Politics," *The Economist,* October 1, 2011, 82. See also Robert G. Kaiser, *So Damn Much Money: The Triumph of Lobbying and the Corrosion of American Government* (New York: Vintage, 2009); David C. Johnston, *Free Lunch* (New York: Portfolio, 2007).

considered equivalent to "insider trading" on sensitive corporate information in the stock market—a practice that is illegal in finance, but not in politics. In the U.S. Congress, politicians regularly provide insider intelligence to corporate, banking, and hedge fund lobbyists on regulatory changes—and on important legislation that affects their operations, their profits, and their power over markets.[199] Political intelligence can also provide a formidable advantage to Wall Street speculators. In one case, for example, political intelligence on a health policy change triggered speculation on the stocks of three health insurance oligopolists—amounting to $662.8 million over a fifteen minute period, which resulted in share price gains of between 2.4 and 8.6 percent.[200] The provision of insider intelligence is helped greatly by the fact that many members of Congress become lobbyists when they retire or lose their seats—a type of occupational recycling that increased much over the past four decades. It was estimated, for example, that in 2012 about half of retiring (or defeated) members of Congress became lobbyists—in the 1970s, by contrast, only 3 percent did so.[201] This occupational recycling from political office to lobbying is important in securing access to thousands of political "insiders"—those who hold important federal positions, or politicians' advisers and staff—who may in turn receive compensation for valuable bits of information.

One case, for example, involved the former Speaker of the U.S. House of Representatives (a multiple-time presidential aspirant), who helped the

---

199. See, for example, Brody Mullins and Susan Pulliam, "Hedge Funds Pay Top Dollar for Washington Intelligence," *Wall Street Journal*, October 4, 2011, B1, and their "Buying 'Political Intelligence' Can Pay Off Big for Wall Street," *Wall Street Journal*, January 18, 2013, A1. Beyond lobbying, government agencies also provide valuable nonpublic information—as in the case of one of one of the wealthiest Wall Street hedge funds, SAC Capital Advisors, and its request for "adverse event reports" on a pharmaceutical company it was considering taking over, using the Freedom of Information Act; see Brody Mullins and Christopher Weaver, "Open-Government Laws Fuel Hedge-Fund Profits," *Wall Street Journal*, September 23, 2013, A1.

200. From the previous day's closing share prices—the stocks of the three oligopolists experienced further increases of between 3.7 and 5.5 percent during the following trading day; see Brody Mullins and Tom McGinty, "Tip on Policy Shift Jolted Health Shares," *Wall Street Journal*, April 4, 2013, A1. An attempt to investigate this incident by federal authorities met major obstacles; see Brody Mullins, Jean Eaglesham, and Devlin Barrett, "Inside-Trading Probe Hits Wall in Capital," *Wall Street Journal*, November 21, 2013, A1.

201. Lawrence Lessig, *Republic, Lost: How Money Corrupts Congress—and a Plan to Stop It* (New York: Twelve, 2011), 99, 123; Robert W. McChesney, "This Isn't What Democracy Looks Like," *Monthly Review*, November 2012, 3.

oligopolistic megabank Credit Suisse gather political insider intelligence on health care policymaking—the sort of information that greatly affects speculation on corporate health care stocks.[202] Credit Suisse, using the valuable insider political intelligence it received, went on to issue a report predicting that certain managed health care corporations would benefit from an initiative by the federal government to reduce costs for Medicare and Medicaid patients. In subsequent stock market transactions, the stock prices of several major health care corporations—all of whom would be affected by the initiative—rose by several percentage points, involving tens of billions of dollars in gains for those who bet on their rising fortunes, based on Credit Suisse's guidance. This high-value political intelligence "industry" has been estimated to be a $100 million annual business in Washington.

Another case involved the successful lobbying effort by six oligopolistic Wall Street megabanks to kill a proposed law that would have split them up. The oligopolistic banks in question were considered to pose a systemic risk to the U.S. financial system, and had to be bailed out in 2008–09 at substantial public expense. The proposed legislation, drafted in 2010, addressed this problem by specifying restrictions on the scale and functions of those banks.[203] Lobbying expenditures by the six megabanks amounted to $29.4 million in 2010, the year the legislation was proposed and discarded—a 33 percent rise over their lobbying expenses in 2006.[204] Lobbying expenditures by the American Bankers Association, the larger lobbying group that comprises the six megabanks in question, increased at about the same rate during 2006–2010—a period when banks fought fiercely against any legislative effort to restrict their influence, despite the massive government bailouts they received during the crisis.

Yet another example—one that combines oligopolistic lobbying power with the 501(c)4-type organizations discussed earlier—involved PhRMA, the pharmaceutical industry's lobbying arm. This organization—which mostly serves oligopolistic pharmaceutical corporations—contributed a substantial

202. Brody Mullins, "Gingrich Firm Gave Guidance to Bank," *Wall Street Journal,* January 13, 2012, A5.

203. See Sherrod Brown (U.S. Senator for Ohio), *Sens. Brown, Kaufman Announce New Bill to Prevent Mega-Banks from Placing Our Economy at Risk* (April 21, 2010), http://brown.senate.gov/newsroom/Press_releases/release/?id=57219a9f-6729-4718-8cc1-1c8286264b07.

204. Center for Responsive Politics, Commercial Banks: Lobbying, and American Bankers Association, http://www.opensecrets.org/industries/lobbying.php?cycle=2012&ind=f03 (accessed February 10, 2012).

sum in the 2010 election cycle to a 501(c)4 organization, American Action Networks—one heavily engaged in supporting right-wing policies and candidates.[205] That contribution, however, was not reported in PhRMA's tax return (which it must publicly provide as a nonprofit organization) until 2011—a year after the 2010 election—meaning that voters and even campaign finance regulators were not aware of it when the election occurred. Because the 501(c)4 organization that received the funds is not required to identify donors at all, the contributions funneled through it to specific candidates were thus never revealed to voters. Similarly, Heritage Action— the 501(c)4 lobbying arm of the powerful Heritage Foundation—never discloses its 61,000 donors despite its important influence on legislation. This lobbying organization ranks members of the U.S. Congress on the basis of how they vote, individually—using a nationwide army of more than five thousand local activists known as "sentinels," to maintain political surveillance on elected officials at all levels (federal, state, local).[206] Another powerful lobbying group, the super-PAC named American Crossroads—a very conservative, pro-corporate organization that helps finance political campaigns—passed most of the $51 million it raised in 2011 to its 501(c)4 organization, Crossroads GPS, with all donors remaining anonymous to voters.[207] These and numerous other cases show how transparency and accountability can be evaded in a corporatocratic state, with the primary beneficiaries being the oligopolistic corporations that generously support their activities.

Lobbying also typically creates valuable channels of influence (and insider information) on powerful government agencies such as the U.S. Federal Reserve Bank—the most important government entity setting macroeconomic and monetary policy—whose decisions affect economic policies and performance around the world. Politically well-connected financial speculators, hedge funds, and Wall Street executives typically gain easy access to top Federal Reserve officials, who provide them with early clues to major policy decisions affecting almost every aspect of the economy—such as interest rate adjustments and economic stimulus actions. Billions of dollars in speculative profit were easily made by one financial speculator alone and her clients, for example, when calls were rapidly placed

205. See Hiltzik, "Artfully Dodging."

206. Patrick O'Connor, "Think Tank Becomes a Handful for GOP," *Wall Street Journal*, July 23, 2013, A4.

207. Hiltzik, "Artfully Dodging."

to clients—after learning directly from Federal Reserve officials that they planned to engage in a massive purchase of long-term U.S. Treasury bonds.[208]

A conduit to receive "advice" from high-level Wall Street executives— the Investor Advisory Committee on Financial Markets—was even set up by the Federal Reserve itself, providing an easy and fast way for Wall Street oligopolists to have access to the highest-level federal officials.[209] This "advisory" body apparently had an important role in pressuring Federal Reserve officials to make decisions and act on the Euro-zone debt crisis in 2011—actions and decisions that ultimately benefited some of the Wall Street oligopolists represented in the committee. Needless to say, Federal Reserve officials are in high demand in oligopolistic Wall Street corporations whenever they leave their posts, because of the valuable contacts and information they possess.[210] Such individuals typically serve as formidable conduits to establish contact with high-level officials—and learn about Federal Reserve decisions early on—before they become known to the public, or even to politicians and other government officials.

Lobbying has also provided immense benefits to oligopolistic corporations and to corporate power in general, in the form of massive corporate welfare—such as tax breaks, loopholes, and subsidies.[211] A study of tax payments by the largest American corporations based on the Fortune 500 classification, for example, found that a majority of them paid far less than

---

208. Susan Pulliam, "Investors Bullish on Fed Tips," *Wall Street Journal,* November 23, 2011, A1.

209. Susan Pulliam, "Wall Street Pushed Federal Reserve for Europe Action," *Wall Street Journal,* December 1, 2011, C1.

210. Luca Di Leo, "New Supply of Former Fed Officials Finds High Demand on Wall Street," *Wall Street Journal,* November 23, 2011, A14.

211. Corporate welfare for the largest oligopolistic corporations is very common—as decried by none other than *The Wall Street Journal,* the most important pro-corporate newspaper in the United States. In one editorial, for example, the *Journal* complained that Boeing, General Electric, and Caterpillar had benefited greatly from the unnecessary and publicly funded U.S. Export-Import Bank, while the so-called sugar lobby gouged three hundred million American consumers through production quotas (and high prices) that benefit only about five thousand farmers; see "A Tale of Two Conservatives," *Wall Street Journal,* June 18, 2012, A12. Lobbying and corporate welfare occur at all levels of government—in California, for example, $286.6 million was spent lobbying in 2011, the largest sum ever, by a record 2,768 entities. Some pundits refer to California lobbyists as "the Third House," to allude to their political and legislative powers (beyond those of the State Senate and Assembly); see, for example, Patrick McGreevy, "Lobbying of Legislators Sets Record: Groups Spent $286.6 Million to Court Lawmakers, Up 6.8% from 2010, Records Show," *Los Angeles Times,* March 6, 2012, AA1.

the corporate federal income tax rate assigned to their annual income—with a large number paying no taxes whatsoever—or receiving tax breaks and government subsidies that amounted to negative tax payments.[212] Among the Fortune 500 group, 280 corporations paid half the official corporate tax rate corresponding to their annual income, while seventy-eight corporations paid no taxes at all or actually had a negative tax rate because of tax breaks and government subsidies. A very large multinational corporation with oligopolistic power over multiple sectors, General Electric—one of the richest American corporations—actually averaged a *negative* 45.3 percent tax rate over three years (2008–2010), due in part to $8.4 billion in tax subsidies. Verizon Wireless, an oligopolist in the telecommunications sector, obtained $12 billion in tax breaks during that period. Wells Fargo, a megabank with considerable oligopolistic power over its sector—which helped create the economic crisis that started in 2007—received almost $18 billion in tax breaks during the same period (2008–2010).[213]

Related to this panorama of fiscal welfare are the tax loopholes on executive compensation that corporations—especially the oligopolies—fiercely lobbied for during the past three decades. Through this long and aggressive lobbying effort, the tax code was effectively rigged so that myriad oligopolistic corporations can deduct massive amounts from the taxes they owe. The vehicle is a tax loophole that allows deductions on "performance-based" chief executive compensation, a very nebulous category that provides wide latitude for interpretation. One study, for example, found that the top five corporations—all of them oligopolies—using this loophole deducted $232 million from their federal taxes in 2011 alone.[214] Compounded over time, and encompassing all the corporations involved, this loophole could account for many trillions of dollars in lost tax revenue during the past two decades. One result of this loophole is that 25 percent of the one hundred highest-paid chief executives in the United States (all

212. Robert S. McIntyre, Matthew Gardner, Rebecca J. Wilkins, and Richard Phillips, *Corporate Taxpayers and Corporate Tax Dodgers 2008–10* (Washington, DC: Citizens for Tax Justice and Institute on Taxation and Economic Policy, 2011), http://www.ctj.org/corpora-tetaxdodgers/ CorporateTaxDodgersReport.pdf; Tiffany Hsu, "Study Finds Many Firms Pay No Taxes," *Los Angeles Times,* November 4, 2011, B2.

213. See McIntyre et al., *Corporate Taxpayers*; Hsu, "Study Finds."

214. Sarah Anderson, Chuck Collins, Scott Klinger, Sam Pizzigati, *The CEO Hands in Uncle Sam's Pocket; How Our Tax Dollars Subsidize Exorbitant Executive Pay,* Institute for Policy Studies, Executive Excess 2012: 19th Annual Executive Survey (Washington, DC: IPS, 2012), http://www.ips-dc.org/reports/executive_excess_2012.

of them with oligopolies) received more compensation than their respective corporations paid in taxes.[215] The average individual compensation for that elite group of one hundred executives was $20.6 million in 2011—more than the taxes paid by each of the companies they headed. Boeing's chief executive, in particular, received $18.4 million in compensation in 2011, while his corporation received a federal tax refund of $144 million based on this loophole.[216] According to one estimate, the total tax breaks provided during 2011 by the lobbied-for "performance-based" executive compensation loophole could have employed 211,732 elementary school teachers in the United States over that entire year—or could have created 241,593 clean energy jobs.[217]

In addition to all these instances of lobbying there stands one entity that serves oligopolistic corporate interests broadly, the U.S. Chamber of Commerce—long considered among the most active and forceful of lobbying organizations. The Chamber took in $189 million in contributions and grants in 2010 alone, allowing it to spend more in political campaigns than any other group, except the two main political parties.[218] The U.S. Chamber of Commerce is thus often considered to be the third most important political party in the United States, given its politicized agenda and its heavy involvement in elections. The vast majority of corporations represented on its board are oligopolists in their sectors or market niches. Oil and pharmaceutical oligopolies, in particular, use it to pursue their lobbying pressure tactics anonymously—thus avoiding the kind of negative public attention that might be attracted if they did so openly. The Chamber's president has even recognized this explicitly, stating frequently that part of the organization's mission is to provide its members with "deniability" on their pressure schemes, games of influence, and other questionable strategies.[219] As a 501(c)6-type nonprofit organization, moreover, the U.S. Chamber of Commerce does not have to provide the names of any donors— in what seems to be an ideal shield from public scrutiny.

The third vehicle through which oligopolistic corporations exercise influence over government is the "revolving door" conduit. This is a fairly common

215. David Lazarus, "Execs Profit at Public's Expense," *Los Angeles Times,* August 28, 2012, B1.

216. Anderson et al., *CEO Hands.*

217. Lazarus, "Execs Profit," B3.

218. "The Chamber of Secrets: The Biggest Business Lobby in the United States Is More Influential than Ever," *The Economist,* April 21, 2012, 77–79.

219. Ibid., 78.

practice that involves high-level corporate executives temporarily serving in government agencies that have regulatory power over their corporations—and over their sector or market niche.[220] The government service involved is typically also high-level and can involve, for example, heading a regulatory agency or holding a presidentially appointed cabinet position that is close to their former corporate endeavors. Through this vehicle, the executives who perform government service can influence or manipulate regulatory policy to help oligopolistic corporate power, in general—and often also the corporation they presided over. After their service in government, these individuals typically return to corporate power as high-level executives—either to the corporation that previously employed them or to others in the same sector.

This vehicle attracted more notice when, in the financial sector in the late 1990s, the head of a Wall Street megabank became U.S. Treasury Secretary—and led the effort to eliminate the Glass-Steagall Act.[221] The elimination of this act contributed greatly to expand financial oligopolists' power over the American economy. Perhaps its most important effect was to remove barriers to the concentration of finance in a handful of too-big-to-fail megabanks—all of which were at the core of the deepest financial crisis since the Great Depression. Almost all of these megabanks had to be bailed out by the government in late 2008, as the crisis threatened to collapse the global financial system. Abrogation of the Glass-Steagall Act also helped raise financial executive compensation greatly, particularly in megabanks and hedge funds. In 2008, the former head of another Wall Street megabank—who was also U.S. Treasury Secretary at that time—was instrumental in leading the bailout of Wall Street banks, including his previous employer.[222] The government rescue packages were most generous, and allowed the top

---

220. See, for example, Alan Zibel, and Victoria McGrane, "JP Morgan Banker Selected for FDIC," *Wall Street Journal,* February 6, 2012, A3; McGinty, "Revolving Door"; Hiltzik, "Door Revolves Quickly"; Frank, "Gulf Spill."

221. Public Broadcasting Service, *The Long Demise of Glass-Steagall,* http://www.pbs.org/ wgbh/pages/ frontline/shows/wallstreet/weill/demise.html (accessed February 7, 2012). U.S. Treasury Secretary Robert Rubin returned to Wall Street in a high-level position at one of the oligopolistic, too-big-to-fail megabanks after his government service in the 1990s. In late 2008 and early 2009, he played a very important advisory role in the bailout of the largest Wall Street banks—including the one he served—using his experience and high-level contacts in government.

222. See William D. Cohan, *Money and Power: How Goldman Sachs Came to Rule the World* (New York: Doubleday, 2011). U.S. Treasury Secretary Henry Paulson headed Goldman Sachs before joining the administration of George W. Bush.

executives to keep their compensation—and their megabanks even made a substantial profit on the use of the rescue funds.[223] After his service as Treasury Secretary, the individual in question returned to a high-level executive position in Wall Street. The practice of employing high-level Wall Street executives as U.S. Treasury secretaries has continued, despite the exposure this practice received during and after the financial crisis.[224]

Attention to the widespread use of the "revolving door" vehicle by the Federal Reserve was the centerpiece of a report by the U.S. Government Accountability Office (GAO) in 2011.[225] The report detailed numerous instances of conflicts of interest, as top corporate executives used their influence as Federal Reserve directors to financially benefit their corporations, and in some cases themselves. The report went on to state that the affiliations of Federal Reserve directors with such oligopolistic corporations as JPMorgan Chase, Lehman Brothers, General Electric, and many others, posed "reputational risks" to the agency. The practice of giving the banking sector—particularly the oligopolistic megabanks—the privilege of providing its own executives to serve as Federal Reserve directors was deemed especially troubling by the report. The GAO report, though widely publicized, had practically no effect on the Federal Reserve's practices—despite the fact that international agencies such as the World Bank, and the U.S. government itself, usually denounce as corrupt governments whose agencies operate with similar conflicts of interest.

A variant of the "revolving door" vehicle involves recruitment and employment—by oligopolistic corporations—of individuals who have long served in high-level regulatory agency positions.[226] Corporate executive positions with substantial compensation packages thus attract those with

---

223. *Bloomberg News*, "Secret Fed Loans Gave Banks $13 Billion Undisclosed to Congress," http://www.bloomberg.com/news/ (accessed January 23, 2012).

224. See, for example, "Treasury Gets a Citibanker: From Wall Street Failure to the Pinnacle of Finance in Four Short Years," *Wall Street Journal*, January 28, 2013, A14.

225. Huma Khan, "Federal Reserve Board Rife with Conflict of Interest, GAO Report," *ABC News*, October 19, 2001, http://abcnews.go.com/blogs/politics/2011/10/; US Government Accountability Office, *Federal Reserve Governance: Opportunities Exist to Broaden Director Recruitment Efforts and Increase Transparency*, GAO-12-18 (October 18, 2011), http://www.gao.gov/assets/590/585807.pdf.

226. See, for example, Ryan Dezember, "Geithner Heads to Private Equity," *Wall Street Journal*, November 16, 2013, A1—on the hiring of a former U.S. Treasury Secretary (also former high-level Federal Reserve official) who wielded considerable power over the bailouts of megabanks in 2008–09, by one of the largest Wall Street hedge funds.

considerable experience in regulation, who can help craft corporate strategies to oppose or evade restrictions. Such individuals can become quite helpful to a corporation's lobbyists by, for example, helping them target specific politicians to influence, or by mapping out how decisions processes work in regulatory agencies. This scheme also provides oligopolistic corporate power with much influence, since the primary function of those individuals is to link up the corporations that employ them with the regulatory agencies that they previously served—by securing inside intelligence on proposed regulations, influencing high-level administrators (their former colleagues), or by helping get executives from the corporations they serve into temporary agency service, to keep the "revolving door" operating.

Another variant of the "revolving door" vehicle is employment of former high-level politicians as lobbyists. The effectiveness of this variant lies in the capacity of those former politicians to influence decision making—by elected officials—on topics that are important to the oligopolistic corporations that finance the effort. One former governor, for example—an erstwhile presidential candidate, who therefore had national recognition—was employed as chief executive (or chief lobbyist) of the Financial Services Roundtable, a lobbying organization that represents one hundred of the largest banking and financial services corporations in the United States—including all the oligopolists in the financial sector.[227] This lobbying entity was vital in securing legislation favorable to the financial sector oligopolists—such as Goldman Sachs, Bank of America, Citigroup, JPMorgan Chase, and AIG—that were bailed out during the financial crisis in late 2008 and early 2009.[228] The former governor who became chief executive of this lobbying organization replaced a former congressman, reflecting how important it is for this body to have former politicians at its helm. The Financial Services Roundtable's chief executive position is one of the highest paid in Washington, with close to $2 million in annual compensation in 2011.[229]

---

227. Jim Puzzanghera, "Ex-Minnesota Gov. Pawlenty to Head Bank Lobbying Group," *Los Angeles Times,* September 21, 2012, B4.

228. The subservience of the federal government to financial sector oligopolists during the crisis was a major point of Neil Barofsky's *Bailout: An Inside Account of How Washington Abandoned Main Street While Rescuing Wall Street* (New York: Free Press, 2012). Mr. Barofsky was the Special Inspector General in charge of oversight for the federal government's Troubled Asset Relief Program (TARP)—the agency that provided bailouts and various forms of corporate welfare during the crisis.

229. Puzzanghera, "Ex-Minnesota Gov. Pawlenty."

The political contribution, lobbying, and "revolving door" vehicles played very important roles in promoting deregulation and the rise of oligopolistic corporate power. These vehicles were aided by mainstream (neoclassical) economic dogma, which became closely allied with neoliberal ideology starting in the late 1970s. *Contestable markets theory*—a staple of neoclassical economics that came into fashion in the late 1970s and throughout the 1980s—made antitrust actions seem unnecessary, thereby promoting the elimination of government regulation in most every sector of the economy.[230] *At its core was the fallacious assumption that economic sectors automatically provide absolute free entry to any firm that might become a competitor to an existing oligopolist*—thus ignoring the many barriers that corporate oligopolies set up to protect their power.[231] Implicit among its various assumptions was *the no less important fallacy that scale economies would not provide any advantage to an existing* oligopolist—and would therefore not pose a barrier to entry for any potential competitor.[232]

The only barriers to free entry into any sector were thus assumed to be government regulation and labor unions. Advocating their elimination became an inevitable policy recipe for anyone who recommended this deeply flawed theory to politicians and public officials. Contestable markets theory was therefore seized by neoliberal ideologues and by the corporate elites as a weapon to justify their views. Labor unions were substantially affected as a result, and many safeguards that protect employees from workplace abuse were taken down. Although the impacts of the theory on policymaking have not been adequately assessed, it served as the basis for practically all of the neoliberal policy positions on oligopolistic corporations and antitrust deregulation. This theory was also used forcefully to promote airline deregulation in the late 1970s, discussed earlier, and was repeatedly employed afterward to back up almost any argument advocating deregulation in other sectors.

Antitrust regulation and law enforcement thus came to be severely crippled, opening the doors to the widespread formation of corporate oligopolies. A major proponent of the disablement of antitrust laws—and of

---

230. See, for example, William J. Baumol, John Panzar, and Robert D. Willig, *Contestable Markets and the Theory of Industry Structure* (New York: Harcourt Brace Jovanovich, 1982).

231. William G. Shepherd, in his *The Economics of Industrial Organization* (Englewood Cliffs, NJ: Prentice-Hall, 1979), identified twenty-two commonly used specific barriers to entry.

232. Scale economies are one of the most important advantages of large enterprise size—a major characteristic of oligopolistic corporations.

regulation writ large—was the neoliberal jurist Robert Bork, a very capable follower and advocate of the precepts of contestable markets theory. His views and policy positions were backed by the free-market ideology of the Chicago School of neoliberal economists—among whom Milton Friedman was most prominent. On oligopolistic market power, Bork opined that laws "should never attack such structures, since they embody the proper balance of forces for consumer welfare," thus enshrining the assumptions of the theory in his vision of jurisprudence.[233] Implicit in this view was the notion that any antitrust action by regulators would harm economic efficiency. In this way, oligopolistic corporate power came to be strongly (and wrongly) equated with economic efficiency, providing a major boost to the neoliberal agenda and to the corporate elites.

The precepts supporting the spread of oligopoly were diffused throughout the planet, becoming enshrined in many nations' economic policies and legal frameworks—and in some cases even in their constitutions. Multinational oligopolistic corporations thus spread far and wide. As a result, the economic weight of a single multinational corporation today is greater than the gross economic product of many individual nations. The influence of oligopolistic corporations over public governance became more important than ever, as the neoliberal economic model based on contestable markets theory—and on the advocacy for greater economic "efficiency" based on oligopolistic power—was applied most everywhere.[234] Control over their social and political milieus became a major objective of these global corporate oligopolies, such that—in the words of two prominent (and prescient) twentieth-century political economists, Paul Sweezy and Paul Baran—they could "buy and sell on specially privileged terms, to shift orders from one subsidiary to another, to favor this country or that depending on which has the most advantageous tax, labor, and other policies—in a word, they want to do business on their terms and wherever they choose."[235]

A major outcome of the spread of oligopolies around the globe is the vast network of very powerful corporations that has emerged. Network

---

233. Robert H. Bork, *The Antitrust Paradox* (New York: Basic Books, 1978), 164.

234. A prescient analysis of the international spread of oligopolistic corporations—and its association with public governance and fiscal crises—was O'Connor's *The Corporations and the State*, chs. 7, 8. See also Barnet and Muller, *Global Reach*; Hymer, *International Operations of National Firms*.

235. Paul A. Baran and Paul M. Sweezy, *Monopoly Capital: An Essay on the American Economic and Social Order* (New York: Monthly Review Press, 1966), 193.

studies at the national level had previously shown that cross-shareholding between large corporations can result in high levels of control over sectors such as automobiles, airlines, steel, and finance.[236] The largest and most comprehensive empirical study ever undertaken on *global* corporate networks—using data from a total of 43,060 multinational corporations—however, has shown just how concentrated oligopolistic corporate power has become.[237] The network analyses showed that only 147 multinational corporations—less than 1 percent of those in the group—controlled 40 percent of the wealth of the total number of companies in the study. All of these corporations were oligopolistic and commanded considerable influence not only in their home nations but also around the world. The most powerful corporations turned out to be oligopolistic megabanks—such as Barclays, JP Morgan Chase, UBS, and Goldman Sachs—reflecting the immense importance of finance to oligopolistic influence. The domination of the global economy by a relatively small number of very powerful oligopolistic corporations has thus become a fact of life in our time.

It does not take much reflection to realize that the vast global economic and political power of these oligopolists is accompanied by immense risk—with the prospect of catastrophic contagion becoming very real when crises occur. Moreover, the supposed diversification of risk that their cross-shareholdings is assumed to provide seems irrelevant, given the immense concentration of power involved, and the similarity of risk evaluation strategies that they—and the megabanks and other financial corporations that sustain them—usually pursue. Those evaluation strategies all too often involve frameworks based on neoclassical economic models, which are inadequate for evaluating risk realistically because of their limited

---

236. See, for example, David Gilo, Yossi Moshe, and Yossi Spiegel, "Partial Cross Ownership and Tacit Collusion," *Rand Journal of Economics* 37 (2006): 81–99; Daniel P. O'Brien and Steven C. Salop, "Competitive Effects of Partial Ownership: Financial Interest and Corporate Control," *Antitrust Law Journal* 67 (1999): 559. Cross-shareholdings between large corporations are often a vehicle for mergers and oligopolistic consolidation—their spread and effects reflected in the rising value of mergers, which reached close to $4.4 trillion worldwide in 2008; see Dealogic, *M&A Analytics*, http://www.dealogic.com/ (accessed December 23, 2013); "The Year in Mergers," *Wall Street Journal*, December 23, 2013, B6.

237. Stefania Vitali, James B. Glattfelder, and Stefano Battiston, "The Network of Global Corporate Control," *Quantitative Finance Papers*, arXiv.org 1107.5728 (September 19, 2011), http://arXiv.org/abs/1107.5728v2. The network analysis in this research comprised 600,508 nodes and 1,006,987 ownership ties. The 43,060 corporations in the study were a sample obtained from 30 million economic entities in the Orbis 2007 database.

ability to deal with uncertainty, and also because they rely heavily on optimality and other general equilibrium assumptions.[238] One result is that the models used for that purpose often become unworkable in the context of suboptimal situations—or end up grossly underestimating the probability of unusual events.[239]

Also, most of those global oligopolistic corporations seek external advice on risk, and on other important aspects of corporate operations, from a very small group of international consulting companies—which tend to provide much the same "best practices" counsel to all.[240] Such counsel depends on the problem or issue being considered, naturally, but to provide anything other than "best practice" advice would expose the consultant to liabilities or blame when outcomes turn out not to be the desired ones. The chances of contagion are thus magnified when crises occur—given that similar practices are usually followed throughout a sector. Longstanding expert-client friendly relations and loyalties also develop, as

---

238. The Black-Scholes-Merton model may be considered an example. Its widespread use was thought to have been responsible for the 1987 stock market crash. Similarly, the use of the Gaussian Copula model—created to measure the chance of default—has been blamed for incurring massive errors in credit ratings and valuations, and for failing to identify the problems with "toxic" structured securities and derivatives—that were behind the deepest crisis since the Great Depression and almost led to a global financial meltdown, in late 2008 and early 2009. See, for example, Pablo Triana, *Lecturing Birds on Flying: Can Mathematical Theories Destroy the Financial Markets?* (Hoboken: Wiley, 2009).

239. See, for example, Nassim Taleb, *Fooled by Randomness: The Hidden Role of Chance in Life and in the Markets* (New York: Random House, 2005); and Taleb, *The Black Swan: The Impact of the Highly Improbable* (New York: Random House, 2010).

240. Three very large global consulting firms—all of them oligopolists in the corporate consulting sector—cater overwhelmingly to the needs of oligopolistic corporations, especially on strategy. These firms—McKinsey, Boston Consulting Group (BCG), and Bain—also provide advice to governments around the world. McKinsey alone employs more than 1,200 consultants, each earning an average of about $1.5 million annually. See Duff McDonald, *The Firm: The Story of McKinsey and its Secret Influence on American Business* (New York: Simon and Schuster, 2013); Andrew Hill, "A Look at Smooth Operators Behind Corporate America," *Los Angeles Times,* October 6, 2013, B3; "The Future of the Firm: McKinsey Looks to Stay on Top of the Heap in Management Consulting," *The Economist,* September 21, 2013, 72, and "Management Consulting: To the Brainy, the Spoils," *The Economist,* May 11, 2013, 67–68. The move of several very large operations consultants and accounting firms into strategy consulting in recent years makes it very likely that further oligopolistic consolidation involving strategy, operations, and accounting consulting will occur; see "Strategic Moves: Big Consulting and Accounting Firms Are Making a Risky Move into Strategy Work," *The Economist,* November 9, 2013, 68–69. One likely result is that a very small group of consulting oligopolies for global oligopolistic corporations will emerge.

corporations and consultants try to avoid uncertainty in their relationships—and corporate clients try to avoid the effort, time, and monetary costs of switching consultants. Consultants tend to become codependent on their corporate clients, because of their own profit needs, the importance of keeping clients, and the longstanding client-consultant relationships that develop. In the United States, for example, almost one-third of the largest one thousand corporations have used the same firm to audit their accounts for a quarter-century or more.[241] These longstanding relationships tend to lead to complacency, and to a reluctance to question dubious decisions taken by corporate clients' top executives.[242] Interrelated webs of professional and personal connections thus develop over time, which influence advice and magnify risk—since the same hired specialists provide similar advice—and refrain from questioning practices that end up becoming commonplace within a sector, or with a set of corporate clients.

Global social networks that informally link the top executives of large oligopolistic corporations—and help mold similar opinions on strategy and practice—are another factor to consider, which can increase the chance of contagion. Global "clubs" of elites from various sectors—especially the top executives of large corporations—often serve as vehicles to exchange and mold views on strategy. They also tend to influence many governments and politicians greatly, by providing policy recipes that favor oligopolistic corporate power. The Mont Pelerin Society—a closed, ultraconservative and corporate-oriented club, for example—often serves as a venue for such exchanges, and for setting strategies that can diffuse throughout a sector and its most powerful corporations.[243] Some global venues, such as the World Economic Forum, held annually in Davos, Switzerland, also help cement those informal social contacts and friendships, which end up influencing how, when and which strategy is followed—along with corporate influence on public policymaking. Corporatocratic governance does, after all, involve games of interpersonal power and influence.

---

241. See, for example, Patrick Krauss, Benedikt Quosigk, and Henning Zülch, *The Relation of Auditor Tenure to Audit Quality Under IFRS and US-GAAP: A German-U.S. Comparison,* Social Science Research Network, December 2011, http://papers.ssrn.com.

242. Jason Zweig, "One Cure for Accounting Shenanigans," *Wall Street Journal,* January 14, 2012, B1.

243. See, for example, George Monbiot, "How the Neoliberals Stitched Up the Wealth of Nations for Themselves," *The Guardian,* August 27, 2007, http://www.guardian.co.uk/; Philip Mirowski and Dieter Plehwe, eds., *The Road to Mont Pelerin: The Making of the Neoliberal Thought Collective* (Cambridge: Harvard University Press, 2009).

In sum, oligopoly capitalism, a fundamental support of corporate hegemony and of corporatocracy, is a predominant feature of our time. This does *not* mean that the set of very powerful oligopolistic corporations that rule society and the economy is monolithic. By and large, those large and powerful oligopolists compete with one another for greater influence over the state, and in some respects even over markets. Their market competition involves not price but cost reductions—achieved through the outsourcing or offshoring of labor tasks and corporate functions, the elimination of unions, improvements in technology (particularly that which eliminates labor), and strategic actions aimed at fencing in new markets or gaining more market share. Price wars—and price cutting—are thus left to small and medium-size companies in the sectors that oligopolies do not yet control.[244] Rather, *price leadership* is the game to play, with the price leader typically establishing a higher price that eventually increases profits for the oligopolistic club as a whole—at least in the sector they control.[245] Thus, the role of price leader is one that any oligopolist in the club is usually welcome to take up, since it will likely benefit all members—even when they compete on costs, technology, and operational efficiency. Competition between oligopolistic corporations in a sector is thus largely "co-respective," in the sense that actions are determined in relation to those of other oligopolists—within the sector—and tacit collusion is resorted to so as to improve group advantage.[246] Such collusion also typically involves influence over public

---

244. Small and medium-size companies that supply oligopolistic corporations in sectors other than their own, may nonetheless find themselves threatened by the payment practices of their oligopolistic clients. Those clients often, for example, withhold or take considerable time to pay their small and medium-size suppliers. The suppliers then have practically no choice but to tolerate it—despite the serious financial troubles they may experience—since taking their oligopolistic client to court will most likely result in the loss of their contract. Payment delays of as many as 120 days by oligopolistic corporations to their small and medium-size suppliers have become commonplace in some sectors; see, for example, Becky Quick, "Insights: A Snack Maker's Unsavory Business Practices," *Fortune,* September 2, 2013, 54. Payment delays can also become part of an oligopolist's strategy to take over its supply chains, by driving out (or under) its small and medium-size suppliers. In addition to the price competition that small and medium-size companies typically experience, they therefore often have to contend with the damaging strategies of their own oligopolistic clients.

245. See Baran and Sweezy, *Monopoly Capital.* Their book—considered by many radical political economists to be a classic—was the most influential conceptual work on oligopolies of the second half of the twentieth century.

246. Co-respective in the sense noted by Joseph Schumpeter in his *Capitalism, Socialism, and Democracy* (New York: Harper and Brothers, 1942), 87–106. See also Paul M. Sweezy, *Modern Capitalism and Other Essays* (New York: Monthly Review Press, 1972); Foster, McChesney, and Jonna, "Monopoly and Competition," 18.

governance in order to benefit the group—even when the specific interests of one or some of the corporations involved have to be subordinated to the interests of the group. *As a result, competition between oligopolists does not lead to price reduction but to cost reduction.* Reduction of costs—most of all, those involving labor—thus becomes the means to greater profit. Also, oligopolistic corporations mostly deploy new technologies when it suits cost reduction and their long-term profit and power strategies, such as the fencing in of new market niches.[247]

Pricing power thus remains paramount, as noted by multibillionaire speculator Warren Buffett—one of the wealthiest individuals in the United States—who greatly favors investment in oligopolistic corporations. In one of his most significant insights, Buffett noted that "the single most important decision in evaluating a business is pricing power. . . . If you've got the power to raise prices without losing business to a competitor, you've got a very good business."[248] This sentiment is echoed by practically all financial specialists, with the erection of barriers to entry becoming a most important vehicle to protect pricing power. A very well-known financial journalist, for example, writing in what is arguably the top financial newspaper in the world, stated that a long-term question for any investor to ask when considering purchasing any stock should be: "Does the company have significant barriers to entry, or could an upstart come in and steal its lunch?"[249]

Beyond sustaining pricing power and erecting barriers to entry, oligopolistic corporations also have major common interests that bring and bind them together—to advance their collective power over the state. This can be readily seen, for example, in the lobbying strategies and political power of organizations that serve whole sectors or industries, as noted earlier in this chapter. Similarly, the vast contributions to political organizations that help numerous candidates get elected—so long as they favor the interests of the donors—is another example of how oligopolistic corporations in a sector, or even at large, can coalesce to protect their common interests. Thus, even when some competition occurs, the pressing *collective need to sustain their power* is enough to bring oligopolistic corporate power together

---

247. A point that is largely contradictory with Schumpeter's key assumption that a "gale of creative destruction" would threaten the existence of large corporations.

248. Andrew Frye and Dakin Campbell, "Buffett Says Pricing Power More Important Than Good Management," *Bloomberg News,* February 17, 2011, http://www.bloomberg.com/news/2011-02-18.

249. Brett Arends, "Upside; Web Stocks: Is It Time for Bargain-Hunters to Dive In?" *Wall Street Journal,* October 13, 2012, B7.

to influence society's governance—particularly when they feel such power to be threatened. *The individual interests of corporate oligopolists may thus be subordinated to their collective interests—in order to enhance group advantage and group power—particularly when it comes to public governance.*

The vast collective power of oligopolistic corporations over the state becomes most obvious in times of crisis, whenever entire sectors of the economy are threatened with collapse. The large size of oligopolistic corporations—and their influence over public governance—practically ensure that the state will intervene in their favor, even when doing so involves immense costs to society. Oligopolies are thus the most important contributors to the emergence of the so-called too-big-to-fail corporations—those that have to be bailed out by government when a crisis drives them into insolvency. The most blatant examples of this disturbing reality were the megabanks that were bailed out by the federal government in 2008–09—a scenario that was repeated over again many times around the world. As we will see in the following chapter, those "too-big-to-fail" oligopolists ended up transferring substantial risks to the state, through their power and influence—making all of society liable for their debts, for their risky strategies, and for the outrageous compensation of their executives.

Implicit in this scenario of subservience of society and governance to oligopoly power is a state that neither provides the people with the means necessary to develop alternatives, nor protects them against the hegemony and the abuses of oligopolists. *The corporatocratic state, in effect, becomes an appendage of corporate power, and, most of all, of oligopolistic corporations.* At most, the state and the political elites look the other way when they see large swaths of the economy falling into oligopolistic control. And we can expect that more often than not, rather than look the other way, they tend to facilitate such control. Money is, after all, a fundamental component of politics and of political campaigns, not only in the United States but also in most of today's world. In the following chapters we will explore other features of corporate hegemony and of corporatocracy, all of which hinge on the emergence of oligopolies as a dominant force in society.

Financialism

The previous chapter dealt with corporate oligopolies and their vast contemporary influence over government and society. A gradual oligopolization of the American economy since the early twentieth century, however, had sown the seeds of a major dysfunction in the central engine of capitalism—the accumulation of capital. Finance capital, which is largely disengaged from production—and that targets speculation as an end in itself—gained greater importance over time. Such capital became more concentrated with the rise of oligopolistic corporations in the financial sector—acquiring greater weight in the economy—while the oligopolization of other sectors allowed speculation to spread far and wide. Rising oligopolistic power throughout the economy thus contributed to a fundamental accumulative dysfunction in advanced capitalism—the overaccumulation of capital—as corporations became heavily involved in finance and as production became both more concentrated and less important.[1]

Periods of crisis revealed aspects of this dysfunction during the first half of the twentieth century. Then, in the 1970s, a deeper crisis involving stagnation, substantial inflation, and higher unemployment shook fundamental beliefs in the sustenance of capitalism. To try to overcome stagflation and greater unemployment, government—following established Keynesian recipes—spent more and resorted to expansionary monetary measures, thereby

---

1. Radical political economists provided the earliest links and analyses between the rising importance of finance, oligopolization—also referred to as *monopoly capitalism* in the literature—and the phenomenon of stagnation (to be dealt with in a subsequent chapter). See Rudolf Hilferding, *Finance Capital: A Study of the Latest Phase of Capitalist Development* (London: Routledge and Kegan Paul, 1981), translated from his *Das Finanzkapital: eine Studie über die jüngste Entwicklung des Kapitalismus* (Vienna: Brand, 1910); Baran and Sweezy, *Monopoly Capital*; Harry Magdoff and Paul M. Sweezy, *Stagnation and the Financial Explosion* (New York: Monthly Review Press, 1987). Their analyses were largely ignored by mainstream (neoclassical) economists, as the field of economics became increasingly narrow and less capable of dealing with the big-picture dynamics of capitalism.

increasing the public debt and fueling inflation.[2] Price shocks in oil and other vital resources triggered further inflation, increasing unemployment and lowering living standards. Manufacturing employment peaked in the United States in 1979 and never recovered, as deindustrialization advanced. The more limited productive investment possibilities that oligopolization generated, along with reduced effective demand—as unemployment and inflation took their toll—also had negative impacts on the economy. One of them was the stock market's prolonged stagnation. During a fifteen-year period (1967–1982), for example, the Dow Jones Industrial average fluctuated barely two hundred points above or below the level it had at the end of 1966.[3] Stagflation, unemployment, declining real incomes, and lower living standards thus became major concerns, and the political and corporate elites began to fear for their hold on power and privilege.[4] Clearly, a new orientation had to be found if capitalism was to have a new lease on life, or a future—any future—at all.

Neoliberalism provided the new orientation, becoming the ideological expression of the corporate and political elites' response to the crisis of the 1970s. Neoliberal interpretations of economic policy by pro-corporate, free-market fundamentalists such as Friedrich von Hayek and Milton Friedman became the ideological beacon, as the elites grappled with the most serious crisis of capitalism since the Great Depression. The neoliberal policy regime—initially tried out in Pinochet's Chile and then in Britain and the United States under Thatcher and Reagan—then sought to dismantle the Keynesian economic policies that had, since the 1930s, tried to provide some balance between the interests of working people and those of the corporate elites. Macroeconomic management was redirected to serve the interests of the elites—by making faster capital accumulation the top priority of public governance. Growth through unfettered capital accumulation thus became the main macroeconomic objective, to try to save capitalism and restore confidence in the political system.[5] Finance provided the key to this

---

2. The scrapping of the Bretton Woods Agreement in 1971 set the stage for expansionary monetary measures, as the U.S. government abandoned the gold standard. See Paul M. Sweezy and Harry Magdoff, *The Dynamics of US Capitalism: Corporate Structure, Inflation, Credit, Gold, and the Dollar* (New York: Monthly Review Press, 1971).

3. StockCharts.com, *Dow Jones Industrial Average (1900–Present Monthly)*, http://stock-charts.com/ freecharts/historical/djia1900.html (accessed February 2, 2012). The Dow Jones Industrials' level was 786 on December 30, 1966 (the closing level for that year).

4. See Harry Magdoff and Paul M. Sweezy, *The End of Prosperity: The American Economy in the 1970s* (New York: Monthly Review Press, 1977).

5. Unfettered capital accumulation rested on the assumption of "market efficiency" as the ultimate, or best, regulator of all economic action—a notion based on general equilibrium

reorientation of public governance, making deregulation, rapid accumulation and monetary measures the central concern of macroeconomic policy.[6]

Deregulation of finance became the prime neoliberal objective to promote growth, starting with bank rates and services.[7] Greater oligopolistic power followed, as bank mergers and acquisitions across U.S. states gained momentum, with risk being shifted to government and taxpayers. The high risk transferred to government became all too obvious during the banking and real estate crisis of the late 1980s and early 1990s, when almost one-quarter of all savings and loan banks in the United States failed—and the total for bailouts during the crisis amounted to almost one-tenth of all 1990 government revenues.[8] Unregulated financial corporations—such as hedge funds—proliferated and became entrenched in the financial system, transferring substantial additional risk to the state.[9] This became obvious again in 1998, when one of the largest hedge funds—Long-Term Capital Management (LTCM)—failed, and a bailout had to be arranged by the U.S. Federal Reserve.[10] Curiously, among the directors of LTCM were two

---

models that became the staple of neoclassical economics starting in the 1950s. The highly unrealistic assumptions behind those models were adopted throughout mainstream economics, and led to a belief in unfettered markets as the solution to most every economic problem—a key prescription of neoliberal policies. See John Cassidy, *How Markets Fail: The Logic of Economic Calamities* (New York: Farrar, Straus, and Giroux, 2009).

6. See, for example, Magdoff and Sweezy, *Stagnation and the Financial Explosion.*

7. The Depository Institutions Deregulation and Monetary Control Act of 1980 and the Garn-St. Germain Depository Institutions Act of 1982 were the early vehicles of financial deregulation; see http://www.bos.frb.org/about/pubs/deposito.pdf and http://www.chicagofed. org/digital_assets/publications/economic_perspectives/1983/ep_mar_apr1983_part1_garcia.pdf.

8. Based on 1990 U.S. federal budget data; see http://www.cbo.gov/budget/data/historical. pdf; Timothy Curry and Lynn Shibut, "The Cost of the Savings and Loan Crisis: Truth and Consequences," *FDIC Banking Review* (2000), http://www.fdic.gov/bank/analytical/ banking/2000dec/brv13n2_2.pdf.

9. Hedge funds' performance, in general, seems to have been much overrated. One experienced financial analyst, for example, estimated that if all money placed in hedge funds had been invested in U.S. Treasury Bonds instead (a very risk-averse investment), the returns would have been twice as high over a twelve-year period (1998–2010); see Simon Lack, *The Hedge Fund Mirage: The Illusion of Big Money and Why It's Too Good to Be True* (New York: Wiley, 2012). Lack also estimated that hedge fund owners kept 86 percent of the returns they obtained using clients' money—because of the high fees charged.

10. See, for example, "Fed Chief Defends Bailout: Greenspan Says Failure of Hedge Fund Could Have Damaged US Economy," *CNN Money*, October 1, 1998, http://money.cnn.com/1998/10/01/ economy/greenspan/. Despite the failure of Long-Term Capital Management, the fees charged and the high risk involved, the hedge fund sector expanded substantially—between 1998 and 2010, for example, total assets under hedge fund management increased from $143 billion to $1.7 trillion. See Lack, *Hedge Fund Mirage.*

prominent advocates of deregulation, who had won the Nobel Prize in economics in 1997 for their "efficient markets" theory—a flawed construct that was one of the most important ideological supports of neoliberal deregulatory policy.[11]

In 1999, the repeal of what remained of the Glass-Steagall Act of 1933—which had compartmentalized insurance, retail, investment, and commercial banking to try to prevent financial crashes—removed all obstacles to the oligopolistic takeover of finance.[12] As a result, for example, by 2010—three years after the start of the worst financial crisis since the Great Depression—the total assets of the six largest bank holding corporations amounted to almost two-thirds of the United States' Gross Domestic Product (GDP)—up from less than one-tenth in the early 1980s.[13] Three of those megabank corporations alone were issuing more than half of all mortgage loans in 2010, and two-thirds of all credit cards—an astounding level of concentration given the size of the American economy.[14] Closely tied to the megabanks, a vast and unregulated "shadow banking" sector

---

11. See Nicholas Dunbar, *Inventing Money: The Story of Long-Term Capital Management and the Legends Behind It* (New York: Wiley, 2000); Roger Lowenstein, *When Genius Failed: The Rise and Fall of Long-Term Capital Management* (New York: Random House, 2000). Efficient markets theory was one of various unproved—but widely accepted—constructs at the core of neoliberal policymaking; see, for example, Yves Smith, *Econned: How Unenlightened Self Interest Undermined Democracy and Corrupted Capitalism* (New York: Palgrave Macmillan, 2010). Among the failings of this and other theories—such as the Black-Scholes model—was the notion that changes in stock prices follow a bell curve (Gaussian or normal) distribution, despite the fact that power-law (skewed) distributions are fairly common in finance; see, for example, George Szpiro, *Pricing the Future: Finance, Physics, and the 300-Year Journey to the Black-Scholes Equation* (New York: Basic Books, 2011). Using the flawed assumptions of the Black-Scholes model, in part, risk analysts at LTCM had estimated that there was a 1 percent chance this hedge fund could lose more than $45 million in a day. By September 1998, however, it was losing between $100 million and $200 million on a regular (often daily) basis until its collapse; see Satyajit Das, *Extreme Money: Masters of the Universe and the Cult of Risk* (New York: McGraw-Hill, 2012).

12. The legislation that repealed the Glass-Steagall Act is known as the Financial Services Modernization Act (or Gramm-Leach-Bliley Act); see http://www.minneapolisfed.org/publications_papers/. Substantial internal changes accompanied the evolution of major banks as their oligopolistic power increased; see, for example, Steven G. Mandis, *What Happened to Goldman Sachs? An Insider's Story of Organizational Drift and Its Unintended Consequences* (Boston: Harvard Business School Press, 2013).

13. Based on financial corporate data from Fortune 500 (http://www.fortunedatastore.com/) and U.S. Census Bureau data (http://www.census.gov/econ/).

14. David Cho, "Banks 'Too Big to Fail' Have Grown Bigger," *Washington Post*, August 28, 2009, http://www.washingtonpost.com/business/.

emerged to process interbank deals involving mortgage-backed securities and numerous other instruments, with transactions estimated at more than $60 trillion as of 2011.[15] The repeal of the Glass-Steagall Act, along with the enactment of the Commodity Futures Modernization Act of 2000, also made it easier for highly complex instruments—such as credit default swaps, repurchase agreements, and myriad types of derivatives—to spread throughout the economy, targeting almost every sector and activity. Securitizing debt through derivatives became the easy road to profits in finance, despite the high risk that most of them carried.[16]

Mountains of debt were created through these instruments, along with a worldwide shadow banking system that lobbied—and bought—politicians almost everywhere, setting the rules of the game for almost everything in finance. By mid-2008, for example, the Bank for International Settlements—the most important organization keeping track of global bank data—reported that the total value of derivatives exceeded one quadrillion dollars worldwide, a magnitude that is practically impossible for most humans to comprehend.[17] In the United States alone, credit derivative contracts issued as of early 2008 were estimated to have a notional value of $455 trillion, while the total value of derivatives outstanding was estimated to be over $600 trillion.[18] Issuance of such instruments created a web of counterparties

---

15. Francesco Guerrera, "Time to Cast More Light on Finance's 'Shadows,'" *Wall Street Journal,* April 10, 2012, C1.

16. Two myths about derivatives have been widely publicized. One of them is that they "expanded credit." However, the excessive accumulation of debt that they promoted—as we will see in this chapter—became a major liability that threatened the entire financial system. The second myth is the notion that they "spread risk." However, most of the risk involved could not be adequately understood or assessed, due to the high complexity of derivatives—and because the three credit rating oligopolies (Fitch, Standard and Poor, Moody's) could not properly evaluate them. In addition, the three credit rating oligopolies had significant conflicts of interest—to be discussed later in this chapter. Risk that cannot be adequately assessed or evaluated becomes a liability, even if it is spread around—and all the more so if the amounts involved are overwhelming.

17. Bank for International Settlements, *Regular OTC Derivatives Market Statistics* (November 13, 2008), http://www.bis.org/statistics/derstats.htm. Notional values of exchange-traded options, futures, and over the counter speculative instruments (such as foreign exchange, interest rate, and credit default swaps) alone were estimated to be about $750 trillion in early 2007 and $800 trillion in early 2011. The crisis that started in 2007, therefore, did not inhibit the growth of these instruments; see "Financial Infrastructure; Of Plumbing and Promises: The Back Office Moves Centre Stage," *The Economist,* Special Report on Financial Innovation, February 25, 2012, 13–15.

18. Editorial, "Financial Insight: Are Credit Derivatives Next? Future Is Looking Gloomier Amid Concern on Collateral, Some Counterparty Worries," *Wall Street Journal,* April 17, 2008, C14; Tim Geithner, "Financial Crisis Amnesia," *Wall Street Journal,* March 2, 2012, A13.

that can magnify and spread almost any problem throughout the financial sector—as occurred during the fall of that year when the entire financial system was threatened with collapse. And, the vast amount of outstanding derivatives has made it very difficult to account for the assets of almost every financial corporation, especially the megabank oligopolies.[19] Further complicating these problems is that derivatives are not cancelled when they no longer have demand—instead, a new derivative that is technically a mirror image of the one no longer wanted is usually created. This means that the failure of even a small group of derivatives can trigger a crisis—when counterparties realize they have taken on more risk than they wanted, and try to unload their holdings as market demand for these instruments collapses.[20]

Debt accumulation through these and other instruments began to masquerade as accumulation of capital, making real capital formation—the one that directly supports the production of goods, services, and resources—subordinate to speculative capital. *High debt worsened the fundamental dysfunction of capital accumulation—overaccumulation of finance capital—but it generated growth, and provided the false impression that a new and more dynamic form of capitalism had been created, driven by financial "innovations."* Growth thus became the great justification for the new neoliberal order, even though its underpinnings were crisis-prone as well as downright unjust—as we will see in this chapter. Among the results of this new reality were further oligopolization of the economy and the emergence of corporatocracy. Placing government at the service of powerful oligopolies—and the corporate and financial elites that owned them—thus engendered corporatocratic governance. Oligopolization and corporatocracy more intensely redistributed wealth and power toward those elites, and toward corporate

---

19. The total 2011 asset value of one oligopolistic (too-big-to-fail) megabank—JPMorgan Chase—for example, could vary by as much as $1.7 trillion depending on how the derivatives it owns are accounted for; see David Reilly, "Deriving the True Size of U.S. Megabanks Is Far from Simple," *Wall Street Journal*, September 24, 2012, C10.

20. An aspect that is further complicated and magnified by the spread of high-frequency trading, a risky and highly speculative strategy that now encompasses more than 70 percent of total equity trading volume, amounting to almost $2.5 trillion annually in the United States alone. See "High-Frequency Trading," *New York Times*, October 10, 2011, http://topics.nytimes.com/topics/reference/timestopics/subjects/; Scott Patterson and Jenny Strasburg, "For Superfast Stock Traders, A Way to Jump Ahead in Line," *Wall Street Journal*, September 19, 2012, A1; Ralph Nader, "Time for a Tax on Speculation," *Wall Street Journal*, November 2, 2011, A17.

power in general, while making finance capital more important and reducing *real* aggregate demand—the kind that is unencumbered by debt. Demand was thus artificially increased through debt—massive amounts of debt that would become an important source of crises.

Debt therefore became a major vehicle for growth, by artificially increasing aggregate demand along with speculation. Increasingly unsustainable debt would become a hallmark of this new era of excesses and high risk, without much consideration of the consequences.[21] As a driver of growth, debt would become less effective over time—in the 1970s, for example, every dollar of new debt increased United States GDP by about 60 cents. By the first decade of the twenty-first century, every dollar of new debt increased GDP by only about 20 cents—a remarkable decline of about two-thirds in its effectiveness as a generator of growth.[22] Debt-laden increases in demand were also helped by the emergence of new technology sectors involving microelectronics, computing, software, telecommunications, biotechnology, nanotechnology, and biopharmacology, for example. Besides becoming new sources of debt-fueled growth—and in some cases productivity—the new sectors also introduced changes in the apparatus of capitalism. Research regimes, creativity, and intellectual property in the new technology sectors became major means and resources for corporate capitalism—much as factory regimes and labor had been under industrial capitalism—a phenomenon I characterized as technocapitalism in other books.[23]

The new technology sectors helped generate growth through high debt and consumerism, but they also redistributed wealth and power toward the corporate and financial elites ever more fiercely. New tech moguls and billionaires joined those elites at the top of the wealth pyramid, becoming icons of corporate culture and role models for executives everywhere. The problem of overaccumulation was then compounded as floods of new capital fed speculation and new crises—the 2000 tech sector crash that

---

21. See William K. Tabb, *The Restructuring of Capitalism in Our Time* (New York: Columbia University Press, 2012); Maria N. Ivanova, "The Great Recession and the State of American Capitalism," *Science and Society* 77 (2013): 294–314.

22. See Foster and Magdoff, *The Great Financial Crisis*.

23. Luis Suarez-Villa, *Technocapitalism: A Critical Perspective on Technological Innovation and Corporatism* (Philadelphia: Temple University Press, 2009); and Suarez-Villa, *Globalization and Tecnocapitalism: The Political Economy of Corporate Power and Technological Domination* (London: Ashgate, 2012).

collapsed the NASDAQ index by 78 percent being the most obvious one.[24] This collapse was the deepest one for a stock market index since the Dow Jones Industrials' crash of 1929, but was possibly more significant in that the NASDAQ comprised thousands of companies—whereas the Dow Jones index comprises only thirty very large ones. The "new" economy that technology was supposedly creating thus proved itself to be as prone to crashes and crises—if not more so—as the economy it was supposedly replacing. The emergence of technocapitalism did not remedy, therefore, the fundamental systemic dysfunction of overaccumulation, but only made it worse by triggering greater speculation, higher indebtedness, and more inequity— along with the oligopolization of the new technology sectors that emerged.

The past three decades have thus witnessed a major transformation of capitalist accumulation, in which finance capital became ever more concentrated through the expansion of oligopolies—aggressively conquering new frontiers, taking over almost every sector of the economy, and spawning a culture of speculation, indebtedness, inequity, greed, and malfeasance that is now a hallmark of contemporary society. Almost every large corporation became involved in finance in some way by, for example, issuing credit, providing insurance, speculating in real estate, packaging its loans into derivatives, or simply compensating executives in stock options—thus making stock price increases a major objective of management—and often relegating such vital aspects as labor relations, production, and supply chain management to a secondary plane. The issuing of shares therefore became an important business in and of itself, above and beyond the functional aspects—or the management—of corporate enterprise. This transformation was part of a long-term evolution from mercantile or factory-based capitalism toward finance-driven capitalism, which began more than one hundred years ago.

The first major transformation of capitalist accumulation can be traced to the last third of the nineteenth century, when a trend toward concentration began—as oligopolies and monopolies started to form—initially in natural resource–related sectors such as oil and minerals, and later in heavy industries. This increasing concentration of accumulation was categorized as "finance capital" at that time, to differentiate it from productive capital—which is closely related to production. Rudolf Hilferding's analyses on this first transformation were most important, noting a consolidation of industrial, mercantile, and banking interests, and their search for a state that

---

24. The NASDAQ index's collapse occurred between March 10, 2000, and October 9, 2002. Twelve years after the collapse, the NASDAQ had barely recovered 20 percent of the 78 percent drop it experienced during that period.

could more effectively support their power.[25] This early effort—to change the purpose of the state to serve large enterprises and their economic interests—can be considered the conceptual embryo of corporatocracy.

The second major transformation of capitalist accumulation that we have experienced during the past three decades is often referred to as "financialization," to denote the overwhelming importance of finance capital in the economy.[26] This phenomenon, however, encompasses a much broader repertory of changes and effects that have so far been overlooked in the literature. For this reason, the second transformation of capitalist accumulation will be referred to as *financialism* in this book, to denote its contemporary multifaceted, wide-ranging nature—one that encompasses social, cultural, ecological, class, political, institutional, economic, and organizational dimensions.[27] This second transformation of capitalist accumulation will therefore be assumed to transcend the importance of finance capital, to take up a much larger scope. Financialism—as defined in this book—*can be associated with the transformation of public governance into corporatocracy—public governance dominated by corporate power, behind a facade of representative democracy—with oligopolistic megabanks and powerful speculators at the top.* Financialism also involves what

---

25. See Hilferding, *Finance Capital*. As the twentieth century advanced, other authors would reflect on the rising importance of finance in capitalism, and its projection on political power; see, for example, Victor Perlo, *The Empire of High Finance* (New York: International Publishers, 1957).

26. The earliest use of the term *financialization* can be traced to Giovanni Arrighi, *The Long Twentieth Century: Money, Power, and the Origins of Our Time* (New York: Verso, 1994), and Kevin Phillips, *Boiling Point: Democrats, Republicans, and the Decline of the Middle Class* (New York: Random House, 1993).

27. The first literal usage of the term *financialism* can be traced to Eamonn Fingleton's *In Praise of Hard Industries: Why Manufacturing, Not the Information Economy, Is the Key to Future Prosperity* (Boston: Houghton Mifflin, 1999), 70, where he referred to it as the tendency for finance to concoct instruments that create profits for itself and its specialists. Lawrence E. Mitchell also used the term in his chapter "Financialism: A (Very) Brief History," in *The Embedded Firm: Corporate Governance, Labor, and Finance Capitalism*, ed. Cynthia A. Williams and Peer Zumbansen (New York: Cambridge University Press, 2011), 42–59—to refer to the advance of stock market speculation in the United States starting in the 1950s, focusing on banking. Edward Hess, in "The Business Revolution That Is Destroying the American Dream," *Forbes*, February 24, 2011, http://www.forbes.com/2011/02/24/, used the term to refer to the narrowly perceived corporate obligation to maximize short-term value—while capital markets are assumed to self-regulate. In all of these instances, the use of the term *financialism* seems to be used as a substitute for—and to be closely related to—the meaning typically attached to "financialization."

may be considered a sustained coup d'état by the financial and corporate elites, to take over the state for their own ends—to redistribute wealth and power for their own benefit, and to the benefit of their oligopolistic corporate interests above everything else. Political systems and the institutions of governance are thus chained to finance, speculation, oligopolies, and corporate power as never before. At the same time, the advance of this phenomenon brings up major social pathologies and dysfunctions—in the domains of institutions, culture, class, ecology, politics, organizations, and the economy—the likes of which humanity has never experienced.

This chapter will consider financialism as a feature of contemporary advanced capitalism and oligopolistic power, and as a major contributor to the crisis of the state. Numerous examples of the overwhelming importance of speculative finance, of its dysfunctions, and of its implications for public governance will be discussed. The disengagement of finance from capitalist production will be addressed, to consider its theoretical significance and its contribution to the occurrence of frequent crises—which require ever larger commitments from the state. Financialism's influence on the deepening of inequalities and social injustices in our time will also be taken into account, to place its character and effects in the context of a larger crisis of governance.

Culturally, financialism represents a distorted and socially corrosive mode of capitalism—one that is largely divorced from production and that depends on financial speculation. Anything and everything that has a probabilistic dimension can become a target for speculation. *Financial speculation becomes both a cultural and a political tool, a vehicle to try to align the interests of oligopolistic corporate power—and of the financial and corporate elites— with the interests of the public at large.* For this purpose, financialism turns speculation into a preferred activity of role models in society. Those "role model" individuals—their wealth, political influence, speculative practices, and showoff luxury consumption—thus become sources for imitation. We can see the effects of this cultural phenomenon, for example, in the kinds of games that preschool children play—in which probability and betting now play major roles—and in what they envision they will do in life when they become adults.[28] We can see it in the interests of the college-age population,

---

28. Such games seem to have superseded salesperson role playing—the prime childhood economic game role in prior decades. Part of this trend may be due to the flood of corporate propaganda and commercials that now target children; see, for example, Joel Bakan, *Childhood under Siege: How Big Business Targets Children* (New York: Free Press, 2011). Numerous games that incorporate some form of gambling or of probabilistic decision making, for example, have been created and are used by food producing oligopolies to target children; see Anton Troianovski, "Child's Play: Food Makers Hook Kids on Mobile Games," *Wall Street Journal,* September 18, 2012, A1.

with finance and speculation becoming a preferred career path, as fields with any connection to these activities attract the largest enrollments. We can also see it in a large number of the adult population who quit their professions and jobs to become day traders—amateur speculators who hope to become wealthy by following the example of the role models that financialism—and the corporate-controlled media—provide.[29]

The social behavior and routines of a large segment of the population are thus transformed, as financialist speculation takes up an ever larger role in human existence. Speculation and the search for speculative targets often become all-consuming—all the more so when large debts are incurred. We can see the cultural effects of this new mode of capitalism in the social pathologies around us, if we care to look. A loss of social identity—a kind of social depersonalization—with many individuals taking actions that are contrary to their own interest—in elections, in social relations, and even in matters affecting their immediate personal well-being. Destructive, hedonic decision patterns that lead to existential fragility and emptiness. Social alienation that manifests itself in myriad forms—from antisocial attitudes to oppressive management in workplaces, to covert hostility and interpersonal sabotage. A lack of solidarity and constructive reciprocity toward others, with aggressive competitism becoming part of our collective consciousness—as the way to get ahead in life, accumulate more, or achieve anything. Such aggressive competitism is now so widespread that it pervades activities that attract much public interest, such as professional contact sports—football, in particular, where players have been paid large bonuses when they cause serious injuries to opponents.[30] Among other effects are a proliferation of fraud, particularly through finance and identity theft, as personal privacy becomes a casualty of profit mining. We can also see them in the innumerable decision processes that, even when individually rational, become collectively self-destructive—especially when their effects are long term and involve all of society. These symptoms and effects are all around us, yet we

---

29. Many also quit their occupations to become "house flippers"—speculating in real estate by purchasing homes and reselling them later at much higher prices—an important component of financial speculation during the 2000s decade. See, for example, Andrew Haughwout, Donghoon Lee, Joseph Tracy, and Wilbert van der Klaauw, *"Flip This House": Investor Speculation and the Housing Bubble,* Federal Reserve Bank of New York December 5, 2011, http://libertystreeteconomics.newyorkfed.org.

30. The largest bonuses being paid for injuries so serious that they cause an opponent to leave a game or forfeit an entire season; see Fran Tarkenton, "Football's Bounty Hunters Must Be Clipped," *Wall Street Journal,* March 7, 2012, A17; Sam Farmer, "Saints Coach Urged Team to Injure," *Los Angeles Times,* April 6, 2012, A1.

seem to have become so accustomed to them that we hardly notice—if we notice at all.

Ecologically, what scientist Richard Levins refers to as "eco-social distress syndrome" is now part of our reality.[31] His concept explains how serious contemporary pathologies of nature are associated with the crises and pathologies of capitalism. The human-made, irreversible damage to the earth's ecosystems and environment that we are witnessing is grounded in our exploitation of nature, in the ways we destroy the environment to accumulate capital, and in the inequalities and injustices that have become a hallmark of our time. Financialism contributes to this reality by turning our ecosystems and the natural environment into targets of financial speculation. Speculation that leads to destruction or damage of nature—as any resource or natural feature with a probabilistic dimension becomes a target. The mere fact that a probabilistic dimension exists, or can be concocted, therefore makes any natural or ecological resource a target. The oxygen we breathe, the water we drink, the soil we tread on, plants, clouds, rain, snow, wind, life itself—any element of nature that affects us in a probabilistic way can be turned into a speculative proposition. Securitizing and turning them into derivatives may be challenging in some cases, but the immense greed and drive to accumulate capital—and to profit—can be counted on to achieve it. After all, most every natural resource that can be turned into a raw material has already become a target of speculation, and most have been securitized—if not already packaged as derivatives. Weather, oil, and ore, for example, can be hedged or bet against, using derivatives—or at the very least using the shares of companies that depend on them. New frontiers for financialist speculation are on the way, as genetically decoding ocean life becomes, for example, a target for speculation based on the patents that will be appropriated. Intellectual property and creativity are, after all, the most valuable economic resources of our time—and if they are associated with nature they become an even more attractive target for speculation.

---

31. See Richard Levins and Richard Lewontin, *The Dialectical Biologist* (Cambridge: Harvard University Press, 1985) and their *Biology under the Influence: Dialectical Essays on Ecology, Agriculture, and Health* (New York: Monthly Review Press, 2007). A pioneer in researching interactions between ecosystems and society, Levins founded the human ecology program at the Harvard School of Public Health. Elected to the National Academy of Sciences in the 1960s, he resigned his membership in protest over what he saw as the academy's link to U.S. government policies that favored war, intervention, and neo-imperial influence; see Richard Levins, "Living the 11th Thesis," *Monthly Review,* January 2008, 29–37.

The social class dimension—a much neglected aspect of society during the past three decades—is very much alive in the financialist economy. Class structure is an integral component of financialism, if the deep inequalities and injustices it promotes are taken into account. In contrast with the first transformation of capitalist accumulation, when the bourgeoisie owned productive capital—industrial or mercantile, often rooted locally—the second transformation that financialism represents enthrones an anonymous oligarchy—the financial and corporate elites—that controls the oligopolies. This oligarchy is global in scope and interests, and anonymous in the sense that personal identities, loyalties, or integrity are often secondary to transactions and speculative schemes. This new oligarchy is at the top of the class pyramid in this second transformation of capitalist accumulation. The wealthiest (and most clever) members of this new oligarchy are the speculators who sell what they do not possess and speculate with what they do not have—property therefore becoming secondary to speculative schemes (or merely their byproduct). In the approach to property we thus find another contrast with the first transformation of capitalist accumulation, and the bourgeoisie's role in it. For the bourgeoisie, property was socially and culturally important, and was often associated with production.[32] Speculating with property was usually negligible, if it occurred at all, and often carried a negative perception. For the wealthiest speculators associated with financialism, on the other hand, property often becomes a mere vehicle or byproduct—to be speculated with, not to be owned, unless ownership somehow facilitates speculation.

The new oligarchic class of financialism is followed by its acolytes—corporate management, think-tank ideologues, consultants, politicians, media managers, for example. The bulk of the middle class occupies the next lower segment of the pyramid, busily running on the treadmill of economic insecurity, high debt, and consumerism, hoping to gain some wealth—just as the gurus of speculation promise everyone can. Upward mobility for this class has largely become a fantasy—but a fantasy that many nonetheless treasure, and that provides some stimulus to stay on the treadmill—with downward mobility becoming increasingly common during

---

32. See, for example, Eric Hobsbawm, *The Age of Capital: 1848–1875* (London: Weidenfeld and Nicolson, 1975), and his *Labouring Men: Studies in the History of Labour* (London: Weidenfeld and Nicolson, 1964); Samir Amin, *The Law of Worldwide Value* (New York: Monthly Review Press, 2010).

economic crises. Working people (those who, long ago, were referred to as "working class") suffer greater insecurity and unemployment, and witness their jobs being outsourced or eliminated—along with pensions, benefits, and employee rights. Problems of health, addiction, or delinquency tend to affect this class greatly, particularly during periods of crisis. Downward economic mobility is all too real for those who become unemployed and stay that way for some time—the long-term unemployed are least likely to find employment with comparable compensation or skills to their previous job, if they are ever employed again.[33] The poor—those with so little income or wealth that they can qualify for public welfare—are at the very bottom of the pyramid. They are best forgotten, as far as the financialist oligarchy is concerned. The homeless are, of course, at the lowest end of this segment and in many places now have the status of fugitives, as city laws are enacted to ban them from public places. Many working people, along with the poor—and undocumented immigrants—make up a reserve army of labor, who perform the dead-end, temporary jobs that have very low pay, no benefits, and are highly insecure. A select few may find employment serving the corporate and financial elites (or their acolytes) as domestic help, and may even get to look after their children, mansions, or vehicles if they are lucky.

Politically, financialism has built deep and widespread webs of influence that have no precedent in American history. Those webs of influence and manipulation aim, first and foremost, to sustain or expand the power of the oligopolistic megabanks and hedge funds that now control finance—and the power of oligopolistic corporations, in general—along with that of the elites associated with them. As noted in the previous chapter, lobbying, campaign contributions, and the "revolving door" vehicle are the usual means for exerting influence and manipulating the political system—reaching up to the highest levels of government. Instances and examples of this dimension of financialism are so extensive that any account is bound to fall short, no matter how comprehensive or detailed it may try to be. Presidential campaigns typically receive their largest contributions from Wall Street—most of all, from oligopolistic megabanks and the richest hedge funds. Almost all members of the most important legislative bodies charged with formulating

---

33. The long-term unemployed are defined officially as individuals who have been looking for work for more than six months after becoming unemployed; see Bureau of Labor Statistics, U.S. Department of Labor, *Economic News Release: Employment Situation Summary*, February 3, 2012, http://www.bls.gov/news.release/empsit.nr0.htm; Shelly Banjo, "Measures Aim to End Bias Against Long-Term Jobless," *Wall Street Journal*, February 24, 2012, A3.

financial laws, such as the U.S. Senate Banking Committee, typically receive substantial political contributions—in most cases the largest contributions in their entire careers—from Wall Street megabanks and other financial corporations.[34] Such politicians also often provide valuable information on legislative initiatives to Wall Street lobbyists and executives. Individuals in charge of financial regulation and policy, at the highest levels of government, ·are typically former top executives from the largest Wall Street megabanks— to which they often return after their government service. Those financial regulatory agencies also provide—as a routine practice—insider information on potential new measures or policies, to the largest Wall Street megabanks that they must regulate—in what is one of the more scandalous, yet legal, examples of collusion between the financial oligopolies and government.

Institutionally, financialism has fundamentally distorted the tax system, turning it into a major source of profit for financial oligopolies. Biasing the tax code to favor financial speculation is an important vehicle for this objective, as the tax rate paid on income derived from speculation was made lower than that obtained from any other source. Thus, for example, an individual who derived all income from capital gains and dividends would, at most, pay a 15 percent tax rate. By contrast, someone who received the same amount of income only from work (or any source other than capital gains and dividends) would pay a 35 percent rate.[35] The tax code also supported indebtedness at the individual and household levels by allowing deductions for mortgages and home equity loans, regardless of how the money is used. A former high-level federal financial official estimated, for example, that the majority of lowest-rated mortgages issued before the financial crisis that

---

34. The Obama presidential campaign in 2008, for example, reportedly received $14.9 million from Wall Street corporations—the largest contribution to any specific campaign in history from that source. No fewer than 86 percent of all members (all of them up for reelection in 2010) of the U.S. Senate Banking Committee—the most important legislative body charged with reviewing proposed financial legislation—reportedly received donations of at least $180,000 each for their campaigns in 2009 from oligopolistic megabanks and other Wall Street interests. See John Bellamy Foster and Hannah Holleman, "The Financial Power Elite," *Monthly Review*, May 2010, http://monthlyreview.org/2010/05/01/the-financial-power-elite#n35; Nomi Prins, *It Takes a Pillage: Behind the Bailouts, Bonuses, and Backroom Deals from Washington to Wall Street* (New York: Wiley, 2009); Timothy P. Carney, "Obama's Cronies Thrive at Intersection of K and Wall," *Washington Examiner*, February 17, 2010, http://washingtonexaminer.com/politics/2010/02/obamas-cronies-thrive-intersection-k-and-wall/.

35. Internal Revenue Service, *SOI Tax Stats: Individual Income Tax Rates and Tax Shares*, http://www.irs.gov/taxstats/indtaxstats/article/0,,id=129270,00.html (accessed March 21, 2012).

started in 2007 were not made to expand home ownership but to obtain cash in a tax-advantaged way—cash that, in many cases, was used for speculation.[36] Financial oligopolists were major beneficiaries of this avalanche of capital since they, in one form or another, profit directly or indirectly from most of the transactions that flow through the stock, bond, housing, and futures markets—not to mention the innumerable types of derivatives and other speculative instruments that they concoct. At the corporate level, the tax system has provided considerable loopholes to exploit, making it possible for most financial corporations—and especially the oligopolies—to pay no taxes, or to secure tax breaks and subsidies that amount to negative tax payments. Those tax loopholes and subsidies also help financial corporations free up capital that can be recycled to boost executive compensation.

Economically and organizationally, financialism promotes oligopolization as it concentrates immense—and increasing—amounts of capital in the coffers of very large financial corporations. This provides easier access to capital for oligopolistic corporations that can be used to acquire other companies—actual or potential rivals, most of all—and lead to further consolidation. At the same time, it also allows the financial oligopolies to charge more for their services, as can be seen in the unprecedented high costs of financial intermediation, which set a historical record in 2010.[37] Larger and better capitalized oligopolistic corporations can also contribute more to political organizations and pay larger compensation to their executives. The oligopolistic megabanks that are so symbolic of financialism, in turn, facilitate this consolidation of power by providing financial services under one roof to their oligopolistic clients, for every imaginable financial activity— from securitization to bond issuance to merger financing, along with retail and personal banking (for the elites associated with those oligopolies). The megabanks, moreover, typically also have a global reach, that can help their oligopolistic clients with outsourcing around the world, along with speculative schemes in foreign stock markets. Megabanks also help oligopolistic corporations erect barriers to entry in their respective sectors, when they

---

36. Sheila Bair, "Want to Spur Growth? For One, End the Home Mortgage Deduction," *Fortune*, March 19, 2012, 88.

37. Thomas Philippon, *Has the US Financial Industry Become Less Efficient?* Stern School of Business, New York University, November 2011, http://pages.stern.nyu.edu/~tphilipp/papers/ FinEff.pdf, and his *The Evolution of the US Financial Industry from 1860 to 2007: Theory and Evidence*, Stern School of Business, New York University, November 2008, http://pages.stern. nyu.edu/~tphilipp/papers/finsize.pdf.

finance takeovers of independent suppliers who might serve new entrants.

Taking these dimensions—the social, cultural, ecological, class, political, institutional, economic, and organizational—into account, financialism may be considered an evolution of capitalism. One in which finance—and the financial oligopolies—reign supreme. Finance, as a vital element of capitalism, however, cannot be divorced from the real economy—the "real" referring here to production, whether in manufacturing, services, or resource extraction. Yet, *financialism has largely removed this fundamental link.* This sets financialism apart from prior transformations of capitalism. The concentration of capital that is a key feature of this phenomenon has also promoted oligopolization—not only in finance but in almost every sector of the economy. And, it has enthroned speculation as the most important means to secure wealth and power, creating an oligarchy that wields much influence through corporatocracy. Speculation and financial scheming are therefore at the core of financialism—much as production and factory routines were at the core of industrial capitalism. During industrial capitalism, however, finance largely supported production—now, finance largely supports speculation.

Financial schemes—such as those based on speculative momentum, imitation, timing, gaming, and subterfuge—are therefore very important in a financialist economy. To put financial schemes to work, an immense variety of speculative vehicles have been concocted that are extremely complex and practically impossible to understand fully. Such vehicles and schemes—and the culture of gaming that pervades financialism—made it possible for fraudsters to emerge and to become highly trusted "market movers," exercising much influence on other speculators and on the trajectory of the financial system. One of those trusted market movers, Bernard Madoff, perpetrated the largest fraud in financial history (estimated at more than $65 billion), cheating his numerous wealthy clients in the United States and abroad—along with friends and his own family—over a period of three decades.[38]

---

38. See Diana Henriques, "Madoff Fraud Rippled around the World," *New York Times,* November 21, 2008, http://www.nytimes.com/2008/11/21/business/; Deborah H. Strober and Gerald S. Strober, *Catastrophe: The Story of Bernard L. Madoff, the Man Who Swindled the World* (Beverly Hills: Phoenix, 2009). Details on how accounts were falsified emerged long after the fraud's revelation, and indicated substantial neglect on the part of regulators; see James Sterngold, "Madoff's Cold Play Outwitted Auditor," *Wall Street Journal,* December 3, 2013, C1, and his "Unraveling the Lies that Madoff Told: Con Man Said He Acted Alone, Had Legit Unit—False on Both Counts," *Wall Street Journal,* December 11, 2013, C1; Ashby Jones, "Jurors Told of Madoff Tricks," *Wall Street Journal,* December 5, 2013, C3, and her "Madoff Fumed at Letter from SEC," *Wall Street Journal,* December 6, 2013, C3.

Due to the opacity so characteristic of the financialist economy—and the close, "revolving door" relationship between regulators and speculation—it took almost one decade for the fraud to be exposed, after a highly experienced financial specialist denounced Madoff's schemes to the U.S. Securities and Exchange Commission (SEC).[39] And this occurred only because Madoff himself revealed his fraud to prosecutors and the media—on his own initiative—in order to try to save his sons (who were his partners) from prosecution, after his schemes unraveled.[40] Only after Madoff's voluntary revelations did the SEC take the case—along with the long-standing prior allegations and evidence—seriously, demonstrating once again how entwined financial regulators and Wall Street "market movers" can become.[41] Also disturbing about the SEC and its ineffective oversight, was the fact that this agency for many years destroyed its own enforcement records and misled another federal agency—the U.S. National Archives and Records Administration—about its record-keeping procedures.[42] The SEC's destruction of its enforcement records was found out only after an internal whistleblower tried, for several years, to call attention to this problem. The investigation of this case started only after the whistleblower's allegations

---

39. Andy Court and Keith Sharman, "The Man Who Figured Out Madoff's Scheme," *CBS News*, June 14, 2009, http//cbs.news.com/stories/2009/02/73/60minutes/main4833667.

40. An important indicator of Madoff's fraud was what some analysts refer to as "unnaturally stable returns," which seemed immune to the usual swings of markets. This peculiarity attracted attention from some analysts but was not sufficient to trigger scrutiny from regulators, despite the fact that all components of Madoff's business—proprietary trading, broker-dealer services, investment advisory—were involved in the fraud; see, for example, Christopher M. Matthews, "Witness: Entire Madoff Business Was Fraud," *Wall Street Journal*, October 30, 2013, C3. Another fraudulent scheme that also disintegrated was that of Russell Wasendorf Sr. This fraud involved $215 million in client funds over nearly two decades through his Peregrine Financial Group; see Jacob Bunge, Scott Patterson and Julie Steinberg, "Peregrine CEO's Dramatic Confession," *Wall Street Journal*, July 14, 2012, A1; Jacob Bunge, Jerry A. DiColo, and Josh Dawsey, "Scandal Shakes Trading Firm," *Wall Street Journal*, July 11, 2012, A1. Financial frauds were not confined to the United States—a scheme similar to Madoff's was discovered in Japan, involving the loss of billions of dollars in clients' funds; see Kana Inagaki, Atsuko Fukase, and Phred Dvorak, " 'Japanese Madoff' Flagged: Industry Newsletter Warned in 2009 About Firm's 'Unnaturally Stable Returns,' " *Wall Street Journal*, February 25, 2012, B1; Atsuko Fukase, "Clients of AIJ Fear for Cash: Japan Firm's Complex Financial Products Befuddled Some Pension Managers," *Wall Street Journal*, February 29, 2012, C3.

41. See, for example, Tom McGinty, "Revolving Door at the SEC: Staffer One Day, Opponent the Next," *Wall Street Journal*, April 5, 2010, C1.

42. Jenny Strasburg and Jean Eaglesham, "SEC Cop to Back Claim: Agency Watchdog to Support Whistleblower's Complaint on Record Destruction," *Wall Street Journal*, October 8, 2011, B1.

became public, in part because he notified some members of Congress and the information leaked out.

Another case involved the misappropriation of about $1.6 billion of client money by MF Global Holdings—a Wall Street fund controlled by billionaire speculator Jon Corzine—to make foreign exchange bets, a form of speculation that started to spread in the late 1990s.[43] MF Global had the highest investment ratings up to the point when it collapsed, reflecting the extent to which both rating firms and regulators can remain ignorant in the financialist economy—even when very risky bets are involved.[44] Beyond its misappropriation of client funds, MF Global drastically disguised its actual debt and risks by consistently engaging in a commonly utilized—and legal— financial trick known as "window dressing."[45] Through this ruse debts can be reduced temporarily—by, for example, using unutilized clients' money to pay off some of the fund's betting debts, or by selling poorly performing bonds and stocks to increase cash holdings—so that debt shows up to be lower before the reporting deadline each quarter. After the end of quarter deadline passes and accounts are reported to clients, regulators, and rating entities, debts are restored by borrowing back the amounts used to pay them off—or by repurchasing the bonds and stocks that were sold. Use

---

43. Jacob Bunge, "Missing at MF: $1.6 Billion," *Wall Street Journal*, February 11, 2012, B18; Julie Steinberg, Aaron Lucchetti, and Mike Spector, "Investigators Probe a Rush at MF Global to Move Cash," *Wall Street Journal*, February 23, 2012, A1, and their "MF Global Autopsy Flags Risks by Corzine," *Wall Street Journal*, June 5, 2012, A1; Aaron Lucchetti and Mike Spector, "The Unraveling of MF Global: With $1.2 Billion Missing, Corzine's Aggressive Strategy Comes Into Focus," *Wall Street Journal*, December 31, 2011, B1; Scott Patterson and Aaron Lucchetti, "Money from MF Global Feared Gone," *Wall Street Journal*, January 30, 2012, A1. MF Global executives were still being paid large bonuses long after the firm's bankruptcy and its misappropriation of client funds became known; see Aaron Lucchetti and Mike Spector, "MF Global Still Set to Pay Bonuses," *Wall Street Journal*, March 9, 2012, C1.

44. See Aaron Lucchetti and Julie Steinberg, "Corzine Rebuffed Internal Warnings on Risk," *Wall Street Journal*, December 6, 2011, A1; Scott Patterson, Julie Steinberg, and Aaron Lucchetti, "Corzine Again in Spotlight: MF Global Hearing to Focus on Ex-CEO, but He Isn't Expected to Be There," *Wall Street Journal*, February 2, 2012, C3; Editorial, "Whodunit at MF Global: New Evidence Casts Doubt on Jon Corzine's Testimony," *Wall Street Journal*, February 27, 2012, A14; Julie Steinberg, Mike Spector, and Aaron Lucchetti, "Fast, Furious at MF Global: In Days Leading Up to Firm's Collapse, $165 Million Transfer Ok'd in a Flash," *Wall Street Journal*, March 1, 2012, C1. A bankruptcy trustee's report concluded that Mr. Corzine deserved much of the blame for the collapse of MF Global—referring to him personally a total of 284 times in the 174-page document; see Aaron Lucchetti and Julie Steinberg, "Corzine Blasted in MF Global Autopsy," *Wall Street Journal*, April 5, 2013, A1.

45. Michael Rapoport, "MF Global Masked Debt Risks: Firm Cut Borrowing Before Reports; Corzine Lobbied Against Trading Curbs," *Wall Street Journal*, November 4, 2011, A1.

of this trick can have a substantial effect on what a fund's end of quarter accounts show—thus providing a false impression of fund performance that can attract new clients, or entice existing ones to put in more money. A two-year analysis, for example, showed that widespread use of "window dressing" by Wall Street funds reduced debts by an average of 42 percent from the peak level for each quarter—a sizable proportion that typically amounted to hundreds of billions of dollars in a single quarter.[46]

Billionaire speculator Jon Corzine, MF Global's owner, is a former chairman of Goldman Sachs—an oligopolistic investment bank that was a major contributor to the financial crisis and had to be bailed out by the U.S. government—who became a U.S. Senator, and subsequently governor of New Jersey during 2006–2010. Corzine used his own vast wealth to finance his political campaigns for senator and governor—$62 million and $40 million—overwhelming all competing candidates through the sheer amount of money he utilized.[47] He had lobbied strongly (and successfully) against a 2010 proposal by the federal Commodity Futures Trading Commission (CFTC) that would have restricted how client money in funds' accounts can be invested—using his vast influence with regulators and his numerous political contacts at the highest levels of government. Corzine's personal involvement with financial regulation and regulators was well known. He was involved, for example, in writing the federal Sarbanes-Oxley financial law in 2002—a major change in accounting regulations that affected (and favored) the largest corporations. Corzine's collaborator in that project was a colleague from Goldman Sachs who, at the time of MF Global's collapse, was chairman of the CFTC—one of MF Global's regulators—in what is another example of the "revolving door" involvement of Wall Street executives with regulation.[48]

Regulators' association with Wall Street made it very difficult to prosecute—or even investigate—wrongdoing in these and many other cases of fraud.[49] However, the impossibility of prosecuting financialist wrongdoing must be seen from a broader perspective. Financial deregulation, starting in the 1980s, made it possible to blame much malfeasance on market

---

46. Rapoport, "MF Global," A2; Steinberg, Lucchetti, and Spector, "Investigators Probe."

47. See, for example, Jonah Goldberg, "Obama's Tainted Bundler," *Wall Street Journal,* April 24, 2012, A11.

48. Editorial, "Mr. Corzine and His Regulators," *Wall Street Journal,* December 1, 2011, A18.

49. Some financial firms have acquired a reputation as "shadow regulators" through their hiring of numerous regulatory agency heads when they leave their posts—all of them individuals who accumulated powerful contacts in government. See, for example, Jean Eaglesham, "SEC Ex-Chief Lands at Consultant: Schapiro is Latest Former US Regulator to Join Promontory Financial," *Wall Street Journal,* April 2, 2013, C1. Conversely, agency staff can experience

changes or poor judgment, thus preempting criminal prosecution.[50] This means that only civil prosecutions could be pursued in most every case of wrongdoing, thereby eliminating the possibility of prison altogether. In many cases—such as that of MF Global—moreover, senior executives cannot even be charged if they are not registered with regulators.[51] Financial penalties—usually amounting to little more than a slap on the wrist, considering the vast profits involved and the impact of malfeasance—became the only consequences, when there were any.[52] No investigation conducted

serious difficulties when their actions or decisions are regarded as too critical by higher-level officials. In one case, for example, an examiner at the Federal Reserve Bank of New York was allegedly ordered to dilute her critical report on conflicts of interest policies at one of the largest Wall Street megabanks, and was fired when she refused to do so; see Julie Steinberg and Dan Fitzpatrick, "New York Fed Is Sued by Ex-Staffer: Former Examiner Says She Was Pressured to Weaken Her Reports on Goldman," *Wall Street Journal*, October 11, 2013, C3.

50. A factor that seems to have induced megabanks to take it for granted that they could get away with conflicts of interest, corruption, lack of transparency in their transactions, and outrageously high executive compensation packages. See Mike Mayo, *Exile on Wall Street: One Analyst's Fight to Save the Big Banks from Themselves* (New York: Wiley, 2012); David Lazarus, "Bankers Scolded for Taking Bad Risks," *Los Angeles Times*, June 15, 2012, B1; Al Yoon, "JP Morgan Talks Show Tangled Web: Mortgage Deals Illustrate Depths of Bank's Subprime Issues; 'Much Worse than Anyone's Expectations,'" *Wall Street Journal*, October 28, 2013, C1. Even obvious cases of wrongdoing, such as the one where a Citibank director concealed from clients to whom he was selling investments in CDOs that the bank was betting heavily against those very same investments, failed in court; see Chad Bray and Jean Eaglesham, "Loss in Citi Case Deals Blow to US," *Wall Street Journal*, August 1, 2012, C3. In many instances, even civil charges became very difficult or impossible to take to court—as in the case of a hedge fund that concocted a vast number of mortgage CDOs which it bet against, and that generated billions of dollars in losses for clients; see Jean Eaglesham, "SEC's Push Loses Steam: Hedge Fund Won't Face Civil Charges Tied to Mortgages," *Wall Street Journal*, August 7, 2013, A1.

51. Jean Eaglesham, Aaron Lucchetti, and Devlin Barrett, "Loophole at MF Global Is Headache for Regulators," *Wall Street Journal*, June 12, 2012, C1.

52. See, for example, Jean Eaglesham, "Financial Crimes Bedevil Prosecutors," *Wall Street Journal*, December 6, 2011, C1; Michael Rothfeld, Jean Eaglesham, and Jenny Strasburg, "SAC Chief Likely to Avoid Charges," *Wall Street Journal*, July 5, 2013, A1. A four-year U.S. Department of Justice investigation of an alleged conspiracy by large—mostly oligopolistic—banks to eliminate competition in the $24.3 trillion credit default swap (CDS) market ended without any penalties or prosecution; see Katy Burne, "CDS Case Nears a Quiet End," *Wall Street Journal*, December 2, 2013, C1. Similarly, the SEC ruled out any action against hedge funds that helped banks create the complex mortgage deals at the heart of the crisis—and profited greatly by betting against the same deals they created. This decision came six years after the start of the crisis, and was considered to be highly favorable to the most powerful financial interests involved. Total penalties charged by the SEC as a result of its bond investigation—about $3 billion—were insignificant, considering the role mortgage bond deals and related instruments had in the crisis; see Jean Eaglesham, "SEC Winding Down Bond-Deal Probes," *Wall Street Journal*, December 13, 2013, C1.

by the Federal Bureau of Investigation, for example, led to the conviction of any high-profile megabank executives after the financial crisis.[53] The Sarbanes-Oxley Act, an important legal tool that was created to hold corporate executives accountable for wrongdoing, was not utilized—despite the fact that it seemed to be an appropriate measure to apply to crisis-related wrongdoing.[54] The SEC, moreover, had no criminal enforcement authority, and typically agreed to "plea bargain" settlements with financial corporations and wrongdoers, allowing perpetrators to avoid any admission of guilt.[55]

Also, the lack of criminal sanctions against deceitful or reckless speculation made it possible to blame losses and damages on mistakes in judgment. Because so many rules and laws were eliminated or diluted through financial deregulation since the 1980s, evidence of intentional misconduct became very difficult—if not practically impossible—to obtain. Federal agencies thus found themselves without any legal grounding to prosecute, even when evidence of willful wrongdoing could be found. The SEC thus had to pursue its first action against a Wall Street investment bank—oligopolist Goldman Sachs—on the basis of civil charges, despite clear evidence that this bank had deceived investors when it sold them its complex

---

53. Jean Eaglesham, "Missing: Stats on Crisis Convictions," *Wall Street Journal,* May 14, 2012, C1; Reed Albergotti and Elizabeth Rappaport, "U.S. not Seeking Goldman Charges," *Wall Street Journal,* August 10, 2012, C1; Becky Quick, "No Perp Walks, No Jail Time: Why Prosecutors are Going Easy on Wall Street," *Fortune,* July 5, 2010, 50. During the savings and loan banking crisis of the late 1980s, by comparison, more than eight hundred bank executives were sentenced to prison; see "Blind Justice: Why Have So Few Bankers Gone to Jail for Their Part in the Crisis?" *The Economist,* May 4, 2013, 71–73.

54. See, for example, Michael Rapoport, "Law's Big Weapon Sits Idle: Sarbanes-Oxley's Jail-Time Threat Hasn't Been Applied in Crisis-Related Cases," *Wall Street Journal,* July 30, 2012, C3. Rules that modified accounting fundamentals to benefit the banking sector—most of all the oligopolies—were also a factor. One such rule, for example, allowed banks to keep losses on long-term bonds out of their profit and loss accounts. As a result, it was estimated that the four largest American banks were able to report more than $20 billion in net income in the second quarter (April-June) of 2013 alone—income they would not have been able to report or claim without this rule; see Dan Fitzpatrick and Shayndi Raice, "Bond Slump Leaves Banks in a Bind," *Wall Street Journal,* August 1, 2013, C1.

55. See Jean Eaglesham, "Challenges in Chasing Fraud: SEC Actions—and Non-Actions—Illustrate the Difficulties of Pinning Blame for Soured Deals," *Wall Street Journal,* June 23, 2011, C1. The SEC is also restricted, under federal law, to a five-year statute of limitations that makes it difficult to pursue cases of fraud and malfeasance—given the extensive time needed to collect evidence; see Jean Eaglesham, Jeannette Neumann, and Reed Albergotti, "Clock is Ticking on Crisis Charges," *Wall Street Journal,* July 12, 2012, C1; Bray and Eaglesham, "Loss in Citi."

mortgage products. The penalty paid by Goldman Sachs to the SEC—$550 million—amounted to only two weeks of profits for this megabank at the time.[56] Goldman Sachs, incidentally, received $12.9 billion in taxpayer funds to cover its losses when insurance oligopolist AIG had to be bailed out by the federal government in 2009.[57]

The SEC also settled—without any assessment of guilt—a case in which one of the largest megabanks (Citigroup) had designed a billion dollar fund to fail, costing clients more than $700 million while obtaining $160 million in profits for itself. The SEC, moreover, had clear evidence that this megabank had bet against the very fund it created and sold to clients, making substantial profits on both ends of the transactions—selling the fund to clients *and* betting against it.[58] Another example was the SEC's settlement with megabank JPMorgan Chase for misleading its clients in a complex mortgage derivatives scheme. The $1.1 billion deal involved Chase's failure to tell its clients that a hedge fund that helped craft this operation also stood to profit if it failed—a fairly common win-both-ways scheme for hedge funds. Chase's clients—which included General Motors' pension plans and various banks in Asia—lost practically all their money when the real estate market declined in 2007–08.[59]

A major justification for the lack of criminal prosecutions against the megabank oligopolies has been their sheer size. Very large size is one outcome of the long trajectory of neoliberal financial deregulation that started in the 1980s, which now seems practically impossible to reverse without triggering a major crisis—not only for the United States but also very likely for the world at large. Thus, it should not surprise that the U.S. Justice Department justifies its inaction on criminal prosecutions on that

---

56. Thomas Catan and Kara Scannell, "Convictions from Crisis Hard: Settlement with Goldman Shows Difficulty in Holding Bankers Accountable," *Wall Street Journal,* July 17, 2010, B2.

57. Paritosh Bansal, "Goldman's Share of AIG Bailout Money Draws Fire," *Reuters,* March 18, 2009, http://www.reuters.com/article/2009/03/18/us-aig-goldmansachs-sb-idUS-TRE52H0B520090318; Michael Hiltzik, "Haste is Waste in 'Fiscal Cliff' Fix," *Los Angeles Times,* December 2, 2012, B1.

58. "A Financial Regulator under Fire: Unsettling Wall Street," *The Economist,* December 3, 2011, 89. See also Chad Bray, Matthias Rieker, and Suzanne Kapner, "Citi Settles Case for $730 Million: Large Payment Resolves Investor Claims That Bank Misled Them in Several Bond, Preferred Offerings," *Wall Street Journal,* March 19, 2013, C1.

59. Jean Eaglesham and Dan Fitzpatrick, "Bank Fine Hints at Feds' Playbook," *Wall Street Journal,* June 22, 2011, A1.

ground. The U.S. Attorney General, for example, testifying before the Senate Judiciary Committee in 2013, argued that it is "difficult to prosecute them when we are hit with indications that if you do prosecute, if you do bring a criminal charge, it will have a negative impact on the national economy. . . . I think it is a function of the fact that some of these institutions have become too large."[60] Large size, a key characteristic of oligopolistic corporations, has therefore become a form of insurance against criminal prosecution, providing the sort of immunity that makes it very attractive for any financial corporation to grow or merge.

Prosecuting the credit rating oligopolies (Standard and Poor's, Fitch, Moody's)—all of which ignored their own standards when assessing speculative schemes at the core of financialism—also proved practically impossible on criminal grounds. Subprime mortgage derivatives that were flawed and very risky often received AAA—the highest—ratings from the three rating oligopolies long before the start of the crisis. Catering to their megabank and hedge fund clients became a major priority, since the three credit rating oligopolies compete with each other for clients—and their own stocks are traded in Wall Street.[61] Also, clients typically engage in a practice known as "ratings shopping," through which they choose the credit rating oligopolist that offers the highest rating—making it implicit that they will take their business to one of the other oligopolists if a rating happens to be low.[62] The three credit rating oligopolists are therefore under pressure to satisfy clients, since their own profits and executive compensation depend on attracting or keeping them.[63] Standard and Poor's ratings of credit derivatives and similar speculative vehicles, for example, accounted for a 300 percent increase in its revenues between 2002 and 2007 (on an annual basis), according to a U.S. Senate report.[64] Efforts to regulate these oligopolies have yielded practically

60. Shan Li, "Banks May Be Too Big to Prosecute, US Says," *Los Angeles Times,* March 8, 2013, B2; U.S. Department of Justice, *Statement of Eric H. Holder, Jr., US Attorney General Before the Committee on the Judiciary, US Senate,* March 6, 2013, http://www.judiciary.senate.gov/3-6-13HolderTestimony.pdf.

61. Jeannette Neumann and Thomas Catan, "US Steps Up S&P Inquiry," *Wall Street Journal,* January 17, 2012, C1.

62. See, for example, Jeannette Neumann, "Fitch Ditched in Bond Dispute," *Wall Street Journal,* April 4, 2012, C1.

63. See, for example, John D. McKinnon and Fawn Johnson, "Credit Raters' Emails Show Concerns," *Wall Street Journal,* April 23, 2010, C3.

64. U.S. Senate Permanent Subcommittee on Investigations, *Wall Street and the Financial Crisis: Anatomy of a Financial Collapse* (Washington, DC: US Senate, 2011), http://hsgac.senate.gov/public/_files/Financial_Crisis/FinancialCrisisReport.pdf.

no results, despite the impact of their past rating practices.[65]

Manipulation of commodities trading has also proven practically impossible to prosecute on criminal grounds, and has led to little more than fines for perpetrators. In one case in 2008, for example, manipulation of oil prices reaped more than $50 million in profits for two commodities speculators who devised an international plot, according to the CFTC.[66] The two speculators, using a common win-both-ways scheme, artificially drove up the value of oil derivatives they already held, pocketing the profits—and then executed similar trades in reverse, thus selling the instruments they had previously purchased—pocketing those profits as well. One result of these and other speculators' actions was a spike in crude oil prices to a record $147 per barrel in July 2008, that caused considerable hardship for hundreds of millions of oil-dependent working people around the world. Also impossible to prosecute criminally were cases of insider trading, including one that authorities described as the most profitable one ever. This case involved a hedge fund led and founded by one of the world's best-known managers, a billionaire Wall Street speculator, who had generated annual returns averaging almost 30 percent during two decades—obtained partly through insider information on the companies that were targeted.[67]

---

65. See, for example, Jeannette Neumann, "Rating Firms Steer Clear of an Overhaul," *Wall Street Journal,* May 13, 2013, C1; Aaron Lucchetti and Serena Ng, " 'Ratings Shopping' Lives On as Congress Debates a Fix," *Wall Street Journal,* May 24, 2010, A1. Almost six years after the start of the financial crisis, federal authorities sued Standard and Poor for $5 billion for providing high ratings to numerous subprime mortgages that eventually collapsed—an amount that was only a fraction of total losses from this type of investment vehicle. The government's evidence was largely based on e-mails and other internal communications; see Jeannette Neumann, Evan Perez, and Jean Eaglesham, "US, S&P Settle In for Bitter Combat," *Wall Street Journal,* February 6, 2013, A1; Michael Hiltzik, "Execs Off the Hook at S&P," *Los Angeles Times,* February 10, 2013, B1.

66. Dan Strumpf and Liam Pleven, "Traders Accused in Oil-Price Plot," *Wall Street Journal,* May 25, 2011, C1. Manipulation of oil prices continued by others after this case, facilitated by the fact that a single corporation—Platt, a division of McGraw-Hill Financial Inc.—controls more than 80 percent of the market for spot-price transactions on oil trades; see, for example, Justin Scheck and Jenny Gross, "Traders Try to Game Oil-Price Benchmark," *Wall Street Journal,* June 19, 2013, A1.

67. Michael Rothfeld, Jean Eaglesham, and Chad Bray, "SAC Hit with Record Insider Penalty: Investment Firm to Pay $616 Million to Settle Two Civil Cases; Other Probes of Hedge Fund Continue," *Wall Street Journal,* March 16, 2013, A1; Tom McGinty, John Carreyrou, and Michael Rothfeld, "Inside a Star Hedge Fund: Lots of Big Bets, Built Fast," *Wall Street Journal,* March 22, 2013, A1; Rothfeld, Eaglesham, and Strasburg, "SAC Chief Likely to Avoid Charges."

Oligopolistic megabanks that perpetrated fraud and abuse on hundreds of thousands of mortgage holders when they zealously foreclosed on mortgages—and misrepresented mortgage derivatives to the clients they sold them to—also incurred civil penalties that amounted to little more than a slap on their wrists.[68] Most of the penalties in this case were actually paid by those who had bought mortgage derivatives from the five megabanks—such as pension funds, retirement plans, and insurance companies, all of whom were the megabanks' clients—and that had not actually engaged in any of the wrongdoing covered by the settlement.[69] Any state that refused to agree to the slap-on-the-wrist penalties negotiated by the federal government and the other states came under pressure to do so—and faced the reality that its own separate litigation would be lengthy, very costly, and possibly unsuccessful, given the legal and political power of the megabanks involved.[70] Compliance with the settlement, moreover, was overseen by an independent monitor who had to rely on the five megabanks' own estimates and data—rather than on independently obtained information. The precedent created by the settlement also set a standard for similar actions involving bank fraud and abuse, as in the U.S. Comptroller of the Currency's case against four megabanks (that were also part of the previously mentioned settlement) involving dishonest mortgage servicing and related activities.[71] Settlements such as these—and the widespread "plea bargain" deals mentioned previously—allowed regulators and politicians to issue self-congratulatory reports and claim success to the media, thereby giving the impression that wrongdoers were being severely prosecuted.

Similarly, other federal agencies have not pursued criminal prosecutions against major financial offenders. The agency that must insure bank deposits—the Federal Deposit Insurance Corporation (FDIC)—for example, only pursued civil charges against wrongdoing—with settlements that typically amounted to a fraction of the losses it incurred. Those losses came to $92.5 billion during 2007–2013, and practically depleted that agency's deposit insurance fund.[72] One settlement with a foreign oligopo-

---

68. See "Foreclosures (2012 Robosigning and Foreclosure Abuse Settlement)," *New York Times,* February 10, 2012, http://topics.nytimes.com/top/reference/timestopics/subjects/f/foreclosures/index.html.

69. Michael Hiltzik, "Deal Gives Banks a Pass," *Los Angeles Times,* February 12, 2012, B1, and his "A Reality Check on Deal with Big Banks," *Los Angeles Times,* March 7, 2012, B1.

70. See, for example, Harold Meyerson, "Deal Breaker," *Los Angeles Times,* November 21, 2011, A13.

71. Hiltzik, "Deal."

72. E. Scott Reckard, "FDIC Keeps Quiet about Settlements: Since the Mortgage Meltdown, the Agency Has Opted to Strike Deals with Banks Rather Than Sue—and Promised not to Tell," *Los Angeles Times,* March 11, 2013, A1.

list—Deutsche Bank—involved a recovery of only $54 million, in contrast with the $13 billion the FDIC had to pay to cover that bank's defaulted loans. The agency, moreover, keeps data on its settlements confidential—a measure that allows its executives to avoid public scrutiny. To obtain records of the FDIC's many settlements, one reporter had to invoke the Freedom of Information Act, for example. After substantial scrutiny of the limited information he was allowed to see, the reporter described the settlement records as "a catalog of fraud and negligence: reckless loans to homeowners and builders; falsified documents; inflated appraisals; lender refusals to buy back bad loans."[73]

With the myriad new vehicles for speculation it spawned, financialism also opened up new channels for malfeasance that are very difficult—if not practically impossible—for authorities to detect or prosecute. One of those channels, for example, involves the so-called "expert network" companies, which claim to sell expertise but in fact often provide access to privileged corporate information that violates securities laws.[74] Such companies typically connect hedge funds with high-level sources at corporations, which can provide sensitive information on anything—from clinical trials to marketing performance, research breakthroughs, and executive decisions, among many other aspects. Related to these activities is another new vehicle for obtaining privileged corporate information—the "channel checker" companies. These firms connect hedge funds and banks with low- or midlevel corporate management, suppliers, and customers, to obtain inside information on sales, supply chain problems, and product usage, for example. Hedge funds, banks, and powerful speculators typically use such "insider" information to bet on the stocks of those corporations—generating vast profits at the expense of small investors who do not have access to it.[75]

Just as questionable is the frequent "insider" trading based on political intelligence obtained from Washington by oligopolistic megabanks and hedge funds, noted in the previous chapter. Such powerful entities enjoy access to top Federal Reserve officials and key politicians in Congress, who provide early clues on policy moves, regulatory action, and upcoming legislation, which are not available to the public or to less well-connected speculators.[76] The actions

73. Ibid.

74. Walter Hamilton and Nathaniel Popper, "Authorities Suspect an Inside Game on Wall St.," *Los Angeles Times*, November 25, 2010, A1.

75. See, for example, McGinty, Carreyrou, and Rothfeld, "Inside a Star Hedge Fund."

76. See, for example, Susan Pulliam, "Investors Bullish on Fed Tips," *Wall Street Journal*, November 23, 2011, A1; Brody Mullins and Susan Pulliam, "Hedge Funds Pay Top Dollar for Washington Intelligence," *Wall Street Journal*, October 4, 2011, A1.

and words of Federal Reserve officials, in particular, have major impacts on markets, while behind-the-scenes contact with—and intelligence from—political insiders often provides important tips for crafting speculative schemes in which regulation plays a key role. Such intelligence and high-level contacts are another indication of corporatocracy at work, and the strong links that exist between oligopolistic power and public governance.

These problems and pathologies, and many others discovered in the course of the crisis that started in 2007, would have been difficult to perpetrate in a system where finance is grounded in production—in the real economy, in other words—rather than in speculative schemes. Those schemes acquire a life of their own in a financialist economy—they largely justify themselves on the basis of paper profits that are a result of a speculative dynamic rather than on the *production* of goods and services. And, they inevitably become models of what-to-do for many people, as large fortunes are made and showoff consumption takes up a prominent place in society. The role model effects of these speculators and their schemes cannot be underestimated, since they typically become models of admiration—giving the impression that great riches are within anyone's reach, if everyone would simply imitate their schemes.

It should not surprise, then, that the financialist economy has been referred to as the "casino" economy—one where gambling rules the day. Gambling that is unlike that of the roulette or the card game in the real casino, and that is much more sophisticated—as it is articulated through the jargon of the financialist technocracy, which can impress many people.[77] It is also a form of gambling that is being automated to an extent that few specialists could have imagined only a decade ago.[78] Financialist gambling

---

77. Betting on young, small companies—the ones most likely to fail even in strong economies—has also become part of the speculative dynamic; see, for example, "Raising Capital Online: The New Thundering Herd—Wanted: Small Sums of Money to Finance Young Companies, Click Here to Invest," *The Economist,* June 16, 2012, 71–72. Among the other myriad, increasingly popular forms of financialist gambling is "spread betting"—gambling on the price movements (or change) of any stock and most every other asset—a type of betting concocted by a Chicago bookmaker; see "Spread Betting: Going Global; A Punt by Any Other Name," *The Economist,* October 26, 2013, 82. Another kind involves securitizing the potential future income of a professional athlete by creating a "tracking stock" through which betting can occur; "Athletic Investment: Skin in the Game," *The Economist,* October 26, 2013, 82.

78. See, for example, Jerry Adler, "Raging Bulls: Wall Street Used to Bet on Companies That Build Things. Now It Just Bets on Technologies that Make Faster and Faster Trades," *Wired,* September 2012, 116–25. Fast trading has also opened new doors to market manipulation; see, for example, Scott Patterson and Jamila Trindle, "High-Speed Trader Pushed to Curb: Financial Cops in US and UK Fine New Jersey Firm for Manipulating Commodities Markets," *Wall Street Journal,* July 23, 2013, C1.

has thus garnered an important place in the collective psyche, as can be readily observed among preschool children in the games they play, or in youngsters who commonly bet on most any event in life or nature that has a probabilistic dimension. The effects of financialism on youngsters can, for example, be seen in the case of two (sixteen-year-old) teenagers, who perpetrated an investment scam on 75,000 people—stock promoters included—that extracted $3.1 million in less than four years.[79] Never before in the history of fraud had a scam been perpetrated by teenagers on so many people, involving so much money. Previously, another (seventeen-year-old) teenager extracted more than $1 million from hundreds of people, using a scam that promised a 2,500 percent "risk-free" annual return.[80] These and other frauds show the extent to which the culture of speculation and greed that accompanies financialism has entered the minds of the young—that most vulnerable segment of society.

In the era of financialism, most anything that has a probabilistic dimension can become an easy target for speculation, if not fraud. Even death—a condition that has a 100 percent certainty of occurrence for all living beings—has been turned into a betting game on the temporal dimension of life—which, unlike death, is subject to uncertainty. Such betting allows those who come into old age and have little income, to obtain and sell their life insurance policies to speculators—who will be paid off as beneficiaries when the death of the insured occurs. In return, speculators commit themselves to pay to keep the policy in effect (or give a loan so the insured can make such payments) and to provide a monthly stipend to their insured subject—while hoping for an early death and the correspondingly higher payoff.[81] One of the most aggressive promoters of this form of gambling—also referred to as "death-betting"—was American International Group (AIG), an insurance oligopolist that had to be bailed out by the U.S. government at substantial expense.[82] AIG's stake in this business was

---

79. Walter Hamilton and Stuart Pfeifer, "Teens Ran Stock-Tips Scam, SEC Says," *Los Angeles Times,* April 21, 2012, A1—the perpetrators of this fraud were based in Britain, but the vast majority of their victims were American.

80. Ibid., A12—the teenage perpetrator in this case was based in California.

81. See Jeff Neal, "Outside the Box: Death Speculation on Senior Citizens Becoming More Popular," *Optionetics,* February 27, 2008, http://www.optionetics.com/market/ articles/19103; Moshe Silver, "The Big Ugly Business of Death," *CNN Money,* February 14, 2011, http://www.finance.fortune. cnn.com/2011/02/14/the-big-ugly-business-of-death/; Marc Lifsher, "Treating Death as a Commodity: A Growing Industry Involves Buying, Selling, and Profiting from Life Insurance," *Los Angeles Times,* February 20, 2008, A1.

82. Leslie Scism, "AIG Tries to Sell Death-Bet Securities," *Wall Street Journal,* April 22, 2011, C1.

estimated to be over $18 billion, comprising almost six thousand policies by the end of 2011—about half the outstanding volume of death-betting policies in effect at that time.[83]

Another example of the casino mindset typical of financialist society involves gambling on lawsuits—with lawyers seeking speculators to bet on the outcomes of their litigation. Such speculation, euphemistically referred to as "alternative litigation funding," promises substantial payoffs to speculators—usually millions of dollars—if they put up funding and the lawsuits are won by the lawyers they bet on.[84] Speculators' share of payouts can be as much as 60 percent, according to one report, attracting hedge funds and oligopolistic megabanks such as Credit Suisse, which created a litigation-finance subsidiary—Parabellum Capital LLC—to target this emerging speculative mode.[85] The creation of international, stock market–traded litigation-speculator companies—such as Burford Capital and Juridica Investments, both based in London but targeting the United States—reflect the rising interest in litigation betting.[86]

Because the probability of winning in court is often low or uncertain—especially if the lawsuit is frivolous—and court proceedings usually take up a long time, attract media attention, and involve significant administrative costs, the objective of lawyers and speculators is to settle all lawsuits out of court. Using funds provided by the speculators who bet on the lawsuit, highly experienced lawyers are hired to pressure the accused party into settling. The amount of money extracted from the accused party then becomes the booty to be shared between lawyers and speculators, based on their initial agreement. Litigation on intellectual property and high-value commercial claims usually provides the largest payoffs to speculators in such out of court settlements, and the accused parties can expect substantial pressure to settle—along with the possibility of frivolous claims—as large amounts of money are made available by speculators. Also, because of the large sums put up by speculators to fund such lawsuits, legal teams can be

83. Leslie Scism, "AIG's Death-Bet Team Departs," *Wall Street Journal*, March 29, 2012, C3.

84. Vanessa O'Connell, "Funds Spring Up to Invest in High-Stakes Litigation," *Wall Street Journal*, October 3, 2011, B1.

85. "Investing in Litigation: Second-Hand Suits," *The Economist*, April 6, 2013, 84–86.

86. Juridica Investments Ltd., *Strategic Capital for Law Markets*, http://www.juridicainvestments.com/ (accessed April 11, 2013); Burford Capital, *Litigation Finance*, http://www.burfordcapital.com/litigation-finance/ (accessed April 10, 2013); "Investing in Litigation," *The Economist*, 84.

strengthened with specialized attorneys—along with extensive data mining to support arguments—thus placing the accused party at great disadvantage. In many cases, lawsuit-betting agreements have also become targets for dispute and litigation—after a case is settled—as the partners (speculators and lawyers) sue each other to try to increase their respective shares of the booty.[87]

The securitization of subprime used car loans provides another example of how the financialist casino economy can encompass almost any activity or human need—in partnership with the financial oligopolies that control or channel most securitization. These loans are made to individuals with ruined credit records—those who cannot qualify for a credit card or any other form of debt—and involve very high-mileage vehicles sold to them at prices that are substantially above their actual market value.[88] Subprime used car loans are thereby turned into derivatives that can be speculated with. A single subprime car loan derivative can comprise as many as tens of thousands of loans—all very risky and with a high probability of default. Total sales of these speculative instruments were estimated to be about $15 billion in 2009 and 2010, with many of the derivatives rated as highly as AAA (the highest rating) by the three credit-rating oligopolists (Standard and Poor, Fitch, Moody's)—under the assumption that they will retain their value even if a significant proportion of the loans in each derivative undergo default.[89]

The subprime used car loans (that are packaged into derivatives) are typically made through what are known as "Buy Here Pay Here" (BHPH) corporations, which provide financing with interest rates as high as 300 percent or more above the usual rates for used car loans.[90] About 25 percent of all sales were estimated to result in a default within a very short period of time, with cars being repossessed and resold immediately—usually by the same dealers that made the initial sales. Average profits on each sale were 38

87. Vanessa O'Connell, "In This Case, Litigation Funding Led to Court Dates for Former Partners," *Wall Street Journal,* October 3, 2011, B4.

88. See Ken Bensinger, "A Hard Road for the Poor in Need of Cars," *Los Angeles Times,* November 3, 2011, A1.

89. Ken Bensinger, "Wall Street Loves Used Cars: Equity Firms Are Buying Dealership Chains, and Auto Loans Are Being Bundled into Securities As Risky Mortgages Were," *Los Angeles Times,* November 1, 2011, A1.

90. Ken Bensinger, "A Vicious Cycle in the Used-Car Business: Sign, Drive, Default, Repossess and Resell—That's the Game at Buy Here Pay Here Dealerships," *Los Angeles Times,* October 30, 2011, A1, and his "Hard Road for the Poor."

percent in 2010, according to the National Alliance of BHPH dealers—a return that is far above those obtained in most Wall Street transactions. The salespersons involved have in many cases received compensation as high as $250,000 annually, as the revolving door scheme involving sales, defaults, repossessions, and resales runs quickly through needy customers—who must typically have a vehicle in order to maintain or find a job. Frequently, therefore, a customer who defaults can quickly obtain another loan and vehicle—but at a much higher interest rate and purchase price than the previous one, thus helping increase sales and profit for the BHPH dealer. Hedge funds such as Altamont Capital Partners, Alpine Investors, and Serent Capital, for example, have speculated with BHPH schemes—given their high returns and the promise of greater payoffs as the numbers of the working poor increase. Altamont, for example, purchased the JD Byrider used car dealership chain, which had sales of $740 million in 2010. Other BHPH used car chains—such as Car-Mart, with 111 locations in nine states and a loan portfolio growth of 30 percent in 2010—have also become targets for hedge funds and Wall Street speculators.[91] Most BHPH corporations are now oligopolists in their own right, and many also have geo-monopolies in numerous local areas.

Some BHPH chains securitize their loan portfolios themselves, thereby obtaining additional profit as they generate derivatives on their own. Drive Time Automotive—a chain with eighty-eight dealerships in seventeen states, for example—generated derivatives valued at almost $500 million in 2011 alone. Each of the derivatives can have as many as fifty thousand loans—all or most classified in the category of "deep subprime," the most risky and prone to default. According to credit rating oligopolist Moody's, more than $7 billion in these kinds of derivatives were issued in the first six months of 2011 alone—a 133 percent increase over the same period in 2010.[92] Perhaps, therefore, it should not surprise that the BHPH used car corporations and their associated Wall Street speculators founded a powerful lobbying vehicle—the Community Auto Finance Association—to influence politicians in the U.S. Congress, with the objective of blocking any regulation of their sector.

Betting on meteorology through weather derivatives—the securitization of weather, essentially—provides yet another example of how anything with a probabilistic dimension can be turned into a gambling proposition

---

91. Bensinger, "Wall Street Loves Used Cars."

92. Bensinger, "Vicious Cycle" and "Wall Street Loves Used Cars."

in the financialist economy. Speculation using weather derivatives was a core activity of the Enron Corporation—an oligopolistic energy speculator—starting in 1997. Its bankruptcy in 2001—after its fraudulent practices were exposed—was the largest ever in American history.[93] This corporation's scandal did not dampen interest in this novel form of speculation, however. Weather derivatives were valued at $45 billion at their peak in 2005–06—shortly before the start of the financial crisis—becoming a new frontier for Wall Street speculation.[94] Climate bets were thus packaged into derivatives—using temperature, rainfall, wind, snow, or sunshine as benchmarks, for example—and were sold to speculators, and to businesses with revenues that depend on weather—such as gas and electricity suppliers, farmers, construction companies, tourism, and outdoor event operators.[95] Catastrophic weather events, such as tornadoes, hurricanes, and floods were already a core business for insurance oligopolists, but weather derivatives became a gambling option that most anyone could participate in—one of many new betting opportunities in the financialist economy, which Wall Street oligopolists began to take over in the 1990s.

An important contributor to the financialist casino economy was the elimination of conventional pensions, and their replacement by employee-funded programs that fundamentally depend on stock and bond market betting to accumulate funds for retirement. A key but usually unmentioned objective of this trend, highly promoted by neoliberal ideologues, was *to align the economic and political interests of the population at large with those of the financial and corporate elites*, by turning almost everyone into a stock market gambler. Making everyone's old-age well-being dependent on speculative corporate finance was the cornerstone of this effort to make public governance—that serves corporate interests above everything else—acceptable to the public. At the same time, eliminating conventional pensions allowed the financial and corporate elites to redeploy capital—which would have gone to support employee retirement—to support lavish executive compensation, including the bonuses, stock options, and "golden handshake" schemes that became so important to those elites.

---

93. See Brian Cruver, *Anatomy of Greed: The Unshredded Truth from an Enron Insider* (New York: Carroll and Graf, 2002); Mimi Swartz and Sherron Watkins, *Power Failure: The Inside Story of the Collapse of Enron* (New York: Doubleday, 2003).

94. "Weather Derivatives: Come Rain or Shine," *The Economist,* February 4, 2012, 77.

95. See, for example, Peter C. Fusaro and Gary M. Vasey, *Energy and Environmental Hedge Funds: The New Investment Paradigm* (New York: Wiley, 2006).

Some authors misleadingly referred to this trend as a "democratization of finance," when in fact what was involved was financializing the public interest, to place it under the control of the financial and corporate elites. A massive redistribution of wealth and power from working people, the middle class, and the poor toward the financial and corporate elites thus accompanied the elimination of conventional pensions.[96] Dispossession of working people, the middle class, and the poor was a result of this process, but was camouflaged by the illusion that attaining great wealth through the stock and bond markets was very much within everyone's reach—if only one would play the financialist gambling game.[97] Turning everyone into a stock and bond market gambler to accumulate money for retirement overlooked the high risk and increasing complexity of financial speculation. This ignorance was promoted by well-known specialists with a vested interest in speculation. One of the best-known mutual fund managers, for example, counseled the public to "stop listening to professionals," adding that "any normal person can pick stocks just as well, if not better, than the average Wall Street expert."[98] Such advice was grounded in the notion that everyone could become a speculator, and that the trajectories of stock and bond markets could be easily figured out by anyone, that those markets are nearly infallible, and that they can self-correct and refloat themselves when crises arise.

The elimination of conventional pensions required structural changes in the social contract and the benefit systems that had supported working people in the United States and in many other nations since the 1940s. Corporations would no longer be responsible for conventional retirement pensions, even as the state's resources to provide old-age support shrank and social security benefits were diminished—partly because of substantially reduced taxes on the financial and corporate elites, and on corporations in general. In the United States, the 401(k) retirement plans were thus enacted by Congress in the 1980s, to allow employers to terminate conventional

---

96. See David Harvey's *A Brief History of Neoliberalism* (Oxford: Oxford University Press, 2005), for an extensive elaboration of this point.

97. The notion that everyone—or anyone—could become a speculator and win large sums of money became part of the American cultural baggage of the 1990s; see, for example, Steve Fraser, *Every Man a Speculator: A History of Wall Street in American Life* (New York: HarperCollins, 2005).

98. Thomas Frank, "Goldman and the Sophisticated Investor," *Wall Street Journal,* May 5, 2010, A19, and his "Please Tread on Us," *Wall Street Journal,* April 21, 2010, A19.

employee pensions—a measure implemented at the same time that financial deregulation gained momentum. Employers would be expected to contribute to these new plans, provided employees also contributed out of their own paychecks, although employer contributions would be much less than those required under conventional pensions. The 401(k) plans were thus essentially employee-managed accounts that fundamentally required stock and bond market betting—to have any chance of providing some income in old age.

Many corporate employers, however, soon started underfunding or eliminating their contributions to employees' 401(k) funds, in what became a cheating game with practically no sanctions or government oversight.[99] A suspension of employer contributions to the 401(k) retirement plans, even for one year, can seriously affect employee retirement balances—in many cases by tens of thousands of dollars when an employee reaches retirement age. Such employer contributions have been estimated to be the single most important factor supporting employee retirement, and are considered to be even more important than household budgets.[100] After 2008, almost one in five American corporations with at least one thousand employees—and almost two-thirds of all corporations with five hundred or fewer workers—had severely underfunded their contributions to their employees' 401(k) plans—as corporate executives got ever-larger compensation packages, bonuses, stock options, and "golden farewell" arrangements.[101] According to one estimate, the corporations that make up the S&P 500 Index—almost all of them oligopolists in their respective sectors or market niches—had a collective $450 billion deficit in their pension funds in 2011, a figure that amounts to about 25 percent of the total funding required to sustain retirement obligations.[102] General Motors, for example—a too-big-to-fail

---

99. See, for example, Ellen E. Schultz, "Who Killed Private Pensions?," *Wall Street Journal,* September 11, 2011, B8.

100. See BlackRock, Inc., *Shifting Focus: From Retirement Savings to Retirement Income; 2011 Defined Contribution Plan Survey,* https://www2.blackrock.com/webcore/ (accessed January 14, 2012); Eleanor Laise and Kelly Greene, "Waiting On Return of 401(k) Match," *Wall Street Journal,* August 3, 2010, C1.

101. Laise and Greene, "Waiting on Return"; Mark Maremont, "McKesson CEO Due a Pension of $159 Million," *Wall Street Journal,* June 25, 2013, B1. Corporations also started lobbying Congress to lower the ratios used to calculate their contributions to employee pension funds, with the objective of saving themselves tens of billions of dollars annually; see Kristina Peterson, "Companies' Pension Plea," *Wall Street Journal,* March 6, 2012, B1.

102. "Too Much Risk, not Enough Reward," *The Economist,* March 17, 2012, 23.

industrial oligopolist that received a $50 billion government bailout in 2009—seriously underfunded its employee pension plan and faced a $25 billion deficit by 2012.[103] This corporation also eliminated all contributions to what remained of its conventional pension program, despite a record annual profit of $8 billion for the previous year—the largest ever in its entire 103-year history. Through its simultaneous government bailout and bankruptcy filing, General Motors also freed itself from its debts and became exempt from paying federal taxes for several years—a corporate welfare tax break estimated to be worth as much as $45 billion.[104]

The risk to employees can be substantial even when 401(k) retirement plans are fully funded by employers.[105] Those risks can involve, for example, employers disowning a retirement plan when a company (or subsidiary) is sold or spun off, or the loss of retirement income because of past inflated (or miscalculated) estimates by the employer.[106] In many cases, employees are induced to take a lump sum payment when they retire—in place of regular retirement payments—as a way to reduce a corporation's obligations. Such lump sum payments are typically insufficient to support retirement if an employee's longevity is average or long—more so if the lump sum funds are invested and incur substantial losses in the stock or bond markets. Also, corporations that run hospitals, schools, charities, universities, nursing homes, and similar institutional entities—many of them oligopolists in their sectors or market niches—have in many cases falsely claimed their retirement plans are "church plans" in order to be exempt from federal pension rules. This means that they are not required to have any retirement plan at all—or make any disclosure—or insure it in any way if they happen to

---

103. Sharon Terlep, "GM Cuts Benefits for Salaried Staff," *Wall Street Journal*, February 16, 2012, B3, and her "GM Acts to Pare Pension Liability," *Wall Street Journal*, June 2, 2012, B3; J. David Anderson, "GM Profit is Easier with Debt, Tax Erased," Letters to the Editor, *Wall Street Journal*, February 17, 2012, A12.

104. Randall Smith and Sharon Terlep, "GM to Get Tax Break Worth Billions," *Wall Street Journal*, November 3, 2010, B1.

105. Such risks can be magnified, for example, when 401(k) funds are used to engage in day trading; see Walter Hamilton, "Anxious Investors Flip Their Nest Eggs: Worries Over 401(k) and IRA Shortfalls Spur Day Trading within the Accounts," *Los Angeles Times*, July 9, 2012, A1. Day-trading using 401(k) funds has attracted interest as individuals' retirement funds decline or become stagnant; see, for example, Richard Schmitt, *401(k) Day Trading: The Art of Cashing In on a Shaky Market in Minutes a Day* (New York: Wiley, 2011).

106. See, for example, Ellen E. Schultz, "Signs Your Pension Plan Is in Trouble," *Wall Street Journal*, February 11, 2012, B9.

have one.[107] The "church plan" scheme places employees at great risk, since they have practically no rights whatsoever if a corporate employer discards a retirement plan.

After conventional pensions for private sector employees were mostly eliminated, neoliberal ideologues and policymakers began to target public sector pensions. The neoliberal push to eliminate conventional pensions for public employees became most strident after the start of the economic crisis in 2007, as government finances were severely impaired—partly because of all the bailouts and subsidies involving corporate welfare, and the tax cuts for corporations and the wealthy—and as public pension systems' stock market funds experienced substantial losses.[108] In addition, the U.S. Federal Reserve's near-zero interest rate policy—which primarily benefited oligopolies and the financial elites—also jeopardized public sector pension systems, by making it impossible to obtain adequate returns on less risky investments.[109] Some state and local governments then started to replace their conventional pension programs with 401(k) plans—much as private sector employers had done earlier.[110] Many public sector pension systems also started to place a substantial amount of their money with highly speculative hedge funds— reaching a quarter-trillion dollars by the end of 2011—to try to increase returns by any means possible, regardless of risk.[111] *Thus, the effort to align the public's interest with the interests of the corporate and financial elites reached a new frontier: public pensions.* This development compounded the ongoing

---

107. See Pension Rights Center, *What Are the Types of Church Pension Plans?*, July 21, 2011, http://www.pensionrights.org/publications/fact-sheet/what-are-types-church-pension-plans; Schultz, "Signs."

108. See, for example, Andrew G. Biggs and Jason Richwine, "Why Public Pensions Are So Rich: Shifting Government Workers to 401(k)-Style Plans Would Offer Greater Transparency and Keep Benefits in Line with the Private Economy," *Wall Street Journal,* January 4, 2012, A13.

109. See George Melloan, "The Year of Governments Living Dangerously," *Wall Street Journal,* December 31, 2011, A15. Issuing more debt to try to cover deficits in employee retirement obligations also became more common; see Nathaniel Popper, "Betting on Bonds to Plug Deficits: Municipalities Issue More Debt to Plug Shortfalls in Employee Retirement Obligations," *Los Angeles Times,* March 29, 2011, B1.

110. See, for example, Editorial, "The Utah Pension Model: The State Adopts 401(k)s for New State Employees," *Wall Street Journal,* January 19, 2011, A14.

111. Michael Corkery, "Pensions Increasing Their Ties: Public Pensions Increase Investments in Private-Equity Funds," *Wall Street Journal,* January 26, 2012, C1, and his "Pensions Bet Big with Private Equity," *Wall Street Journal,* January 25, 2013, A1; Lack, *Hedge Fund Mirage.*

redistribution of wealth and power from the working and middle classes toward those elites, and toward oligopolistic corporate power in general.

The widespread adoption of 401(k)-type plans means that any significant gains in pension and old-age income will have to occur through stock and bond market bets by individual employees—thereby *shifting all risk and blame for shortfalls in retirement funds to the individual*. This massive transfer of risk to individual employees for old-age support relieved oligopolistic corporations and the corporate elites from a major, costly obligation that had been part of the social contract in the United States (and in most rich nations) for many decades. This shift also allowed oligopolistic corporations to free up capital to spend on greater executive compensation, and to lobby or co-opt politicians to do their bidding.[112] An individual employee's failure to accumulate enough money for retirement could now therefore be blamed on poor personal betting choices, flawed decision making, bad luck, or even personal stupidity—even though the speculative choices available to individuals through 401(k)-style programs are usually quite limited.[113]

In this way, the system—financialist capitalism—was absolved of any blame, along with the financial and corporate elites that controlled the corporatocratic state—and the politicians who run it at their behest. Keeping everyone busy on this betting treadmill to accumulate money for retirement became a great way to try to prevent social and political awareness—of the sort that could threaten the power built up by the financial elites. This betting treadmill was further sped along by rising economic insecurity for employees—due to the outsourcing of jobs, the layoffs of older employees to avoid funding their healthcare benefits, and the redeployment of internal funds that could support employee benefits to enhance corporate income accounts (or increase executive compensation). Such insecurity helped create reserve armies of labor—the unemployed—during economic downturns, allowing many corporations to pay substantially lower salaries if or when workers were rehired.[114] Economic insecurity also took up a new dimension, as many elderly people found that they could not afford to retire at

---

112. See Ellen E. Schultz and Theo Francis, "Companies Tap Pension Plans to Fund Executive Benefits: Little-Known Move Uses Tax Break Meant for Rank and File," *Wall Street Journal*, August 5, 2008, A1.

113. See, for example, Barbara Ehrenreich, *Nickel and Dimed: On (Not) Getting By in America* (New York: Picador, 2011); Jack Hough, "Getting the Most from a Lame 401(k) Retirement Plan," *Wall Street Journal*, October 8, 2011, B7.

114. An aspect explored in Bertram Gross, "The Reserve Army of the Insecure," *Monthly Review*, May 1995, 43.

all—and would thus never be able to get off the treadmill.[115] *This massive induction of employees and workers into the financialist betting economy tacitly transferred much risk from corporations to government,* since employees who failed to secure sufficient old-age support would invariably end up in the lap of government—as welfare recipients or as wards of the taxpayer-supported U.S. Pension Benefit Guaranty Corporation (the government agency that insures employer-provided pensions).

Among the other neoliberal schemes aimed at aligning the economic interests of the population with those of the financial and corporate elites are proposals to end Social Security by transforming it into either savings accounts to be held by private banks—especially the oligopolistic megabanks—or into stock market betting accounts that would depend heavily on speculation and corporate power. Such proposals ignore the fact that Social Security has all along had a surplus from employee contributions and interest due, and that it has saved many millions of people from poverty in old age since it was created seven decades ago—making it the most successful government program in U.S. history.[116] Curiously, the neoliberal ideologues who favor making Social Security part of the financialist betting economy never advocate billing Wall Street megabanks, hedge funds, and the financial elites for the vast sums it cost the public treasury to bail out the financial sector. Proposals to privatize Social Security are, moreover, often rife with conflicts of interests—as in the case of a key member of the National Commission on Fiscal Responsibility and Reform who was drawing $335,000 in part-time annual compensation as a director of Wall Street megabank Morgan Stanley (one of the too-big-to-fail banks that was bailed out in 2008–09).[117]

One long-standing argument used by neoliberal ideologues to try to privatize Social Security and incorporate it into the financialist casino economy is what may be referred to as *generational discrimination.* This scheme separates the younger from the older segments of the American workforce—in what is basically a game of divide and conquer—by proposing to substantially cut future benefits to the younger segment when they reach retirement age, while maintaining current benefits to those already retired and those who are not too far from retirement. An intended effect of

---

115. See Kelly Greene and Anne Tergesen, "More Elderly Find They Can't Afford Not to Work," *Wall Street Journal,* January 21, 2012, A1.

116. See, for example, Michael Hiltzik, *The New Deal: A Modern History* (New York: Free Press, 2011).

117. Michael Hiltzik, "Cutting Deficit with Ideology: Deficit-Cutting 'Patriotism' Wouldn't Hit Wall Street," *Los Angeles Times,* November 14, 2010, B1.

this scheme is to effectively make Social Security irrelevant to the younger segment of the workforce, given the substantially reduced retirement benefits that they would receive. This would cause Social Security to lose support among that younger segment of the labor force—so that they can be induced to agree to the privatization of the program. The ideas behind generational discrimination for Social Security date to 1983 when two neoliberal ideologues, distressed over the Reagan administration's failure to privatize the program, published them in a conservative think tank's journal.[118] Their divide-and-conquer scheme has become a staple of neoliberal proposals on Social Security during the past three decades.[119]

Another proposed scheme for aligning the economic interests of the population with those of the financial and corporate elites would involve turning Medicare into a coupon program, which would force elderly Americans to become "clients" of large, oligopolistic insurance corporations in order to receive any medical care. This scheme is partly based on the so-called consumer-driven health plans that became common as corporations stopped providing health coverage—thus forcing employees to purchase their own health insurance from the oligopolists that control this sector, and to pay for many treatments out of their own savings and salaries.[120] A result of this trend has been a rapid accumulation of debt by those who seek care, and the aggressive pursuit of those who cannot pay by debt collection corporations.[121] In many cases, hospital corporations—most

---

118. Stuart Butler and Peter Germanis, "Achieving Social Security Reform: A 'Leninist' Strategy," *Cato Journal* 3 (1983), http://www.cato.org/pubs/journal/cj3n2.html.

119. See Michael Hiltzik, "Behind Social Security 'Reform': The Agenda Behind 'Fixes' to Social Security, Medicare," *Los Angeles Times,* January 15, 2012, B1.

120. The elimination of health coverage provision by corporate employers and the switch to "consumer-driven health plans" parallels the elimination of conventional pensions and the switch to 401(k) retirement programs. A major problem is that contributions by employers did not keep up with rising health care costs—in much the same way that employer contributions to 401(k) programs usually do not keep up with rising inflation or cost of living increases. The result is that employees end up having to pay for more of their health care costs out of their own salaries or savings, much as 401(k) retirees end up finding out that their balances cannot support them adequately when they retire. See "Health Care in America: Shopping Around for Surgery," *The Economist,* February 4, 2012, 70; Anna Wilde Mathews, "Big Firms Overhaul Health Coverage," *Wall Street Journal,* September 27, 2012, A1.

121. Medical bills have been one of the largest causes of personal bankruptcies in the United States. See, for example, Lucette Lagnado, "Twenty Years and Still Paying: Jeannette White Is Long Dead but Her Hospital Bill Lives On; Interest Charges, Legal Fees," *Wall Street Journal,* March 13, 2003, B1; Anna Wilde Mathews, "Surprise Health Bills Make People See Red," *Wall Street Journal,* December 4, 2008, D1.

of them oligopolists in their sector, if not also geographically—denied care to those who could not come up with cash before nonemergency procedures, especially if their credit reports were judged to be less than excellent.[122] This kind of privatization of Medicare would immensely enrich the financial and corporate elites further—and the oligopolies they control—while reducing coverage and raising out-of-pocket costs for those who qualify.[123] At the same time, since Medicare per-person costs have tended to increase less rapidly than those of private insurance, a privatization of Medicare would likely inflate costs and burden taxpayers further.[124] Not surprisingly, legislative proposals that seek to reform Medicare by privatizing it typically exclude any possibility of raising taxes for corporations or the wealthy, as a way to ensure full coverage.[125] Generational discrimination is also part of this general scheme, and targets the younger segment of the population by raising their qualifying age, reducing benefits, and increasing premiums. Medicare premiums would likely increase because raising the qualifying age for the younger population would make the pool of recipients older over time—and thus more likely to be receiving costly medical care. Higher premiums would in turn make Medicare less attractive to the younger segment of the population, inducing support for privatization.[126]

122. See Barbara Martinez, "Cash Before Chemo: Hospitals Get Tough," *Wall Street Journal,* April 28, 2008, A1, and her "Healthy Funding at M. D. Anderson," *Wall Street Journal,* April 28, 2008, A15; Sarah Rubenstein, "Why Hospitals Want Your Credit Report: Many Are Using Personal Data to Assess Your Ability to Pay; Concerns About Denial of Care," *Wall Street Journal,* March 18, 2008, A1.

123. See, for example, Noam N. Levey, "GOP Plan Raises Costs, Agency Says: An Analysis Finds Rep. Paul Ryan's Proposal to Privatize Medicare Would Have Seniors Paying Almost Double," *Los Angeles Times,* April 8, 2011, A10.

124. During 2000–2010, per-person costs for private health insurance increased more rapidly than for Medicare; see John Holahan and Stacey McMorrow, "Medicare and Medicaid Spending Trends and the Deficit Debate," *New England Journal of Medicine* 367 (August 2012): 393–95; Chapin White and Paul B. Ginsburg, "Slower Growth in Medicare Spending—Is This the New Normal?" *New England Journal of Medicine* 367 (August 2012): 1073–75.

125. See, for example, Lisa Mascaro, "GOP Is Back with a Revised Medicare Overhaul," *Los Angeles Times,* March 17, 2012, A1; Lisa Mascaro and Michael A. Memoli, "GOP Revisits Medicare Reform: A Rough Budget Plan Includes a Proposal to Create a Voucher-Like System for Those Who Are 56 or Younger," *Los Angeles Times,* March 3, 2013, A1.

126. See, for example, Kaiser Family Foundation, *Raising the Age of Medicare Eligibility: A Fresh Look Following Implementation of Health Reform* (Menlo Park, CA: KFF, 2011), http://www.kff.org/medicare/8169.cfm; Hiltzik, "Behind Social Security."

A likely result of the privatization of Medicare would be to leave a larger proportion of the population with less access to old age medical care. Benefits would also likely be reduced, as the oligopolistic corporations that would most likely end up in charge of the program try to reduce costs and increase profits by any means possible. Another result would be the co-optation of politicians and regulators to guarantee profit margins to those corporations, at taxpayers' (and Medicare recipients') expense. Privatization of Medicare and Social Security—to corporatize and incorporate them in the financialist betting economy—is undoubtedly of great interest to Wall Street's hedge funds and megabanks. A rich and deep mine of profits—and speculation—lies beneath the population's need for old age support and health care. For the population at large, the most likely effect would be greater economic uncertainty—a faster-running treadmill of insecurity that would likely keep many people's minds off any thought of seeking social justice, fairness, or economic rights—while at the same time transferring more risk from corporations to government and to individual citizens.[127]

In the financialist economy, whenever crises occur, corporate power and the financial elites tacitly assume that government will come to their rescue. Thus, if old-age support through stock and bond market betting becomes insufficient, the financial and corporate elites assume that their control over public governance—corporatocracy—will resolve the problem by reducing the public's expectations, raising taxes and fees for working people and the middle class, and eliminating labor unions. When much of the population becomes unemployed or falls into the social safety net, government will therefore be expected to pick up the cost—as occurred, for example, when federal spending on means-tested social programs (such as Food Stamps and Medicaid) rose by 60 percent (to over $700 billion) during 2007–2011.[128] *This massive shifting of systemic risk from the financial and corporate elites—and from oligopolistic corporate power—to the state is one of the hallmarks of financialism—and of corporatocracy.*

The corporatocratic state is, after all, the bailor, subsidizer, profit guarantor, and lender of last resort to the oligopolies—especially the too-big-to-fail financial corporations—which rule the economy and soci-

---

127. See Loïc Wacquant, *Punishing the Poor: The Neoliberal Government of Social Insecurity* (Durham: Duke University Press, 2008).

128. "Who Are the Real 'Freeloaders': The Poor or the Old?" *The Atlantic*, February 10, 2012, http://www.theatlantic.com/business/archive/2012/02/252894/.

ety.[129] The financial crisis that started in 2007 was estimated to have cost about $17 trillion worldwide over the following three years, in government bailouts of failed corporations, in stimuli, subsidies, and various forms of corporate welfare. The U.S. government's stimulus program alone amounted to 4 percent of gross domestic product (GDP) as the crisis deepened (in February 2009). By contrast, the Roosevelt administration's New Deal stimulus programs, in any year during the 1930s, amounted to 1.5 percent or less of GDP.[130] Total U.S. Treasury debt outstanding mushroomed to $15 trillion in 2011 from $10.6 trillion three years before—an increase of 42 percent, unprecedented for such a short period of time.[131] Substantial increases in government expenses also occurred in Europe and Japan, and in many less developed nations. The prime beneficiaries of this immense increase in government spending were the financial elites tied to oligopolistic financial corporations—both those bailed out and those that were not—and the ones that would have collapsed in the cascade of failures, had Wall Street not been rescued. The losers were many millions of working people around the world, who lost their well-being, their jobs, their homes, and incomes—and the masses of taxpayers who became responsible for the emergency corporate welfare programs that governments created.

This shift of systemic risk has been mostly ignored, as it happened gradually and in fragmented ways. And the rising importance of financialism during the past three decades led many to believe that a new economy—a new form of capitalism, implicitly—was emerging. But the financialist economy was in fact grounded in an excessive accumulation of *debt* at all levels. In the late 1970s, for example, total outstanding debt—incurred by consumers, private businesses, and government—in the United States was about 1.5 times annual GDP. Three decades later, it was close to four times annual

---

129. In the early 1970s—four decades ago—James O'Connor, in his *The Fiscal Crisis of the State* (New York: St. Martin's Press, 1973), foresaw this situation and noted its inevitability, along with its role as a source of fiscal crises.

130. Michael Grunwald, *The New New Deal: The Hidden Story of Change in the Obama Era* (New York: Simon and Schuster, 2012). The American Recovery and Reinvestment Act— which funded the stimulus program—was estimated to cost $787 billion at the time it was signed into law (February 2009), and has raised substantial questions about its effectiveness; see, for example, Michael Grabell, *Money Well Spent? The Truth Behind the Trillion Dollar Stimulus, The Biggest Economic Recovery Plan in History* (New York: PublicAffairs, 2012).

131. Mary Bottari, "Money Still Owed in Federal Bailout: $1.5 Trillion Still Owed to Treasury, Federal Reserve," *PR Watch*, August 3, 2011, http://www.prwatch.org/news/2011/08/10924/.

GDP—an unprecedented expansion of total debt.[132] This overwhelming importance of debt in the financialist economy is reflected in speculators' frequent efforts to manipulate debt markets. One case, for example, involved the manipulation of a type of interest rate that affects hundreds of millions of loans around the globe—the London Inter-Bank Offered Rate (LIBOR).[133] This rate is typically used to price myriad derivatives, corporate debt, home mortgages, and auto loans, all of which were valued at over $350 trillion worldwide in 2011.[134] Cities and local governments around the world are greatly affected, since a manipulation of the rate can cost them billions of dollars annually in additional interest payments. Speculators at some of the world's largest banks—all of them oligopolists—used their inside knowledge and external networks to coordinate bets, and make artificially high or low quotes, on derivatives and loans linked to the LIBOR interest rate—reaping hundreds of millions of dollars in profit between 2007 and 2010.[135] Networks of speculators in megabanks, who engage in such manipulations, are most difficult to trace or prosecute because of their international reach, and the inability of regulators to monitor their schemes.

The accumulation of excessive government debt is also a major outcome of financialism. Total U.S. government debt mushroomed after the late 1970s, reaching almost 155 percent of GDP by 2011 ($22.1 trillion) when

---

132. See Foster and Magdoff, *Great Financial Crisis*. In 1954, the ratio of total U.S. indebtedness to GDP (government, corporate, institutional, consumer) was 1.3; over six decades, total U.S. indebtedness nearly quadrupled in relation to GDP. During the coming two decades, the projection is for U.S. government debt alone to double in size, relative to GDP; see U.S. Congressional Budget Office, "CBO's Long-Term Budget Outlook," June, 2012, http://cbo.gov/publication/41486.

133. See, for example, Ramaa Vasudevan, "'Liboring Under the Market Illusion," *Monthly Review,* January 2013, 1–12.

134. Vasudevan, "Liboring Under"; Jean Eaglesham, Paul Vieira, and David Enrich, "Traders Manipulated Key Rate, Bank Says," *Wall Street Journal,* February 17, 2012, C1.

135. See, for example, Jean Eaglesham and Max Colchester, "Interest Rate Probe Escalates: Barclays Agrees to Pay Record Fine; Emails Show Traders Tried to Manipulate Libor," *Wall Street Journal,* June 28, 2012, A1; "The LIBOR Probes: An Expensive Smoking Gun," *The Economist,* April 14, 2012, 80–82, and "Fixed Harmony: An Admission of Collusion Banks to Further Legal Woes," *The Economist,* December 7, 2013, 79; David Enrich, "Libor Case Ensnares More Banks: UK Prosecutors Allege Staff from JP Morgan, Deutsche Bank, and Others Tried to Fix Rates," *Wall Street Journal,* June 21, 2013, C1; David Enrich and Jenny Strasburg, "UK to Name Others in Libor Probe," *Wall Street Journal,* October 18, 2013, C3. Frequent manipulation of rates other than LIBOR by the world's largest banks is also suspected; see, for example, "Rigging Currency Markets: The FX Is In; Are Foreign-Exchange Benchmarks the Latest to be Manipulated by Bankers?" *The Economist,* October 12, 2013, 88.

federal agency debt ($7.5 trillion) is included in the total.[136] Taking into account that total annual U.S. government revenues were about $2.3 trillion in 2010, this means that the U.S. government's share of debt to income was about 961 percent, the largest debt-to-income load ever. The transfer of corporate risk to government—through deregulation, corporate welfare, bailouts, substantial reductions in taxes for corporations and the elites, and the growth of speculation—was greatly responsible for this unprecedented growth of public debt.

Government deficits also increased to unprecedented proportions, fueling the debt load noted previously. In the twelve months between mid-2007 and 2008, for example, the U.S. government deficit tripled, and then it tripled again during 2008–09. By 2011, the government's annual deficit was the largest ever, at $1.5 trillion—a figure that later increased, and could increase substantially with another economic crisis.[137] To cover those deficits, the U.S. government was forced to borrow heavily—to unprecedented levels—with total borrowing to cover the 2011 deficit alone amounting to over 40 percent of all the funds expended that year, for example.[138] The U.S. government's deep dependence on creditors—especially foreign—is illustrated by the fact that in 2011 the amount owed was four times greater than that owed when the American economy previously plunged into recession in 2000. In the 2000s decade—when financialism's speculative frenzy was quite intense—the U.S. government became more dependent on creditors than ever. Its unfunded liabilities, moreover, were projected at about $40 trillion over the next seven decades—an amount that, to be covered, would require continuous budget surpluses of at least 1.8 percent annually over that period of time—an extremely unlikely prospect. Massive amounts of corporate welfare, along with substantial tax cuts for the corporate elites, accelerated these dramatic increases in deficits and debt.

Mountains of debt are also accumulated by individuals and households, as financialism expands and turns much of the population into stock market

---

136. See John Steele Gordon, "A Short Primer on the National Debt," *Wall Street Journal,* August 29, 2011, http://online.wsj.com/article/; Alex J. Pollock and Anthony Davies, "National Debt Is Larger, More Subtle Than Thought," Letters to the Editor, *Wall Street Journal,* September 8, 2011, A14; Foster and Magdoff, *Great Financial Crisis,* 45–46.

137. Congressional Budget Office, *Budget and Economic Outlook: Fiscal Years 2011 to 2021,* January 26, 2011, http://www.cbo.gov; Gordon, "Short Primer."

138. U.S. Government Accountability Office, *Fiscal Year 2011 Financial Report of the United States Government,* http://www.gao.gov/financial/fy2011financialreport.html (accessed February 10, 2012).

gamblers. Household debt, for example, rose to more than 130 percent of income, on average, by the mid-2000s—a level that had no precedent in American history.[139] Most worrisome, the U.S. Federal Reserve—America's central bank—practically ignored this trend, and the dangers posed by the highly speculative mortgage loan market.[140] Money to speculate was garnered through mortgage equity loans, personal loans, pension fund loans, credit cards, and other debt vehicles, in what became a frenzy of debt accumulation driven by the greedy expectation of accumulating more money—based on speculation alone. This frenzy of speculation was also driven by economic anxiety, as incomes declined and debt ended up being used to sustain both stock market gambling and personal consumption—an aspect of financialism that became painfully obvious as incomes sank 7 percent (in real terms) between 2000 and 2010, for the U.S. population at large.[141] This decline in incomes—and the massive amounts of debt incurred to sustain consumption—were partly a result of a redistribution of wealth from working people and the middle class toward the financial and corporate elites, an aspect that will be discussed later in this chapter.

Some hedge funds targeted their business models to profit from this massive increase in household debt—and the anxiety it created—by mak-

---

139. See Geithner, "Financial Crisis Amnesia"; Foster and Magdoff, *The Great Financial Crisis*. The long-term rise in household debt also became a vehicle to transfer profits to the financial sector—especially the oligopolies—from nonfinancial activities; see Fletcher Baragar and Robert Chernomas, "Profits from Production and Profits from Exchange: Financialization, Household Debt, and Profitability in 21ˢᵗ-Century Capitalism," *Science and Society* 76 (2012): 319–39.

140. Dr. Ben Bernanke—the Federal Reserve's chairman—for example, stated publicly in March 2006: "Again, I think we are unlikely to see growth being derailed by the housing market"; and once again in May (2006): "We are seeing, at worst, an orderly decline in the housing market." His remarks came barely a year before the start of the worst decline in U.S. housing markets, and the worst economic crisis since the Great Depression; see Jon Hilsenrath, Luca Di Leo, and Michael S. Derby, "Little Alarm Shown at Fed at Dawn of Housing Bust," *Wall Street Journal*, January 13, 2012, A1.

141. Phil Izzo, "Bleak News for Americans' Income: Pay Fell 7% in Last Decade and Economists Say It Won't Catch Up Before 2021; Even College Graduates See Salaries Slide," *Wall Street Journal*, October 14, 2011, A6. The total amount of debt used to bet in the stock and bond markets (known as "margin debt") reached $381.4 billion in the United States in July 2007—just before the start of the crisis—a historical record. Also disturbing is that by March 2013, this type of debt was valued at $379.5 billion—very close to the record set six years earlier (just before the start of the crisis); see Alexandra Scaggs and Steven Russolillo, "Investors Rediscovering Margin Debt," *Wall Street Journal*, May 10, 2013, C1.

ing deals with numerous banks to sell superfluous "protection" programs to credit card holders. The programs involve recurring monthly fees that are built into credit card holders' bills, and that can generate tens of millions of dollars in monthly revenue for the hedge funds. Two hedge funds, Apollo Management and General Atlantic Partners, for example, made an agreement with Citibank that enlisted this megabank to sign up its twenty-one million North American credit card account customers for their Watch-Guard Preferred security service.[142] The trail of ownership and control leading from the hedge funds to the "security service" offered by Citibank was disguised by making it a subsidiary of other subsidiaries—all of them also owned by the hedge funds—to forestall lawsuits or public exposure. Thus, ownership of Watch-Guard Preferred was held by a company named Trilegiant, which was in turn owned by another company named Affinion Group—the one actually owned by the hedge funds. Affinion Group itself owns dozens of such "security" programs that go by numerous different names, and provide "protection" for consumers in such diverse areas as prescription medications, travel, shopping clubs, and identity theft. To get its credit card customers to sign up for Watch-Guard Preferred (and collect its own commission for the service) Citibank even provided a pre-checked box in the bills for all its credit card customers, thus creating the opportunity to sign them up automatically—betting that they would not bother to check their statements thoroughly (and un-check the box). Only when some states took Affinion to court for billing customers without prior consent, did this scheme become a matter of public record. Even so, the "protection" scheme continued to enroll credit card customers from numerous banks, in states that allowed the scheme to operate.[143]

For those who damaged their credit through excessive indebtedness or personal bankruptcy, debt service corporations and banks created the possibility of "resurrecting" expired debt as a way to allow them to pile up more debt. Through debt resurrection, individuals are issued new credit that allows them to obtain loans and credit cards if they agree to repay a portion of an expired debt—that which can no longer be legally collected because it falls under a statute of limitations. Debt resurrection is a form of subprime lending that involves high risk, since the targeted parties are

142. David Lazarus, "Citi's Pitch Doesn't Check Out," *Los Angeles Times,* June 19, 2012, B1; Gilman Law LLP, *Apollo, Affinion, Trilegiant TLG Scam Alert,* http://www.gilmanlawllp.com/consumer-protection/ (accessed June 19, 2012).

143. Lazarus, "Citi's Pitch."

likely to default again on the new debts they incur. Corporations and banks involved in this business nonetheless eagerly targeted individuals with ruined credit, in order generate new revenue streams that typically involve high fees and higher than average interest rates. One leading debt resurrection corporation, CompuCredit, for example, collected $15 million in newly resurrected debt and fees from individuals with badly damaged credit during the first nine months of 2011 alone—in what amounts to a refloating of debt-based consumption by inducing consumers to pile on more debt on top of already defaulted debt.[144] Debt resurrection companies typically agree to cover losses to banks if borrowers stop paying, despite the inherent risk that both they and the banks involved will end up insolvent when a significant number of debtors cannot pay their new debt.

Among other frantic attempts to refloat consumption through debt— adding to the mountains of debt accumulated before the economic crisis that started in 2007—is the case of automobile loans to individuals with damaged credit records. In the first nine months of 2011, for example, it was estimated that 205,000 loans were issued to borrowers who had partially or completely defaulted on their home mortgage loans. This figure was 156 percent higher than that for a similar period in 2006—before the crisis started—according to credit bureau Experian.[145] One major corporation that had to be bailed out in 2008—General Motors Financial (GMAC)—even started to ignore or downplay mortgage delinquencies and defaults when evaluating applicants for loans. Interest rates for such borrowers can be as high as 20 percent per year, compared to about 5 percent for those with the best credit rating, thus providing a substantially higher revenue stream to lenders despite the high risk. This practice was thought to have helped automobile sales considerably, which were up more than 10 percent in 2011 compared to the previous year. Similarly, credit cards issued to borrowers who had partially defaulted on their mortgage loans or experienced a foreclosure increased by 36 percent between 2007 and 2011, according to Experian.[146] These and many other cases reflect the frantic effort to refloat the financialized economy by any and all means, even at the risk of incurring deeper and more catastrophic crises later on. Such efforts also echo govern-

---

144. Jessica Silver-Greenberg, "Bringing Expired Debt Back to Life," *Wall Street Journal,* December 31, 2011, A1.

145. Ruth Simon, "Auto Lenders Speeding Past Mortgage Troubles," *Wall Street Journal,* January 5, 2012, C1.

146. See ibid., C2.

ment policies—most of all, the U.S. Federal Reserve's monetary schemes and money-printing measures—aimed at providing very high liquidity to try to lift the economy through debt-based consumption.

High indebtedness does generate some growth for the financialist economy—growth that would otherwise disappear or become insignificant—but typically only over the short term. And economic growth was, after all, what the financial, corporate, and political elites badly sought after the crises, stagnation, and inflation of the 1970s—growth that was urgently needed to save capitalism from a prolonged period of decline and potential upheaval. That such urgently needed growth had to occur through debt mattered little back then, given the urgency of the situation and the fact that debt loads were not overly burdensome at that time. An important observation from this close association between financialism and debt is that its economy can do without debt no more than a heroin addict can do without the drug—without incurring crises and upheaval. Creation of massive amounts of debt is thus closely linked to growth in the financialist economy, in much the same way that needles and heroin are associated with addiction.

Speculative organizations, such as hedge funds, are not much different from individuals in generating debt—except for the fact that they control vast amounts of money, usually in the billions of dollars, and can easily become "market movers" due to the large amounts they can speculate with.[147] These large and rich speculative organizations can affect the production of goods, services, and resources—the real economy—but often with very harmful consequences to the interests of employees and to working people at large.[148] This occurs, for example, when they take over companies through the speculative games they set in motion, and, most of all, by incurring immense debt to gather the purchase capital they need.[149] One such case, among a vast array of examples, was the takeover of jet maker

147. See Lack, *Hedge Fund Mirage*; McGinty, Carreyrou, and Rothfeld, "Inside a Star Hedge Fund." Hedge funds became known in the 1980s, as speculation and takeovers spread throughout the American economy, and are often referred to as "private equity" or "leveraged buyout" funds—indicating the crucial importance of debt (or leverage) for their existence.

148. See, for example, Richard Trumka, "It's Time to Restrict Private Equity," *Wall Street Journal*, April 13, 2010, A17.

149. By some estimates, for example, high debt has accounted for as much as one-half of hedge fund returns; see Viral V. Acharya and S. Vish Viswanathan, "Leverage, Moral Hazard, and Liquidity," *Journal of Finance* 66 (2011): 99–138; "Private Equity under Scrutiny: Bain or Blessing?" *The Economist*, January 28, 2012, 74.

Hawker Beechcraft by Goldman Sachs Group's private equity unit and hedge fund Onex Partners in 2007 (just before the start of the financial crisis) for $3.3 billion—obtained through debt. Hawker Beechcraft incurred substantial losses afterward, including a net loss of $630 million in 2011 alone, and had to reduce its 9,300 labor force by almost 25 percent over a three-year period—all of which led regulators and creditors to question its chances of survival.[150] In another case, hedge fund 3G Capital's $3.4 billion takeover of Burger King (the fast food service corporation) in 2010 resulted in the loss of half of all jobs at that company's headquarters, while this same hedge fund's takeover of food manufacturer H. J. Heinz in 2013 (for $3.3 billion, with Berkshire Hathaway as partner) was projected to double the taken over company's debt to more than $12 billion, lowering its credit rating to junk status as a result—with the eventual likely loss of many jobs.[151]

Given the large amounts of money hedge funds can speculate with, it is possible for them to target a company and to take it over simply by buying a large portion of its issued stock. Shareholders of the targeted buyout companies may end up with offers to purchase their stock that are below the prices they paid, thus incurring losses. Realizing that the companies whose stock they own will be taken over and that they are powerless to stop it, the shareholders must either sell or face the prospect of receiving lower offers if they hold out. Prices offered to shareholders are usually low because hedge funds team up with management to preempt competing bids, thus making sure that shareholders have no alternative but to sell to them.[152] When dividends are paid to shareholders as part of a buyout deal, they often siphon much-needed capital from the targeted company, weakening their finances and setting them up for eventual bankruptcy and employee layoffs. This practice—commonly known as "company stripping"—can trigger a subsequent buyout of the weakened company, generating more profits for the hedge fund that originally gained control.[153]

Transaction fees charged for buyouts are usually high, moreover, generating substantial profit for the hedge funds involved—and the oligopolistic

150. Mike Spector, "Hawker Nearing Chapter 11: Jet Maker Labored Under Debt From a Goldman-Onex Buyout," *Wall Street Journal*, May 3, 2012, B1.

151. Julie Jargon, Ryan Dezember, and Serena Ng, "Heinz Takes on Heavy Load: Substantial Acquisition Debt in $23 Billion Deal Could Lead to Cost-Cutting," *Wall Street Journal*, February 16, 2013, B3.

152. See, for example, Josh Kosman, *The Buyout of America: How Private Equity Will Cause the Next Credit Crisis* (New York: Portfolio, 2009).

153. See Robert Lenzner, "Why Warren Buffett Disdains the Private Equity Crowd," *Forbes*, January 14, 2012, http://blogs.forbes.com/robertlenzner/page/4/.

banks arranging the deals—no matter how the targeted companies fare.[154] Also, it is common for hedge funds to charge the buyout target substantial amounts for the "privilege" of being purchased—and then charge addition-al annual sums for management and "advisement." TXU (Energy Future Holdings)—a takeover target—for example, had to pay its suitor $300 mil-lion for the "privilege" of being acquired, and over $35 million annually to be managed and advised by its new owner.[155] Such vast payouts all too often cause the taken-over company to cut employment substantially— and require clever financial engineering—to keep the company afloat.[156] Buyouts typically make hedge fund speculators very wealthy—hedge fund owners are now among the richest people in the world, according to the Forbes 400 directory and similar reports. The three owners of hedge fund Carlyle Group, for example, received $400 million in compensation jointly for 2011, while the top five executives of another major hedge fund—the Blackstone Group—jointly received $771.5 million.[157] Nine of the ten larg-est buyouts in financial history occurred between 2006 and 2008, reflecting the powerful role of hedge funds in the speculative economy of financialism.

The companies that hedge funds take over are often saddled with immense debt—the debt the speculators incurred in order to take over the company. The targeted, debt-saddled companies can be found today in almost any sector or economic activity, from manufacturing to used car sales and commercial real estate, for example.[158] The taken-over companies must then cope with their high debt loads, and typically resort to drastic

---

154. See, for example, Matt Wirz and Sharon Terlep, "Dell Buyout is a Fee-for-All: Banks Advising and Financing the Deal Could Reap More than $400 Million," *Wall Street Journal,* April 5, 2013, C1.

155. "Private Equity's Mega-Deals: Too Big to Veil," *The Economist,* August 4, 2012, 67.

156. See, for example, Peter Morris, *Private Equity, Public Loss?* (London: Centre for Study of Financial Innovation, 2010).

157. Gregory Zuckerman and Ryan Dezember, "Carlyle's 3 Founders Share $400 Million-Plus Payday," *Wall Street Journal,* January 12, 2012, A4.

158. See, for example, Maura Webber Sadovi, "Goldman's New York Story," *Wall Street Journal,* January 11, 2012, C6. Debt loads can be exacerbated whenever future interest rates are expected to rise—as hedge funds rush to increase their taken-over companies' debt in order to fund payouts to themselves. During the first six months of 2013, for example, it was estimated that $47.4 billion of new loans and bond debt were incurred by companies in order to pay dividends to their hedge fund owners, according to data provider S&P Capital IQ LCD; see Ryan Dezember and Matt Wirz, "Private-Equity Payout Debt Surges: Companies Owned by Buyout Shops Rush to Loan, Bond Markets in Anticipation of Rate Increase," *Wall Street Journal,* August 16, 2013, C1. Such debt, when added to a company's high debt load or to poor quality preexisting debt, will typically have a very low (or "junk") rating.

efforts to cut costs by laying off employees, outsourcing, offshoring work to low-cost nations, or by declaring bankruptcy in order to be rid of pension obligations, labor contracts, and part of the debt that their new owners incurred through the takeover—and loaded on them. An acquisition or merger dynamic can also become part of this process, if the weakened enterprise is then taken over by another company—perhaps controlled by the same speculators who previously took it over, or by a rival company—leading to further employment cuts, much outsourcing or offshoring of work, and more consolidation. This situation is fairly common with many mergers and acquisitions—and often leads to the formation of oligopolies, as the weakened companies are consolidated in order to dominate entire sectors or market niches.

This convergence of financialism with the real economy—the economy of production—therefore occurs through speculation, and is one example of how oligopolistic finance can take over nonfinancial sectors of the economy. *Thus, finance—an essential and necessary part of a capitalist economy—ends up turning many other sectors into accessories, or mere betting chips, of financialism.* The interests of the companies that are taken over are often harmed in the process—not only because their employees (usually the most valuable resource of an enterprise), their creativity, their skills, their compensation, and their benefits tend to be shortchanged—but also because the companies often end up being damaged financially and operationally in order to satisfy the greed of the speculators who took them over. In this way, as noted earlier in the discussion on oligopolies, newspapers end up being taken over by speculators who have little or no regard for journalism, or education is taken over by online diploma corporations whose prime objective is profit and high executive compensation rather than education.

Another example of how financialism corrodes the real economy can be found in the common practice by corporations of buying back their own shares, in order to artificially boost the value of the remaining outstanding stock—a scheme that results in a smaller total pool of shares, which can gain greater value in a rising stock market. Between the beginning of 2007 (the peak year for "buybacks") and the middle of 2011, for example, the thirty large corporations listed in the Dow Jones Industrial Index disbursed $614 billion to buy back shares, a historical record for this practice.[159] JPMorgan Chase—one of the "too-big-to-fail" oligopolistic megabanks—

---

159. Maxwell Murphy, "Buying Shares, Buying Trouble," *Wall Street Journal*, October 12, 2011, B1.

spent $8 billion alone in stock buybacks during the financial crisis—at a time when it was being bailed out by the U.S. government.[160] This bank's top executives were also paying themselves more than a hundred million dollars in annual compensation during that time. In another oligopolistic corporation, IBM, this buyback scheme reduced total outstanding shares by 20 percent between the end of 2006 and the middle of 2011, while its stock price nearly doubled—a very unusual outcome given the economic crisis that started in 2007, and the reduction in demand for most of IBM's products and services.[161] These buyback schemes are highly favored by corporate executives because they reduce their accountability, as the total number of outstanding shares (and of shareholders) declines—while gratifying the remaining shareholders by increasing stock prices. They also allow executives to boost their own personal compensation, by claiming credit for the improved performance that they artificially engineer through the buyback scheme.

The transformation of a capitalist economy into a financialist one, which all these schemes and trends represent, can be linked to the rise of oligopolization discussed previously in this book. Concentration of production through oligopolistic control allows greater emphasis on speculation through stocks, bonds, derivatives, and other instruments in the financialist economy. Share buyback schemes are only one of the many tools available in the arsenal of the corporate oligopolies, as they seek to manipulate stock prices, artificially boost returns, and increase their power over markets and society. The example provided earlier—on how hedge funds target companies—also ties in with oligopolization, as mergers and acquisitions lead to larger companies and greater market power. Consolidation through takeovers thereby becomes a vehicle for oligopoly formation. *Thus, the speculative schemes at the core of financialism often end up generating oligopolistic power—and oligopolistic power, in turn, ends up generating political power*—through lobbying, the "revolving door" scheme of corporate executives' employment in regulatory agencies, and the large amounts of money that oligopolistic corporations bestow on politics.

Debt growth is intimately related to this dynamic. The rising importance of debt in the financialist economy transformed capital accumulation,

---

160. See "Dimon's Reserve Spooks Banks," *Wall Street Journal*, October 14, 2011, C8, and the "Overheard" section, *Wall Street Journal*, C8. For the megabanks, share buybacks have become a strategic tool to boost returns on equity; see, for example, Justin Baer, "Big Bank Gets Set for More Buybacks," *Wall Street Journal*, October 29, 2013, C1.

161. See Murphy, "Buying Shares."

by making ownership of paper shares more important than the ownership of real capital—that is, capital based in the actual production of goods, services, and resources. The ownership of paper shares thus became more important than ever, supported by ever larger amounts of debt (also known as "leverage" in financialist jargon). Speculation was thereby made possible by large and growing amounts of debt—which hedge funds, oligopolistic megabanks, and myriad speculators compete to obtain and in many cases to issue as well. Such debt then boosts the speculative accumulation of money, leading to the ownership of paper shares—that in turn generate yet more speculative money. Thus, the productive base of the economy—production of goods, services, and resources (the real economy, in other words) becomes largely separated from real finance—finance that provides the capital that supports the real economy. *Real finance is thereby displaced by financialist capital—capital that supports speculation for its own sake, and that usually provides higher returns merely because of the speculative dynamic.*[162]

Long ago, in the mid-nineteenth century, Karl Marx referred to speculative capital as "fictitious" capital because it involved the sort of capital accumulation that was not grounded in the real economy—the production of goods or services—but in speculation for its own sake, foreseeing what would become a major phenomenon of our time.[163] In this way, he noted

---

162. Under competitive conditions, mechanisms used in real finance—such as options and futures—support capitalist production; see, for example, John E. Parsons, "Bubble, Bubble, How Much Trouble? Financial Markets, Capitalist Development, and Capitalist Crises," *Science and Society* 52 (1988): 260–89. However, under financialism—which is inherently oligopolistic—those mechanisms largely become mere betting outlets, and lose (or greatly diminish) their supportive role for production. Options and futures, instead, usually end up helping oligopolists sustain their power over pricing—as well as making mergers, acquisitions, entry barriers, and market lock-in easier to set up. At the core of this reality is that financialist speculation is easier to do and can potentially extract higher returns than production. Financialist speculation has also been made easier than ever by automation. Most stock and bond market speculation (including the one targeting options and futures) is now automated—"algorithmic" trading now accounts for more than 70 percent of all stock trading and 50 percent of all futures trading, for example. See "High-Frequency Trading: The Fast and the Furious" Special Report on Financial Innovation, *The Economist*, February 25, 2012, 11–13; Jim McTague, *Crapshoot Investing: How Tech-Savvy Traders and Clueless Regulators Turned the Stock Market into a Casino* (New York: FT Press, 2011); Louise Bedford, *Trading Secrets: Killer Trading Strategies to Beat the Markets and Finally Achieve the Success You Deserve* (New York: Wiley, 2012); Patterson and Strasburg, "Superfast Stock Traders."

163. See Karl Marx, *Capital: A Critique of Political Economy*, Vol. 3: *The Process of Capitalist Production as a Whole*, ed. F. Engels (New York: International Publishers, 1974; orig. publ. Hamburg: Verlag von Otto Meissner, 1867), Part V, ch. XXV, 400–13. Marx's critique of David Ricardo's theory of accumulation also provided insights related to this point; see Karl Marx, *Theories of Surplus Value* (New York: Prometheus, 1999), ch. XVII, 470–546.

the potential for a split between finance that is linked to—and supports—
production, and speculative finance that does not. Marx's prescient observation was based on his understanding of the tendencies of capitalism as a
system—the *systemic* character of capitalist accumulation, specifically—and
the relations of power at the core of capitalist society. In his view, an important tendency of capitalism involved the possibility for capital to transform
itself into "pure money"—speculative capital, in other words—in which case
money begat money for its own sake, without linkage to production (to the
real economy). In this form, Marx wrote, "capital reaches its most superficial
and fetishized form," becoming a source of crises that would create severe
strains and injustices in the capitalist economy.[164] Marx's observations are all
the more interesting and significant today, given that financial speculation
in his time was quite limited, and could hardly be considered a precursor
of the complex phenomena of financialism that we now witness.

To place the split between productive and speculative finance—and
its association with crises—in perspective, one must refer to Marx's outline of the fundamental accumulation dynamic of capitalism, which can
be specified as:

$$M \rightarrow C \rightarrow C' \rightarrow M', \text{ where } M' = M + \Delta m$$

—with M as money-capital, C as all inputs (commodities) used in manufacturing or service production, C' as the product (or new commodities, generated through production), while M' represents new money capital derived
from the sale of the product (C'), and Δm is surplus value (also variously
interpreted as profit).[165] This fundamental dynamic of capitalist accumulation breaks down when M' becomes insufficient to provide for the start of
a new cycle—such that commodities (C) can be purchased and production
(embedded in C $\rightarrow$ C') sustained. Negative surplus value (Δm) would cause
M' to be insufficient to provide for a new cycle—a condition that may also
occur when Δm happens to be nil, if the cost of commodities (C) needed
to start a new cycle increases. In such cases, finance would be essential to
start a new cycle. Finance may also be vital in helping expand production,

---

164. Marx, *Capital*, Vol. 3, Part V, 402.

165. A capitalist can therefore be defined as an individual or entity that owns a sufficient
amount of M (money-capital) to set up production (in manufacturing or services), such that
$M \rightarrow C \rightarrow C'$ can be undertaken. All or part of M can be obtained through credit—in
that case, a financial entity will (directly or indirectly) become involved in this dynamic.
It was this rising involvement of finance with capitalist production that Rudolf Hilferding
noticed during the first decade of the twentieth century; see Hilferding, *Finance Capital*.

such that M' can be increased. And, the cost of any financing obtained to add to M—or to expand or make up for any shortfalls in M'—would have to be paid for out of any future production. *This is the supportive role of finance for capitalist production.* Productive finance must therefore help sustain production, such that the dynamic cycle of accumulation can be continued. His understanding of this dynamic led Marx to observe the need for production and finance to be closely integrated in the capitalist economy.

Implicit in this presentation of the accumulation dynamic is the assumption of competitive conditions. Although Marx noted an incipient tendency for larger enterprise size, oligopolies were rare in his time. Consolidation leading toward oligopolies and monopolies would not start to attract attention until the last quarter of the nineteenth century—mostly in some natural resource sectors. Modifying the accumulative dynamic noted above, to take oligopolistic power into account:

$$M \rightarrow C \rightarrow C' \rightarrow M^N, \text{ where } M^N = M + \Delta m + \Delta N$$

—with ΔN as the oligopolistic surplus, above and beyond the surplus (Δm) that would be obtained under competitive conditions, while M^N is the new oligopolistic money-capital obtained from the sale of the product (C'). M^N—the new, oligopolistic money-capital—would typically be greater than M'—the money-capital obtained under competitive conditions—given the nature of oligopolies. The oligopolistic surplus (ΔN) is the source of the typically high profitability of oligopolistic corporate power, noted in the previous chapter. Beyond pricing power—the main characteristic of oligopolies—this surplus depends on the apparatus of capacity control, mergers, regulatory influence, standards setting, entry barriers, and market lock-in that characterizes oligopolistic conditions. *The oligopolistic surplus is also intimately related to the split between productive and speculative finance—as much of the profits derived through oligopolistic control typically becomes part of the vast pool of speculative capital in the financialist economy.* Oligopolistic power therefore feeds substantial amounts of capital to speculative finance—an aspect that can be readily observed today in the vast number of financial schemes that corporate oligopolies engage in, in almost every sector of the economy.

The growing split between speculative and productive capital was widely noticed in the 1920s, as unfettered speculation created the conditions that triggered the Great Depression. Among those who tried to understand the causes of the crisis was John Maynard Keynes—possibly the best-known economist of the twentieth century.[166] Like Marx, Keynes understood the

---

166. See John Maynard Keynes, *Collected Writings*, Vol. 13 (London: Macmillan, 1973).

split between speculative and productive finance to be a potential source of crises—a thought that motivated his attempt to formulate a monetary theory that could orient policymaking.[167] Much of Keynes's work was also based on his disagreement with Jean Baptiste Say's nineteenth-century assumption that supply creates its own demand—later to be known as Say's Law—a disagreement that Marx had expressed seven decades earlier. Keynes, who was no expert on Marx (nor much friendly to his ideas), thus agreed with his critique of Say's Law—through which Marx argued for the necessity to integrate production and finance in the capitalist economy.[168] Keynes's construction of a monetary theory—his most influential work—was largely based on these premises, as can be seen in his writings and lectures on accumulation, aggregate demand, and the monetary system of his time.[169] Keynes thus recognized the possibility for capital accumulation to acquire a speculative dynamic of its own—outside of $M \rightarrow C \rightarrow C' \rightarrow M'$—such that money capital would be turned into more money capital *without the production of any goods or services.*

In this sense, therefore, the accumulative dynamic would become:

$$M_f \rightarrow M'_f, \text{ where } M'_f = M_f + \Delta f$$

—with M_f and M'_f representing speculative money-capital (initial and new), and Δf the speculative surplus obtained—assuming competitive conditions. This is the accumulative dynamic of speculative finance that both Marx and Keynes understood to be a potential trigger of crises in

---

167. See, for example, John Maynard Keynes, "A Monetary Theory of Production," in his *Collected Writings,* Vol. 13; Dudley Dillard, "Keynes and Marx: A Centennial Appraisal," *Journal of Post Keynesian Economics* 6 (1984): 421–25; Peter Kenway, "Marx, Keynes, and the Possibility of Crisis," *Cambridge Journal of Economics* 4 (1980): 23–36; John Bellamy Foster, "The Financialization of Accumulation," *Monthly Review,* October 2010, 3–6. It has been noted that Keynes believed stock market activities to be similar to a casino's, due to the spread of speculative finance in his time—see *The Economist,* "Spread Betting."

168. See Karl Marx, "The Chapter on Capital," in *Grundrisse: Foundations of the Critique of Political Economy* (London: Penguin, 1973), 243–69, and his *Capital,* Vol. 3, Part IV, 267–337.

169. See Keynes's *Collected Writings,* 408–11, and his *The General Theory of Employment, Interest, and Money* (New York: Harcourt, Brace, 1936). See also Steven Kates, "A Letter from Keynes to Harlan McCracken dated 31st August 1933: Why the Standard Theory on the Origins of the *General Theory* Needs to Be Rewritten," *Working Paper Series of the Social Science Research Network,* October 25, 2007, http://ssrn.com/abstract=1024388; Harlan McCracken, *Value Theory and Business Cycles* (Binghamton, NY: Falcon, 1933), 45–48; Dillard, "Keynes and Marx."

capitalist accumulation. This dynamic underlies the split between speculative and productive capital, as it operates in parallel with (or in replacement of) the productive dynamic of capitalist accumulation ($M \rightarrow C \rightarrow C' \rightarrow M'$). Under oligopolistic conditions—a major feature of financialism—this dynamic is transformed into:

$$M_f \rightarrow M^F_f, \text{ where } M^F_f = M_f + \Delta f + \Delta F$$

—with M^F_f as new oligopolistic (speculative) money-capital, and ΔF the oligopolistic surplus—above and beyond the surplus (Δf) that would be obtained under competitive conditions. This oligopolistic surplus is a product of the myriad speculative schemes undertaken by powerful financial corporations—such as megabanks and the larger hedge funds—which have overwhelming control over the pricing and design of speculative transactions. It can therefore be expected that M^F_f—new oligopolistic (speculative) money-capital—will typically be greater than M'_f—speculative money-capital under competitive conditions—given the power of oligopolistic corporate finance. To sustain the accumulative dynamic of financialism, new oligopolistic (speculative) money-capital (M^F_f) must provide for the start of a new cycle, by replenishing or increasing the money-capital dedicated to speculation (M_f).

This distortion of the dynamic of capitalist accumulation is a fundamental characteristic of financialism—as money is merely used to accumulate more money through speculation. *A most essential feature of capitalism—the use of commodities (C) to generate their transformation (through production) into new commodities (C')—thus becomes less important under financialism.* Production and productive capital become largely subservient to speculative capital in the economy—with megabanks and the larger hedge funds gaining immense power. This situation is understood to be a trigger of crises in capitalism—one that violates the accumulative dynamic involving production. Thus, *commodification*—a fundamental feature of capitalist production—which requires appropriation of a commodity for it to be transformed through a productive process, loses importance in the financialist economy.[170] This loss negates the systemic productive character of capitalism—and of commodities. Speculative schemes therefore take the place of production.

---

170. For the importance of commodification to the dynamic of capitalist accumulation see Marx, *Grundrisse*, "The Chapter on Money," 165–68.

Speculative schemes—such as those described earlier in this chapter—are *not* commodities, by any means, since they cannot be appropriated. They are, at best, heuristics based on common sense, game playing, or subterfuge, and cannot be appropriated even when built into the rules or algorithms that are used to speculate. Thus, claiming a property right over something that is fundamentally common sense or a rule of thumb, long used already by millions of speculators in diverse ways—and therefore in the public domain—is practically impossible. Unlike patents, for example, which do provide a property right, speculative schemes cannot claim uniqueness or novelty—all the more so when they are already in use in the public domain, and when their reliability under many situations evaporates—as often occurs when market conditions change.[171]

Speculative schemes do *not* involve production, since they do not comprise any transformation of commodities. Also, they cannot be considered production because the speculative results they generate—through $M_f \rightarrow M^F_f$ (or $M_f \rightarrow M'_f$ under competition)—cannot be exchanged as commodities (C'). That possibility is preempted by the fact that speculative schemes cannot be appropriated—as a commodity would be. *The impossibility of grounding the myriad speculative schemes of financialism in production, or in any sort of commodification* (as occurs when a commodity is appropriated), *therefore makes the financialist economy systemically dysfunctional. In this sense, financialism breaks down the fundamental accumulative dynamic of capitalism, as speculative accumulation takes the place of productive accumulation.*

Financial speculators and mainstream economists have sought to downplay the crises triggered by financialism, by portraying them as exceptional or rare events, when in fact they are frequent products of the systemic nature of this phenomenon (and of capitalism, in general). A notable exception was Hyman Misky, who in his analysis of financial instability tried to fit crises into business cycle theory, thus taking up a short-term vision of this phenomenon.[172] Minsky called attention to the tendency of capitalism to

---

171. A point forcefully made by Nassim Taleb in his *Fooled by Randomness: The Hidden Role of Chance in Life and in the Markets* (New York: Random House, 2005).

172. See Hyman Minsky, "The Financial Instability Hypothesis," Working Paper no. 74 (May 1992), Levy Economics Institute, Bard College, www.levyinstitute.org/pubs/wp74.pdf; Piero Ferri and Hyman Minsky, "Market Processes and Thwarting Systems," *Structural Change and Economic Dynamics* 3 (1992): 79–91. For critiques of Minsky's views—relevant to the financial crisis that started in 2007—see Thomas Palley, "The Limits of Minsky's Financial Instability Hypothesis as an Explanation of the Crisis," *Monthly Review*, April 2010, 28–43; John Bellamy Foster and Robert W. McChesney, "Listen Keynesians, It's the System!" *Monthly Review*, April 2010, 44–56.

generate financially driven crises and booms, but his mechanistic approach failed to grasp the fundamental flaws inherent to capitalist accumulation— and the larger system of which it is part. By blaming crises on specula- tors' misperceptions, circumstantial influences, supply and demand factors, or business cycle parameters, he ended up shifting attention to narrow, short-term aspects that shed little light on the big-picture dynamic of why and how crises arise. Minsky's work thus evaded fundamental problems of capitalist accumulation, such as the role of oligopolies, the relations of power behind corporatocracy, or the rising influence of corporate capital over society and governance.

Unlike Marx and Keynes, neoclassical (mainstream) economists have ignored the systemic dimension of financialism, and interpret crises—such as the multifaceted one that started in 2007, the "dot-com" crash of 2000, the banking, real estate, and derivatives crises of the early and mid-1990s, the "junk bond" crash of 1987, and the debt crises of the late 1990s, for example—as freakish events to be considered in isolation, without reference to the larger systemic flaws of capitalism and of financialism.[173] This posi- tion has become increasingly difficult to sustain, however, as crises become deeper and have greater impact on economies around the world. More than $50 trillion in global assets were erased, for example, between September 2007 and March 2009 (an eighteen-month period)—including $6 trillion in housing and $7 trillion in stock market wealth in the United States alone. The Dow Jones Industrial average had, by early March 2009, dropped to its 1966 level (adjusted for inflation)—the deepest collapse since the Great Depression.[174] The higher frequency and depth of crises during the three decades since the emergence of financialism, therefore, indicate that there is a serious systemic problem at work. During 1981–2004, for example, there

173. The rare exceptions among mainstream economists are Joseph Stiglitz's *Freefall: America, Free Markets, and the Sinking of the World Economy* (New York: Norton, 2010); Nouriel Roubini and Stephen Mihm's *Crisis Economics: A Crash Course in the Future of Finance* (New York: Penguin, 2010); Carmen M. Reinhart and Kenneth S. Rogoff's *This Time is Different: Eight Centuries of Financial Folly* (Princeton: Princeton University Press, 2009). Speculators and mainstream economists subscribe instead to what may be described as the "black swan" assumption—regarding the crises of financialism (and of capitalism in general); for a critique of this view see Taleb, *The Black Swan*.

174. See Sam Jones, "A Trillion Dollar Mean Reversion," *Financial Times*, July 15, 2008, http://ftalphaville.ft.com/blog/2008/07/15/14504/a-trillion-dollar-mean-reversion/ (based on estimates by James Reid of Deutsche Bank); John Bellamy Foster, "The Age of Monopoly Finance Capital," *Monthly Review*, February 2010, 1–13.

were 114 sovereign debt crises around the world, compared to twenty-three between 1941 and 1980. Those four decades between 1941 and 1980—which preceded the emergence of financialism—also witnessed little in the way of crashes, deep recessions, and speculative fraud, compared to what we have experienced since the early 1980s.[175]

To try to avoid financial crises, governments have typically resorted to debt guarantees. Ever-larger guarantees, mostly through bank deposit insurance or corporate bailouts, have been at the core of federal financial policy in the United States since the Great Depression.[176] This has resulted in an unsustainable accumulation of government debt obligations—that now threaten the financial apparatus not only of the United States but also the world. Government debt guarantees have been a major source of American corporate welfare, as could be most readily seen during the crisis that started in 2007. One financial specialist has estimated the U.S. government's debt guarantee burden to amount to nine out of ten dollars of debt in the American economy—an excessive amount considering the size of the economy and the massive debt load that the government already carries, noted earlier in this chapter.[177]

Government-guaranteed debt mushroomed since the start of financialism in the early 1980s, as financial deregulation spawned too-big-to-fail megabanks and hedge funds, which now pose major systemic risks to the economy. Much of that risk occurred through the evasion of capital requirements by hedge funds and megabanks—as they pooled together massive amounts of very risky debt that was securitized and misleadingly classified as "AAA" by the credit rating oligopolies. Such debt was then used as a speculative vehicle (typically derivatives) that implicitly or explicitly carried government guarantees. The U.S. Federal Reserve, for example, held close to $900 billion in government-guaranteed, mortgage-backed securities (mostly as derivatives) by the end of 2011—all of them acquired through bailouts of failing oligopolistic mortgage corporations and insurance companies in

---

175. See, for example, Foster and Magdoff, *Great Financial Crisis*; Edward S. Herman, *The Roller Coaster Economy: Financial Crisis, Great Recession, and the Public Option* (New York: Sharpe, 2010).

176. The guarantees contribute to the growth of government spending, particularly during economic crises and recessions, thus setting the stage for fiscal crises when expenses surpass revenues; see O'Connor, *Fiscal Crisis*.

177. John H. Cochrane, "The Fed's Mission Impossible," *Wall Street Journal,* December 29, 2011, A15.

2008–09, along with the insolvent government-owned mortgage insurers Federal National Mortgage Association (FNMA, also known as "Fannie Mae") and the Federal Home Loan Mortgage Corporation (FHLMC, also known as "Freddie Mac").[178] One outcome of this prolonged and massive expansion of government-guaranteed, speculative debt is the great difficulty of measuring and regulating credit exposure in the financial sector—a major problem, since any attempt to measure credit exposure that judges a too-big-to-fail bank or hedge fund to be in trouble could trigger a panic, or at least a serious crisis.

This difficulty is compounded by the fact that financial corporations (such as the insurance oligopolies) which must keep up payments to government-guaranteed obligations (such as guaranteed-return pensions), would have to be bailed out—along with too-big-to-fail banks and hedge funds—when a crisis occurs. An example of this was the frantic $125 billion government bailout of insurance oligopolist AIG (American International Group) in 2009.[179] This corporation had the most sound credit over the span of several decades and, right up to the time of its collapse, was considered to be the ideal counterparty for Wall Street megabanks and hedge funds. AIG was bailed out by U.S. Treasury Secretary Henry Paulson—previously the top executive of Goldman Sachs.[180] Goldman Sachs, in turn, was AIG's most important counterparty in Wall Street—another sign of the deeply entwined relationships between Wall Street oligopolists—and between them and government, through the "revolving door" vehicle discussed in the previous chapter. The government's bailout of AIG was a most profitable one for the corporation's executives, its shareholders, and Wall Street counterparties, given its $19.8 billion profit in the fourth quarter of 2011—almost all of it based on a tax-related accounting gain, in what amounted to a "stealth" taxpayer-funded bailout (the second one in less than three years).[181] The failure of AIG would have had major political implications, since its vast number of annuity and pension recipients would have most certainly blamed

---

178. See George Melloan, "For the Fed, There's No Easy Exit," *Wall Street Journal*, February 27, 2012, A15.

179. See, for example, Roddy Boyd, *Fatal Risk: A Cautionary Tale of AIG's Corporate Suicide* (Hoboken: Wiley, 2011).

180. "The Financial Crisis: Hank's for the Memory," *The Economist*, April 30, 2011, 89.

181. "Earnings Roundup; AIG: Bailed-Out Insurer Earns $19.8 Billion," *Los Angeles Times*, February 24, 2012, B5; Jim Puzzanghera, "4 Former Bailout Watchdogs Criticize Tax Break for AIG," *Los Angeles Times*, March 13, 2012, B5.

the politicians in power for the collapse of their well-being, had the corporation not been bailed out.[182] Financialism thus greatly entwines government with corporate power—by making it politically impossible (and politically catastrophic) for a too-big-to-fail oligopolist to collapse or be dismantled.

Major legislation in response to the crisis—such as the Dodd-Frank financial law—virtually guaranteed that the too-big-to-fail oligopolists that now rule American finance will preserve or increase their corporatocratic power—as they grow larger and their collapse becomes politically impossible to fathom.[183] Instead of splitting up the too-big-to-fail banks and hedge funds to forestall another major crisis (as the repealed, 1930s-era Glass-Steagall Act had prescribed)—or nationalizing them to prevent larger future bailouts—the Dodd-Frank legislation left them in place, thus ensuring that the status quo will continue indefinitely.[184] One provision of this legislation, in particular, seems quite unrealistic—the requirement that too-big-to-fail banks should divine in advance (on their own) how they would split themselves up when a financial panic or major crisis occurs. The situation created by this provision might be compared to the case of a heroin addict who, after being diagnosed with cancer, is required to decide on his own which organs must be extracted—along with the heroin withdrawal program to be enforced.

In a severe crisis, a too-big-to-fail bank that tries to split itself up will likely collapse—and take the rest of the financial system down with it. Other oligopolistic corporations that also pose systemic risks would thus likely collapse as well. Times of crisis and panic are least propitious to split up a major financial enterprise, if the long history of corporate capitalism is any guide. Since the Dodd-Frank law also prohibits bailouts of failing

---

182. See U.S. Congress, House Committee on Oversight and Government Reform. *The Federal Bailout of AIG* (Washington, DC: U.S. Government Printing Office, 2011).

183. See Jim Puzzanghera, "Several Banks Once Deemed Too Big to Fail Are Even Bigger," *Los Angeles Times,* September 17, 2013, B1; "The Anointed: The Number of Too-Big-to-Fail Institutions Gets Bigger," *The Economist,* June 8, 2013, 79; U.S. Congress, *Dodd-Frank Wall Street Reform and Consumer Protection Act* (Washington, DC: U.S. Government Printing Office, 2010). A simulation of the likely scenarios in a serious crisis showed that none of the options available under the Dodd-Frank law may work; see "Fright Simulator: How to Deal with a Collapsing Bank under the Dodd-Frank Rules," *The Economist,* November 12, 2011, 86.

184. Even though it might make sense from a shareholder perspective to split up the megabanks; see Sheila Bair, "Why It's Time to Break Up the 'Too Big to Fail' Banks," *Fortune,* February 6, 2012, 56.

megabanks, government would be able to do little more than watch from the sidelines as the financial system implodes (assuming the law is observed). In that event, lowering interest rates to zero and implementing monetary tricks—such as the Federal Reserve's "quantitative easings" and other money-printing and bond-buying schemes—may do little to salvage the banks or the financial system. Similarly, the imposition of clearing houses for derivatives—to monitor transactions between buyers and sellers—would most likely not do much to avert crises. Clearing houses are themselves likely to pose immense systemic risk as massive amounts of derivatives accumulate—all the more so since they are inadequate for reducing the risks posed by the more illiquid and complex derivatives, which are the ones most likely to threaten the financial system.[185] The Dodd-Frank law's prohibition of megabank bailouts, and its imposition of derivatives clearing houses, was symptomatic of how financialism has driven the state into a corner—which may provide no room except for an eventual financial collapse and economic calamity for the vast majority of the population.

One notable aspect of the Dodd-Frank financial legislation was the so-called Volcker rule that prohibits banks from betting with any funds guaranteed by the federal government—particularly if the bank is so systemically important that it might collapse the financial system when its bets go wrong.[186] Essentially, therefore, this rule would prevent banks from gambling at taxpayers' expense, and it would potentially limit government debt guarantees over the long term. Loopholes in this rule, however, render its eventual effectiveness uncertain—especially in the case of global megabanks that have substantial operations abroad. Risks and substantial losses from those operations can be ultimately transferred to American taxpayers—given the interconnected nature of the financial system, its global reach, and the impossibility of providing adequate oversight of what a bank with guaranteed government funds does abroad.[187] The Volcker rule was fiercely opposed

---

185. See, for example, "All Clear? Clearing-Houses are Meant to Solve Problems in Derivatives Markets; They Create them Too," *The Economist*, April 7, 2012, 14.

186. See U.S. Commodities Futures Trading Commission, *XXVIII: Volcker Rule*, http://www.cftc.gov/LawRegulation/DoddFrankAct/ (accessed January 22, 2012).

187. See Jim Puzzanghera, "Regulator Failed to Spot Big Bank Loss: Despite 65 Examiners at JPMorgan, US Agency Missed the Huge Blunder," *Los Angeles Times*, June 7, 2012, B1. Concerns were also raised by two regulatory officials shortly before the Volcker rule's implementation deadline; see Scott Patterson and Andrew Ackerman, " 'Volcker Rule' Faces New Hurdles: Objections from SEC, CFTC Officials That Measure Is Too Soft on Banks May Delay Startup," *Wall Street Journal*, November 20, 2013, C1.

by the banking sector, since it would curtail the amount of money that can be used in speculative schemes—most of all, the vast government-guaranteed sums that they have long used for that purpose.[188] Executive compensation would likely suffer as a result of this rule, since any reduction of speculation will encroach on profits and lower the value of a bank's stock—not to mention the stocks of other banks with which it might speculate. It is very likely, however, that powerful lobbying by Wall Street will eventually dilute or neutralize this rule, given the dependence of the financial system on government-guaranteed money—a dependence that cannot be curtailed without affecting bank profits, executive compensation, and the competitiveness of American banks with similar institutions around the globe.[189]

One clever way for a bank to neutralize some of the provisions of the Volcker rule—and transfer risk to the government—involves moving accumulated derivatives to a subsidiary that has government-guaranteed

---

188. See, for example, Michael Hiltzik, "Bankers Dislike New Rule? Big Surprise." *Los Angeles Times,* January 11, 2012, B1.

189. Efforts to neutralize the Dodd-Frank Act (and especially its Volcker rule) started immediately after passage; see, for example, David Enrich and Laura Stevens, "Deutsche Avoids Dodd-Frank Rule: German Bank Restructures US Unit to Avoid New Capital Requirements; Regulators Don't Object," *Wall Street Journal,* March 22, 2011, C1; John Carreyrou, "Goldman in Push on Volcker Limits," *Wall Street Journal,* October 10, 2012, C1; Victoria McGrane and Scott Patterson, "Timeline Reset for 'Volcker Rule,'" *Wall Street Journal,* April 20, 2012, C3; Lynn Stout, "When Banks Can't Quit Gambling," *Los Angeles Times,* May 22, 2012, A13; Deborah Solomon, Robin Sidel, and Aaron Lucchetti, "Big Banks Push Back Against Tighter Rules," *Wall Street Journal,* May 9, 2013, A1; Craig Karmin and Justin Baer, "Goldman Skirts Ban in Volcker," *Wall Street Journal,* December 23, 2013, C1. In a way that is reminiscent of 1933 and how a Supreme Court challenge was orchestrated against President Roosevelt's efforts to reform the economy, some highly influential conservative groups and individuals raised "unconstitutionality" as an argument against the Dodd-Frank Act; see, for example, C. Boyden Gray and Jim R. Purcell, "Why Dodd-Frank Is Unconstitutional," *Wall Street Journal,* June 22, 2012, A17. Some state governments whose politicians were influenced by financial and corporate interests also joined the "unconstitutionality" effort; see, for example, Jim Puzzanghera, "3 States Join Suit Against Key Part of Dodd-Frank," *Los Angeles Times,* September 22, 2012, B2. Lobbying efforts by oligopolistic megabanks—and the financial sector in general—also enlisted well-known former politicians as lobbyists, to try to limit enforcement and impacts of the Dodd-Frank Act; see, for example, Jim Puzzanghera, "Ex-Minnesota Gov. Pawlenty to Head Bank Lobbying Group," *Los Angeles Times,* September 21, 2012, B4. The Dodd-Frank Act's Volcker rule was finally approved by regulators in December 2013— setting off substantial lobbying efforts to dilute its requirements; see Justin Baer and Julie Steinberg, "Bank Rule Challenges Wall Street," *Wall Street Journal,* December 11, 2013, A1; Ryan Tracy, James Sterngold, and Stephanie Armour, "'Volcker' Rule Battle Lines are Drawn," *Wall Street Journal,* December 12, 2013, C1.

deposits. Bank of America, for example, sought to move derivatives from its Merrill Lynch unit to a subsidiary with substantial FDIC-insured deposits in 2011, after it received a downgrade from one of the three credit rating oligopolies.[190] This bank's $75 trillion in accumulated derivatives posed a risk to its financial well-being after its credit was downgraded—and after its counterparties demanded that Merrill Lynch place them under the insurance umbrella provided by the FDIC. The ratings downgrade held serious negative implications since, for example, most pension funds would have to forgo purchases of the bank's stock or divest if they held any—to comply with rules that typically restrict purchases and stock holdings to those of the highest-rated entities. Also, the bank's market capitalization would suffer greatly if risk-averse speculators shunned or sold its stock as a result of the downgrade. Although restrictions to such transfers of risk to the government already existed, the Federal Reserve had granted exemptions in 2009—to help the too-big-to-fail megabanks that were on the brink of failure.

The vast bailouts and the frantic efforts of the U.S. Federal Reserve Bank during the most recent crisis, if anything, provide much evidence on how dependent the financialist economy has become on corporate welfare. At the same time, the crisis revealed the extent to which government has been captured by the financial sector.[191] Between 2007 and 2009, the Federal Reserve distributed a total of $1.2 trillion to 407 individual banks, which involved more than fifty thousand transactions and seven different financial mechanisms.[192] The Federal Reserve, moreover, sought to keep part of this information secret, refusing to reveal which banks received funds under two of the seven mechanisms, and the news agency that divulged the data had to file a request under the Freedom of Information Act to obtain it. The banks that received such welfare were estimated to have made a net profit of about $13 billion—after paying off all the interest on their loans—in what is a vivid example of corporatocracy at work.[193]

---

190. Bob Ivry, Hugh Son, and Christine Harper, "BofA Said to Split Regulators over Moving Merrill Derivatives to Bank Unit," *Bloomberg News,* October 18, 2011, http://www.bloomberg.com/news/2011-10-18/.

191. The word *captured* was used by none other than the Special Inspector General in charge of the federal Troubled Assets Relief Program (TARP), to describe the command that Wall Street megabanks exercise over government; see Neil Barofsky, "Fraud 101," in *Bailout,* 1–19.

192. "The Fed's Secret Liquidity Lifelines," *Bloomberg News,* http://www.bloomberg.com/news/(accessed January 6, 2012).

193. "Secret Fed Loans Gave Banks $13 Billion Undisclosed to Congress," *Bloomberg News,* http://www.bloomberg.com/news/(accessed January 23, 2012).

With guarantees included, the Federal Reserve and the Treasury committed a total of $7.8 trillion as of March 2009 to rescue the U.S. financial system—an amount that, even when adjusted for inflation, dwarfs any other rescue effort ever undertaken.[194] Bailout funds targeted Wall Street megabanks and other financial corporations, mortgage lenders, and some automotive corporations—all of them oligopolists in their sectors.[195] Loans and loan guarantees carried little or no interest, and bailouts actually turned a profit for many banks—as noted previously. Among the specific beneficiaries, for example, bailout funds received by megabank JPMorgan Chase ($48 billion) amounted to twice its total cash holdings in early 2009. Bank of America received $86 billion—an amount that prevented its collapse and guaranteed high compensation packages for its executives. In a time of severe financial crisis, when deep asset losses could be expected, the total assets held by the six largest banks—Citibank, JPMorgan Chase, Bank of America, Wells Fargo, Goldman Sachs, Morgan Stanley, all of them oligopolists—rose instead by almost 40 percent during 2006–09 (end of September data), from $6.8 to $9.5 trillion—as a result of massive government help.[196] The majority of the funds used to help the financial sector came from the Federal Reserve, which exercised the bailouts using an obscure section of its charter.

This effort—aimed at propping up the megabanks and other financial corporations that triggered the crisis—provides a stark contrast to the measly $2 billion the U.S. Treasury spent to help homeowners avoid foreclosure through the Home Affordable Mortgage Program—a failed effort given the magnitude of foreclosure filings that occurred after its creation. Similarly, less than $218 million had been disbursed to homeowners by the Hardest Hit Fund Program two years after it was created—with leftover funds from the TARP (Troubled Assets Relief) corporate welfare program—in what was yet another failed effort to help homeowners.[197] Curiously, the main reason for these programs' failure was that the megabanks—most of all, those that had been bailed out by government—refused to accept a plan to reduce outstanding mortgage balances for unemployed and financially strapped homeowners. The deep contrast between the amounts spent on corporate

194. *Bloomberg News,* "Fed's Secret Liquidity."

195. See Bottari, "Money Still Owed."

196. Cho, "Banks Grown Bigger"; Puzzanghera, "Banks Once Deemed Too Big to Fail"; "The Anointed," *The Economist.*

197. E. Scott Reckard and Alejandro Lazo, "Foreclosure Funds Largely Go Untapped," *Los Angeles Times,* March 3, 2012, A1.

bailouts, and the foreclosure aid—aimed at helping working people and the struggling middle class—makes it quite clear who holds the power in a corporatocratic society.

Adding to this panorama of bailouts and crisis is the fact that too-big-to-fail megabanks have been taking increasing risk by providing ever larger amounts of money for corporate takeovers. JPMorgan Chase, for example, a megabank that had to be bailed out, financed on its own $20 billion of AT&T's proposed takeover of Deutsche Telekom's T-Mobile U.S. wireless unit in 2011.[198] This takeover deal would have been financed in the past by a consortium of banks, thus spreading the risk among numerous parties. The proposed takeover by AT&T, incidentally, would place 80 percent of the U.S. wireless market for contract customers under the control of two oligopolists (AT&T and Verizon Wireless), demonstrating once again the close association between Wall Street banks and oligopolistic corporations that has become a hallmark of the American economy. It is hard to imagine that a bank would have funded this large a deal on its own if it did not feel that its oligopolistic weight and the vast systemic risk it posed would not guarantee a bailout from government—when the next crisis strikes. Executives at megabanks have reportedly even marketed their immense systemic risk as a benefit to prospective clients in very large deals—usually those involving multibillion-dollar amounts—believing it to be a guarantee against failure.[199]

Even with the restrictions imposed by new financial legislation, it seems that ever-larger government guarantees and low-cost federal financ-

---

198. James Saft, "The Power of Being Too Big to Fail," *International Herald Tribune*, March 23, 2011, 20.

199. See "In the Fed's Sights: The Importance of Being Enormous," *The Economist*, April 14, 2012, 84. Their apparent immunity from failure also motivated the megabanks and large hedge funds to engage in the same speculative schemes that triggered the crisis. See, for example, Sheila Bair and Barney Frank, "Watch Out: The Mortgage Securities Market is At It Again," *Fortune*, June 10, 2013, 69; Katy Burne, "One of Wall Street's Riskiest Bets Returns," *Wall Street Journal*, June 5, 2013, A1; Ryan Dezember, "Buyout Firms Throw Toggle: A Precrisis Debt-Financing Tool Resurfaces in Neiman Marcus Deal," *Wall Street Journal*, October 23, 2013, C4; Katie Benner, Scott Cendrowski, and Marty Jones, "After the Fall: Five Years After the Collapse of Lehman Brothers Triggered the Worst Economic Catastrophe Since the Great Depression, Life Seems Mostly Normal—Which Is One Reason Some Fear It Could All Happen Again," *Fortune*, September 16, 2013, 145–59; Holman W. Jenkins, "Rewriting the Lehman Postmortem," *Wall Street Journal*, September 21, 2013, A13; Alan S. Blinder, "Five Years Later, Financial Lessons Not Learned," *Wall Street Journal*, September 11, 2013, A15.

ing are the only remedies in store when a new crisis comes along. The dependence of the financialist economy on corporate welfare is simply too deeply seated, and the risks posed by all the speculative schemes to generate profits and growth are too great, to think that government debt guarantees, low-cost financing, and other public subsidies can be limited. Also, it seems very unrealistic to expect that the corporatocratic nexus between financialism, public governance, and oligopolistic corporate power will not trigger other crises. Since government resources are finite—and are already deeply strained by the vast and rising quantum of accumulated debt and deficits—it does not seem too fanciful to imagine that a major and prolonged crisis could potentially collapse both the corporate ecology of financialism and corporatocracy. Symptoms of the unsustainable nature of this panorama of crises, financialism, and corporatocracy, are already apparent in the unprecedented and deep-seated range of inequalities generated during the past three decades.

The distribution of income is usually the most unequal component of human existence—above and beyond any other type of socially generated human inequality. One of the more nefarious effects of financialism has been its contribution to dramatically increase inequality to levels seldom seen before. In the United States—the cradle of financialism and of the neoliberal dogma that underpinned it—income and wealth inequality have gained historical importance, becoming a threat to societal well-being and just governance. *This dramatic rise in inequality is a hallmark of financialism, of oligopolistic corporate hegemony, and of corporatocracy.*

The three decades since the start of financialism resulted in a cycle of inequality that has practically no parallel in American history.[200] Previous periods of rapidly rising inequality can only be found in the late 1920s (before the Great Depression), in the early 1910s (before World War I), and in the early 1860s (before the Civil War).[201] All of those periods were

---

200. See, for example, Steven Greenhouse, *The Big Squeeze: Tough Times for the American Worker* (New York: Knopf, 2008); Thomas Frank, "Our Great Economic U-Turn," *Wall Street Journal*, May 14, 2008, A23.

201. See, for example, Michael Perelman, *The Confiscation of American Prosperity: From Right-Wing Extremism and Economic Ideology to the Next Great Depression* (New York: Palgrave Macmillan, 2007), 13; Peter Lindert and Jeffrey Williamson, *American Inequality: An Economic History* (New York: Academic Press, 1980). Rising inequality has been considered by some authors to be one of the causes of the financial crisis that started in 2007; see Raghuram Rajan, *Fault Lines: How Hidden Fractures Still Threaten the World Economy* (Princeton: Princeton University Press, 2010); "Is a Concentration of Wealth at the Top to Blame for Financial Crises?" *The Economist*, March 17, 2012, 87.

relatively brief, however, compared to the three decades-long span associated with financialism. The inequalities they created were also relatively shallow, compared with the depth of the inequalities generated during the past three decades. One result is that total after-tax income of the top 1 percent of the population (those with $398,000 or higher annual income in 2007)—the privileged segment that comprises the financialist elite—rose by 275 percent between 1979 and 2007.[202] This was more than four times the income increase of the rest of the top 20 percent—the top quintile of the income scale—during the same period. By comparison, after-tax income for the 60 percent of households that are in the middle of the income scale ($15,000 to $70,000 annual income in 2007) rose by 35 percent between 1979 and 2007. Also, this middle income segment sank deeper into debt during this period, in order to sustain their consumption and living standard.[203] Economic mobility also dropped substantially, as it became much harder to climb out of both the lower and middle segments of the income scale.[204]

Related to the panorama of downward economic mobility and rising inequality is the alarming amount of uncompensated work that corporate employers customarily extract from American workers. This is a form of exploitation that is commonplace in contemporary corporate capitalism, and that can be associated with the emergence of the corporatocratic state. It has been estimated, for example, that more than $100 billion annually in work-time value goes uncompensated—income taken from employees, therefore—by corporate employers.[205] This involves a vast range of actions, such as requiring employees (often tacitly) to work time for which they are not compensated—a very common practice during probationary periods or after hiring occurs, or during times of rising unemployment. In many cases, it also involves inducing employees to take work to do at home which is

202. U.S. Congressional Budget Office, *Trends in the Distribution of Household Income Between 1979 and 2007,* October 2011, http://cbo.gov/ftpdocs/124xx/doc12485/10-25-Householdincome.pdf.

203. Michael Hiltzik, "Saving the Middle: The Occupy Movement Speaks to Downward Mobility," *Los Angeles Times,* January 1, 2012, B1.

204. See John E. Silvia, Tim Quinlan, and Joe Seydl, *Economic Mobility: Is "Rags to Riches" Still Possible?* Economics Group, Wells Fargo Securities, November 15, 2011, https://www.wellsfargo.com/; Walter Hamilton, "Escaping Poverty Gets More Difficult," *Los Angeles Times,* December 1, 2011, B1.

205. Kimberley A. Bobo, *Wage Theft in America: Why Millions of Working Americans Are not Getting Paid—And What We Can Do About It* (New York: New Press, 2009).

uncompensated (or not fully compensated). Using unpaid "interns"—those who work for free hoping to be hired eventually—is another example, even though it often breaks labor laws (which typically go unenforced). Every year, more than a half-million individuals work as unpaid interns in the United States, with corporations receiving a bonanza through this form of unpaid labor—a practice typically disguised as a provision of "learning experience"—while another half-million interns are paid poorly, or far below the compensation level for the work they do.[206] Failing to pay minimum wage is another common practice, particularly for less skilled occupations—the ones filled mostly by working people and the working poor. Failing to pay overtime wage differentials is also common—one that seems to occur more frequently when other employees are being laid off, and that plays on individuals' fear of unemployment and poverty. With the decline of labor unions, employees typically have no bargaining power and no protection against these forms of abuse. Weak or ineffective workplace oversight and regulation—as can be expected in a corporatocratic society—virtually guarantee that government will do nothing. Those who complain (the "whistleblowers")—or try to organize against these abuses—can easily find themselves downgraded, their promotions denied, or fired and tacitly blacklisted as troublemakers.

The rise in income inequality is very noticeable when the share of total pretax income of the top 1 percent is compared with that of the bottom 20 percent of all households (the poorest). In 1979, for example, the total income of the top 1 percent was thirty times the income of the bottom 20 percent—by 2007, it was over one hundred times.[207] Also, after-tax household income in the United States was substantially more unequal in 2007 than in 1979. The poorest of the poor—those at 50 percent or less of the official poverty level (annual incomes of $5,570 or less for an individual, or $11,157 or less for a family of four)—comprised one in fifteen people in the United States in 2010, the highest level on record since such

206. See Beenish Ahmed, "Unpaid Interns: Real World Work or Just Free Labor?," *NPR*, November 16, 2011, http://www.npr.org/2011/11/16/142224360/unpaid-interns-real-world-work-or-just-free-labor.

207. Some analysts have referred to this deep cleavage in incomes and wealth as "plutonomy"; see Ajay Kapur, Niall Macleod, and Narendra Singh, *Plutonomy: Buying Luxury, Explaining Global Imbalances*. Citigroup Research, October 16, 2005, http://cryptome.org/0005/rich-pander.pdf.

statistics started to be compiled.[208] The equalizing effect of federal taxes was also much smaller in 2007 than in 1979, due to the shift away from income taxes and toward payroll taxes—which are less progressive—and the fact that the average federal income tax rate declined through cuts that favored the wealthy.[209]

Between 1979 and 2007, a notable shift in the composition of the top 1 percent segment was the growth of financial occupations.[210] Investment bankers, hedge fund owners, wealthy speculators, and finance-linked corporate lawyers displaced corporate executives at the very top of the U.S. income ladder. By 2009, for example, the twenty-five richest hedge fund speculators got roughly six times the combined total income of all the chief executives of the 500 corporations listed in the S&P 500 stock index.[211] A striking feature about this most privileged group (within the top 1 percent) of the population was their economic stability and security throughout the three-decade span—a condition that the vast majority of the population has practically no chance of attaining in their lifetime.[212] Thus, the vast majority of individuals in that most privileged group (within the top 1 percent) typically remain in that category over the long term, if not throughout their lifetime. All of these trends reflect a redistribution of income away *from* working people, the middle class, and the poor *toward* the richest segment of the population—a hallmark of financialism and of corporatocratic governance.

At the global level, income inequalities between nations also increased dramatically. In the period from 1950 until the mid-1970s, for example, disparity in per capita GDP (an indicator of income) between the richest and poorest groups of nations in the world decreased from fifteen to one to thirteen to one. Since the late 1970s, however, this measure of inequal-

---

208. U.S. Census Bureau, *Population Profile of the United States* (November 2011), http://www. census.gov/population/; Associated Press, "Poorest Population Segment Grows to a Record Size," *Wall Street Journal,* November 4, 2011, A5.

209. See Jim Puzzanghera, "The Rich Are Getting Richer, US Confirms," *Los Angeles Times,* October 27, 2011, B2.

210. See Foster, "Financialization of Accumulation."

211. "Income Inequality: Who Exactly Are the 1%?" *The Economist,* January 21, 2012, 31.

212. See Emmanuel Saez, *Striking It Richer: The Evolution of Top Incomes in the United States (Update with 2007 Estimates)* (August 5, 2009), http://elsa.berkeley.edu/; Thomas Piketty and Emmanuel Saez, "Income Inequality in the United States, 1913–1998," *Quarterly Journal of Economics* 118 (2003): 1–39; Steve Kaplan and Joshua Rauh, "Wall Street and Main Street: What Contributes to the Rise in the Highest Income," *Review of Financial Studies* 23 (2010): 1004–50.

ity rose to twenty to one.[213] Comparisons between countries that strongly followed financialist policies and those that did not also revealed substantial internal—and growing—income disparities.[214] The spread of financialism around the world had much to do with these growing disparities, as the speculative schemes pioneered in Wall Street sought new frontiers—and unfettered speculation took over finance in many nations. Much surplus capital generated in less-developed nations—especially those that became export-dependent since the late 1970s—flowed to rich nations, most of all, the United States, and became part of the casino economy. Important financialist betting hubs also developed—Hong Kong, Dubai, and Singapore, for example—taking in some of the surplus capital while serving as proxies for the larger financial centers in rich nations.

The result was that much capital accumulated in less developed nations helped inflate speculative bubbles, as well as growth, in rich nations—especially the United States—while speculative booms also developed in some less developed nations.[215] All this occurred behind a mask of high consumption and apparent prosperity. Also, wages in most less-developed, export-dependent nations were kept low—through wage repression and the elimination of labor unions—in order to accelerate capital accumulation.[216] Oligopolistic financial corporations—most of all, the megabanks—followed on the steps of the (also oligopolistic) multinational corporations that had, decades before, established their footholds by creating vast webs of subsidiaries, branches, and shared holdings. Income disparities in less developed nations therefore increased dramatically, as credit systems copied from the rich nations—most of all, the United States—stimulated stock market gambling and created debt-laden, financialized economies.

Wealth inequality—which includes all personal property, such as real estate, bank accounts, stocks, bonds, and other accumulated assets—followed the dramatic rise in American income inequality during the three decades after the 1970s. As a result, the wealthiest 20 percent of the population in

213. Branko Milanovic, *Worlds Apart: Measuring International and Global Inequality* (Princeton: Princeton University Press, 2005); Angus Maddison, *The World Economy: A Millennial Perspective* (Paris: OECD, 2001).

214. See, for example, Thomas Piketty and Emmanuel Saez, "The Evolution of Top Incomes: A Historical and International Perspective," *American Economic Review*, Papers and Proceedings 96 (2006): 200–205.

215. See Richard Peet, "Contradictions of Finance Capitalism," *Monthly Review*, December 2011, 18–32.

216. See Foster, "Financialization of Accumulation," 14.

the United States now owns more than 93 percent of all wealth.[217] Never before was there such a high concentration of wealth in the hands of a small elite in American history.[218] The top of the wealthiest 20 percent segment is largely composed, as in the case of income, by the financial and corporate elites associated with the rise of financialism.[219] Millionaires make up less than 1 percent of that top 20 percent segment, yet they control 40 percent of all wealth, a historical record.[220] Average net worth—the sum of all assets, such as housing equity and property, minus debt—for millionaires in the United States increased threefold during the decade of 2000–09. In contrast, during the same decade the average net worth of the population at large declined by 13 percent, the largest drop since data on net worth started to be compiled.[221] Most American families had two working adults during that decade, yet most had to borrow in order to maintain their standard of living, accumulating an unprecedented amount of debt.[222]

The rising mountains of debt, greater wealth inequality, and economic insecurity also had effects in many aspects of life for working people, the poor, and the middle class. One of them was a deterioration of access to health care for many people in the bottom half of the wealth scale.[223] Health care became progressively less affordable as the insurance oligopolies that took over this sector placed profits over people and their

217. See Peet, "Contradictions," 19–25; Perelman, *Confiscation*; Congressional Budget Office, *Trends*.

218. Joyce Appleby, "The Wealth Divide," *Los Angeles Times*, November 7, 2011, A15.

219. See, for example, Arthur B. Kennickell, *Ponds and Streams: Wealth and Income in the US, 1989 to 2007*, Federal Reserve Board Working Paper 2009-13 (2009): 55–63.

220. Boston Consulting Group, *Shaping a New Tomorrow* (Boston: BCG, 2011).

221. Based on data compiled by the U.S. Department of Commerce and the U.S. Bureau of Economic Analysis, available at www.commerce.gov and www.bea.gov; Tim Rutten, "It Was the Worst of Times," *Los Angeles Times*, January 2, 2010, A27.

222. See, for example, Peter Gosselin, *High Wire: The Precarious Financial Lives of American Families* (New York: Basic Books, 2008); Wacquant, *Punishing the Poor*. Some researchers believe that luxury goods and services consumption by wealthy elites has generated a "trickle-down" imitation effect, inducing those who can least afford to accumulate debt—working people and the middle class—to do so; see Marianne Bertrand and Adair Morse, *Trickle-Down Consumption*, http://faculty.chicagobooth.edu/adair.morse/research/bertrand-morsetrickle2011dec7.pdf (accessed March 23, 2012).

223. See Grace Budrys, *Unequal Health: How Inequality Contributes to Health or Illness* (Lanham, MD: Rowman and Littlefield, 2009); Wacquant, *Punishing the Poor*.

health.[224] Many employers simply refused to provide or pay for it, and many workers were faced with the dilemma of sustaining consumption *or* spending an ever-increasing amount of their wages on health insurance. Those who chose to pay for their insurance not only became poorer, but also found that coverages were usually insufficient and required large amounts of out-of-pocket cash to cover many treatments.[225] Children were also affected, as rising wealth inequality and insecurity took their toll on working families and the poor. One study, for example, estimated that about 50 percent of all children in the United States would be dependent on food stamps at some point during their childhood.[226]

An important contributor to wealth inequality was the credit system— an integral part of financialism and of the casino economy it engendered—in which oligopolies play a major role. The credit system became a major vehicle for the accumulation of wealth *by* the financial elites and the financial corporations they control—*from* the population at large.[227] This occurred through an immense accumulation of debt by the population—most of all, by working people and the middle class—through the various means provided by the credit system. According to one estimate, for example, the working poor—those with incomes at, or barely above, the poverty level set by the federal government—pay surcharges amounting to more than $30 billion annually for the financial services they use.[228] Secondary mortgages based on home equity, along with consumer loans, personal borrowing, retirement plan loans, credit card debt, and stock market gambling loans were the more important means for this phenomenon. At the same time, the stagnation of wages in most sectors of the economy—along with the erosion

---

224. A trend that started in the 1980s; see Noam Chomsky, *Profits Over People: Neoliberalism and the Global Order* (New York: Seven Stories Press, 1998); Budrys, *Unequal Health*; Gosselin, *High Wire*.

225. See Martinez, "Cash Before Chemo"; Rubenstein, "Hospitals Want Credit Report"; Mathews, "Surprise Health Bills."

226. Paul H. Wise, "Children of the Recession," *Archives of Pediatrics and Adolescent Medicine* 163 (2009): 1063–64; Liz Szabo, "Study: Half of US Kids Will Receive Food Stamps," *USA Today*, November 2, 2009, http://www.usatoday.com/news/health/2009-11-02-food-stamps_N.htm.

227. See Gary Rivlin, *Broke, USA: From Pawnshops to Poverty, Inc.; How the Working Poor Became Big Business* (New York: Harper, 2010); David Harvey, *The Enigma of Capital* (London: Profile, 2010).

228. Rivlin, *Broke, USA*, 45.

of minimum wages—guaranteed that immense debt would be accumulated by the public, to try to sustain consumption and their standard of living.[229]

One rapidly rising category of debt, beyond consumption sustenance, that affects the middle class and working people greatly is the unprecedented accumulation of student debt, which reached a total of over $1 trillion in the United States in 2010—a result of cuts in public education funding and of rising tuition costs that were far above increases in the cost of living.[230] One-third of all student loan borrowers were estimated to be carrying a past-due balance in early 2012, the highest delinquency rate ever.[231] Rising student loan debt also forced many students to drop out. As a result, for example, only about 40 percent of all students enrolled in public universities that serve primarily working people and the middle class, such as the California State University System, end up completing a degree.[232] Also, for the first time in American history, children today are projected to receive less education than their parents throughout their lifetime.[233] Adopting the

229. In 2008, total US household debt—mortgages, auto loans, credit cards, student loans—was $12.7 trillion, the highest ever. Five years later, the total stood at $11.28 trillion and continued to rise—by $127 billion alone during the July–September quarter, 2013 (the largest quarterly increase since 2008)—despite considerable distress since the start of the crisis and the fact that the recovery was very weak; see Neil Shah, "Consumer Borrowing Picks Up," *Wall Street Journal*, November 15, 2013, A4. Many middle class individuals who incurred substantial debts—and became unemployed—also discovered they were unable to qualify for welfare; see Molly Hennessy-Fiske, "Middle-Class Jobless Run Into a Welfare Wall; After Shock of Having to Apply for Social Aid, Many Are Jolted Again: They Don't Qualify," *Los Angeles Times*, March 26, 2009, A1. At the same time, downward economic mobility was compounded by an array of policies and measures that penalized those who found themselves unemployed and poor; see Barbara Ehrenreich, "When All Else Fails, Rob the Poor," *Los Angeles Times*, May 17, 2012, A19.

230. See "University Challenge," *The Economist*, December 10, 2011, 74; Josh Mitchell and Maya Jackson-Randall, "Student-Loan Debt Tops $1 Trillion," *Wall Street Journal*, March 22, 2012, A5; Josh Mitchell, "Student Debt Hits the Middle-Aged," *Wall Street Journal*, July 18, 2012, A6; Adam B. Wolf, "Heading for the Student Debt Cliff," *Los Angeles Times*, June 23, 2013, A20.

231. Ruth Simon and Rachel L. Ensign, "Risky Student Debt is Starting to Sour," *Wall Street Journal*, January 31, 2013, C1; Federal Reserve Bank of New York, *US Credit Conditions: Student Loans*, http://data.newyorkfed.org/creditconditionsmap/ (accessed March 13, 2012).

232. Don Lee, "College Debt a Looming 'Time Bomb,'" *Los Angeles Times*, March 6, 2012, B1; Josh Mitchell, "Student Debt Rises by 8% as College Tuitions Climb," *Wall Street Journal*, June 1, 2012, A5.

233. See David Wessel and Stephanie Banchero, "Education Slowdown Threatens US," *Wall Street Journal*, April 26, 2012, A1.

spirit of financialism and corporatocracy, many universities have become more like corporate enterprises—eagerly searching to increase revenue by any means, raising tuition at unprecedented rates—while treating education as a commodity.[234] The U.S. Bureau of Labor Statistics, for example, estimated that tuition costs per student rose five times more than the rate of inflation between 1983 and 2010.[235] The period 2001–2010 alone saw the cost of a university education rise from 23 percent of median annual income to 38 percent—an unprecedented increase for such a short time span—that reflects the corporate mindset of university executives, the need to pay for their generous compensation packages, and the debts they have loaded onto operating budgets.[236] The spread of the corporate mindset to many public university systems has also made enrollment cuts a priority—much as factories that cut raw materials and supplies—thereby restricting access while increasing tuition.[237] Thus, education—a key to society's long-term well-being—has become increasingly out of reach for working people, the middle class, and the poor.

Inequality is also reflected in the deep and growing cleavage between the financial and corporate elites and the average wage earner. In the late 1970s, for example, total compensation for the top 10 percent of corporate chief executives was about fifty times that of the average wage earner in the American economy.[238] Three decades later, corporate chief executive com-

234. See, for example, Marc Bousquet, *How the University Works: Higher Education and the Low-Wage Nation* (New York: New York University Press, 2008); Jennifer Washburn, *University, Inc.: The Corporate Corruption of American Higher Education* (New York: Basic Books, 2005).

235. U.S. Bureau of Labor Statistics, *Back to College* (September 2010), http://www.bls.gov/spotlight/2010/college/pdf/college.pdf.

236. "Higher Education: Not What It Used to Be; American Universities Represent Declining Value for Money to their Students," *The Economist,* December 1, 2012, 29–30; Douglas Belkin and Scott Thurm, "Deans List: Hiring Spree Fattens College Bureaucracy—and Tuition," *Wall Street Journal,* December 29, 2012, A1; U.S. Bureau of Labor Statistics, *Back to College.*

237. See, for example, Larry Gordon, "CSUN Told to Cut Students or Lose $7 Million," *Los Angeles Times,* January 28, 2012, AA3; Carla Rivera, "College to Offer Two-Tier Course Pricing," *Los Angeles Times,* March 14, 2012, A1, and her "CSU to Freeze Spring Student Rosters," *Los Angeles Times,* March 20, 2012, A1.

238. See Task Force on Inequality and American Democracy, *American Democracy in an Age of Rising Inequality* (Washington, DC: American Political Science Association, 2004).

pensation was 475 times that of the average wage earner.[239] In the financial sector, chief executive compensation reached as high as 700 times that of the average salaried employee in the sector, and the gap was not reduced much by the financial crisis that started in 2007.[240] One hedge fund owner, for example, received $3.7 billion in compensation alone in 2007—74,000 times the median household income in the United States—while the five top executives of another one received $771.5 million in cash distributions alone in 2006.[241] The onset of the financial crisis in 2007 did not reduce much hedge fund executive compensation. In 2012—the worst year for hedge fund executive compensation since 2008—for example, the top twenty-five hedge fund managers received a total of $14.1 billion in compensation.[242] All of these extremely rich, high-compensation hedge funds were responsible for the loss of tens of thousands of jobs in the companies they took over since the start of the financial crisis, as numerous reports have pointed out. The support provided by the federal government to the financial sector in 2008 and 2009 benefited them greatly, since they are all linked—as clients and speculators—to the oligopolistic megabanks that were bailed out.

Substantial compensation disparities can also be found between executives of financial and nonfinancial corporations—a reflection of financialism's growing importance. Between 1948 and 1982, for example, average executive compensation in American financial corporations ranged between 99 and 108 percent of the average level in all nonfinancial corporations.[243] By 2007, this proportion had risen to 181 percent of the average for all nonfinancial corporations. In 1988, none of the ten best-compensated corporate executives were in financial corporations—by 2007, financial corporations accounted for four out of the top five best-compensated executives in the United States. Financial corporations also contributed a rapidly growing

---

239. Perelman, *Confiscation,* and data on executive compensation for the largest American corporations as reported by *Fortune* magazine in its annual "Fortune 500" reports, 1979–2011. See also Edward N. Wolff, *Recent Trends in Household Wealth in the United States: Rising Debt and the Middle-Class Squeeze; An Update to 2007,* Levy Economics Institute, Working Paper 589 (March 2010); Raghuram G. Rajan, *Fault Lines* (Princeton: Princeton University Press, 2010).

240. Steve Eder and Gregory Zuckerman, "Paulson Fires Back at Critics," *Wall Street Journal,* October 12, 2011, C3; Foster, "Financialization of Accumulation," 13.

241. See Zuckerman and Dezember, "Carlyle's 3 Founders."

242. Stephen Taub, "The Rich List: Our 12th Annual Ranking of the World's Top-Earning Hedge Fund Managers," *Institutional Investor's Alpha* (April 15, 2013), http://www.institutionalinvestorsalpha.com/; "Hedge Funds: Launch Bad," *The Economist,* April 20, 2013, 79.

243. Perelman, *Confiscation*; Foster and Holleman, "Financial Power Elite."

proportion of the wealthiest segment of the population. In 1982, for example, less than one-fifth of the four hundred wealthiest individuals in the United States had obtained their wealth through finance—by 2007, almost one-third had done so. By contrast, barely one-fifth of the wealthiest individuals derived their wealth from technology corporations in 2007, despite the brisk growth of new technology sectors during the prior two decades.[244]

In almost every financial corporation bailed out by the U.S. government, executives continued to pay themselves astounding multimillion dollar compensation packages that were among the highest for all corporate executives.[245] Nine oligopolistic banks that received government bailouts, for example, paid their executives $33 billion in bonuses in 2008, including more than $1 million individually to five thousand employees—despite the huge losses they incurred that year.[246] In 2009 alone, major U.S. banks and financial corporations paid $145 billion in compensation to their executives, while at the top thirty-eight financial corporations executive compensation rose by 18 percent that year (compared with the previous year).[247] The chief executive of Citigroup (the holding company that controls Citibank), for example, was compensated $38 million in 2009—the year after this corporation had to be bailed out by the federal government.[248] The chief executive of Goldman Sachs (the most important Wall Street investment bank) was paid $69 million and $54 million in 2007 and 2006—the largest pay packages for the head of a Wall Street financial corporation in those years. The same chief executive received more than $21 million in total compensation for 2012—three years after his megabank was bailed out—while its top twelve executives received almost $100 million in restricted share compensation alone for that year.[249] The chief executive of Morgan Stanley (another oligopolistic Wall Street investment bank) was paid $40

244. Matthew Miller and Duncan Greenburg, "The Richest People in America," *Forbes*, September 30, 2009, http://www.forbes.com/2009/09/30/forbes-400-gates-buffett-wealth-rich-list-09_land.html; Kennickell, *Ponds and Streams*.

245. See Foster and Holleman, "Financial Power Elite."

246. Susanne Craig and Deborah Solomon, "Bank Bonus Tab: $33 Billion; Nine Lenders That Got US Aid Paid at Least $1 Million Each to 5,000 Employees," *Wall Street Journal*, July 31, 2009, A1.

247. Stephen Grocer, "Banks Set for Record Pay," *Wall Street Journal*, January 15, 2010, A1.

248. Aaron Lucchetti and Matthew Karnitschnig, "On Street, New Reality on Pay Sets In," *Wall Street Journal*, January 31, 2009, B1.

249. Liz Rappaport and Liz Moyer, "Big Payday for Goldman CEO: Stock Bonuses Jumps to $13.3 Million; On Track for $21 Million in Compensation," *Wall Street Journal*, January 19, 2013, B1.

million in stock and options alone in 2006, the largest bonus awarded to any Wall Street executive at the time.[250]

The chief executive of Lehman Brothers, one of the most important Wall Street investment banks until it collapsed in 2008, was compensated a total of $480 million between 2000 and 2008. Lehman Brothers and its chief executive had an important role triggering the financial meltdown of 2008–09. Its fifty highest-paid executives—the elite of the bank—received $700 million in compensation in 2007, an amount that amazed even Wall Street veteran executives.[251] Lehman was allowed to fail by federal regulators, leaving tens of thousands unemployed and wiping out most of the funds of anyone who had invested in it (including pension funds). Its failure triggered a panic that nearly collapsed the financial system, and caused all other failing banks to be bailed out by the government. Lehman Brothers' chief executive, however, kept his compensation, while the total notional value of the bank's unresolved derivatives eighteen months after its failure was estimated at $40 trillion—almost three times the total U.S. annual GDP for 2009.[252] Very high compensation over long periods of time was another aspect of Wall Street megabanks that became noticed during the crisis. Between 1999 and 2008, a member of the board of directors of Citigroup was paid a total of $115 million, for example. Before 1999, this individual was the chief executive of another Wall Street megabank before becoming U.S. treasury secretary during the Clinton presidency—a good example of the two-way "revolving door" relationship between corporate power and government. This individual was quite influential in orchestrating the bailout of Wall Street banks by the U.S. government in 2008 and 2009, using his considerable experience and powerful contacts to benefit Wall Street. The staggering compensation packages—and the webs of political influence that accompany them—reflect the excesses that financialism generated, and the subservience of government to corporate interests.[253]

---

250. Lucchetti and Karnitschnig, "On Street"; Floyd Norris, "To Rein in Pay, Rein in Wall Street," *New York Times*, October 30, 2009, B1.

251. Walter Hamilton, Andrew Tangel, and Stuart Pfeifer, "Lehman Elite Stood to Get $700 Million: Bankruptcy Case Reveals Pre-Crash Pay for 50 Employees that Shocks Even Wall Street Veterans," *Los Angeles Times*, April 27, 2012, A1.

252. Michael Corkery and Katy Burne, "Rattled By Lehman—Again," *Wall Street Journal*, June 13, 2011, C1.

253. To reduce public—and shareholders'—attention to high executive compensation, a growing number of corporations started to provide alternative measures for reporting their top

No less astounding are the very low taxes that the financial and corporate elites pay—another aspect of the vast inequalities that accompany financialism. These elites project their influence right up to the top of the U.S. government, to Congress, to the regulatory agencies that affect their activities, to the nation's judicial system—and they can also have the last word on tax policy.[254] Tax cuts for the wealthiest segment of the population—the financial and corporate elites—in the United States were estimated to have been about $700 billion alone during the decade that started in 2001.[255] And, on top of it all, their privileged businesses are bailed out when crises occur, at taxpayer expense—yet, the financial and corporate elites usually pay less than the average working person does.[256] Thus, for example, one of the two richest individuals in the United States, billionaire speculator Warren Buffett, casually remarked in an interview that he paid a much lower share of taxes than his receptionist—a total rate of 17.7 percent on his annual taxable income ($46 million) in 2006, compared to his receptionist's 30 percent.[257] And, this occurred despite the fact that Buffett (by his own admission) was not engaged in tax avoidance schemes, and had no tax shelter to protect his income.

This situation is mirrored in the case of tax payments by the largest financial corporations—the ones largely responsible for the financial crisis that started in 2007. A study of tax payments, for example, found that the largest Wall Street corporations—all of them oligopolists in their sector—paid no taxes whatsoever, *or* had tax breaks and subsidies that actu-

executives' pay. As a result, the total compensation reported for the same chief executive by the same corporation can be tens of millions of dollars less than that reported to government agencies (such as the Securities and Exchange Commission). And, to make executive compensation more opaque, the diverse ways the "alternative" measures are calculated makes them unsuitable for making comparisons between companies; see Emily Chasan, "Executive Pay Gets New Spin," *Wall Street Journal,* September 25, 2012, B1.

254. See, for example, Lisa Mascaro, "Bush-Era Tax Cuts Still Loom Large: A Decade Later, the Breaks for the Wealthy Figure in Every Round of the Budget Fights," *Los Angeles Times,* November 28, 2011, A1. 255. Donald L. Bartlett and James B. Steele, *The Betrayal of the American Dream* (New York: PublicAffairs, 2012).

256. See, for example, Walter Hamilton and Nathaniel Popper, "How the Wealthy Get Tax Breaks," *Los Angeles Times,* January 24, 2012, B1.

257. Alex Crippen, "Warren Buffett and NBC's Tom Brokaw: The Complete Interview," *CNBC,* October 31, 2007, http://www.cnbc.com/id/21553857/; Tomoeh Murakami Tse, "Buffett Slams Tax System Disparities," *Washington Post,* June 27, 2007, http://www.washingtonpost.com/wodyn/content/article/2007/06/27/.

ally amounted to negative tax payments.[258] Those that paid taxes typically contributed far less than the federal income tax rate corresponding to their incomes. Wells Fargo, for example, received almost $18 billion in tax breaks during the three-year period that started in 2008, while its executives continued to pay themselves dozens of millions of dollars annually in total compensation.[259] Other large financial corporations enjoyed tax breaks that essentially amounted to negative tax payments—a condition that reflects both the power of the oligopolies driving financialism and the deep injustice engendered by three decades of neoliberal socioeconomic engineering.[260]

Tax breaks helped free up money that could be recycled to bolster executive compensation.[261] Such breaks were responsible, for example, for making corporate tax receipts (as a share of profits) the lowest in forty years, saving corporations more than $110 billion in 2010 and 2011.[262] It should not surprise, then, that while corporate tax payments declined, the twenty highest-paid corporate executives in the United States received an average $36 million annually in compensation during 2000–09, a substantial increase over the previous decade.[263] Lower tax payments and loose regulations on employee benefits also allowed corporate executives to redirect funds that would have gone to support employee retirement, health care, and other benefits, to fund their own salaries, bonuses, stock option plans, and all the "golden handshake" and "golden farewell" schemes that augmented their personal wealth—often without any correlation to their actual performance as executives.[264] One such golden-farewell scheme, for example, provided a $255.4 million severance package to one executive, while another provided $85 million—despite the

---

258. Robert S. McIntyre, Matthew Gardner, Rebecca J. Wilkins, and Richard Phillips, *Corporate Taxpayers and Corporate Tax Dodgers 2008–10* (Washington, DC: Citizens for Tax Justice and Institute on Taxation and Economic Policy, 2011), http://www.ctj.org/corporatetaxdodgers/CorporateTaxDodgers Report.pdf.

259. Ibid.

260. Tiffany Hsu, "Study Finds Many Firms Pay No Taxes," *Los Angeles Times,* November 4, 2011, B2; McIntyre et al., *Corporate Taxpayers.*

261. See Schultz, "Who Killed Private Pensions?"

262. Damian Paletta, "With Tax Break, Corporate Rate Is Lowest in 40 Years," *Wall Street Journal,* February 3, 2012, B1.

263. See, for example, Phred Dvorak, "Poor Year Doesn't Stop CEO Bonuses," *Wall Street Journal,* March 18, 2009, B1.

264. See Ellen E. Schultz and Tom McGinty, "Pensions for Executives on Rise: Arcane Techniques, Generous Formulas Boost Payouts as Share Prices Fall," *Wall Street Journal,* November 3, 2009, C1.

large losses and poor performance during his tenure (both corporations are oligopolists in their sectors).[265] Some of the most richly paid corporate executives in the United States, in fact, were also the worst performers in terms of profitability, productivity, revenue streams, and stock prices.[266]

Executives at twenty-one of the largest one hundred corporations that went through bankruptcy in 2010, for example, received more than $350 million in salaries, bonuses, stock grants, and severance pay—compensation paid when those corporations filed for bankruptcy proceedings, or just after.[267] The median compensation of chief executives at each of those failing twenty-one corporations (most of them oligopolists in their sectors) was $8.7 million in the year they filed for bankruptcy—very close to the $9.1 million median chief executive compensation for *all* chief executives of the corporations listed in the S&P 500 directory during the same year. Corporations also found ways to evade legally a 2005 federal law that limits bonus pay during bankruptcy—by crafting "incentive plans" that are outside the scope of that law. In one corporation that filed for bankruptcy, cut more than twenty thousand jobs, and wiped out all its shareholders, for example, top-level executives and managers received $20.6 million in bonuses—including $5.4 million for its chief executive.[268]

---

265. "Fortune Favours the Boss: Big, Controversial 'Golden Goodbyes' to Bosses Are Probably Here to Stay," *The Economist,* December 7, 2013, 66–67; Mark Maremont, "How Some Firms Boost the Boss's Pension," *Wall Street Journal,* January 23, 2009, A1. Elite attorneys are usually employed by corporate chief executive candidates to negotiate their hiring and the severance packages they will receive. Thus, because such compensation is contracted for at the time of hiring, corporate boards typically consider it less troublesome to pay up when the chief executive leaves than to contest the severance package. A common justification is that any such litigation would likely scare away candidates who might fill the vacancy.

266. See, for example, Lucian Bebchuk, "Congress Gets Punitive on Executive Pay: We Want Compensation Tied to Performance," *Wall Street Journal,* February 16, 2009, http://online.wsj.com/. In fact, politicians managed to do nothing about this issue—their concern proved to be quite temporary, and was driven by the need to attract attention from the media as the economic crisis deepened in late 2008 and early 2009. One vivid example of the disconnection between executive pay and corporate performance was the case of MF Global—a hedge fund that misappropriated $1.6 billion in client funds—whose top executive approved for himself a multimillion dollar pay package as the firm was about to collapse; see Patrick Fitzgerald and Mike Spector, "Corzine Pay Plan Topped $8 Million," *Wall Street Journal,* May 22, 2012, C3.

267. Mike Spector and Tom McGinty, "The CEO Bankruptcy Bonus: Firms Sidestep Rule That Limits Rewards for Executives," *Wall Street Journal,* January 27, 2012, A1.

268. Ibid.

The vast amounts involved in corporate chief executive compensation—along with the inequalities they engendered—seem to have been based on the relations of power, which favored corporate executive interests, and the larger apparatus of oligopolistic power. They also reflect a larger dysfunction of the state, in the sense that corporate hegemony over politics and the public interest became the norm, twisting and shaping the priorities—as well as the purpose—of public governance, to serve corporate power above everything else. *In many respects, this reflects a long, drawn out coup d'état by the financial and corporate elites against just public governance.* In this way the state and the politicians who rule it were enlisted in the financial and corporate elites' agenda to eliminate labor unions, to lower taxes on their own income and wealth, to erode minimum wages and benefits for the working population, to reduce welfare benefits for the poor, to boost wage repression through outsourcing and offshoring, to eliminate or dilute regulations that posed an obstacle to their expanding power over the economy and over governance, and to prevent any scrutiny of the injustices that their rising power entailed.[269]

The consequences of the long-running coup d'état by the financial and corporate elites against social justice are nowhere more visible than in the world capital of financialism, New York City—the home of Wall Street.[270] Among American metropolises, New York has the most unequal income distribution, with 1 percent of households claiming almost half of all income by 2010—a level that is about twice that of the wealthiest 1 percent of all households nationally. Average household income for the wealthiest 1 percent of the population in New York City rose by about 120 percent between the mid-1990s and 2010, while the median hourly wage fell by almost 10 percent in real terms during the same period.

---

269. Aspects that are explored in, for example, Matt Taibbi, *Griftopia: A Story of Bankers, Politicians, and the Most Audacious Power Grab in American History* (New York: Spiegel and Grau, 2011); Robert W. McChesney, "This Isn't What Democracy Looks Like," *Monthly Review,* November 2012, 1–28. The overwhelming power of high finance (and its elites) over public governance and regulation is thought to be a major factor in the decline of corporate integrity; see, for example, Jonathan K. Macey, *The Death of Corporate Reputation: How Integrity Has Been Destroyed on Wall Street* (Upper Saddle River, NJ: FT Press, 2013).

270. See Christopher Ketcham, "The Reign of the One Percenters: Income Inequality and the Death of Culture in New York City," *Orion Magazine,* September-October 2011, http:// www.orionmagazine.org/ index.php/, and his "The New Populists?" *Los Angeles Times,* October 6, 2011, A19; David Harvey, *Rebel Cities: From the Right to the City to the Urban Revolution* (London: Verso, 2012).

Middle-income households—those with annual incomes between $29,000 and $170,000—saw their earnings decrease by almost 20 percent during the same period, in real terms, while almost 12 percent of the total population of New York City were classified as living in deep poverty—according to federal guidelines.[271] Almost one-third of all children in New York City were living in poverty by 2010, while almost one-fourth were in households living in deep poverty. The total number of homeless people on New York City streets—those requiring overnight stays at municipal shelters—rose to an average of 120,000 nightly by 2010—a record number for all American metropolises, and the largest among all metropolises in rich nations around the world. Just as important, from a cultural and legal perspective, were the city laws that practically turned the homeless into fugitives in order to drive them out of public sight—something that New York City pioneered and that was imitated by many other cities in the United States.[272] Also, new laws in many American cities made it practically impossible for demonstrations that protest social injustice to occur, after corporations pressured local governments to ban them in their districts.[273]

A very disturbing aspect of this panorama of inequality and social injustice is the federal government's attempt to refloat financialism by any and all means—through measures that essentially try to turn the clock back to the time prior to the crisis. Wielding its regulatory powers, this is what the U.S. Federal Reserve and the Treasury Department did after the debacle of 2008–09—with the most powerful Wall Street oligopolies pulling the strings—in what is one of the more obvious symptoms of

---

271. Ketcham, "Reign"; U.S. Department of Health and Human Services, *Poverty Guidelines, Research and Measurement* (January 31, 2011), http://aspe.hhs.gov/poverty/; Jessie Willis, *How We Measure Poverty: A History and Brief Overview* (Silverton, OR: Oregon Center for Public Policy, 2000), http://www.ocpp.org/poverty/how.htm; Barbara Garson, *Down the Up Escalator: How the 99 Percent Live* (New York: Doubleday, 2013).

272. See Barbara Ehrenreich, "Occupational Hazards," *Los Angeles Times,* October 22, 2011, A35, and her *Nickel and Dimed.* By January 2013—more than six years since the start of the economic crisis—one source estimated that an average of fifty thousand people were still being housed nightly in New York City's homeless shelters; see Michael H. Saul, "New York City Leads Jump in Homeless," *Wall Street Journal,* March 5, 2013, A6.

273. See Frank Shyong, "Occupy's Ironic Legacy: Limits on Protests; Cities Have Tightened Restrictions on Demonstrators in Ways That Opponents Say Threaten Free Speech," *Los Angeles Times,* December 6, 2012, A1; Amory Starr, Luis Fernandez, and Christian Scholl, *Shutting Down the Streets: Political Violence and Social Control in the Global Era* (New York: New York University Press, 2011).

corporatocracy at work. Countless secret meetings by the Federal Reserve, for example, ensured that the "new" rules of the game it drafted favored the most powerful Wall Street interests—the megabank oligopolies, the hedge funds, the wealthiest speculators, and the elites associated with them. The Federal Reserve even broke with a long history of airing regulatory matters at open meetings, making sure that the new rules it was writing were known to no one but itself and the powerful Wall Street interests who would be affected.[274] Frequent consultation with groups of high-level executives from Wall Street oligopolies, along with the "revolving door" vehicle of influence, allowed those privileged parties to know about—and influence—the rules being drafted before anyone else.

To refloat financialism, the Federal Reserve lent massively to oligopolistic megabanks that could not (or were not willing to) borrow from each other. Such lending, predictably, carried negative interest rates (when adjusted for inflation), thus amounting to a subsidy and, as noted previously, resulted in substantial profits for recipients. Many loans and much debt were also guaranteed by the federal government, so that the megabanks could resume lending to each other. As a result, the new loans and debt increased the federal government's obligations by trillions of dollars, in what is one more poignant example of the massive shifting of risk from oligopolistic corporate power to public governance. Then, the federal government borrowed massively, issuing trillions of dollars in new debt (by printing U.S. Treasury Bonds) so that those oligopolistic megabanks—which had triggered the worst crisis since the Great Depression—could buy part of that debt and also make a profit doing so. The profits were easily arranged for, by allowing the megabanks to purchase the Treasury Bonds with the massive amounts of money provided to them by the Federal Reserve—at negative real interest rates—while the said banks were earning interest income—at positive rates, above inflation—from the bonds printed by the Treasury.[275]

The Federal Reserve itself joined the oligopolistic megabanks in buying that debt, as part of its "quantitative easing" scheme—through which massive amounts of dollars were printed in order to buy the Treasury Bonds—

274. See, for example, Victoria McGrane and Jon Hilsenrath, "Fed Writes Sweeping Rules from Behind Closed Doors," *Wall Street Journal*, February 21, 2012, A1.

275. By that time, the oligopolistic megabanks were resuming much the same activities that had triggered the crisis—feeling confident that the government would refloat the financialist economy that had so favored their interests. See, for example, Matt Wirz, "Banks Are Back in Takeovers," *Wall Street Journal*, October 24, 2011, C1; Puzzanghera, "Several Banks Once Deemed"; Blinder, "Five Years Later"; Bair and Frank, "Watch Out."

in what amounts to a "right arm of government buys what left arm of government sells" scheme. Its objective was to try to drive down interest rates throughout the economy by buying up massive amounts of Treasury Bonds on its own, so that everyone would find it easier to borrow—and pile on more debt on top of the vast amounts already accumulated, to refloat financialism.[276] One result of this policy was a further increase in the accumulation of very risky debt, such as junk-rated corporate bonds.[277] Debt—and its massive accumulation—a key feature of financialism during the past three decades, was therefore the key to the refloating strategy. This meant that the credit system also had to be refloated—at public expense, with working people and the middle class becoming liable for the consequences. Also, any inflation triggered by the massive "quantitative easing" and money-printing schemes would erode the middle class and working people's savings and savings income—especially when negative real interest rates are imposed over many years. The possibility that this could lead to the empoverishment of the vast majority of the population seemed to have been lost on the Federal Reserve. *These and other measures would result in a substantial transfer of wealth from working people and the middle class to the most affluent—a key feature of financialism and the corporatocratic state.*[278]

This panorama of social injustice is part of the multifaceted reality of financialism. Oligopolistic corporate power underlies and sustains it. More than at any other time in history, oligopolies today control the agenda of finance. The transfer of financial risk from oligopolies to the state, the effort to align the public interest with that of the financiers, the accumulation of vast amounts of debt that overwhelmingly benefit oligopolies, the financialist coup d'état that continually dispossesses the vast majority of the population

276. The Federal Reserve also tacitly assumed that lower interest rates on Treasury Bonds would make it easier for the government to finance its massive deficit and debt, and that speculators would be driven to buy stocks. These hoped-for effects drove similar central bank policies in other countries; see, for example, "Quantitative Easing: Just More of the Same? The Bank of England's Monetary Easing Could Be Bolder; It May Well Need to Be," *The Economist*, February 11, 2012, 59.

277. Over $75 billion in "junk" bonds were sold during the first three months of 2012 alone, by 130 junk-rated corporations—as speculators were driven to them by negative real interest rates, and the desire to increase returns by any means possible, no matter the risk; see Matt Wirz, "Junk Bonds Feed a Hungry Market," *Wall Street Journal*, March 30, 2012, A1; Katy Burne and Matt Wirz, "Market Chilled by Crisis Sees a Thaw," *Wall Street Journal*, April 5, 2012, C1.

278. See, for example, Mark Spitznagel, "How the Fed Favors the 1%," *Wall Street Journal*, April 20, 2012, A13.

by redistributing wealth to the elites, the wholesale (and legal) corruption of the political system, and the crisis-prone disengagement of finance from the real economy of production—all are part of this reality.

In this panorama of injustice engendered by financialism lies a major manifestation of the crisis of the state—a state in which the interests of oligopolistic corporate power are served above everything else. A state that is increasingly corporatocratic in deed and spirit, and that crafts its laws to suit the interests of oligopolies. A state that fails to look after the well-being of its citizens as its prime priority, and that seems to be primarily of, by, and for the financial and corporate elites—and for oligopolistic corporate power—rather than of, by, and for the people. Abraham Lincoln's most famous words thus seem to have become practically meaningless, in a system of governance where the interests of the public have been subordinated to the interests of oligopolistic corporate power.

Fundamental Split

The severance of finance from the real economy, discussed in the previous chapter, is accompanied by another, very important split. This second split involves the functional organization of corporate capitalism. It is quite relevant to oligopoly formation and deals with corporate control over the most vital productive resources of our time. It helps explain why public governance, politics, and society became major targets for oligopolistic influence, and it helps us understand why corporate power seeks oligopolistic control. The crisis of the capitalist state that we are witnessing is partially grounded in this phenomenon, although its importance and ramifications are not yet well understood.

In contrast with financialism, this fundamental split is based in the "real" economy—the economy of production. *It involves the severance of reproduction from commodification—two vitally important processes for corporate capitalism.*[1] It affects all productive activities, given the crucial role these two processes have for appropriating and transforming resources, and for obtaining profit. Research-dependent sectors that generate or use new technologies are most heavily impacted, but practically all other sectors—whether in manufacturing or services—are also affected, as creativity, knowledge, and other intangibles have become vitally important for almost every

---

1. Reproduction and commodification (sometimes also referred to as commoditization) have long been central concepts in Marxian political economy. In Marx's seminal critique of capitalism, both terms were conceptualized as key aspects of the process of capitalist production; see Karl Marx, *Capital: A Critique of Political Economy*, ed. F. Engels (New York: International Publishers, 1967; orig. publ. Hamburg: Verlag von Otto Meissner, 1867), Vol. I, *The Process of Capitalist Production* (chs. 1, 23), and Vol. II, *The Process of Circulation of Capital*, Part III (chs. 18–21). The initial use of the term *reproduction* mostly referred to capital—the most scarce resource in the early phase of industrial capitalism. Commodification's initial usage, however, comprised labor as well as capital and raw materials. See, for example, Eric Hobsbawm, *The Age of Capital: 1848–1875* (London: Weidenfeld and Nicolson, 1975).

corporate endeavor.[2] Corporate oligopolies are now heavily dependent on these intangibles to sustain their power and wealth, and to extend their influence over society and public governance.

This chapter will consider both reproduction and commodification in contemporary corporate capitalism, their severance in the corporate domain, and the vital role that intangibles now play in this phenomenon. Both processes will be defined, taking into account their historical evolution, their most significant contemporary features, and their placement in the fundamental dynamic of capital accumulation. The relationship between oligopolistic concentration and the severance of reproduction from commodification will be addressed throughout, along with the social pathologies and dysfunctions engendered, and their effect on the contemporary crisis of governance. The approach adopted in this chapter is unusual in politico-economic studies of the state and capitalism, because it addresses aspects that that are usually relegated to the microlevel sphere of the enterprise—and that are seldom related to the larger panorama of societal governance.

At the core of the severance of reproduction from commodification is that the reproduction of intangibles is socially mediated, depending greatly on societal relations that are external to the corporate domain—and therefore largely out of the control of corporate power. Myriad societal influences are required to regenerate and deploy intangibles, most of all, creativity, making it practically impossible for reproduction to be effectively carried out internally. The reproduction of some tangible resources is also evading corporate control, as in the case of skilled labor in manufacturing and service production—where skills must increasingly be regenerated outside the corporate domain, through socially mediated networks and influences. In manufacturing and service production, such externally developed skills have gained paramount importance for corporate power, leading to major changes in the workplace.[3] Commodification, on the other hand, remains mostly under corporate control, and involves both tangible and intangible resources—with appropriation as the single most important objective of corporate management.[4] *The*

---

2. The most research-dependent sectors are those at the vanguard of what I refer to as *technocapitalism*; see Luis Suarez-Villa, *Technocapitalism: A Critical Perspective on Technological Innovation and Corporatism* (Philadelphia: Temple University Press, 2009), 1–30.

3. Particularly in service activities that involve much office work; see, for example, Joan Greenbaum, *Windows on the Workplace: Technology, Jobs, and the Organization of Office Work* (New York: Monthly Review Press, 2004); Ursula Huws, *The Making of a Cybertariat: Virtual Work in a Real World* (New York: Monthly Review Press, 2003).

4. Appropriation—and the high level of control it requires—greatly influences workplace technology and how work is performed; see Harry Braverman, *Labor and Monopoly Capital*

need for societal mediation to reproduce resources therefore separates reproduction from commodification in the contemporary corporate domain, setting up major contradictions that affect oligopolistic power and its influence over public governance. These contradictions, as we will see in this chapter, contribute to the crisis of the state.

External reproduction is vitally important for corporate oligopolies engaged in manufacturing or service production. Intangible resources are today the single most important source of value, accounting for as much as 80 percent—if not more—of the value of most manufactured products and services.[5] In many sectors, intangibles such as creativity, knowledge, and experience are typically deployed in many activities within the corporate domain—involving research, design, marketing schemes, or the articulation of services, for example. As a result, intellectual property has become a most important source of value for corporate power.[6] Intangibles also affect the provision of tangible goods, resources, and labor more than ever before, especially in the richest nations. One of their effects is the technological substitution of physical labor, in ways that have deeply changed employment and the nature of work. In the United States, for example, waves of automation have left only the most essential personnel in manufacturing—those which computers and machines could not yet replace.[7] Much the same trend

---

(New York: Monthly Review Press, 1974); David F. Noble, *Forces of Production: A Social History of Industrial Automation* (New York: Knopf, 1984).

5. See Suarez-Villa, *Technocapitalism,* 31–55. The overwhelming value of intangibles for corporate power has motivated many efforts to come up with management formulas to enhance them; see, for example, Ahmed Bounfour, *The Management of Intangibles: The Organisation's Most Valuable Assets* (London: Routledge, 2003).

6. Intellectual property rights, in particular, are a vehicle for corporate power to appropriate the results of creativity; see Michael Perelman, *Steal This Idea: Intellectual Property Rights and the Corporate Confiscation of Creativity* (New York: Palgrave Macmillan, 2004). Patents—beyond serving as tools to appropriate creativity—have also become strategic financial assets for many corporations—most of all, those in high tech sectors; see, for example, Shira Ovide and John Letzing, "Tech Patents Soar in Value," *Wall Street Journal,* April 10, 2012, B1.

7. The widespread deployment of flexible production methods in the last quarter of the twentieth century was an important factor in this trend. See, for example, Tony Smith, *Technology and Capital in the Age of Lean Production: A Marxian Critique of the "New Economy"* (Albany: State University of New York Press, 2000), and the contributions in Jim Davis, Thomas Hirschl, and Michael Stack, eds., *Cutting Edge: Technology, Information, Capitalism, and Social Revolution* (London: Verso, 1998). Automation, in particular, was found to have had a major negative impact on the semiskilled manufacturing labor force in the 1990s; see David H. Autor, David Dorn, and Gordon H. Hanson, "Untangling Trade and Technology: Evidence from Local Labor Markets," Economics Department, MIT (March 2013), http://economics.mit.edu/files/8763.

has taken root in services, leaving mostly personnel whose work could not be replicated by machines and software—or those with very low skills (and the lowest wages).[8]

The rising importance of intangibles is therefore at the core of the split between reproduction and commodification. This is a relatively recent development in the temporal dimension of capitalism that, as I noted in other books, is related to its systemic evolution.[9] Intellectual property and rights, which are intimately related to intangibles, had little importance throughout the nineteenth and early twentieth centuries.[10] Early industrial capitalism, with its emphasis on capital, labor, and raw materials, placed relatively little value on intangibles.[11] Intangible-rich forms of property and rights started to gain importance with the rising power of corporate oligopolies in the twentieth century.[12] Intangibles are thus deeply associated with oligopolistic corporate power, as they provide new frontiers of value—and profit—that help increase concentration. The search for new forms of value involving intangibles has therefore become a key feature of contemporary capitalist accumulation. As a result, for example, today any form of life that can be turned into intellectual property is very likely to be targeted in the corporate quest for greater power and profit, by the oligopolies that rule the real economy of production—and the speculative one of financialism.[13]

---

8. See, for example, Julie Jargon, "Latest Starbucks Buzzword: 'Lean' Japanese Techniques," *Los Angeles Times,* August 4, 2009, A1.

9. Luis Suarez-Villa, *Globalization and Technocapitalism: The Political Economy of Corporate Power and Technological Domination* (London: Ashgate, 2012), and his *Technocapitalism.*

10. See, for example, Michael Perelman, "The Political Economy of Intellectual Property," *Monthly Review,* January 2003, 29–37, and his *Steal This Idea*; Hobsbawm, *Age of Capital.*

11. Marx, in *Capital,* concentrated his attention on capital and labor. Works in political economy—Marxist or otherwise—subsequently focused on these two resources as the critical drivers of the capitalist mode of production. See, for example, Eric Hobsbawm, *Labouring Men: Studies in the History of Labour* (London: Weidenfeld and Nicolson, 1964), and his *Age of Capital*; Michel Beaud, *A History of Capitalism: 1500–2000* (New York: Monthly Review Press, 2001).

12. After the 1910s, the overarching tendency toward greater corporate concentration became known as *monopoly capitalism,* reflecting the initial importance of monopolies in various sectors. See, for example, Baran and Sweezy, *Monopoly Capital,* and Baran's *The Theory of Capitalist Development* (New York: Monthly Review Press, 1956); John Bellamy Foster, *The Theory of Monopoly Capitalism: An Elaboration of Marxian Political Economy* (New York: Monthly Review Press, 1986).

13. Genetics, in particular, has become a major target, not only for corporate appropriation (through patenting) but also for financial speculation—a trend that became noticeable by the end of the twentieth century. See, for example, Naomi Aoki, "New Alchemy: Patents Aim to Turn Genes into Biotech Gold," *International Herald Tribune,* September 1, 2000,

One symptom of the high importance of intangibles in contemporary capitalism is the rising value of patents, and their use as speculative vehicles.[14] Companies known as "patent trolls" that profit, litigate with, and speculate on inventions that they had no role whatsoever in creating have become common.[15] These companies typically purchase and accumulate a large number of patents for the purpose of licensing them to others, to litigate over them and extract large amounts of money—or to pressure anyone who might use any related ideas to buy a license (or face expensive litigation). In one case, for example, a patent troll corporation—Round Rock Research—purchased 4,200 patents from a semiconductor oligopolist—Micron Technology—and subsequently negotiated numerous licensing agreements with other companies for the acquired patents.[16] Patent trolls that market themselves as "aggregators" are also selling protection from lawsuits—a scheme that is typically presented as a defensive strategy—if they pay an annual fee and buy a blanket license to use any patent in the aggregator's portfolio.[17] Corporations, usually oligopo-

---

10; David S. Ross, "Bioinformatics: Trying to Swim in a Sea of Data," *Science,* February 16, 2001, 1260–61. A new frontier for genetics appropriation is being provided by deep ocean life; see, for example, Gautam Naik, "Census Uncovers Oceans' Deep Secrets: Survey Names More than a Thousand New Species, but Scientists Are Most Surprised by Huge Variety of Microbial Level," *Wall Street Journal,* October 5, 2010, A8. Court decisions that have eliminated challenges to the corporate appropriation of human DNA indicate how important this resource has become for corporate power, even when such appropriation interferes with research and medicine; see, for example, Brent Kendall, "Court Rules Biotech Firm Can Patent Human Genes," *Wall Street Journal,* August 17, 2012, B3.

14. The keen search for value in any and all forms—and the prime importance of patents for corporate power—was reflected in some of the management literature of the late 1990s, in works such as Kevin G. Rivette and David Kline, *Rembrandts in the Attic: Unlocking the Hidden Value of Patents* (Boston: Harvard Business School Press, 2000). Since then, patent litigation—a symptom of the growing importance of intellectual property—has intensified greatly, particularly among advanced technology companies; see, for example, Don Clark and Shayndi Raice, "Tech Firms Intensify Patent Spats," *Wall Street Journal,* October 4, 2010, B3; Ashby Jones and Jessica E. Vascellaro, "In Silicon Valley, Patents Go on Trial: Tech Giants Near a Landmark Jury Trial over Provenance of an iPhone; Is It Innovation or Litigation?" *Wall Street Journal,* July 24, 2012, B1, and their "Patent War Pits Two Legal Stars: Apple's Veteran Litigator Squares Off against Samsung's Rising Star in Silicon Valley Courtroom," *Wall Street Journal,* August 3, 2012, B1; Ashby Jones, "Patent War Flares Anew," *Wall Street Journal,* November 4, 2013, B5.

15. Ashby Jones, "Patent 'Troll' Tactics Spread," *Wall Street Journal,* July 9, 2012, B1; "Trolls on the Hill: Congress Takes Aim at Patent Abusers," *The Economist,* December 7, 2013, 66.

16. Jones, "Patent 'Troll,'" B7.

17. Beyond the aggregators, new companies that promise "protection" from patent-related lawsuits also seek to gain clients with large patent portfolios; see, for example, Don Clark, "New Venture Enters Patent Fray: San Francisco Startup Plans to Recruit Companies to Deter Legal Threats against Its Members," *Wall Street Journal,* April 8, 2013, B3.

lists, that own a substantial number of patents are also spinning off units to try to sell licenses to other companies—pressuring those who use any idea that remotely resembles the ones they own to buy a license—and suing them if they refuse. Five technology oligopolists—Apple, Microsoft, Sony, Ericsson, and Research In Motion—for example, spent a combined $4.5 billion to purchase more than six thousand patents from the bankrupt Nortel Networks Corporation in 2011, placing most of them in a new, jointly owned venture— Rockstar Consortium—to license them to others or to litigate over their use.[18]

Prior eras of capitalism—the industrial and mercantile—did not witness a split between reproduction and commodification, mainly because of the relatively low importance of intangibles in their time.[19] Reproduction and commodification could *both* occur within the corporate domain, as tangible resources—raw materials, labor, monetary and physical capital— were relatively easy to appropriate, control, and exploit, and were not as influenced by intangibles as they are now. This was obvious in the industrial enterprises that sprung up in the late nineteenth and early twentieth centuries. In the automotive industry, for example, vertical integration was the norm, with a single company controlling pretty much everything it needed, from raw material supply chains to the furnaces that made the steel it used, to the manufacturing of tires, transmissions, engines, and even the seats fitted in the vehicles.[20] Product chains were similarly under the control of the same company, and often included ownership of dealers, marketing, distribution channels, and even shipping logistics.[21] Tangible resources were at the core of all operations—given the overwhelming importance of factory production—and those resources could be both commodified and reproduced in-house. In the case of labor, for example, the reproduction of

---

18. Jones, "Patent 'Troll,'" B1.

19. See Hobsbawm, *Labouring Men,* and his *Age of Capital*; Stephen Meyer, *The Five Dollar Day: Labor Management and Social Control in the Ford Motor Company, 1908–1981* (Albany: State University of New York Press, 1981).

20. Ford Motor Company's River Rouge (Michigan) plant, for example, had all the equipment needed to turn raw materials into finished vehicles (the entire chain). It comprised sixteen million square feet of factory floor, one hundred miles of railroad track, its own docks for shipping, and employed about one hundred thousand workers. See, for example, Ford Motor Company, *The Ford Industries: Facts About the Ford Motor Company and Its Subsidiaries* (Detroit: Ford Motor Company, 1925), and its *Ford at Fifty: 1903–1950* (New York: Simon and Schuster, 1953); General Motors, *General Motors, The First 75 Years* (New York: Crown, 1983); Robert F. Freeland, *The Struggle for Control of the Modern Corporation: Organizational Change at General Motors, 1924–1970* (Cambridge: Cambridge University Press, 2001).

21. See Elizabeth Studer-Noguez, *Ford and the Global Strategies of Multinationals: The North American Auto Industry* (New York: Routledge, 2003); Ford, *Ford at Fifty*; Freeland, *Struggle for Control.*

skills could occur within the corporate domain, given the relatively simple tasks that were performed in the factories of that time.[22] Programming the reproduction of labor skills was an internal operation, with Frederick Taylor's "scientific management" and the piece rate system providing templates.[23]

Mass production, made possible by Taylor's ideas, helped keep reproduction in-house, by limiting the development of skills—as labor tasks were turned into mind-numbing, repetitive routines.[24] Creativity in factory production routines was unnecessary, and could easily become an enemy of production efficiency. Its potential disruption of production programs and the imposed protocols was a threat to managerial control, even when its exercise might enhance a product. Knowledge and experience were acquired and reproduced on the job, in-house, requiring little education and external influence. Their enhancement beyond the simple requirements of the job—the repetitive, physical actions that were so much a part of factory labor in those days—was also a potential threat to managerial control. Labor unions tried to fight this reality with very limited success, despite their victory in having child labor banned from the factory floor.[25]

Concentration, a key feature of oligopoly—and the fundamental importance of intangibles—makes it practically impossible to undertake both commodification and reproduction internally. The high concentration that is so characteristic of oligopolistic control often generates excessive scale, making operations more difficult to manage.[26] This can preempt

---

22. See, for example, Hobsbawm, *Labouring Men*; Sumner H. Slichter, *The Turnover of Factory Labor* (New York: Appleton, 1919); Philip S. Foner and David R. Roediger, *Our Own Time: A History of American Labor and the Working Day* (London: Verso, 1997).

23. See Frederick W. Taylor and Frank B. Copley, *Two Papers on Scientific Management: A Piece-Rate System and Notes on Belting* (London: Routledge, 1919); Robert Kanigel, *The One Best Way: Frederick Winslow Taylor and the Enigma of Efficiency* (New York: Viking, 1997). Templates based on Taylor's ideas and measures most of all enhanced managerial control, and eventually contributed to de-skilling—although they initially made it easier to reproduce labor skills internally. The piece-rate system, in particular, set the stage for a substantial de-skilling of factory work as labor was reduced to performing very simple tasks—an outcome denounced by Braverman in his *Labor and Monopoly Capital*.

24. See Meyer, *Five Dollar Day*; Freeland, *Struggle for Control*.

25. See, for example, Philip S. Foner, *History of the Labor Movement in the U.S.* (New York: International Publishers, 1987); Braverman, *Labor and Monopoly Capital*.

26. Even in the Japanese *keiretsu*—often presented as models of efficient management throughout the late twentieth century—large scale led to serious multiple problems involving coordination, distribution, product targeting, quality control, marketing, and research, among other areas; see, for example, Kenichi Miyashita and David Russell, *Keiretsu: Inside the Hidden Japanese Conglomerates* (New York: McGraw-Hill, 1994).

reproduction from occurring internally, even when the resources available within the corporate domain are substantial. One common strategy to try to overcome this problem is to spin off units—as separate companies that operate autonomously—which are owned and controlled by the oligopolistic parent.[27] Vertical disintegration of related operations is another strategy, which can occur in combination with spinoffs.[28] Outsourcing and offshoring, especially to subsidiaries located in lower cost locales or nations, are also often attempted to try to cope with this problem.[29] An atomization of units that belong to the same oligopolistic corporation may therefore result from these strategies, creating substantial coordination problems for the parent company. The usual outcome is even greater external dependence for reproduction—in the operations that are spun off, vertically disintegrated, or outsourced—since those enterprises are typically no more capable of reproducing intangibles on their own than the parent oligopolist.

Examples of this trend can be found throughout the oligopolistic spectrum, in most every sector. Pharmaceutical oligopolists, for example, try to overcome the difficulties of large scale—and of reproducing biotech research creativity—by spinning off research units as autonomous enterprises.[30] When they acquire biotech research companies—which are usually small—they very often maintain them as autonomous units or subsidiaries.[31]

---

27. Spinoffs were a fairly common tactic to try to induce intracorporate growth and reduce internal inefficiencies in the late twentieth century. See, for example, S. Shiva Ramu, *Restructuring and Break-Ups: Corporate Growth Through Divestitures, Spin-Offs, Split Ups, and Swaps* (Thousand Oaks, CA: Sage, 1999); Andrew S. Grove, "What Detroit Can Learn from Silicon Valley," *Wall Street Journal*, July 13, 2009, A13.

28. Networks are a common vehicle for this strategy. The emergence of Business-to-Business (B2B) networks after the start of the Web, in particular, helped this process; see, for example, Harry B. DeMaio, *B2B and Beyond: New Business Models Built on Trust* (New York: Wiley, 2001). Achievement of trust in B2B networks seems to depend more on the social (collective) exposure to peers provided by the network, than on bilateral arrangements between companies.

29. Offshoring by oligopolistic multinational corporations became noticed in the mid-twentieth century, as they expanded globally; see, for example, Stephen H. Hymer, *The Multinational Corporation: A Radical Approach* (New York: Cambridge University Press, 1979); Richard J. Barnet and Ronald E. Müller, *Global Reach: The Power of the Multinational Corporations* (New York: Simon and Schuster, 1974). See also Mary C. Lacity and Leslie Willcocks, *The Practice of Outsourcing* (London: Palgrave Macmillan, 2009).

30. See Ernst and Young LLP, *Beyond Borders: Global Biotechnology Report* (New York: Ernst and Young LLP, 2011 and various years); Jack W. Plunkett, *Plunkett's Biotech and Genetics Industry Almanac* (Houston: Plunkett Research, 2010 and various years), and his *Plunkett's Health Care Industry Almanac* (Houston: Plunkett Research, 2010 and various years).

31. In part, because this facilitates the discovery process; see, for example, Tamas Bartfai and Graham V. Lees, *Drug Discovery: From Bedside to Wall Street* (Burlington, VT: Elsevier, 2005).

Oligopolistic old-tech industries seem to be no less susceptible to this trend, and often depend on external networks to sustain spinoffs.[32] Automotive oligopolists, for example, try to cope with the difficulty of reproducing design creativity and knowledge by outsourcing design projects to small, specialized firms.[33] Research to create automotive technologies, such as electric or fuel-cell propulsion systems, is often carried out by smaller enterprises. Reproducing skills needed in factory and services production (as opposed to research) is no less problematic. To try to cope with the difficulty of reproducing labor skills, for example, automotive oligopolists typically outsource segments of the production chain to smaller subcontractors or to subsidiaries.[34] Similarly, service sector oligopolists often outsource training programs meant to enhance service production skills, to external firms or consultants—or to training centers outside their corporate domain—all of which are typically small, or at least much smaller than the subcontracting corporation. Although none of the smaller enterprises involved are able to reproduce intangibles on their own, they may nonetheless help if they can operate with greater flexibility, and can tie in more effectively with the kind of external societal networks that affect intangibles.

The high concentration that is a key feature of oligopolization is, in a dialectical sense, also a result of the corporate inability to control reproduction. The lack of control over reproduction induces concentration, as a way to protect accumulated power, generate growth and surplus value, and increase executive compensation. Influencing important external entities that help oligopolies sustain their power—such as capital and product markets, politics, and public governance—is a way of compensating for the loss of internal control over reproduction. Such influence is at the core of corporatocracy, and of the oligopolies' power over society. The resources that must be reproduced externally—such as creativity, knowledge, and skills—are, after all, a corporation's most precious asset. The lack of control over their reproduction is most unsettling to corporate power, since it creates much uncertainty and risk. Adding to this scenario of distress is the fact that the uncertainty and risk that accompany external reproduction are usually difficult to anticipate in any complete sense—given the qualitative nature of

32. See Suarez-Villa, "Networks as Mediators" and "Decomposing the Corporation," in *Technocapitalism*, 56–85 and, 86–122.

33. See Vincent P. Barabba, *Surviving Transformation: Lessons from GM's Surprising Turnaround* (New York: Oxford University Press, 2004); Studer-Noguez, *Ford and the Global Strategies*.

34. Particularly in large corporations; see, for example, Jack W. Plunkett, *Plunkett's Outsourcing and Offshoring Industry Almanac* (Houston: Plunkett Research, 2010 and various years).

intangibles. Their qualitative character makes it very difficulty to measure, control, value, or appropriate them, compared to tangible resources.

External networks, which are usually of great importance for the reproduction of intangibles, also provide another motive for oligopolistic concentration. External networks usually add to the uncertainty of reproduction—and to the risk of losing yet more control—by neutralizing or uprooting the links that remain between intangible resources and the oligopolistic corporate domain.[35] Greater concentration may thus seem necessary to an oligopolist in order to offset the loss of internal control, the risk, and the uncertainty of being dependent on external networks—for something as vital to corporate power as reproduction. Also, the larger the extent of an external network, the more challenges it poses for the corporate oligopolist.[36] These challenges typically involve, for example, greater complexity for coordinating external-internal interphases, a higher chance of failing to appropriate ideas that can be turned into intellectual property—if they are leaked or end up in the public domain—and the loss of highly skilled personnel. Larger external network extent can, however, be very positive because of the more diverse social influences that help regenerate and enrich intangibles, and because it can diffuse new ideas and methods more quickly and widely.

An example of how external networks can collapse corporate control over reproduction can be found in the case of Open Source networks, which are vital for reproducing creativity in such sectors as software, biotechnology, industrial design, engineering services, news media, and education, among others.[37] The usually large extent and nonproprietary character of such networks means that it is practically impossible for any oligopolistic corporation—no matter how large—or a combination of such corporations, to control them. Open Source networks, moreover, tend to be global, self-organizing, and fluid, with vast numbers of members who participate as their

---

35. Partly because hierarchies can be diluted or collapsed; see Suarez-Villa, "Networks as Mediators," in *Technocapitalism,* 67–72.

36. Larger network extent usually increases uncertainty and risk; see Suarez-Villa, "Network Extent," in *Technocapitalism,* 57–67.

37. See, for example, Janet Hope, *Biobazaar: The Open Source Revolution and Biotechnology* (Cambridge: Harvard University Press, 2008); "When Code Can Kill or Cure; Medical Technology: Applying the 'Open Source' Model to the Design of Medical Devices Promises to Increase Safety and Spur Innovation," *The Economist,* Technology Quarterly, June 2, 2012, 20–22; Johan Söderberg, *Hacking Capitalism: The Free and Open Software Movement* (New York: Routledge, 2007); Joseph M. Reagle, *Good Faith Collaboration: The Culture of Wikipedia* (Cambridge: MIT Press, 2010).

time allows, without set agendas, and with frequent changes in the topics that are pursued.[38] The fact that all work and ideas are shared freely for anyone to see, work on, or evaluate means that they are impossible for any oligopolist—or group of oligopolists—to appropriate. Also, innovations generated by Open Source networks immediately become part of the public domain, thus making it impossible for corporate power to stake any claim on them, even when their employees or workers participate.[39] Open Source networks are therefore outside the control of corporate power, and their trajectories tend to be dynamic and fluid—yet they are a very important vehicle for reproducing individual creativity, knowledge, and skills.

The loss of corporate control over reproduction, and the trend toward greater oligopolistic concentration, have also been affected by deindustrialization—a long-running phenomenon that has severely diminished the industrial base. Deindustrialization, coupled with automation and the offshoring of industrial jobs, reduced American manufacturing labor by almost one-quarter—relative to the total labor force—during the past five decades, despite the domestic emergence of high-tech industries in the 1970s and 1980s.[40] This phenomenon also contributed to disarticulate the economy, internally and structurally—as manufacturing disappeared. One result was the weakening of multiplier effects that induce growth between sectors during economic upswings, along with the stagnation of workers' incomes.[41] High tech sectors began to be affected shortly after their emergence, through the shift of assembly operations offshore.[42] Intense pressure to reduce costs,

---

38. Their fluidity, diverse uses, and seemingly chaotic character also make it very difficult for any one entity to influence them for long; see Axel Bruns, *Blogs, Wikipedia, Second Life, and Beyond: From Production to Produsage* (New York: Lang, 2008).

39. Corporations can, however, use the results of Open Source networks—even though this may preclude appropriation.

40. See Steven C. High and David W. Lewis, *Corporate Wasteland: The Landscape and Memory of Deindustralization* (Ithaca: ILR Press, Cornell University, 2007); Jefferson Cowie and Joseph Heathcott, *Beyond the Ruins: The Meanings of Deindustrialization* (Ithaca: ILR Press, Cornell University, 2003). For early accounts of this long-running phenomenon, based on insights from the 1970s, see Barry Bluestone and Bennett Harrison, *The Deindustrialization of America: Plant Closings, Community Abandonment, and the Dismantling of Basic Industry* (New York: Basic Books, 1982); John P. Hoerr, *And the Wolf Finally Came: The Decline of the American Steel Industry* (Pittsburgh: University of Pittsburgh Press, 1988).

41. See Richard Peet, "Contradictions of Finance Capitalism," *Monthly Review,* December 2011, 28–29.

42. See, for example, Andrew Ross, *Fast Boat to China: High-Tech Outsourcing and the Consequences of Free Trade; Lessons from Shanghai* (New York: Vintage, 2007).

coupled with the emergence of lower-cost manufacturing locales around the world, were major catalysts for this phenomenon. Also, the rapid oligopolization of high tech made it easier to offshore production, as larger companies could exercise greater influence on foreign authorities. Because of deindustrialization, intangibles—and their reproduction—gained greater importance in the industries that remained in the United States. Only some of the most intangible-dependent industrial jobs had any chance to avoid being swept out by deindustrialization and offshoring.[43] And, at the same time, the reproduction of skills in those jobs became ever more dependent on external social mediation, networks, and other societal influences that are largely out of corporate control. This increasing dependence on external social mediation for reproduction, in the remaining industries, influenced the tendency toward greater oligopolistic concentration—as a means to offset the loss of control over this most vital process of capitalism.

At the same time, deindustrialization placed greater weight on the need to influence politics, society, and public governance. Such influence became vital for oligopolistic, multinational corporations to keep government from trying to contain deindustrialization—through laws that might protect industrial jobs at home, for example.[44] For oligopolists, moving production capacity abroad—to lower-cost locales—became a way to try to offset the lack of internal control over reproduction at home. After all, the threat of offshoring jobs can be a powerful source of anxiety for employees, and can help limit the autonomy from corporate control that they may seek through external reproduction. The ineffectiveness of government-funded

---

43. Among the intangibles-dependent industrial job categories less likely to be lost was computer programming—especially for automated production systems. Many of the industrial job categories that remained were thus related to factory automation, directly or indirectly. Automation often advanced corporate control over workers whose occupations were not offshored, through the threat of job loss. This aspect tacitly played a prominent role in what David Noble refers to as the "machine design" aspect of automation; see Noble, "Social Choice in Machine Design," in *Forces of Production*, 79–194.

44. The so-called Washington Consensus, for example, was a prime sponsor of this corporate-inspired agenda, in the United States and abroad. "Integration" into the global trading system—based on flawed neoclassical economics–grounded rules that touted the superiority of free trade and favored corporate interests—became a fundamental argument. The creation of the World Trade Organization (WTO), an entity strongly supported by the Washington Consensus, was largely intended to impose rules based on this perspective. See, for example, Jan Kregel, "The Discrete Charm of the Washington Consensus," *Journal of Post-Keynesian Economics* 30 (2008): 541–60; Richard Peet, *Unholy Trinity: The IMF, World Bank, and WTO* (London: Zed, 2009).

efforts to retrain the unemployed, moreover, helped restrain employees from seeking more autonomy through external reproduction—given the likelihood of long-term unemployment should they lose their jobs.[45] Moving production abroad also became a means to increase surplus value and profit by lowering costs, and at the same time reduce the power of labor unions at home.[46] Unions, the historical archenemy of oligopolistic corporate power, would thus see their power severely diluted as deindustrialization gained momentum.[47] As a result, labor unions all too often caved in to oligopolistic demands—or had little to show in the end when they decided to strike.[48] In these respects, deindustrialization at home became an important ally of oligopolistic power, allowing the latter to offset some of the loss of control that external reproduction entailed.

The loss of control over reproduction also bolstered financialism, as production—the real economy—became more difficult and complex. External reproduction—an absolute necessity for corporate power to sustain production in our times—poses many challenges to corporate power, leading to greater uncertainty and risk, noted earlier. The casino economy that financialism fosters, on the other hand, seems relatively easy to engage

---

45. See, for example, Ianthe Jeanne Dugan and Justin Scheck, "US Faces Uphill Battle in Retraining the Jobless," *Wall Street Journal,* August 1, 2012, A1. Adding to this problem was the fact that legislation that required corporations to provide at least sixty days' advance notice of large-scale layoffs—the 1988 Worker Adjustment and Retraining Notification Act—was often sidestepped by issuing layoffs in small numbers over time. Also, only corporations planning to lay off five hundred or more employees were covered by this law, and those who had worked fewer than six months over a twelve-month period—or had worked fewer than twenty hours per week—were not covered; see U.S. Department of Labor, Employment and Training Administration, *The Worker Adjustment and Retraining Notification Act* (Washington, DC: Government Printing Office, 1988).

46. See Kim Moody, *An Injury to All: The Decline of American Unionism* (London: Verso, 1988); Michael Goldfield, *The Decline of Organized Labor in the United States* (Chicago: University of Chicago Press, 1987). The link between union decline and greater corporate profitability has often been overlooked.

47. The overwhelming power of oligopolistic corporations, and the declining well-being of the American labor force—partly because of the economic crisis that started in 2007—has, in recent times, raised awareness of the need for unions; see Michael Yates, *Why Unions Matter* (New York: Monthly Review Press, 2009).

48. As occurred, for example, in the case of strikes against Caterpillar, American Crystal Sugar, Lockheed Martin, AT&T, and Verizon—all oligopolies—during the first eight months of 2012. See Bob Tita and James R. Hagerty, "Caterpillar Union Bows to Demands," *Wall Street Journal,* August 18, 2012, B1.

in by comparison. The vast majority of betting schemes targeting the stock, bond, currency, and options markets, for example, are now easily automated using software robots to make decisions and execute trades.[49] More than three-quarters of all financial trades today are decided and executed in this way.[50] Derivatives are relatively easy to trade, in contrast to the operations of the real economy, and do not require any real understanding of their great complexity to do so—a curious contradiction that has attracted many people to financial speculation.[51] Easy credit, despite the mountains of debt it created, also enthroned financial speculation as the easier alternative to production. The high profile of financialism, and its takeover of almost every sector, can thus be considered a partial result of the growing complexity, uncertainty, and risk associated with the real economy—to which the severance of reproduction from commodification contributed greatly.

At this point, our consideration of this phenomenon must address its relationship with the larger panorama of capitalist accumulation. Pinpointing the differences between commodification and reproduction should also help us consider how their severance in the corporate domain is a source of contradictions and social pathology. Commodification involves corporate *appropriation* of a resource for the purpose of transforming it—through manufacturing or service production—such that a commercial transaction can eventually occur (involving exchange or sale), to obtain new money-capital. Appropriation—a necessary companion of commodification—typically involves control, if not outright ownership of a resource. Recalling the fundamental accumulation dynamic of capitalism introduced in the previous chapter—assuming oligopolistic conditions:

$$M \rightarrow C \rightarrow C' \rightarrow M^N, \text{ where } M^N = M + \Delta m + \Delta N$$

—where M represents the initial money-capital expended to purchase a commodity (C), such that production can be undertaken, C' is the product (or newly transformed commodity), M^N is the oligopolistic money-capital

---

49. See, for example, McTague, *Crapshoot Investing*; Bedford, *Trading Secrets*.

50. "High-Frequency Trading: The Fast and the Furious," Special Report on Financial Innovation, *The Economist*, February 25, 2012, 11–13; Bedford, *Trading Secrets*.

51. This contradiction also underlies the vast systemic risks they pose to the economy. See Dick Bryan and Michael Rafferty, *Capitalism with Derivatives: A Political Economy of Financial Derivatives, Capitalism, and Class* (New York: Palgrave Macmillan, 2006); Laurent L. Jacque, *Global Derivative Debacles: From Theory to Malpractice* (Singapore: World Scientific, 2010).

to be obtained from the exchange of the product, and ΔN represents the oligopolistic surplus received—beyond the surplus value (Δm) that would be obtained under competitive conditions. *Commodification therefore occurs when a commodity (or resource) is appropriated such that it can be transformed into a new commodity through manufacturing or service production* ($C \rightarrow C'$).[52] This dimension—appropriation and transformation through manufacturing or service production—also involves other operations that precede or occur concurrently with production, such as research and development (R&D) or design, which are vitally important to contemporary corporate capitalism.

Commodification of *tangible* resources involves simple appropriation, with money-capital (M) being used to purchase a commodity (C)—a raw material or labor, for example—such that corporate ownership or control over it can be established. The physical, quantitative, and measurable nature of tangible resources makes it easy for them to be appropriated, controlled, and programmed. Tangible resources are a known entity because of their inherent characteristics—and their usage is typically codified. They are also easy to safeguard, through measures that are grounded in their physical character. Well-defined standards and markets exist for them to be evaluated and priced—and their performance can usually be determined a priori with a high degree of certainty. This means that risk can be reduced greatly, provided they are adequately managed.[53]

The commodification of *intangible* resources—such as creativity, knowledge, experience—also involves appropriation. Their commodification is complex, however, because of their qualitative character. Also, markets for intangibles often do not exist, are not well established, or cannot provide codified ways to evaluate the resources involved. Because of these features, corporate control is usually difficult or practically impossible to impose with much certainty. The qualitative nature of intangibles therefore translates into elusiveness and uncertainty—as well as risk. Corporate power tries to reduce the inherent uncertainty and risk of appropriation, by trying to standardize

---

52. For the earliest conceptual insights on commodification see Karl Marx, *Grundrisse: Foundations of the Critique of Political Economy* (New York: Penguin, 1973; orig. published as *Grundrisse der Kritik der Politischen Ökonomie*, 1939), 140–53—this work was based on Notebooks I and II, dating from 1857–58. See also Marx, *Capital*, Vol. I, ch. 1.

53. Management that usually involves precise evaluations of quantity, quality, and process of transformation. The origins of many management practices involving tangible resources can be traced to late-nineteenth and early-twentieth-century efforts to systematize production. See, for example, Kanigel, *One Best Way*; Dan Clawson, *Bureaucracy and the Labor Process: The Transformation of U.S. Industry, 1860–1920* (New York: Monthly Review Press, 1980).

or codify them as much as possible. This effort, however, often shortchanges intangibles and can be self-defeating, especially when rare human qualities are involved. Such qualities typically depend on larger influences that are external to the corporate domain, and almost any attempt by corporate power to seize or program them often impairs their quality.[54]

In the case of creativity, for example—an intangible resource that depends greatly on external social mediation—corporate power tries to appropriate it by imposing employment contracts that severely restrict sharing. The covenants—which are now commonplace—dictate terms that prohibit employees' disclosure of any new ideas, methods, processes, tools, gadgets, or formulas, which typically make up an invention or innovation and result from the exercise of their creativity.[55] Such restrictions usually also cover any results obtained by an employee outside the corporate domain, even when the exercise of creativity involves resources not provided or not owned by the employer. Collaborating with others outside the corporate domain—who are not in any way connected to the employer—is also typically prohibited, especially when the exercise of creativity involves any products or services that can be remotely associated with what the employee does within the corporate realm—or that result in intellectual property (such as a patent award). This means that any and all intellectual property awarded to the employee must be signed over to the employer. Violations of such contracts result in firings and tacit blacklisting among a corporations' affiliates, suppliers, or subsidiaries (and in many cases also competitors), and effectively end careers. Those contracts and prohibitions usually shortchange employees' creativity, skills development, knowledge, or experience, and are counterproductive—even for the corporate employer—but are nonetheless imposed to try to appropriate creativity, a most precious resource for the corporate oligopolies of our time.

Commodification of both tangibles and intangibles involves several steps, which are important for our understanding of the split between reproduction and commodification. *Structuring* the operations that must transform the appropriated resources (tangible or intangible) is one step. Those operations involve production (manufacturing or services), but can also comprise

---

54. Programming often involves imposing analytical templates. See, for example, David Rosenberg, "The Brainstormer," *Wall Street Journal,* May 13, 2002, R14; Jacob Goldenberg, David Mazursky, and Sorin Solomon, "Creative Sparks," *Science* 285 (September 3, 1999): 1495–96.

55. Employment contracts typically reinforce corporate appropriation, beyond and above the tendency of intellectual property rights and laws to favor corporate power; see Perelman, *Steal This Idea.*

research, design, or any combination of them. In production they typically comprise organizing assembly or refinement routines, supply logistics, quality controls, and the features of the products or services to be provided. In research they may involve, for example, the elaboration of experiments, testing, or the interpretation of results.[56] Design usually involves the reconceptualization of an existing product or service, or the creation of a new one—targeting its styling, packaging, or functional operation. Research and design may work closely together, depending on the targeted product or service.

Fragmentation and compartmentalization of production, research, or design operations is of fundamental importance, to reduce uncertainty and impose managerial control. Fragmentation typically involves splitting up activities and routines in order to structure a production process, such that control can be established. Compartmentalization encompasses the systemic organization of fragmented activities and routines into operational units. Such units usually form part of a larger system of production—in manufacturing or services—and become essentially important for achieving a specified objective—the transformation of C into C' being the overarching priority. An important companion of fragmentation and compartmentalization is systematization. Systematization aims at ensuring that compartmentalization will achieve its specified objective within a definite period of time. Systematization also typically requires standardization, to reduce uncertainty and improve the measurability of all aspects—such that performance can be determined. The larger aim of systematization is to therefore produce a steady stream of output (new commodities or C')—with a predetermined level of performance—that can be ultimately exchanged for new money-capital (M^N) in the shortest possible time.

Systematization, an essential component of commodification, however, usually shortchanges intangibles—most of all, creativity. The regimentation it introduces—and the rigidities it imposes—are often lethal for this most precious of resources. Also, systematization and its byproduct—standardization—typically reflect the relations of power between corporate management and employees.[57] Corporate power favors systematization and standardization in order to obtain new money-capital (M^N) as rapidly as

---

56. See Suarez-Villa, "Creativity as a Commodity," in *Technocapitalism*, 31–55.

57. Relations of power that typically favor managerial priorities—embedded as rules and technical protocols in production processes—over which employees have little or no control. Historically, those rules sought to implement criteria—greater efficiency being most commonly cited—formulated by "experts" hired by corporate management, to further its control. See Braverman, *Labor and Monopoly Capital*; Clawson, *Bureaucracy and the Labor Process*; Kanigel, *One Best Way*.

possible. Employees, however, might—if allowed to decide on their own—opt for ways that exercise more of their creativity, and that can be more fulfilling—but which create more risk and uncertainty for corporate management. Projects that require cross-fertilization of ideas and substantial experimentation are an example.[58] This is often the case in research, and it involves creativity, experience, and accumulating more knowledge—all of which are important for employees' self-development and their enjoyment of work—but which complicate the overarching corporate objective of obtaining new money-capital. Management also often places inter-employee competition over collaboration, as a means to sustain its control over the corporate domain—even though collaboration may be more self-fulfilling and may allow employees to exercise more of their creativity, knowledge, and experience. As a result, the intrinsic rewards of creative endeavors, skills deployment, experience gains, knowledge accumulation, and other aspects of self-development are often shortchanged—partially or completely.

The three component features of the first step—fragmentation, compartmentalization, systematization—influence greatly how commodification is structured. They help provide a supportive platform upon which specific production tasks and activities are built. Without them, appropriation of a commodity would yield few results and, most likely, the production process embedded in $C \rightarrow C'$ would fail. Appropriation of a commodity or resource must therefore be followed by the structuring of production, such that a commodity (C) can be transformed, and a new commodity (C') eventually produced and exchanged for new money-capital (M^N) in a specified period of time. The amount of the new money-capital must cover the initial money-capital (M) expended in order to sustain production. Under oligopolistic conditions, however, the new money-capital can be expected to eventually yield a surplus ($\Delta m + \Delta N$), thus allowing the oligopolist to secure a profit and expand a new cycle of production—if all or part of the profit is reinvested. In this regard, the oligopolistic surplus (ΔN) is particularly important, as it reduces uncertainty and risk involving production. Continuity in production is essential, and this dynamic typically occurs without interruption.

---

58. Particularly those that require multidisciplinary approaches, and must depend on open, cross-consultation among people in diverse specialties—including those outside the corporate domain. Such approaches have been shown to be effective in dealing with complex research problems; see, for example, Julie T. Klein, *Transdisciplinarity: Joint Problem Solving Among Science, Technology, and Society; An Effective Way for Managing Complexity* (Basel: Birkhäuser, 2001).

A second step of commodification involves the *disengagement* of fragmented aspects of production (including research, design, and other activities related to production within the corporate domain) from their authors—from employees, in other words. This is a key aspect of commodification, without which corporate power cannot establish appropriation. Those fragmented aspects and components of production (and of research or design) are assembled as "products" (manufactured or service) that are typically tied to corporate "brands." They are thus taken over by corporate power, regardless of whether they are tangible—physical products—or intangible—services, new ideas, intellectual property, designs—and become disengaged from those who created them. Through corporate appropriation, they take an existence that is independent from the production—or the research and design—processes, and from the individuals who created them. The end result for those individuals who exercised their skills, creativity, knowledge, and experience is alienation. Alienation from the results of their work, and from the results of the exercise of their creativity, knowledge, skills, and experience—the intangibles that are central to production in our time.[59]

The third step of commodification involves *exchange,* to turn the new commodity (C') into new money-capital (M^N). Exchange is expected to generate a surplus ($\Delta m + \Delta N$)—an outcome that gains greater certainty under oligopolistic conditions, as pricing and capacity controls are applied.[60] At the very least, the exchange of the new commodity must generate an amount

---

59. Alienation, however, has a broader meaning within the context and reality of capitalism. See Bertell Ollman, *Alienation: Marx's Conception of Man in Capitalist Society* (Cambridge: Cambridge University Press, 1977). The social alienation of those who provide intangibles such as creativity and new knowledge is in many ways analogous to that found among industrial workers in Marx's writings—even though the settings, tools, and context are markedly different.

60. The surplus (in this case surplus value *and* the oligopolistic surplus) is often considered analogous to profit. Conceptually, however, the definition of the surplus is broader than that of profit. See Marx, *Grundrisse,* 381–86, 549–602—Marx's notes in this work, originally drafted in 1857–58, were the basis of his discussion on surplus value in *Capital,* parts III, IV, and V. Marx defined two types of surplus value: *absolute* and *relative*—the absolute kind being generated by structuring production processes such that employees are forced to work harder and longer for the same wage. In this case, a productivity increase occurs without any additional compensation for the worker—while the capitalist appropriates the results of the unpaid additional work and productivity. Relative surplus value is generated by modifying the division of labor—restructuring the organization—of production, a tactic that often leads to greater specialization. Relative surplus value can also be generated by equipping employees with more efficient tools (this can include new technology), or by providing training to acquire more skills and knowledge.

equivalent to the initial money-capital (M) used to acquire a commodity (C) and undertake production—if losses are to be avoided. Market exchange is therefore at the core of this final step of commodification. Any notion that "free" markets rule this step must be dispelled, however, since oligopolists can easily influence or determine pricing through capacity controls. Greater relative scarcity can thus be generated by throttling production whenever demand slackens in order to sustain prices—and generate the oligopolistic surplus (ΔN) that virtually guarantees a profit. Much the same tactic can be pursued whenever the oligopolist seeks to increase the price of the new commodity—a scenario that is typically welcomed by other oligopolists, as it will most likely also increase their surpluses. Whenever this occurs, follow-the-leader price increases can be expected. Purchasers of the new commodity thereby end up disadvantaged, as the lack of price competition guarantees that they will have to pay more. In addition, the new owners of the product or service (the new commodity C') that is exchanged typically bear no relationship whatsoever to those who created it—the employees and workers engaged in production, research, or design. The result is further alienation of creators from the product and from the production (or research and design) process involved—a trajectory that started with the corporate appropriation of their talents, skills, knowledge, experience, and labor.

Underlying the three steps of commodification is the fundamental corporate need to recreate the dynamic of accumulation—$M \rightarrow C \rightarrow C' \rightarrow M^N$—such that the production cycle can continue indefinitely. *This fundamental cyclical dynamic is at the core of capitalist accumulation.* For corporate oligopolies, it is as essential as it is for any corporation, but their power and size makes it all the more important that it operate continuously. Any interruption (or major diminution) of the cycle translates into crisis—particularly if the breakdown is long lasting—as might occur during depressions.[61] Recalling from the previous chapter, this cyclical dynamic—so vital for capitalism—is largely collapsed by financialism, which turns it into M_f

---

61. Crises, in the form of depressions and prolonged, deep recessions can trigger major overhauls of capitalism, as occurred during the Great Depression in the United States. Crises can be triggered by a systemic breakdown of the accumulative dynamic, whenever sufficient new money-capital fails to be generated to cover the initial money-capital needed to start a new productive cycle—over the long term. Profit rates in that scenario—under both competitive and oligopolistic conditions—can be expected to decline. Ernest Mandel's work on long waves showed that long-term tendencies in the rate of profit—rather than free markets—are decisive in triggering downturns. See Ernest Mandel, *Long Waves of Capitalist Development* (Cambridge: Cambridge University Press, 1980).

$\rightarrow M^F_f$—thus voiding production. Commodification is therefore eliminated through financialism, and what takes place is mere appropriation of money to generate more money through speculation—or, using paper money to obtain more paper money.

Whereas appropriation is central to commodification, *reproduction involves the regeneration of resources, such that production can occur.* Reproduction is an essential and inevitable companion of commodification—without *both* of these processes, production cannot be sustained. Accumulation is also vital for reproduction, since resources that are regenerated—especially intangibles—typically gain value as they accumulate. The compounding of that value—which accumulation allows—often determines, for example, whether a corporation that produces much the same kind of product as another can gain a qualitative advantage and establish a niche for its product. Such qualitative advantages are often important for oligopoly formation—as securing a market niche can provide sufficient surplus to not only sustain or expand the productive cycle, but also to acquire competitors and set up entry barriers. Reproduction is therefore fundamental to corporate power, to its control over production, and to its ability to sustain the accumulative dynamic—$M \rightarrow C \rightarrow C' \rightarrow M^N$—which is at the core of capitalism. The meaning of reproduction used here corresponds with that of expanded reproduction in Marxian political economy—as opposed to simple reproduction.[62] Marx's original use of the term *reproduction* referred to capital—and in the case of expanded reproduction it referred to growth and the reinvestment of the surplus—such that the accumulative dynamic can be sustained.

In its original usage, reproduction targeted a tangible resource—money-capital (M). Because of its fundamental importance in Marx's analysis of capitalist production, this tangible resource took center stage. At that time—the mid-nineteenth century—money-capital was the most scarce resource, and it was also the one element that made capitalism distinctive from previous socioeconomic modes. Oligopolies and monopolies were not yet part of the economic reality. Intangibles, by comparison, were relatively unimportant at that time. The factory system of that era—focused almost entirely on production and on tangible resources—made it possible for both

---

62. See Marx, *Capital,* Vol. I, ch. 23 ("Simple Reproduction"), and Vol. II, Part III, chs. 18–21 (particularly chapter 20, "Simple Reproduction," and chapter 21, "Accumulation and Reproduction on an Extended Scale"—the term *extended* here refers to Expanded Reproduction).

reproduction and commodification to occur internally, within the corporate domain. In that context, reproduction of capital was the prime concern of corporate power.[63]

Insofar as tangible resources—other than money capital—are concerned, how reproduction addresses their regeneration and accumulation depends on their use in production. With physical (nonmonetary) capital, for example, reproduction deals with the expansion, renovation, or reconfiguration of buildings, facilities, and equipment used in production. The accumulation of physical capital is vital for production and is especially relevant to operational scale. Larger scale—a hallmark of oligopolistic power—thus typically requires greater accumulation of physical capital, while such capital also acquires greater importance in sustaining production. Almost every production regime in existence today depends on a timely accumulation of physical capital. Shortfalls in the accumulation of this vital tangible resource would force a company to depend on others—subcontractors, for example—to increase or sustain production. In the case of physical labor, reproduction involves the regeneration of the capacity to work, such that it can be deployed in production as continuously as possible. Such regeneration is achieved by limiting the amount of working time, and by providing the support (internal and external) to sustain a certain living standard such that work can be effectively accomplished.[64] Accumulation for this important tangible resource refers to the amount of physical labor employed, such that a certain level of production can be sustained. Raw materials are typically expended in production, and reproduction in this case refers to any byproducts—of raw materials used in production, in the form of physical matter, gases, liquids—that can be reused in some form to sustain production. The recycling of raw materials embedded in products that can be reused in production may also be considered part of reproduction—in the sense that it helps sustain production by replenishing the stock of raw material inputs.

The reproduction of intangible resources—such as creativity, knowledge, experience—involves recurrent regeneration, such that they can be

---

63. See, for example, Hobsbawm, *Age of Capital*.

64. Marx discussed in *Capital* the important (but subjective) nature of the "subsistence wage" as a socially necessary cost for the capitalist employer to sustain production; see Marx, *Capital*, Vol. I, Part VI, "Wages." In the context of contemporary capitalism, we have seen how oligopolistic corporate power tries to reduce that "socially necessary cost" as much as possible, by shifting production abroad, eliminating labor unions, using interns and temporary workers, and otherwise reducing benefits.

recreated, deployed, and exercised continuously. Their exercise in production (or in related functions, such as research and design) is of fundamental importance for the accumulative dynamic. Oligopolistic corporations are more dependent than ever on such resources to sustain their power. *Intangibles such as creativity and knowledge are usually decisive in a crucial area where oligopolistic corporations do compete with one another—technology.* Invention and innovation—in products and production processes, or in design—are all too often the key to sustaining oligopolistic control over a market niche. *An oligopolist's unassailable control over pricing is thus usually due to the quality of its technology—and the inventive and innovative creativity of the research and design operations that drive it.* Superb quality control and highly efficient manufacturing are of little help if an oligopolist's product technology is obsolete—or is surpassed by that of a competing oligopolist.

For this reason, the reproduction of intangible resources is of paramount importance to an oligopolistic corporation. Reproduction of intangibles today typically occurs through *social mediation outside the corporate domain*, and is therefore largely out of the control of corporate power. *Social relations and the societal context thus acquire vital importance, and how strong a role they play in reproduction influence greatly the quality of the intangibles used to support the productive operations embedded in C →* C'. On this key aspect of our contemporary reality rides the severance of reproduction from commodification—one becoming largely external to the corporate domain while the other remains internal. This is a phenomenon of contemporary advanced capitalism and of the evolution of its accumulative dynamic, and cannot be considered a result of the three-decades-old neoliberal era—although neoliberal policies have no doubt influenced it. For oligopolistic corporations, so accustomed to exercising power over entire sectors or market niches, this phenomenon is as unsettling as it is difficult (if not impossible) to resolve. Partly because of this phenomenon, oligopolistic power tries to accumulate intangibles rapidly and voraciously—an example being the widespread hoarding of intellectual property and the creation of subsidiaries exclusively dedicated to that purpose.

The accumulation of intangibles is thus also of crucial importance for oligopolistic corporate power. Accumulating intangibles has become a new form of accumulation in its own right—an aspect I addressed in another book.[65] A major contributor was the massification of higher education that started in the late 1940s, through the creation and expansion of public

---

65. See Suarez-Villa, "Fast Accumulation," in *Globalization and Technocapitalism*, 44–54.

university systems—a phenomenon that is now threatened by declining access, rapidly rising tuition, and privatization. Massive investments in educational infrastructure over five decades accompanied this phenomenon—involving a vast array of facilities that support education, directly or indirectly.[66] These investments have benefited corporations—most of all, oligopolies—immensely, since it is society at large that pays for their vast, cumulative cost.[67] Large investments in higher education over such a long period of time made it possible for two new accumulative modes to emerge—the accumulation of tacit knowledge and of codified knowledge—as noted in a previous book.[68] These two modes have been at the core of two fundamentally important intangibles for contemporary corporate capitalism—creativity and new knowledge. Invention and innovation depend immensely on these two intangibles—without them, the emergence of high technology sectors, and the resulting (high tech) oligopolies that began to form in the late 1970s, would not have been possible. Emerging new technologies—in biotechnology, nanotechnology, biopharmacology, advanced software, bioinformatics, for example—depend greatly on them.[69] One result—intimately related to the overwhelming importance of intangibles—is the emergence of intellectual property as a major corporate property

---

66. For intangibles, the creation and expansion of public research university systems was particularly important. A hierarchy of universities developed in the United States since the early 1950s, with many of the new public university systems rising to the higher levels of the academic pyramid—in relatively short periods of time. See Hugh D. Graham and Nancy Diamond, *The Rise of American Research Universities: Elites and Challengers in the Postwar Era* (Baltimore: Johns Hopkins University Press, 2004). Nonetheless, the post-1950s era of university expansion in the United States was preceded by an earlier—and little known—period of growth in higher education that coincided with the emergence of oligopolies; see Clyde W. Barrow, *Universities and the Capitalist State: Corporate Liberalism and the Reconstruction of American Higher Education, 1894–1928* (Madison: University of Wisconsin Press, 1990).

67. American universities—and U.S. higher education in general—have also internalized many aspects of oligopolistic corporate culture; see, for example, Sheila Slaughter and Larry L. Leslie, *Academic Capitalism: Politics, Policies, and the Entrepreneurial University* (Baltimore: Johns Hopkins University Press, 1997); Marc Bousquet, *How the University Works: Higher Education and the Low-Wage Nation* (New York: New York University Press, 2008). The spread of oligopolistic corporate power has largely helped turn higher education into a commodity, in order to make it more malleable and attuned to its interests; see, for example, Wesley Shumar, *College for Sale: A Critique of the Commodification of Higher Education* (Washington: Falmer Press, 1997).

68. See Suarez-Villa, *Globalization and Technocapitalism*, 44–54.

69. See Suarez-Villa, "Creativity as a Commodity," in *Technocapitalism*, 31–55.

right. For most oligopolistic corporations, intellectual property has become the single most important type of property they can own—reflected in the dramatic increase of intellectual property litigation in recent times.[70]

The reproduction and accumulation of intangibles are influenced greatly by three factors that are external to the corporate domain. All of them involve social mediation on a large scale—the kind that only society can provide. *Networks* are one factor, and are especially important for acquiring and sustaining access to tacit knowledge—the cornerstone of individual and group creativity. Networks also play a vital role in providing access to the kind of social mediation that allows sharing, counsel, and collaboration—all of which are crucially important for creativity and knowledge. Open Source networks, for example—which lie typically outside of corporate control—can play a major role in this regard. Such networks can also help employees gain greater independence from their corporate employers—and serve as vehicles to switch employment. The worldwide spread of communication networks—made possible by digitization, the Internet, and the Web—provides speed and multidimensional interactions that cut across hierarchies, making it easier for social mediation to enlarge its scope and scale.[71] Although none of these aspects is necessarily inimical to oligopolistic power, the fact that mediation networks can operate independently from its control is a major source of concern.

A second factor is *social legitimation*. Legitimacy is important for reproduction, because it provides vital social, psychological, and moral support to those who exercise intangibles—most of all, creativity. Social legitimation can occur in numerous ways, especially when networks are utilized. Among the various sources of legitimation are professional communities, which can provide support and help form alliances to collaborate. Collaboration is often vital for regenerating creativity, since it often leads to the cross-fertilization of ideas—a frequent vehicle to create new methods, tools, or processes.[72] Forming coalitions is another means to obtain social legitimation. Coalitions often lead to the creation of interest groups that can promote collectively beneficial objectives—such as lobbying for rights,

---

70. See, for example, Perelman, *Steal Ihis Idea*; Clark and Raice, "Tech Firms Intensify"; Jones and Vascellaro, "Patent War Flares"; Vandana Shiva, *Protect or Plunder? Understanding Intellectual Property Rights* (London: Zed, 2001).

71. The dualistic character of networks can also counter social mediation in some situations; see Suarez-Villa, "Networks as Mediators," in *Technocapitalism*, 56–85.

72. See Klein, *Transdisciplinarity*.

protection of employees' intellectual property, exposure of abuses, or the formulation of rules that safeguard the public interest. All of these aspects pose threats or limitations to oligopolistic control over employees who, after all, are the providers of creativity and knowledge.

The third factor affecting the reproduction and accumulation of intangibles operates at the *individual* level and involves social influences on how an individual works, and on attitudes toward others—especially those who exercise similar skills—and toward the exercise of intangibles in general. With this factor, interpersonal relations, interaction, counsel, and self-realization—aspects that are greatly influenced by social mediation— help develop certain qualities, such as persistence in the face of adversity, personal discipline, and methodical ways of exercising skills. These qualities are important in regenerating and developing intangibles at the individual level. They help sustain creativity and the motivation to acquire new knowledge. Social mediation at the individual dimension is also influenced by institutions that support skills development, such as schools, universities, and training centers. Social networks can, as in so many other aspects, also play an important role, as in the case of Open Source network collaboration and their positive influence on creative self-development and skills training.[73]

One observation emerging out of this discussion of reproduction and commodification is how different these two fundamental processes are from each other. One—reproduction—is inherently external, depending on societal mediation to be fulfilled, while the other—commodification—is internal to the corporate domain and depends on corporate control. This creates a major problem for corporate power, since it impedes the accumulative dynamic represented by $M \rightarrow C \rightarrow C' \rightarrow M^N$. At the very least, it involves a serious complication—which makes the production of new commodities (C') more uncertain and risky. At its worst, it can collapse the accumulative dynamic—by making it impossible to manage transformation in effective or timely ways. The transformation of commodities, embedded in $C \rightarrow C'$—the production process and related activities—is where reproduction and commodification must come together if there are to be any products that can be exchanged. Yet, that is precisely where these two vital processes come apart and generate major contradictions, not only for oligopolistic power but also for society at large.

---

73. An important feature of such networks is that collaborative work is freely and openly shared between participants—and with the rest of society. See Söderberg, *Hacking Capitalism*.

Outlining how these processes evolve within C → C' can illustrate their differences, and the contradictions they generate for corporate power, especially oligopolies. *Reproduction* can be outlined as: C → Social mediation → Regeneration and accumulation → Transformed commodity (partial), with social mediation playing a most important role once a commodity (C) is obtained. This applies most strongly to the case of intangibles—such as creativity and tacit knowledge—that typically cannot be reproduced internally within the corporate domain. *Commodification,* on the other hand, can be outlined as: C → Appropriation → Structuring and disengagement → Transformed commodity (partial), with internal management playing a major role. Here, appropriation refers to the capacity to actually take over a resource, such that its transformation can be structured. It does not necessarily refer to the acquisition of a resource or commodity (C)—the transaction embedded in M → C—which involves purchase for ownership or for license to use (as in the case of leasing and employment). Structuring and disengagement are essential components of a managerial regime—the apparatus of control, rules and procedures under which production occurs. Clearly, *neither of these strands can complete the process of transformation on its own,* such that a new commodity (C') can emerge. A product or service cannot be created and exchanged, therefore, so long as transformation remains incomplete.

The completion of that transformation is of utmost importance for corporate survival, most of all, for large-scale enterprises which have much capital and other resources tied up with it. Without its completion, there can be no exchange—C' → M^N—such that new money capital can be obtained. A breakdown of C → C' therefore entails failure for corporate power—of its essential rationale for existence, which is the sustenance of accumulation. For oligopolies, a failure of the accumulative dynamic has the most severe consequences, since the entire apparatus of concentration and control can come crumbling down. *The very existence of the corporatocratic state is also placed at risk by a failure of the accumulative dynamic, given the overwhelming influence of oligopolies. And, to the extent that the state must step in to sustain it—through bailouts and assorted forms of corporate welfare—public governance also becomes engulfed in crisis.*

Research, a most important component of contemporary corporate capitalism, is embedded in C → C'. Invention, innovation, and the creation of new technologies have largely become outcomes of oligopolistic corporate research—as individual invention declined during the last six decades. Also, the research productivity of small and medium-size companies became less significant, as oligopolies acquired a vast number of them—merging their research operations with their own. Alternatively, some medium-size companies grew and attained oligopolistic power—acquiring small, research-oriented companies in the process. Because of the great importance of research today, a breakdown of the accumulative cycle has major implications for technology. New technologies created through C → C' are fundamental for accomplishing the "constant revolutionizing of production" that Marx considered to be a major feature of capitalism.[74] Joseph Schumpeter—tacitly following up on Marx's observation more than a half-century later—placed innovation at the core of economic transformation, triggering what he thought to be a process of "creative destruction" that swept away established sectors and made it possible for new ones to emerge.[75] Schumpeter assumed that waves of innovations could transform economies "from within" (endogenously)—with oligopolies as the most likely agents of that transformation. He also assumed that rivalries between oligopolists would create the need to innovate, and that any failure to do so would weaken their power. These arguments point to the fundamental need for transformation (C → C') to be completed—research, invention, and innovation included—in order to sustain the accumulative dynamic.

The severance of reproduction from commodification therefore poses a most difficult challenge to corporate power. Not only does it generate the real possibility of failure for the accumulative dynamic, but it also creates the conditions for major societal dysfunctions. *Those dysfunctions are different from the ones generated by financialism—and possibly also less visible—but in some ways they are more difficult because they are grounded in the real economy.* This makes them all the more critical for public governance, as the real economy seems to be the only one that can sustain capitalism over the long term. And, the real economy is crucial for corporatocracy's survival. The breakdown of a fundamental aspect of the accumulative dynamic— the process of transformation embedded in C → C'—therefore becomes potentially catastrophic.

---

74. Marx, *Grundrisse*, 85–88; Karl Marx and Friedrich Engels, *The Communist Manifesto* (New York: Monthly Review Press, 1964), 7.

75. Schumpeter, *Capitalism, Socialism, and Democracy,* 83, 87–106; John Bellamy Foster, "Theories of Capitalist Transformation: Critical Notes on the Comparison of Marx and Schumpeter," *Quarterly Journal of Economics* 98 (1983): 327–31; John Bellamy Foster, Robert W. McChesney, and R. Jamil Jonna, "Monopoly and Competition in Twenty-First Century Capitalism," *Monthly Review,* April 2011, 18.

The dysfunctions generated by the split between reproduction and commodification can be grouped into several categories. All of them are sources of crisis, not only for public governance but also for society at large. *The first and most prominent dysfunction is the all-important quest of corporate oligopolies to control public governance.* This is a partial outcome of the failure to control reproduction and to sustain it in-house—within the corporate domain. This loss of control over a fundamental aspect of accumulation creates a most disturbing situation for oligopolistic corporate power, which it tries to overcome by increasing its influence over government. *Oligopolistic influence over public governance results in a shift of risk to the state,* which involves not only the growth of spending to unsustainable levels but also the setting of corporate needs as the uppermost priority of governance.[76] Thus, failing to control reproduction, corporate oligopolies turn to control public governance as a way to safeguard their power. *This dysfunction is at the core of the crisis of the state—and of its pathologies.* Greater control over government means that regulations, laws, and institutions must be largely aligned with, and subservient to, the interests of the oligopolies. *The ultimate objective of this game of influence is to make society—and its governance—"safe" for oligopolistic corporate power.*

This objective is at the heart of corporatocracy. Lobbying, political contributions, and the "revolving door" mechanisms of corporate influence, discussed in an earlier chapter, are the common vehicles. The vast amounts spent on lobbying annually in the United States are now larger than the gross economic product of many nations. The large sums given as political contributions, directly and indirectly, are also larger than most government budgets around the world. Clearly, the sustenance of corporatocracy has turned into an industry of sorts, in its own right. Corporate oligopolies are at the heart of these vehicles, with the vast amounts of money they contribute—and the high stakes they have in making sure public governance becomes an appendage of their power. This is a collective interest on the part of corporate oligopolies—one that stands above any rivalries. Their collective interest, as a group, is therefore what is really at stake, over and above the narrow interests of any specific actor.

A second source of dysfunction generated by the split between reproduction and commodification is the effort to align the interests of the population with

---

76. A situation foreseen by James O'Connor in his *Corporations and the State: Essays in the Theory of Capitalism and Imperialism* (New York: Harper Colophon, 1974) and *The Fiscal Crisis of the State* (New York: St. Martin's Press, 1973).

those of oligopolistic corporate power. Making everyone's well-being dependent on corporate power's fortunes is at the heart of this vehicle. The casino economy of financialism proved to be a formidable tool for this purpose, making stock markets the prime betting venue of the United States and much of the world. Stock markets are, after all, where corporate oligopolies get most of their capital to support their games of power and hegemony. Eliminating conventional pensions—and tying old-age support to corporate performance in the stock market—was only the first step in this direction. Getting many individuals into stock market betting on their own—to try to make a living out of it—was another. Getting much of the public to accept, tacitly or not, that massive corporate contributions to politics—and having politicians serve corporate interests above all—are part of "democracy" was also very important. Clearly, this was a masterful—and largely successful—operation, orchestrated through three decades of neoliberal propaganda, corporatist indoctrination, the gullibility and greed of many who simply followed and questioned nothing, and the legions of corrupt (but law-abiding) politicians who were all too eager to uphold corporate interests as their uppermost priority.

In the mid-1970s (shortly before the start of the neoliberal era), two business school academics—neoclassical economists both—came up with a concept known as "agency theory."[77] This concept, which would become a major tool and justifier of neoliberal measures—and of corporate hegemony—tried to show that shareholders' interests are best served when theirs and those of corporate management are perfectly aligned.[78] The "alignment" rested on the notion that management—much like politicians in a corporatocracy—should act solely as "agents." Extrapolating agency theory to the case of corporatocracy, *the interests of politicians—the agents—are to be aligned with those of oligopolistic corporate power.* And, much as profit optimization was stipulated by agency theory to be the uppermost objective of agent-managers, so optimizing the interests of the oligopolies who own corporatocratic governance would be the main objective of the agent-politicians.

---

77. Michael C. Jensen and William H. Meckling, "Theory of the Firm: Managerial Behavior, Agency Costs, and Ownership Structure," *Journal of Financial Economics* 3 (1976): 305–60.

78. In spite the fact that shareholders are not actually owners of a corporation—they merely own shares and only have a claim to a portion of the profits. And that following the recipes prescribed by agency theory often harms a corporation's employees and the public; see Lynn Stout, *The Shareholder Value Myth: How Putting Shareholders First Harms Investors, Corporations, and the Public* (San Francisco: Berrett-Koehler, 2012); Suarez-Villa, *Technocapitalism,* 114–15.

Much of what goes on in a corporatocracy may thus be considered an application of agency theory on a grand scale—on steroids, in a manner of speaking, involving society at large—where agent-politicians' interests must be aligned with those of the owners of public governance—the corporate oligopolies. The extrapolation of agency theory's interest-alignment vision to corporatocracy thus requires *the additional alignment of the interests of the public at large with those of the corporate oligopolies that rule over public governance.* Such an alignment has been a major element in the rise of financialism, noted in the previous chapter, and of oligopoly capitalism. *A double set of alignments must therefore be created, without which corporatocracy and oligopolistic corporate power cannot be considered "safe."* These alignments make democratic public governance a farce—one concocted to conceal the nature of corporatocracy. This sort of masquerade has been advertised as "representative democracy" in the United States, and seems to be part of an effort by the most powerful oligopolistic corporations to impose corporatocratic governance around the world.[79] Governance that actually aims *not* to be representative of the interests of the people, but of the corporate oligopolies that rule some societies—and now aim to rule the globe. How far this farce has been taken—and legitimized—can be seen in the policies and practices of international organizations—such as the IMF, the WTO, the World Bank, and the OECD, among others—who now routinely impose it on nations as a condition for aid, recognition, and financial support.[80]

A third source of dysfunction generated by the split between reproduction and commodification involves the theft of intellectual rights—and the violation of employee workplace rights—by corporate power. This dysfunction involves corporate oligopolies most, because of their immense power and the high stakes they have in appropriating resources—most of all, intangibles. Because of their power and influence, and because of inadequate regulatory oversight, corporate oligopolies are usually able to get away with the kind of malfeasance that is part and parcel of this dysfunction.[81] As with the other

---

79. An effort that has benefited from the support of the so-called Washington Consensus since the late 1980s. See Kregel, "Discrete Charm"; Narcís Serra and Joseph Stiglitz, eds., *The Washington Consensus Reconsidered: Towards a New Global Governance* (New York: Oxford University Press, 2008).

80. See Suarez-Villa, *Globalization and Technocapitalism*, 177–207; Peet, *Unholy Trinity.*

81. See Perelman, *Steal This Idea*; Pat Choate, *Hot Property: The Stealing of Ideas in an Age of Globalization* (New York: Knopf, 2005); Joel Bakan, *The Corporation: The Pathological Pursuit of Profit and Power* (New York: Free Press, 2004).

dysfunctions, this one can be considered a result of the effort to make up for the loss of control over reproduction. This dysfunction all too frequently revolves around intangibles, their fundamental role in research and development (R&D), and their overwhelming importance for corporate power. Intellectual rights theft here refers to the stealing of ideas from employees, as well as patent infringements, corporate espionage, and intercorporate theft of intellectual property. A diverse range of strategies, actions, and schemes is involved in this dysfunction—a range that keeps getting deeper and more diverse as intangibles become more important and their reproduction becomes more dependent on external social mediation.

Theft of employees' intellectual rights typically occurs through commodification and the inevitable corporate appropriation of resources—intangibles and their exercise, most of all—that must occur if production of services and manufactures (embedded in $C \rightarrow C'$) is to reach completion. Beyond this fundamental aspect, such appropriation is the key to exchange ($C' \rightarrow M^N$) that inevitably helps decide corporate performance and profitability. Corporate confiscation of the results of employees' exercise of creativity and knowledge is central to this appropriation process. Such confiscation and appropriation are grounded in employment and whatever salaries and benefits corporate power grants to employees. With the rise of oligopolies and the elimination of unions, compensation truly becomes a grant on the part of corporate power—which involves little or no real negotiation, and whatever employee workplace rights corporate power wishes to tolerate. The compensation involved is typically a very small fraction of the ultimate, accumulated surplus that an oligopolistic corporation will derive from appropriation.[82] All the more so when the results of employees' exercise of their creativity and knowledge can be reproduced *serially*—in large quantities or for a long period of time, without their further involvement or exercise of creativity—as all too often occurs in the case of corporate intellectual property, most of all, with oligopolies. In that case, which is now the norm, *corporate power will have essentially confiscated employees' intellectual rights,*

---

82. Legally binding clauses in employee contracts—and the threat of blacklisting and reprisals—make it very difficult to publish or report abuses in this area. When litigation does occur, settling a lawsuit typically requires confidentiality on the part of the employee, as a precondition. One of the very few published reports on this form of abuse is J. Rodman Steele's *Is This My Reward? An Employee's Struggle for Fairness in the Corporate Exploitation of His Inventions* (West Palm Beach: Pencraft, 1986). Letters are also rarely published detailing problems in this area—one exception was "Letters: The Problem with Patents," *Science* 308 (April 15, 2005): 353.

usually deriving a vast amount of revenue over time—which will not be shared (fairly or at all) with those who created it.

Even when employees are granted shares or stock options by their employer, the value and accumulated revenue of the corporate intellectual property they create is usually far out of line with such compensation. Levels of employee compensation and benefits granted by corporate power are all the more distressing when disparities with executive compensation are taken into account.[83] Adding to this panorama of inequity are the limited retirement benefits employees receive, compared to the "golden farewell" benefits and vast lump-sum amounts granted to executives when they retire or depart. As noted in the previous chapter, disparities between executive and employee compensation have grown dramatically during the past four decades—a fact that reflects the overwhelming power of oligopolistic corporate management over employees, their rights, and their work. Employees who try to redress this situation and claim their rights typically face unsurmountable odds, given the elimination of labor unions and the lack of any real bargaining power.[84] It has been noted, for example, that even in the best of circumstances the chances of forming a union or similar rights organization is less than one in five in our contemporary, oligopoly-dominated society.[85] In the

---

83. Beyond the question of intellectual property–related compensation it has been estimated, for example, that corporate employers take away more than $100 billion a year (in 2009 dollars) from employees, through various means—such as requiring employees to work time they are not compensated for, or failing to pay minimum wage and overtime wage differentials. See Kimberley A. Bobo, *Wage Theft in America: Why Millions of Working Americans Are Not Getting Paid—And What We Can Do About It* (New York: New Press, 2009); Ehrenreich, "When All Else Fails, Rob the Poor," A19. In a landmark case that shows how the judicial system favors corporate interests, the U.S. Supreme Court ruled in 2012 that pharmaceutical corporations can forgo compensating their sales representatives for overtime work. This ruling alone allowed the corporations to potentially keep hundreds of millions of dollars in employee compensation—funds that can be used to compensate executives lavishly instead, among other uses; see Brent Kendall, "No Overtime for Drug Reps as Industry Wins Big Ruling," *Wall Street Journal,* June 19, 2012, B1.

84. Whistleblowers, in particular, face immense odds against the complaints they raise and usually end up paying for their efforts with dismissals or demotion; see, for example, Jennifer Levitz, "Whistleblowers are Left Dangling: Technicality Leads Labor Department to Dismiss Cases," *Wall Street Journal,* September 4, 2008, A3. Even in government agencies that offer protection to whistleblowers, reprisals can occur; see, for example, Ricardo Alonso-Zaldivar, "FDA Scientist Says He Faces Retaliation: Star Witness Who Criticized His Agency's Drug Safety Record Contends He's under Pressure to Be 'Exiled' to a Different Job," *Los Angeles Times,* November 25, 2004, A26.

85. Robert B. Reich, "Power in the Union," *Los Angeles Times,* January 26, 2009, A13.

rare cases when such organizations are created, their chances of survival are grim—and those that are formed typically collapse within a short period of time. Intimidation and threats by corporate power can be expected whenever such efforts are mounted, along with reprisals for those who publicly expose problems in the workplace. Those who refuse to bend to corporate pressures can expect to be fired or demoted and, if that should occur, they can also expect to be tacitly blacklisted as troublemakers and undesirables—effectively ending their careers.

The destruction of employee workplace rights also involves the legal dimension—"legality" being defined in terms always favorable to oligopolistic power—a key feature of corporatocracy.[86] Employment contracts that require secrecy, and that practically eliminate an employee's right to discuss, share, or consult with others outside the corporate domain are one vehicle—despite the fact that such external relations are usually essential to employee self-development, professional fulfilment, and the advancement of individual creativity or knowledge. External sharing and consultation are typically also stepping stones to employee recognition in a professional community. External employee recognition is all too often detrimental to the interests of corporate power, however, in the sense that it increases the likelihood that individuals will request more compensation and benefits, or leave the corporation altogether. Partly for these reasons, more than 90 percent of all technical and managerial employees in the United States are made to sign "non-compete" employment contracts, which prevent them from working for a rival for two years or more after leaving.[87] Contracts also often involve "confidential information" and "pre-invention assignment" requirements, which prevent employees from leaving to work for a rival altogether (without time limits), and impose wide-ranging corporate claims—including ownership—over their inventions, even if they were being

---

86. See, for example, Kendall, "No Overtime"; Perelman, *Steal This Idea*. One of the more blatant examples of how employee rights have eroded—and how much workplace "legality" favors corporate power—involves startup companies, where so-called "fail fast" dismissals have become the norm. This practice typically provides no recourse to contest the decision or seek redress, and has been described as "firing people before the ink is dry on their employment contracts"—Stephanie Gleason and Rachel Feintzeig, "At Startups, Pink Slips Come Early and Often," *Wall Street Journal*, December 13, 2013, B1.

87. "Ties That Bind: The Market for Smart People Is Clogged Up by All Manner of Dubious Legal Restrictions," *The Economist*, December 14, 2013, 76. See also Orly Lobel, *Talent Wants to Be Free: Why We Should Learn to Love Leaks, Raids, and Free Riding* (New Haven: Yale University Press, 2013).

worked on long before joining the company, or were created during spare time or after leaving. Intimate knowledge of the corporate memory and of an organization's workings, of its creative capabilities, of its schemes, malfeasance, plans, and projects can reveal the internal reality of a company to outsiders—discrediting its propaganda and spin campaigns, while embarrassing politicians who are paid off. In the context of financialism, such insights can also become valuable "insider" knowledge to speculators, who can use it to bet on a corporate entity.[88]

Suppression of employee talents that do not fit into preestablished corporate templates—and can make appropriation and commodification more difficult—are also part of the general panorama of workplace rights abuse. Corporate management accomplishes commodification by systematizing and standardizing tasks.[89] This helps streamline commodification, while reducing uncertainty and risk. It also makes it easier to manipulate employee routines and operations, such that $C \rightarrow C'$ can be completed faster—or at least the part of it that is relevant to commodification. This means that employee talents, such as those that involve critical understanding and action—but which are inimical to the interests of corporate power—are banished from the workplace. Critical talents that are typically considered adversarial by corporate power are very diverse. One of them, for example, involves creating and deploying a new invention to increase social benefit above—or in place of—corporate profit. Creating new software that does not expire and can be used indefinitely, as opposed to one with an automatically expiring time window—that requires repurchase for continued use—is one such case. Designing greater simplicity into a product—such as an automobile or home appliance—to reduce maintenance or postpone replacement is another. Creating vaccines that can last a lifetime, as opposed to those with limited time effectiveness—which require payment for extensions of immunity—is

---

88. Although illegal, trading based on "insider" information is commonly practiced and can be done in ways that are very difficult to detect by authorities—especially when former employees are the source of information. Also, when politicians—or their friends and relatives—are involved and use such information for financial speculation, insider trading usually becomes more difficult to prosecute. See, for example, Peter Schweizer, *Throw Them All Out: How Politicians and Their Friends Get Rich off Insider Stock Tips, Land Deals, and Cronyism That Would Send the Rest of Us to Prison* (Boston: Houghton Mifflin Harcourt, 2011).

89. Systematization and standardization are largely antithetical to creativity, but are nonetheless at the core of commodification and production. See Suarez-Villa, "Creativity as a Commodity," in *Technocapitalism*, 31–55, and his "Commodification," in *Globalization and Technocapitalism*, 72–78.

another example. A result of suppressing critical talents is further alienation of employees from the exercise of their creativity, knowledge, and experience. Such alienation often results in a lack of self-fulfillment, and in pressures by corporate management that enthrone interpersonal (and intergroup) competition in place of collaboration, sharing, and mutual assistance—qualities that are vitally important for socially constructive action or outcomes.[90]

Corporate espionage typically includes myriad strategies aimed at stealing ideas, processes, methods, or formulas—that can lead to inventions, innovations, and new products or services—from other companies or from individuals outside the home corporate domain.[91] It can also involve access to other corporations' secret plans regarding markets, takeovers, supply chains, or product distribution. Strategies involving corporate espionage are typically aimed at reducing uncertainty and risk for the perpetrator. For oligopolistic corporations, less uncertainty and risk often translate into cost reductions—one of the most important aspects of competition between oligopolies. R&D activities are particularly targeted—due to the loss of control over reproduction, and the high value of intangibles for invention and innovation and their importance for cost reduction. Other operational aspects that tend to be targeted are internal measures that affect production efficiency, product quality, and costs. Preventing others from entering a market niche or from strengthening a contested one are common objectives, especially when the new entrants have lower costs. Small companies seeking to enter a market controlled by oligopolists usually attract special attention, and may easily find themselves targeted for takeover by any of the corporations controlling the niche. The history of corporate capitalism is filled with cases of promising, well-run small companies that did not survive long enough to become large, because they were taken over by an oligopolist to prevent them from becoming established in its market.

---

90. Forced ranking of employees has been one of the tactics used by corporate management to promote interpersonal competition—it was widely copied after oligopolistic conglomerate General Electric implemented it in the 1980s; see Robert Slater, *Jack Welch and the GE Way: Management Insights and Leadership Secrets of the Legendary CEO* (New York: McGraw-Hill, 1999). Among the many imitators were Microsoft and insurance oligopolist AIG.

91. For an overview of the many possibilities involving corporate espionage, see Hedieh Nasheri, *Economic Espionage and Industrial Spying* (Cambridge: Cambridge University Press, 2005); Adam L. Penenberg and Marc Barry, *Spooked: Espionage in Corporate America* (Cambridge, MA: Perseus, 2000); Choate, *Hot Property*; Perelman, *Steal This Idea*; Bakan, *The Corporation*.

Theft of intellectual property—especially that related to new inventions and innovations—can involve various strategies. One of them, for example, is the fairly common practice of reverse engineering competitors' products—to save resources, funds, and time that would otherwise have to be expended in R&D.[92] This strategy provides shortcuts and helps reduce the uncertainty and risk of research—making it possible for the perpetrator to appropriate ideas, processes, methods, or formulas that lead to inventions and innovations. It is a strategy that can be considered part of a heightened corporate emphasis on development (the D in R&D), as opposed to research—reflecting the higher priority placed on short-term/lower-risk/fast-profit improvements over long-term, high-risk but potentially more significant research. Corporate oligopolies spearheaded this emphasis—and the reverse engineering strategy—in most every R&D-intensive sector during the past three decades. Their power made it possible for them to practice it on a regular basis—and get away with it. Reverse engineering—also referred to as "teardown"—has become so common that it can be outsourced to firms that specialize in this activity.[93] Criminal sanctions do not exist for reverse engineering—or for almost any kind of intellectual property theft—and the vast resources available to almost every oligopolistic corporation ensure that litigation, should it occur, will not pose significant financial difficulties. Also, the potential rewards of an innovation obtained through reverse engineering are typically more significant—especially when compounded over time—than the likely costs of litigation. Innovations extracted and appropriated through reverse engineering are also very difficult to prove—if they are sufficiently tweaked or disguised from the original, as they usually are.

Reverse engineering can be considered part of a larger corporate strategy—second-mover research—that attempts to reduce uncertainty, risk, and potential failure by pilfering others' work.[94] Appropriation—a key feature of

---

92. See, for example, Carl Hoffman, "The Teardown Artists," *Wired,* February 2006, 136–39.

93. Among the companies specializing in teardowns in the electronics sector are, for example, iSuppli and UBM TechInsights; see "The Business of Dissecting Electronics: The Lowdown on Teardowns," *The Economist,* January 23, 2010, 62–63. The rising value of intangibles has made reverse engineering more important—in electronics, for example, the vast majority of a product's value lies in intellectual property and services, rather than manufacturing.

94. Second-mover research has become an important component of corporate strategy, as development work takes a higher priority than research. See, for example, "Out of the Dusty Labs: Technology Firms Have Left the Big Corporate R&D Laboratory Behind, Shifting the Emphasis from Research to Development. Does It Matter?" *The Economist,* March 3, 2007, 74–76. See also Nasheri, *Economic Espionage*; Choate, *Hot Property.*

commodification—is central to this strategy, as it is with reverse engineering. Second-mover research helps secure a shortcut to C' by seizing inventions and innovations that help complete production (in C → C'). Second-mover research and reverse engineering can also be part of an effort to substitute reproduction. They can be advantageous to those who undertake them and manage to achieve results, since they might help evade external social mediation—and reduce the accompanying risks, uncertainties, and loss of control. Second-mover research can become a priority when a corporation decides to forgo external networks and social mediation, since it restores some control over reproduction—control based on malfeasance, but which can be attractive to oligopolistic power depending on the potential gains. First-mover companies—those that have spent the funds, time, and effort to generate original inventions and innovations—are therefore shortchanged and can be upstaged by second-movers, who often profit more from the pilfered inventions than they do.[95] Imitation that does not involve pilfering can also be considered a second-mover tactic—especially when the most important features of the original idea are replicated.[96]

Second-mover schemes are often part of another strategy that may be referred to as malicious opportunism. This strategy involves external, intercorporate arrangements that are structured for the nominal purpose of cooperation. Intercorporate relations of power are at the core of this strategy, and research collaboration is a frequent target. Such arrangements are usually pursued to try to regain some control over reproduction and evade social mediation—thereby substituting intercorporate collaboration for the societal networks that are vital for reproducing intangibles. Malicious opportunism is often engineered through alliances, joint ventures, or research unit to research unit (R2R) arrangements aimed at specific (or narrow) projects and tasks.[97] These intercorporate arrangements then become a breeding ground for theft and malfeasance involving ideas, intellectual property, and other

---

95. One of the earliest published works to provide empirical findings on this aspect was William L. Baldwin and Gerald L. Childs, "The Fast Second and Rivalry in Research and Development," *Southern Economic Journal* 36 (1969): 18–24.

96. Imitation that follows closely on others' original ideas and inventions has become a major component of corporate strategy; see, for example, "Pretty Profitable Parrots: For Businesses, Being Good at Copying Is at Least as Important as Being Innovative," *The Economist*, May 12, 2012, 76.

97. Strategic alliances seem to be an important vehicle. See, for example, Wilma N. Suen, *Non-Cooperation: The Dark Side of Strategic Alliances* (New York: Palgrave Macmillan, 2005); Suarez-Villa, "Pathology of Decomposition," in *Technocapitalism*, 108–21.

intangibles—litigation now having become fairly common among those engaged.[98] Diverse actions and schemes are often involved. Among them, for example, is relegating a partner to do the most difficult parts of a research project—thereby creating an asymmetrical situation that reduces risk and costs for the perpetrator. Another one involves learning key details about a corporate partner's research operations and projects, to use such information for a takeover. This is an important tactic used by oligopolists to increase their power—or by those that hope to grow larger and control a market niche. It is also attractive to hedge funds if they happen to control a corporation involved in this arrangement, as it can provide advantages when they target any of the other participants.

Clearly, the third source of dysfunction—theft of intellectual rights and workplace abuse—is therefore a multifaceted one, comprising a vast array of strategies and actions. How entrenched this dysfunction has become in corporate strategy can be seen in the kind of counsel dispensed by prominent corporate strategy consultants—the ones that typically advise corporate oligopolies in the United States and around the world. The work of two widely known consultants—leaders of what is possibly the top global consulting company on corporate strategy, with strong links to one of the world's top business schools—provides a vivid example. These individuals came up with fundamental advice—which they characterize as "hardball"—comprising five strategic principles that, in their words, are listed as: (1) "Devastate Rivals' Profit Sanctuaries," (2) "Plagiarize with Pride," (3) "Deceive the Competition," (4) "Unleash Massive and Overwhelming Force," and (5) "Raise Competitors' Costs."[99] All of these principles are practiced today—in diverse ways and intensities—by corporate oligopolies, and can be considered to be at the heart of our contemporary corporate culture.[100] Strategic principles (2) and (3), in particular, are directly related

---

98. See Perelman, *Steal This Idea*; Bakan, *The Corporation*; Suen, *Non-Cooperation*; Choate, *Hot Property*.

99. George Stalk Jr., and Robert Lachenauer, "Hardball: Five Killer Strategies for Trouncing the Competition," *Harvard Business Review* (April 2004): 62–71. A more extensive treatment can be found in George Stalk Jr., Robert Lachenauer, and John Butman, *Are You Playing to Play or Playing to Win?* (Boston: Harvard Business School Press, 2004).

100. A culture based on an outlook that seems aggressive and authoritarian—relentlessly seeking to take advantage of any means to appropriate, control, or vanquish. The words of the best-known business school academic on corporate strategy can probably summarize it best: "[S]imply making that set of [strategic] choices will not protect you unless you're constantly sucking in all of the available means to improve your ability to deliver." Keith H. Hammonds,

to elements in the third source of dysfunction discussed here—theft of intellectual rights and property, espionage, reverse engineering, second-mover schemes, and malicious opportunism. Principle (5) is closely related to oligopolistic production, which typically targets cost reduction as a major internal objective. This principle, however, aims to turn cost performance into an external weapon. Principles (1) and (4) seem better suited to war than to constructive economic action, and appear to be particularly anti-social in scope and practice. In various ways, these principles reflect the kind of pathology that characterizes the contemporary oligopolistic quest for power and profit—not only over entire economic sectors but also over public governance.

A product of the third source of dysfunction is an unprecedented amount of corporate litigation. Because of the overwhelming importance of intangibles, the most profitable (and sought-after) specialty in the legal profession is intellectual property litigation. Lawsuits in this area have skyrocketed to such magnitude that some specialists are now calling for the elimination of patenting. The annual litigation budget of one large corporation, Intel—an oligopolist in the microprocessor sector—for example, is said to be about one billion dollars.[101] The costs of intellectual property litigation in the United States are now estimated to exceed the profits corporations obtain from licensing their patents to others.[102] In many ways, this reflects the extent to which pilfering and theft—the kind that result

---

"Michael Porter's Big Ideas," *Fast Company,* March 2001, 150–55. See also Michael Porter, "Don't Collaborate, Compete," *The Economist,* June 9, 1990, 17. This outlook has also become established in management education and practice; see, for example, Walter Kiechel, *The Lords of Strategy: The Secret Intellectual History of the New Corporate World* (Boston: Harvard Business School Press, 2010); Matthew Stewart, *The Management Myth: Why the Experts Keep Getting It Wrong* (New York: Norton, 2009); *Business 2.0* magazine cover, Special Global Issue—Steal These Ideas: What You Can Learn from the Most Innovative Companies and Smartest People on the Planet, August 2004.

101. Robert P. Colwell, *The Pentium Chronicles: The People, Passion, and Politics Behind Intel's Landmark Chips* (New York: Wiley-Interscience, 2006). See also Perelman, "Political Economy of Intellectual Property," 34.

102. L. Gordon Crovitz, "Why Technologists Want Fewer Patents," *Wall Street Journal,* June 15, 2009, A13. Also, since the early 1980s, the number of lawsuits per patent application (or filing) has increased threefold, while litigation over intellectual property infringements has increased sixfold; see James Bessen and Michael J. Meurer, *The Direct Costs from NPE Disputes,* Boston University School of Law Working Paper 12-34 (Boston: Boston University School of Law, 2012); *Economist,* "Trolls on the Hill."

in litigation—have trumped licensing. Seeking a license to use someone's intellectual property—the legal way to secure usage—seems quaint or even foolish in a corporate culture where the previously mentioned "hardball" strategies become the norm.

Also related to this panorama of malfeasance and pathology—and to the growing importance of intangibles and intellectual property—is the astronomical rise in litigation over mergers and acquisitions. Mergers and acquisitions are the main vehicle for greater oligopolistic concentration, and a most important reason to seek a merger or an acquisition is the intellectual property (or the intangible resources) possessed by the targeted party. Malfeasance by corporate suitors—such as providing insufficient compensation to shareholders of targeted companies—has become a common trigger for lawsuits. In 2005, for example, 39 percent of all merger and acquisition deals in the United States were challenged by lawsuits.[103] By 2011, lawsuits were filed in 96 percent of mergers and acquisitions worth more than $500 million, and each merger deal involved an average of more than six lawsuits.[104] Attorneys are the main beneficiaries of this astounding amount of litigation—gaining about $1.2 million per settlement in 2011. It can be argued that the massive transfer of money to attorneys through this kind of litigation could be employed in more socially useful ways—such as raising employee compensation and benefits or creating jobs—which are vital for improving living standards and economic security. In a society dominated by oligopolies, however, mergers and takeovers—and legal disputes over their execution—predominate over such considerations.

The fourth source of dysfunction generated by the split between commodification and reproduction involves secrecy and subterfuge as strategic tools. Secrecy and subterfuge become vital to corporate power to protect itself from the dysfunctions mentioned before. With litigation reaching such high levels, secrecy becomes indispensable. Theft, malfeasance, and abuse always need to be covered up—even when they are not illegal—lest they trigger costly lawsuits, unfavorable bets in the stock or bond markets, or some negative coverage in the media. Just as troublesome is that such media coverage may end up implicating politicians who serve the corporate perpetrator, and

---

103. "Mergers and Lawsuits: Shark Attack," *The Economist*, June 2, 2012, 78–79.

104. Robert M. Daines and Olga Koumrian, *Recent Developments in Shareholder Litigation Involving Mergers and Acquisitions: March 2012 Update* (Palo Alto: Cornerstone Research, 2012), http://www.cornerstone.com/files/.

whose money they take for campaigns.[105] Secrecy is essential for corporations to safeguard their appropriation of intangibles—a most important aspect of commodification—and to ensure that the process of transformation embedded in C → C' is completed as rapidly as possible. Secrecy's importance as protection against other corporate predators cannot be overestimated, particularly when new cost-reducing production techniques are adopted. In this area, secrecy and subterfuge are as important to an oligopolist as teeth and fins are to a shark.

In corporate research, secrecy is fundamental today. Keeping secret any new ideas, designs, processes, formulas, methods, or tools—and any experiments that lead to them—is vitally important. And, given oligopolistic power's dependence on R&D, secrecy and subterfuge help reduce risk.[106] Non-oligopolistic companies also rely on secrecy, particularly when they are targeted by oligopolists wielding the "hardball" strategies noted before. The workings of R&D units are thus typically shrouded in secrecy—all the more so if any malfeasance is going on in them. With reverse engineering and second-mover research schemes being common, secrecy becomes paramount to avoid costly litigation. With the first-to-file rule in U.S. patenting—which eliminates from consideration anyone who is not first to apply for the same (or similar) invention—research secrecy has also gained greater priority.[107] Openness and diffusion in research are therefore practically impossible to reconcile with the workings of the corporate domain.

---

105. Covering up has become a major preoccupation for corporate power—most of all, oligopolies—given the high stakes involved in their influence over politicians and public governance. Public relations campaigns are vitally important in this regard, and are typically designed to deploy all resources to present a favorable view to the public, regardless of how nefarious the perpetrator's acts are. See, for example, William Dinan and David Miller, *Thinker, Faker, Spinner, Spy: Corporate PR and the Assault on Democracy* (London: Pluto, 2007).

106. The success of systematized research regimes—a key aspect of corporate R&D—depends greatly on secrecy; see Suarez-Villa, "Experimentalist Organizations," in *Technocapitalism*, 123–51. High tech oligopolists have taken R&D secrecy to new heights, creating elaborate measures that enthrone it as a major element of strategy; see, for example, Adam Lashinsky, *Inside Apple: The Secrets Behind the Past and Future Success of Steve Jobs' Iconic Brand* (London: Murray, 2012); Robert Slater, *Microsoft Rebooted: How Bill Gates and Steve Ballmer Reinvented Their Company* (New York: Portfolio, 2004); Karen Southwick, *Everyone Else Must Fail: The Unvarnished Truth About Oracle and Larry Ellison* (New York: Crown Business, 2003); Randall E. Stross, *Planet Google: One Company's Audacious Plan to Organize Everything We Know* (New York: Free Press, 2008).

107. See U.S. Patent and Trademark Office, *General Information Concerning Patents* (November 2011), http://www.uspto.gov/patents/resources/.

Corporate research's secrecy and subterfuge therefore make it incompatible, as partner, with academic research. Yet, universities—because they are sources of tacit knowledge, a fundamental prerequisite for creativity—are increasingly important to oligopolistic corporate power. Universities are also repositories of codified knowledge—a vital support for skills training and development. It should not surprise, therefore, that corporations—especially oligopolists—are more involved today with universities than ever before.[108] At no previous time have corporate power, and corporate money, been as entwined with academia as they are now. University "research parks," aimed at linking up corporate and academic research, are commonplace. Oligopolistic corporations are more willing than ever to open their coffers to university administrators, who seem all too eager to ignore ethical conflicts, and to name buildings, schools, professorial positions, and even walkways and benches after their corporate patrons—or the wealthy elites tied to them.[109] Money has gained paramount importance in the agenda of

---

108. Corporate culture has penetrated universities and academia in diverse ways. One of them involves an intense search for money and revenues, which often alienates the educational mission; see, for example, Bernard Wysocki Jr., "Ivory Tower: Once Collegial, Research Schools Now Mean Business," *Wall Street Journal,* May 4, 2006, A1. Another one involves the convergence of university administration with corporate executive culture; see, for example, John Hechinger and Rebecca Buckman, "The Golden Touch of Stanford's President: How John Hennessy's Silicon Valley Connections Reap Millions for the University—and Himself," *Wall Street Journal,* February 24, 2007, A1. For public universities, the penetration of corporate culture has introduced many contradictions that diminish their mission and their importance to society; see, for example, Rick Wolff, "The Decline of Public Higher Education," *Monthly Review,* February 16, 2007, www.monthlyreview.org/mrzine/; James R. Brown, "Privatizing the University—the New Tragedy of the Commons," *Science* 290 (December 1, 2000): 1701–1702.

109. See, for example, Benjamin Ginsberg, *The Fall of the Faculty: The Rise of the All-Administrative University and Why It Matters* (New York: Oxford University Press, 2011); Bousquet, *How the University Works*; Jennifer Washburn, *University, Inc.: The Corporate Corruption of American Higher Education* (New York: Basic Books, 2006); Slaughter and Leslie, *Academic Capitalism.* Closer association between universities and corporate power, and massive corporate donations, have had noticeable effects on academic debate; see, for example, Michael Hiltzik, "Campus is Oddly Silent on BP," *Los Angeles Times,* August 1, 2010, B1. Also, university administrations have been adopting many of the same elements of corporate management—one of them, for example, is the "chief marketing officer," a position that is often second in importance to—and carries salaries close to that of—the university president. Individuals in these positions typically have corporate backgrounds; see, for example, Emily Glazer and Melissa Korn, "Colleges Must Learn to Make the Sale: Universities Hire Marketing Chiefs to Prove They're Worth the Money; Critics Call It Just More Bloat," *Wall Street Journal,* August 16, 2012, B10.

academic administrators, who view their positions as analogous to those of corporate executives and spare no effort to attract corporate funding. Behind the facade of tax-deductible philanthropy is the ever more pressing corporate need to seize intangibles that can sustain reproduction—and complete that all-important process of transformation embedded in C → C'.

The intangibles that universities generate are very important for that crucial objective—and they can also help corporate R&D units turn out new inventions and innovations. University research—when it can be influenced or manipulated to cater to corporate priorities—can therefore be used to try to regain some control over the reproduction of intangibles. And, although universities—on their own—cannot reproduce intangibles, they can nonetheless help provide some of the social mediation needed. There is a fundamental contradiction here, however, in that university research must be open and diffused to anyone and everyone as rapidly as possible. Such diffusion is also vital for the careers of the individual researchers involved, for their professional recognition and advancement, and for the benefit of society at large. Corporate research, on the other hand, is secretive by nature and necessity, being primarily targeted at appropriation, exploitation, and profit. Invariably, therefore, the relations of power come to the fore when the two—university and corporate research—are meshed together.[110] The typical result is a serious conflict of interest, that cannot be resolved conclusively except by separating the two.[111] Such separation all too often kills whatever

---

110. The asymmetrical nature of the relations of power can create major public controversies, particularly on joint research that has major implications for human well-being; see, for example, Alan P. Rudy et al., *Universities in the Age of Corporate Science: The UC Berkeley-Novartis Controversy* (Philadelphia: Temple University Press, 2007); Seth Shulman, *Owning the Future* (New York: Houghton Mifflin, 1999).

111. A way for corporate power to evade this conflict of interest is to allow joint corporate-university projects to be based on Open Source platforms. In this way, a corporation can later modify the research results and appropriate them, or it can simply incorporate them into its products—on a nonproprietary basis. Because they would be derived from Open Source collaboration, a corporation can thus evade sharing any revenue with its university partner—while profiting greatly from the products it based on such collaboration. This Open Source–based partnership has become common in some technology fields, such as computing and software; see, for example, Stephen Ceasar, "UCI Anchors New Intel Research Center: Project Applies Social Science, Humanities to Design and Analysis of Digital Information," *Los Angeles Times*, June 27, 2012, AA4. The link of Open Source networks to corporate profitability and capital accumulation raises major issues regarding the social benefits of this medium; see Daniel Ross, "The Place of Free and Open Source Software in the Social Apparatus of Accumulation," *Science and Society* 77 (2013): 202–26.

benefit a joint academic-corporate research project might have—for corporate power. Inevitably, details and results are bound to be diffused—or will end up being leaked—even when some separation can be engineered into the projects. For this reason, most such joint corporate-academic ventures become a conduit for oligopolistic power to entice researchers to join its domain and leave academia. The joint projects thus become a sort of brain drain vehicle to benefit corporate power—all the more so when the particular kind of creativity and tacit knowledge needed is unique or unusual.

For universities, the benefits of joint research with corporations seem rather limited. Similarly, university incubations of new companies appear to have had little success. Although comprehensive data on these ventures are difficult to find, it seems that universities seldom realize much gain from joint research and any new companies they help incubate.[112] Also, successful incubated companies become candidates for takeover by corporate oligopolists that dominate the sectors they try to enter—especially when they have promising inventions. Such acquisitions typically wipe out or dilute heavily whatever stake the university has in an incubated company. The corporate oligopolists that take over such companies are often, curiously, the ones that donate to the universities that serve as incubators. If the universities happen to be public—or receive government grants—taxpayers' resources are usually part of the assets expended in the joint research projects or incubations. In such cases, what started out as an incubation project or joint corporate-university research becomes part of a closed loop of support for corporate power—corporate welfare of a kind—at public expense. Helping corporate power reproduce intangibles thereby turns into another scheme of corporate welfare.

Patents obtained from joint corporate-university research can yield some royalties for universities, but those are often ephemeral or do not generate enough income to justify the costs and time taken up—or the ethical issues raised by conflicts of interest. In many cases, undertaking the research projects through Open Source–type networks can yield greater benefits—for society and the university—than if they are taken up with corporations. Open Source–type projects can also magnify the openness and rapid diffusion that are at the core of academic research—and benefit

---

112. See Eilene Zimmerman, "Assessing the Impact of Business Incubators," *New York Times*, August 12, 2013, http://boss.blogs.nytimes.com/2013/08/12/; Alejandro S. Amezcua, *Boon or Boondoggle? Business Incubation as Entrepreneurship Policy; A Report from the National Census of Business Incubators and their Tenants* (Syracuse: Whitman School of Management, Syracuse University, 2010), http://www.maxwell.syr.edu/uploadedFiles/news/BoonOrBoondoggle.pdf.

society more—through the immediate sharing and cross-fertilization they foster.[113] The costs of undertaking Open Source network projects are also typically low, compared to the funding expended in joint corporate-university research. Most of all, Open Source projects prevent the sort of secrecy and subterfuge that are intrinsic to corporate research. Helping corporate power gain some control over reproduction thus seems hardly worth the benefit that it provides universities, compared to the ethical and monetary costs, and the loss of public trust involved.

At the core of the severance of reproduction from commodification—and of these dysfunctions—is the social dimension of reproduction and the loss of control that it entails for corporate power. *This social dimension is at the core of the crisis of public governance, to the extent that corporate power's influence over the state becomes a means to make up for that loss.* The intangibles needed by corporate power to achieve reproduction and complete transformation thus acquire a societal dimension. The results of reproduction thus belong to society. *Those results can be considered part of the commons, belonging to no one in particular, and to everyone at large.* It is this dimension that sets our contemporary, oligopoly-driven capitalism apart from previous eras. *The dysfunctions that are associated with the split between reproduction and commodification result, by and large, from the denial of this fundamental aspect.* Those dysfunctions are now becoming a hallmark of the twenty-first century, and their multidimensional character—and deep association with oligopolistic power—ensure that they will affect many aspects of governance in coming decades. They therefore pose major dilemmas for the state, for corporate power, and for society—dilemmas that require resolution if we are to prevent governance from becoming a tool of the privileged few to dispossess the rest of society.

The social dilemmas posed by the split between reproduction and commodification are potentially pathbreaking, in the sense that a choice that defies the status quo can have consequences that are systemic and long lasting. The resolution of the split between reproduction and commodification thus presents a very difficult, perhaps impossible, choice for corporate power—most of all, for oligopolies. *To achieve a resolution of the split, corporate power must necessarily place the social dimension of reproduction above its narrow, self-serving interests.* Such placement brings up two dilemmas that require action, and involve *appropriation* and *control*. The

---

113. Particularly the life sciences and with projects that cut across diverse disciplines and fields; see, for example, Hope, *Biobazaar*; Klein, *Transdisciplinarity*.

appropriation dilemma involves strategic decisions that can either sustain the status quo—with all its dysfunctions and pathologies—or set a new course that is socially coherent, and that addresses the fundamental human need for just governance. Two courses of action can decide the fate of this dilemma. Corporate power can appropriate the results of the exercise of intangibles—especially creativity—to extract profit and power for its own interest, above all else, *and* thereby shortchange their benefit to society (the status quo position). *Or,* corporate power can provide those results freely to society, to become part of the commons—of the collective heritage of society and humankind—such that they benefit society above all else *and* thereby compromise its power over public governance and society. Clearly, the second course would likely mark the end of corporatocracy, and possibly also of oligopolistic corporate power. It is a course that will most probably be identified as an existential threat by oligopolistic corporate power—and that it is bound to struggle against with all its might.

The *control dilemma* also poses difficult strategic decisions that have much relevance for our governance and for society, given the social character of reproduction. It involves the corporate domain itself, however, and the governance of this domain by corporate power. At stake are the reproduction and commodification of the most precious resources of our time—intangibles such as creativity and new knowledge. Corporate power can attempt to control their reproduction, by trying to internalize it within the corporate domain, *and* thereby end up shortchanging commodification. *Or,* it can forgo such control—letting society take over their reproduction—such that its social dimension is placed above corporate interests, *and* thereby lose control over *both* reproduction and commodification. Giving up control over reproduction to society would trigger this dual loss, since once it is given up it seems practically impossible to turn a social resource—one that belongs to society at large—into a corporate commodity. The resources thus reproduced would, in a very real sense, be in the public domain—rather than the corporate domain. Neither of the two courses of action is favorable to oligopolistic corporate power, in the sense that both would eliminate its long-term influence over public governance and society. In either case, that fundamental process of transformation embedded in C → C' would remain incomplete. Corporate power—most of all, the oligopolies—may thus be expected to evade any resolution of this dilemma altogether, and to continue with actions, schemes, and strategies that generate social dysfunctions and pathologies. So long as those actions, schemes, and strategies complete the process of transformation in C → C'—regardless of the dysfunctions and pathologies they generate—it may be expected that corporate power will consider either course of action to be an existential threat, one to be opposed by any and all means.

The result of a continuation of the status quo is simply more dysfunction, and greater efforts to exercise control over the state—and over society at large. Can oligopolistic corporate power be expected to give up its power over governance, in order to resolve the severance of reproduction from commodification? This is a fundamental question for the corporatocratic state, and for the public at large. Although the appropriation and control dilemmas are at the core of the split between reproduction and commodification, the larger question of societal governance seems unavoidable. When corporate power appropriates intangibles, the public is dispossessed. This is a dispossession that, in our time, becomes part of that redistribution of wealth from the public at large—the vast majority of people—to oligopolistic corporate power and its associated elites. And, it is a dispossession that has become so common and routine that hardly anyone notices, and that most people take for granted—as integral to contemporary public governance.

Stagnation

A long-term tendency toward slow or minimal growth is a feature of oligopoly capitalism. This tendency, which we can call *stagnation,* poses major problems for the corporatocratic state. Slow long-term growth in advanced capitalism tends to generate greater economic insecurity, downward mobility, debt, and a redistribution of wealth toward the wealthiest segments of society. A dependence on financialism to concoct growth through speculation is also related to this phenomenon. At the same time, greater dependence on intangibles and the structural dysfunctions considered previously make it more difficult for the real economy to sustain growth, especially over the long term.

This chapter will refocus our attention back to the macrolevel panorama of oligopoly capitalism and its association with the crisis of the corporatocratic state. Major features of long-term stagnation will be considered first, taking into account vital indicators that reflect the enduring presence of this phenomenon. Government policies and strategies that attempt to deal with stagnation, and the socioeconomic dysfunctions they create, will also be considered—along with their theoretical and historical underpinnings. The emergence of new sectors and technologies will be taken into account, to address how and whether they might affect long-term stagnation. The dynamics of oligopoly capitalism—and of oligopolistic control over the state—will provide the general frame of reference throughout this chapter, bringing together aspects of financialism and the microlevel severance of reproduction from commodification that are important to understand why and how stagnation occurs.

Stagnation in advanced capitalism is not a product of speculative crashes—although it can and does occur in their sequel—or of business cycle downturns. *It is a systemic, long-term tendency generated largely by oligopolistic concentration.* Stagnation occurs because as oligopolies become dominant, they compound a major problem of advanced capitalism: *the*

223

overaccumulation of capital. This phenomenon, a serious flaw in what is a most important component of capitalism—accumulation—results from the rising surplus that accompanies oligopolistic concentration. The surplus manifests itself in a vast amount of available capital—the result of oligopolistic control over pricing and the profitability it generates. Technological improvements and cost cutting also contribute to overaccumulation through higher profitability. At the same time, the myriad tax loopholes and corporate welfare vehicles of the corporatocratic state make it easier to accumulate capital. More capital is thus accumulated than can be productively invested in the real economy—the economy of production. It is therefore a problem of excess—an embarrassment of riches, in a manner of speaking—which underscores the remarkable capacity of oligopoly capitalism to accumulate.

The overaccumulation of capital that accompanies oligopolistic concentration is also a product of the intense and continuous effort to cut or keep wages low as a means to reduce costs. Offshoring and outsourcing jobs, and weakening labor unions—along with the productivity gains obtained through new production technologies and internal restructuring—play an important part in this regard. The result is a tendency toward stagnant or declining wages—in real terms and over the long term—that in turn generates stagnant aggregate demand as economic insecurity rises and consumption is curtailed.[1] Fiscal austerity compounds this tendency by increasing unemployment, reducing real incomes, and further contracting aggregate demand. Sustaining aggregate demand and consumption through debt sets the stage for future credit crises, as noted earlier in this book. Stagnant aggregate demand in turn generates stagnant productive capacity—and occasionally overproduction—thus reducing the need to invest in productive activities.[2]

---

1. Aggregate demand, a Keynesian concept, refers to the collective (or macro) scale. This interpretation of demand was necessary to frame Keynes's ideas on monetary theory and policies, and is therefore largely a product of his work; see Keynes, *The General Theory of Employment, Interest and Money.*

2. Reduced aggregate demand is assumed to lead to less production, but it must be noted that the inverse can also occur. Under oligopolistic conditions, less production may also lead to lower consumption—as prices are sustained or increased to support profits. Although oligopolies were rare in his time, Marx was first to outline this inverse dynamic, noting that "production, for its part, correspondingly (1) furnishes the material and the object for consumption. Consumption without an object is not consumption; therefore, in this respect, production creates and produces consumption. (2) But the object is not the only thing which production creates for consumption. Production also gives consumption its specificity, its character, its finish. . . . (3) Production not only supplies a material for the need, but it also supplies a need for the material." See Karl Marx, *Grundrisse: Foundations of the Critique of Political Economy* (New York: Penguin, 1973; orig. published as *Grundrisse der Kritik der Politischen Ökonomie*, 1939—based on Notebooks I and II, dating from 1857–58), 92.

The trend toward long-term stagnation manifested itself in the American economy after the 1950s—as oligopolies became more important and growth in gross domestic product (GDP) declined. Thus, a 4.4 percent average real GDP growth rate during the decade of the 1960s declined to 3.2 percent in the 1970s, 3.0 percent in the 1980s and 1990s, and 1.6 percent during the first decade of the new century.[3] Similar slowdown trends, toward minimal real GDP growth, occurred in the other two major world zones of advanced capitalism: Western Europe and Japan—Western Europe seeing consecutive, declining rates of 4.9 percent (1960s), 3.5 percent (1970s), 2.4 percent (1980s), 2.0 percent (1990s), and 1.4 percent (2000s); while Japan experienced rates of 9.9 percent (1960s), 4.6 percent (1970s and 80s), 1.4 percent (1990s), and 0.7 percent (2000s)—at a time when oligopolies were gaining greater importance in their economies.[4] The troika of advanced capitalism—the United States, Western Europe, and Japan—therefore experienced similar general slowdown trends, despite their different historical trajectories.

American industrial production followed this long-term slowdown trend, with average annual growth declining from 9.4 percent in 1954 to 6.7 percent in 1960, 5.1 percent in 1970, 4.6 percent in 1980 (at the start of the neoliberal era), 2.8 percent in 2000, and on down to 1.8 percent by 2010—in what became a long downward slide with no lasting upswings.[5] Western Europe and Japan also experienced long-term slowdown trends in industrial production—Japan's being more severe, with an average growth rate of 16.7 percent during the period 1960–1970, declining to 0.04 percent during 1990–2010.[6] Long-term annual averages in U.S. manufacturing

---

3. U.S. Bureau of Economic Analysis, *National Income and Product Accounts* (Washington: BEA, various years), http://www.bea.gov/national/nipaweb/SelectTable.asp. Percent change from preceding period in real gross domestic product.

4. World Bank, *WDI Database* (Washington: World Bank, various years), http://www.databank.worldbank.org. See also Stephen D. King, *When the Money Runs Out: The End of Western Affluence* (New Haven: Yale University Press, 2013). The prospects for long-term stagnation in Western Europe increased substantially after the start of the economic crisis in 2007—including Germany, which had been the strongest and most dynamic economy since the creation of the European Union; see "Die Grosse Stagnation," *The Economist*, November 30, 2013, 14–16.

5. Average annual estimates based on twenty-year moving averages, provided by the Federal Reserve Board of St. Louis, Economic Research Division, *Industrial Production Index (INDPRO)* (St. Louis, Federal Reserve Board, various years), http://research.stlouisfed.org/fred2. See also John Bellamy Foster and Robert W. McChesney, "The Endless Crisis," *Monthly Review*, May 2012, 15.

6. World Bank, *WDI Database*; Council of Economic Advisers, *Economic Report of the President Transmitted to the Congress* (Washington, DC: Government Printing Office, various years).

capacity utilization confirm this general trend, declining from 84.2 percent in 1970 to 83.1 percent in 1980, 79.8 percent in 2000, and down farther to 77.7 percent by 2010—a long declining trend that was also practically devoid of any lasting upturns.[7] Annual percent changes for real investment in manufacturing structures—an indicator of industrial facility construction spending (including both new and refurbished plants)—also reflects this downward trajectory, declining from an average annual growth of 28.1 percent in 1952 to 16.2 percent in 1960, 9.3 percent in 1970, 5.3 percent in 1980, zero growth in 2000, and down to minus one percent by 2010.[8] These long-term trajectories toward very slow or negative growth reduced productive investment possibilities along the way, by building on a dynamic of contraction and decline—and contributing to the problem of overaccumulation.

The offshoring of production along with deindustrialization—a five-decade phenomenon—also contributed to the long-term industrial slowdown. One consequence of this long trend seems to be a *disarticulation* of the American economy—the weakening of domestic multiplier effects that induce growth when aggregate demand increases.[9] Thus, an increase in aggregate demand does *not* generate much growth domestically—but triggers it elsewhere, since so much production serving the U.S. economy is now abroad.[10] A decline of almost one-quarter in U.S. manufacturing jobs—relative to the total labor force—during the past five decades was another

---

7. Based on twenty-year moving averages; see Council of Economic Advisers, *Economic Report*.

8. Based on average annual (twenty-year moving average framework) data for real investment in manufacturing structures (percent change from preceding year in real private fixed investment in structures, by type) provided by the Bureau of Economic Analysis, *National Income and Product Accounts* (various years), http://www.bea.gov/national/.

9. See Richard Peet, "Contradictions of Finance Capitalism," *Monthly Review*, December 2011, 28–29.

10. After the 1960s and '70s, the United States became the world's consumer market of last resort as many American industries closed, relocated abroad, or offshored their jobs—and as consumerism took off through substantial increases in credit and debt. The U.S. economy has thus incurred permanent trade deficits for decades, which were partly financed by inflows of capital from abroad—a process helped by the dollar's position as the prime international trading currency. Numerous specialists have questioned the sustainability of this situation over the years; see, for example, Catherine L. Mann, *Is the US Trade Deficit Sustainable?* (Washington: Institute for International Economics, 1999); Richard A. Illey and Mervyn Lewis, *Untangling the US Deficit: Evaluating Causes, Cures and Global Imbalances* (Northampton, MA: Elgar, 2007).

effect, which slowed domestic aggregate demand over the long term.[11] And this long-winded dynamic of deindustrialization and manufacturing job off-shoring now seems ripe for replication in many service activities. It has been estimated, for example, that potentially 160 service occupations—employing more than thirty million Americans—are very vulnerable to offshoring during the next ten years.[12] The loss of industrial production and jobs noted before occurred despite the emergence of high technology industries in the 1980s, and the information technology (IT) revolution of the 1990s.[13] The rise of new high tech sectors was a very significant development—which most likely would have made the long-term slowdown worse had it not occurred. It seems, therefore, that high tech and IT could neither stop nor reverse the long-term trend toward stagnation, despite their importance for the American economy.

It is also significant to note that the long-term trend toward stagnation occurred despite substantial reductions in taxes. In the 1950s and on through the mid-1960s, the top federal individual income tax rate was about 90 percent. It declined to about 70 percent from the mid-1960s to the early 1980s—about a 20 percent reduction—and then to less than 40 percent from the mid-1980s to 2011—more than a 50 percent reduction compared to the 1950s.[14] The lowest tax rate also declined, from about 20 percent in the 1950s to less than 10 percent by 2011. Between the top and the lowest tax rates—the ones that affect the middle class most—declines also occurred depending on income. Despite these substantial tax rate reductions,

---

11. See, for example, Steven C. High and David W. Lewis, *Corporate Wasteland: The Landscape and Memory of Deindustralization* (Ithaca: ILR Press, Cornell University, 2007). The larger panorama of a crumbling social contract and its effects on employment must also be taken into account; see George Packer, *The Unwinding: An Inner History of the New America* (New York: Farrar, Straus, and Giroux, 2013).

12. Donald L. Bartlett and James B. Steele, *The Betrayal of the American Dream* (New York: Public Affairs, 2012).

13. In many cases, the new technologies associated with IT also eliminated jobs, by making automation and offshoring easier. Employment losses at U.S. wireless carriers during 2006–2011, for example, were estimated at 40,400—bringing total employment in this sector to 166,600 by 2011, a twelve-year low—despite revenue growth of 28 percent during that period; see, for example, Anton Troianovski, "Wireless Jobs Vanish," *Wall Street Journal,* July 18, 2011, B1.

14. Internal Revenue Service, *SOI Tax Statistics: SOI Bulletin, Historical Tables and Appendix* (2012), http://www.irs.gov/taxstats/article/id=115033,00.html.

the long-term stagnation trend continued unabated, as noted previously. This contradicts a major neoliberal assumption that has become a standard message of political campaigns since the early 1980s—that tax reduction will promote growth, and that tax rate reductions for the wealthiest will result in greater growth, since they are more likely to invest than the rest of the population. Thus, insofar as the top tax rate is concerned—the one paid by the highest-income segment—this does not seem to be borne out if one takes the long slide toward stagnation into account. Much the same applies to the other income segments of the population, for which the tax rate reduction should have led to increases in aggregate demand. For corporations, the top marginal federal income tax rate also declined, from about 52 percent in the mid-1950s to 35 percent by 2011—a reduction of 17 percent.[15] However, most corporations—especially the oligopolies—pay little or no tax by taking advantage of loopholes, subsidies, and various forms of corporate welfare.[16] Nonetheless, this significant reduction in the top corporate tax rate—which applies to the most profitable corporations—did not reverse or stop the long-term slide toward stagnation.

A long-term decline in U.S. net private nonresidential fixed investment—an indicator of business investment possibilities—further confirms the long slowdown trend. During the decade of the 1970s, the average for this indicator stood at 4 percent of GDP. It subsequently declined to 3.8 percent during the 1980s, 3 percent during the 1990s, and on down to 2.4 percent during the first decade of the new century.[17] The long-term decline of this indicator is important because it includes investment in services-related activities, in addition to manufacturing—and therefore serves as a barometer of business investment that takes the private sector

15. Internal Revenue Service, *Corporate Income Tax Brackets and Rates, 1909–2002,* http:// www.irs.gov/ pub/irs-soi/02corate.pdf (accessed August 20, 2012).

16. The top five corporations in the United States—all of them oligopolists—using an executive performance–based compensation tax loophole, for example, had a combined $232 million in federal tax deductions in 2011 alone. By one estimate, the total amount of corporate tax deductions provided by this particular loophole alone could have employed 211,732 elementary school teachers for all of 2011. See Sarah Anderson, Chuck Collins, Scott Klinger, and Sam Pizzigati, *The CEO Hands in Uncle Sam's Pocket; How Our Tax Dollars Subsidize Exorbitant Executive Pay.* Institute for Policy Studies, Executive Excess 2012: 19th Annual Executive Survey (Washington, DC: IPS, 2012); David Lazarus, "Execs Profit at Public's Expense," *Los Angeles Times,* August 28, 2012, B1.

17. Bureau of Economic Analysis, *National Income and Product Accounts,* based on data from "Gross and Net Domestic Investment by Major Type" (revised August 2011); http://www.bea.gov/national/.

as a whole into account. Its decline is significant because the population was growing during those decades—a fact that should have contributed to additional demand and investment. The emergence of high tech sectors and IT should have also increased investment, yet their impact could not offset the slowing dynamic. Also important is that financialism—with all its unfettered speculation and emphasis on growth—did not reverse the long slowdown trend. These important features of the American economy since the 1970s should have more than offset the negative investment impacts of production offshoring, deindustrialization, and any shortfalls in aggregate demand—yet they did not. An explanation of the slowing trajectory must therefore consider *the reduction of investment possibilities as a contributor to the overaccumulation of capital.*

Greater oligopolistic concentration by itself reduces the number and variety of productive investment possibilities, as small or medium-size companies are acquired by the oligopolies—or as mergers take out competing companies. Acquisitions and mergers thus create more concentration, larger scale, greater pricing power, more surplus, and more profits—leading to greater capital accumulation.[18] The acquired companies are usually also taken out of stock markets, thus reducing the spectrum of investment possibilities. The dynamic of acquisitions and mergers is made all the more feasible by high oligopolistic surpluses, which provide ample funding—often leading to the payment of excessive amounts for a merger partner or acquired company. Oligopolistic overaccumulation thus builds on its own dynamic, using the surplus capital to further strengthen oligopolistic control—which in turn allows more capital accumulation to occur. Barriers to entry set up by existing oligopolists also prevent new companies from emerging or growing larger—preempting new investment possibilities. The result is a vast amount

---

18. Larger scale—achieved through mergers and acquisitions—is a powerful incentive for increasing profits and market power. In investment banking, for example, oligopolies with the largest shares of trading volume become much more attractive as trading counterparties—because of their greater liquidity; see "Investment Banking," *The Economist,* September 15, 2012, 66–67. High profits—a key characteristic of corporate oligopolies and a major contributor to the overaccumulation of capital—are essential for mergers. The resulting consolidation eventually leads to even greater profitability, thus increasing capital accumulation—while compounding overaccumulation. See Shawn Tully, "A Year of Frenzied Activity: Flush with Profits, America's Biggest Companies Put Their Money to Work in 2012, Fueling a Surge in M&A," *Fortune,* May 20, 2013, 250–52. Although the problem of capital overaccumulation has been acknowledged by bankers, its oligopolistic roots have been ignored; see, for example, Daniel Alpert, *The Age of Oversupply: Overcoming the Greatest Challenge to the Global Economy* (New York: Penguin, 2013).

of accumulated capital that finds limited or no investment outlets—or that increases much faster than the productive investment possibilities available.

Hedge fund takeovers further compound the reduction of investment possibilities, since the acquired companies are usually withdrawn from stock markets—a process that is referred to as being taken "private" in financial parlance. During a three-year period (2005–07), for example, more than three thousand companies were acquired by hedge funds (also known as "private equity" or "leveraged buyout firms") in the United States.[19] Also, the very possibility that a company might be targeted for takeover by a hedge fund often acts as a deterrent to prospective investors. Existing investors often do not fare well when a company is taken over, since the relations of power involved tend to be stacked in favor of the hedge fund suitor—all the more so when management becomes its accomplice. The majority of taken-over companies are also laden with debt by their hedge fund acquirers, thus making them less attractive as future investment possibilities. Equally important is that an increasing number of sales of taken-over companies between hedge funds—also known as "secondary deals"—usually leads to investors (those not connected to the hedge funds involved) being fenced out. Such "secondary deals" amounted to more than $51 billion in 2007 alone, and are becoming fairly common in the largely unregulated hedge fund sector.[20]

The lack of investment possibilities that contributes to overaccumulation is also a product of an excessive short-term focus by corporate executives, shareholders, and investment fund managers. Immediate gains are typically their top priority and, for corporate executives, personal benefit is often also an important factor. Engaging in share buybacks to drive up stock prices, for example, provides a better opportunity for executive promotion than making productive investments that will only pay off over the long

---

19. David Benoit and Ryan Dezember, "This Buyout Boom Is an Inside Job: Companies Swapping One Private-Equity Owner for Another," *Wall Street Journal*, September 14, 2012, C1; Tom McGinty, John Carreyrou, and Michael Rothfeld, "Inside a Star Hedge Fund: Lots of Big Bets, Built Fast," *Wall Street Journal*, March 22, 2013, A1. "Leveraged buyout firm" was the original term used to refer to hedge funds—reflecting their high dependence on debt (or "leverage"); see Sebastian Mallaby, *More Money than God: Hedge Funds and the Making of a New Elite* (New York: Penguin, 2010); Richard M. Bookstaber, *A Demon of Our Design: Markets, Hedge Funds, and the Perils of Financial Innovation* (Hoboken: Wiley, 2007).

20. According to data obtained from Dealogic by Benoit and Dezember, "Buyout Boom"; "Dealogic Investment Bank Rankings," *Financial News*, September 15, 2012, http://www.efinancialnews.com/.

term.[21] To further boost stock prices and the value of existing holdings, a common tactic is to avoid issuing new shares—thereby further limiting investment possibilities.[22] In many cases, top executives also make sure that they personally control the majority of shareholding votes, even when they own a minority of shares—effectively skewing voting outcomes to favor their own short-term interest.[23] Productive investments that will only pay off over the long term, moreover, tend to be complicated and carry risks that are usually impossible to anticipate. The payoffs for those investments are also typically out of the time frame of most executives' expected tenure.

For shareholders, short-term results are primordial, and investments that mostly yield results over the long term are out of their performance time frame. By one estimate, for example, the average time that shareholders own a stock on the New York Stock Exchange plummeted from eight years in 1960 to four months in 2010.[24] Also, investing in oligopolistic corporations seems less risky to many potential shareholders, because of their market power—and the perception that this will make it easier to obtain higher immediate returns. For fund managers who invest in the corporate oligopolies, short-term results are very important, since they determine how their performance will be judged by their clients—and whether incoming

---

21. See Jean-Pierre Danthine and John B. Donaldson, *Executive Compensation and Stock Options: An Inconvenient Truth,* Swiss Finance Institute Research Paper no. 08-13 (Geneva: Swiss Finance Institute, 2008); Xavier Gabaix and Augustin Landier, "Why Has CEO Pay Increased So Much?," *Quarterly Journal of Economics* 123 (2008): 49–100. Share buybacks to drive up the stock price—and increase executive compensation—can also involve secrecy, when corporate directors with vast holdings sell them back; see John A. Levin, "Secret Buybacks are Unfair to Shareholders," *Wall Street Journal,* December 31, 2013, A11. Adding to the attraction of share buybacks and short-term horizons is that corporate chief executives' average tenure declined by half during the 2000s decade, compared to the previous one; see "Going Off the Rails: Companies Need to Keep an Eye on Their Bosses for Signs of Destructive Behaviour," *The Economist,* November 30, 2013, 67.

22. "Taking Stock: Why Equity Markets Have Forgotten Their Function," *The Economist,* July 28, 2012, 65.

23. See Michael Hiltzik, "Like It or Not, He'll Get His Way," *Los Angeles Times,* May 20, 2012, B1. According to Hiltzik, Facebook's Mark Zuckerberg, for example, owns 28 percent of the company but controls 57 percent of shareholder voting; Google's Larry Page and Sergey Brin together control two-thirds of shareholder voting and, to sustain their power, issue shares that have no voting rights; Zynga's Mark Pincus owns shares that carry seventy votes each, thus allowing him and his insider associates to control 98 percent of shareholder voting.

24. "Taking the Long View: The Pursuit of Shareholder Value Is Attracting Criticism," *The Economist,* November 24, 2012, 75.

money flows will increase or decline.[25] Such flows have a major impact on fund managers' careers—at a time when short-term performance makes all the difference between professional success or failure. Also, short-term performance-enhancing schemes—such as share buybacks—are quite popular with both shareholders and fund managers, since they can boost results immediately. All of these factors limit productive investment possibilities—given the herd-driven nature of speculation, and the all-important emphasis on limiting risk and boosting immediate returns.[26]

The pervasive emphasis on the short term on the part of executives, shareholders, and fund managers also reflects an alignment of interests consistent with the tenets of "agency theory"—a concept taught widely in business schools since the late 1970s, which has become entrenched in management. As noted in the previous chapter, this concept was introduced by two neoclassical economists—business school professors both—in the mid-1970s.[27] Agency theory stipulates that shareholders are best served when their interests and those of corporate management are completely aligned. This means that, according to this widely practiced concept, corporate management should—and must—act primarily as "agents" of shareholders, who are in turn considered to be the "owners" of the corporation.[28] The prime objective for management, by the tenets of agency theory, is profit maximization—a goal that is stipulated as the highest priority of shareholders, and that typically has a short-term focus. The overwhelming emphasis on the short term—which ends up withdrawing investment possibilities and

25. A single investment fund manager may be in charge of hundreds of billions of dollars in clients' money, and typically experience substantial pressure to increase returns over the short term. See, for example, Kirk Kazanjian, *The Market Masters: Wall Street's Top Investment Pros Reveal How to Make Money in Both Bull and Bear Markets* (New York: Wiley, 2005); Susan Long and Burkard Sievers, *Towards a Socioanalysis of Money, Finance, and Capitalism: Beneath the Surface of the Financial Industry* (London: Routledge, 2012).

26. Hedge funds' practices, involving very short-term horizons and fast trading, also compound this aspect; see, for example, McGinty, Carreyrou, and Rothfeld, "Inside a Star Hedge Fund," A12; Mallaby, *More Money than God*; Bookstaber, *Demon of Our Design*.

27. Michael C. Jensen and William H. Meckling, "Theory of the Firm: Managerial Behavior, Agency Costs, and Ownership Structure," *Journal of Financial Economics* 3 (1976): 305–360.

28. A point that has been disputed by legal specialists and researchers, who argue that agency theory fallaciously treats shareholders as "owners" of the corporation whose stock they purchase, when in fact they only own shares—and their sole claim is to a fraction of the profits. It is also argued that putting agency theory into practice usually works against the best interests of employees, since they are a corporation's most valuable resource—given the overwhelming importance of intangibles. See Suarez-Villa, *Technocapitalism*, 114–15; Lynn Stout, *The Shareholder Value Myth: How Putting Shareholders First Harms Investors, Corporations, and the Public* (San Francisco: Berrett-Koehler, 2012).

contributing to overaccumulation—may therefore be seen as an outcome of the practice of this concept. Also, the narrow focus on profit maximization is an engine for overaccumulation and for oligopolistic consolidation, as larger corporations usually generate more profit and surplus capital—part of which can be redistributed to shareholders as dividends.

Adding to the limited investment possibilities for surplus capital—beyond the excessive emphasis on the short term—is the severance of reproduction from commodification in productive activities. The complication of production that this split creates is all the more worrisome for executives, shareholders, and investment fund managers, since it magnifies uncertainty and risk—even when the payoff prospects are not long term. When returns can only be expected over the long term, adding any consideration of this split can be deadly for an investment project. Even oligopolistic power and the presumed safety of large enterprise size cannot overcome this concern. The overarching importance of intangibles also adds much uncertainty to any long-term proposition. The qualitative nature of intangibles—especially creativity—and the uncertainty regarding their results and availability, tend to make short-term payoffs seem much safer. This adds to the shortage of productive investment outlets for surplus capital, since projects that depend greatly on intangibles tend to be costly, especially on wages—the main cost item for most productive activities.[29]

It should not surprise, then, that the long-term stagnation trend also manifests itself through declining real wages. When productive investment outlets for surplus capital are lacking or insufficient, a most important aspect of the economy—wages—tend to stagnate or decline. For the vast majority of the population, declining or stagnant wages are a major blow to their well-being given their dependence on work income. Average U.S. hourly real wages for production and nonsupervisory employees remained stagnant between January 1990 and April 2011, growing by less than 0.5 percent annually over that period (from $7.94 to $8.76).[30] This reflects the disadvantage experienced by the vast majority of the population during those two decades—an important period of the neoliberal era—as labor

29. Intangibles are part of another dimension of overaccumulation: intellectual property—of which invention patents are a major element. More than 90 percent of all invention patents awarded in the United States are never put to any economic use, and therefore lie idle—or seek applications and investment opportunities that never materialize.

30. See Fred Magdoff and Harry Magdoff, "Disposable Workers: Today's Reserve Army of Labor," *Monthly Review,* April 2004, 18–35; John Bellamy Foster, Harry Magdoff, and Robert W. McChesney, "The Stagnation of Employment," *Monthly Review,* April 2004, 3–17. Also, the share of wages in the U.S. economy (as a proportion of total economic product) fell over time, contributing to greater inequality; see, for example, Joseph E. Stiglitz, *The Price of*

unions declined, worker protections were scrapped, and oligopolistic corporations gained immense power over almost every aspect of employment.
The economic crisis that started in 2007 then deepened this trend, with
average corporate profits per employee increasing by over one-third between
2008 and 2012—while the proportion of companies providing cost-of-living
adjustments to employees declined from 20 to 11 percent, and those offering
retiree healthcare coverage declined from 32 to 24 percent.[31] The decline
of wage bargaining—a product of weaker unions and greater oligopolistic
power—also affected nonunion workers and wages.[32] The minimum wage
level—an important economic benchmark for the low-income population—
declined in real terms between 1960 ($5.20) and 2000 ($5.00) by 3.8
percent.[33] The erosion of earnings for those who depend on such wages was

---

Inequality: How Today's Divided Society Endangers Our Future (New York: Norton, 2012). This
dynamic is reflected in estimates of U.S. median real household income—between January
2000 and May 2013, for example, this indicator declined by almost 10 percent (seasonally
adjusted); see Gordon Green and John Coder, *Household Income Trends: May 2013*, Sentier
Research LLC, http://www.sentierresearch.com.

31. Alana Samuels, "Efficient and Exhausted: As Companies Push Down Costs, They Squeeze
Employees Harder Even as Rewards that Once Came Standard Have Faded Away," *Los Angeles
Times*, April 7, 2013, A1; Society for Human Resource Management, *2012 Employee Benefits:
The Employee Benefits Landscape in a Recovering Economy* (Alexandria, VA: SHRM, 2012),
http://www.shrm.org/ research/; Sageworks Blog, "Profits per Employee Increase," http://www.
sageworks.com/blog/ (accessed April 7, 2013). Also, 85 percent of all fifty-five-year-old—and
older—workers laid off in, or after, 2009 had not been able to find any employment four years
later; see Carl E. Van Horn and Cliff Zukin, *The Long-Term Unemployed and Unemployment
Insurance: Evidence from a Panel Study of Workers Who Lost a Job During the Great Recession*,
Heldrich Center for Workforce Development, Rutgers University (New Brunswick, NJ:
Heldrich Center, 2011); Walter Hamilton and Shan Li, "How a Family's Path Veered," *Los
Angeles Times*, September 22, 2013, A1; Neil Shah, "Household Incomes Level Off," *Wall
Street Journal*, September 18, 2013, A3; Hedrick Smith, "Middle-Class Mayday," *Los Angeles
Times*, August 4, 2013, A25.

32. See Bruce Western and Jake Rosenfeld, "Unions, Norms, and the Rise in US Wage
Inequality," *American Sociological Review* 76 (2011): 513–37.

33. Based on data provided by the Economic Policy Institute, http://www.epinet.org/content.
cfm/; Foster, Magdoff, and McChesney, "Stagnation of Employment"; Magdoff and Magdoff,
"Disposable Workers." See also Ralph Nader, "America's Miserly Minimum Wage Needs an
Upgrade," *Wall Street Journal*, April 16, 2013, A15; Michael Hiltzik, "Minimum Wage Debate
Reignites Age-Old Arguments," *Los Angeles Times*, June 30, 2013, B1. Declining real minimum wages also required many workers to seek public benefits to supplement their income;
see Sylvia A. Allegretto and Steven C. Pitts, *To Work with Dignity: The Unfinished March
toward a Decent Minimum Wage* (Washington, DC: Economic Policy Institute, 2013); Carl
Bialik, "Fast Food, Low Pay—and Sometimes a High Cost," *Wall Street Journal*, November
2, 2013, A6.

much greater between 1980—the start of the neoliberal era—and 2000, as the real minimum wage level declined by more than 24 percent.

Despite the well-known neoliberal claim that raising mininum wages reduces employment, U.S. labor force participation rates actually stagnated as the real minimum wage declined. Labor force participation increased slightly from about 63.5 percent in 1980 to a maximum of about 67.3 percent by 2000—less than four percentage points over two decades—and then declined to about 63.4 percent by early 2012—about the same level where it was more than three decades before.[34] Stagnant levels of participation hurt working people the most—and reflect two aspects of economic insecurity that usually accompany downward mobility. One is long-term unemployment, especially for those whose skills become less marketable over time and cannot retrain—a problem exacerbated by budget cuts inspired by neoliberal policies. The other aspect involves dropout by workers in preretirement middle age, and second-income earners in households. As far as can be determined, this occurred due to low-paying jobs that did not provide sufficient income to meet needs—a problem of declining real minimum wages—or a lack of employment opportunities (most of all, during economic downturns). Stagnant labor force participation can be considered another facet of the larger panorama of stagnation that characterizes advanced capitalism.

The disturbing wage and labor force participation data discussed before are confirmed by the longstanding erosion of the middle class—another symptom of the long-term stagnation trend. In 1971, for example, about 61 percent of all Americans were considered to be middle-class—this proportion then declined to 59 percent by 1981, and eroded farther to 51 percent by 2010, three decades after the start of the neoliberal era.[35] This long decline

34. Civilian labor force participation rate; see Bureau of Labor Statistics, U.S. Department of Labor, "Databases and Tools" (accessed September 8, 2012), http://data.bls.gov/timeseries/LNS11300000/. Declining participation rates attracted attention in the aftermath of the economic crisis that started in 2007; see, for example, Ben Casselman, "Long-Term Jobless Left out of the Recovery," *Wall Street Journal,* September 3, 2013, A4; William A. Galston, "The Incredible Shrinking Workforce," *Wall Street Journal,* October 30, 2013, A13; Editorial, "Another Jobs Lull: The Labor Force Participation Rate Falls to its Lowest Level Since 1978," *Wall Street Journal,* September 7, 2013, A14; Mortimer Zuckerman, "A Jobless Recovery Is a Phony Recovery," *Wall Street Journal,* July 16, 2013, A15.

35. Pew Research Center, *The Lost Decade of the American Middle Class: Fewer, Poorer, Gloomier* (August 22, 2012), http://www.pewsocialtrends.org/2012/08/22/the-lost-decade-of-the-middle-class/1/. This research was based on a representative national survey of 1,287 adults, supplemented by data from the U.S. Census Bureau and the Federal Reserve—defining middle-class status as households comprising a family of three with incomes ranging from $39,000 to $118,000 in 2011 dollars. See also Smith, "Middle-Class Mayday"; Hamilton and Li, "Family's Path"; Shah, "Household Incomes."

was largely a product of downward socioeconomic mobility, rather than any significant shift upward from the middle class to the wealthy segment—as some neoliberal pundits have tried to claim. Downward socioeconomic mobility that was accompanied by a substantial redistribution of wealth *from* the vast majority *toward* the wealthiest segment of the population.[36] The median net worth of middle class families, for example, increased only 2.3 percent between 1983 and 2010—an increase that was far behind that of the cost of living during that twenty-seven-year period—another symptom of long-term stagnation. It declined by 28 percent during 2000–2010, the worst decade for middle-class households' net worth—an unprecedented drop since such data started to be recorded.[37] In 1971, the middle class accounted for about 62 percent of overall household income in the United States, but by 2010 its share had declined to 45 percent. For the 2000–2010 decade alone, middle-class median household income dropped almost 5 percent (8 percent for all households)—confirming the long-term erosion of wages noted earlier.[38] At the same time, the wealthiest 1 percent of the population increased their share of national income substantially. In 1976, for example, the wealthiest 1 percent owned 8.9 percent of all U.S. income, but by 2007—just before the start of the economic crisis—their share had climbed to 23.5 percent, a level last seen in 1928 (just before the start of the Great Depression).[39]

---

36. Joseph Stiglitz noted that "much of the growth of income and wealth at the top in recent decades has come from what economists call rent-seeking—activities directed more at increasing the share of the pie they get rather than increasing the size of the pie itself"—see his "Level the Playing Field: To Fix the Economy, We Must Boost Demand; To Do That, We Have to Address Inequality," *Los Angeles Times,* July 22, 2012, A26, and *The Price of Inequality: How Today's Divided Society Endangers Our Future* (New York: Norton, 2012). See also Charles A. Murray, *Coming Apart: The State of White America, 1960–2010* (New York: Crown Forum, 2012).

37. Between the start of the economic crisis in 2007 and the end of 2010, middle-class households' net worth declined by 39 percent; see Pew Research Center, *Lost Decade.* One associated aspect is the growing insecurity that now accompanies some of the more prominent professions—which in the past provided entry into the middle class; see, for example, Vanessa O'Connell, "Lawyers Settle . . . for Temp Jobs: As Clients Seek to Cut Costs, the Field of 'Contract' Attorneys Expands," *Wall Street Journal,* June 15, 2011, B1.

38. Rebecca Trounson, "Middle Class Erodes to 51%: The Core US Belief in Economic and Social Mobility Is Not Necessarily True Anymore, a Study Says," *Los Angeles Times,* August 23, 2012, AA1; Pew Research Center, *Lost Decade;* Sentier Research LLC, *Changes in Household Income During the Economic Recovery: June 2009 to June 2012* (August 23, 2012), http://www.sentierresearch.com/reports; Barbara Garson, *Down the Up Escalator: How the 99% Live in the Great Recession* (New York: Doubleday, 2013).

39. Emmanuel Saez, *Striking It Richer: The Evolution of Top Incomes in the United States (Update with 2007 Estimates)* (August 5, 2009), http://elsa.berkeley.edu/; Piketty and Saez, "Income Inequality in the United States, 1913–1998," 1–39.

The long-term erosion of the middle class that accompanied stagnation was also evident in the aftermath of the economic crisis that started
in 2007. Sixty percent of all jobs lost during the crisis were estimated to
have paid midlevel wages ($13.84 to $21.13 per hour). During the three
years (2009–2012) following the start of the recovery, however, only 22
percent of all jobs created were in this wage category. In contrast, almost
60 percent of all new jobs created during that period were in the low-
est-paying category ($7.69 to $13.83 per hour).[40] This disturbing job and
wage trajectory was accompanied by declining household incomes across the
United States.[41] In 2011 alone, for example—four years after the start of
the crisis (and two years into the recovery)—median real U.S. household
income declined by 1.3 percent, to $50,502—a level last reached in the
mid-1990s. This decline of median household income was accompanied
by a rapidly increasing number of households who fell below the federally
established poverty level.[42] The crisis thus not only accelerated downward
mobility but also exacerbated demand for public assistance, in the form of
welfare and food stamps.[43]

---

40. National Employment Law Project, *The Low-Wage Recovery and Growing Inequality*
(New York: NELP, 2012), http://www.nelp.org/page/-/Job_Creation/LowWageRecovery2012.
pdf?nocdn=1; Jim Puzzanghera, "Most Jobs Created in Recovery Found to be Low-Paying,"
Los Angeles Times, September 1, 2012, B2.

41. U.S. Bureau of the Census, *American Community Survey* (Washington, DC: U.S.
Government Printing Office, various years), http://www.census.gov/acs/; Josh Mitchell,
"Incomes Fell or Stagnated in Most States Last Year," *Wall Street Journal*, September 20,
2012, A6. One result of this trend is a projected retirement crisis—as many working individuals end up having insufficient savings and investments to provide an adequate income
in old age; see, for example, Kelly Greene and Vipal Monga, "Workers Saving Too Little
to Retire," *Wall Street Journal*, March 19, 2013, A1; Employee Benefit Research Institute,
Retirement Confidence Survey (RCS) (Washington, DC: EBRI, 1996–2013), http://www.ebri.
org/surveys/rcs/.

42. For a family of four, $23,021 (2011). Between 2009 (the recovery's starting year) and
mid-2013, individuals classified as poor increased by 2.9 million; see William A. Galston, "In
Defense of Food Stamps," *Wall Street Journal*, November 6, 2013, A13. In California—the
most important economy in the United States—335,760 people fell below the poverty level in
2011 alone, raising this state's poverty rate to almost one-fifth of the population; see Census,
American Community Survey; Mitchell, "Incomes Fell."

43. By mid-2012, 46.7 million people in the United States were receiving food stamps under
the federal government's Supplemental Nutrition Assistance Program—an increase of almost
42 percent from 2009; see U.S. Department of Agriculture, Food, and Nutrition Service,
Office of Research and Analysis, *Building a Healthy America: A Profile of the Supplemental
Nutrition Assistance Program* (Washington, DC: U.S. Department of Agriculture, 2012),
http://www.fns.usda.gov/ora/SNAP.htm; Garson, *Down the Up Escalator*.

The decline of midlevel wage jobs that resulted from the crisis contributed to long-term stagnation by throttling aggregate demand and consumption. And to maintain consumption as wages eroded, the vast majority of the population incurred vast—and unsustainable—amounts of *debt*. Financialism made this possible through easy credit and the securitization of debt on an unprecedented scale.[44] Mortgage debt was particularly important in this dynamic. Almost everyone seemed to ignore the high risk it carried as housing prices increased rapidly—with mortgage corporations, banks, and speculators feeding the notion that they could, and would, go on rising forever. In this way, the vast majority of the population could be desensitized—collectively anesthetized, in a manner of speaking—about the long-term erosion of income they were experiencing. This turned into a cultural trend of sorts during the 1990s and 2000s, as super-consumerism became a paramount objective for the majority of the population. At the same time, the notion that borrowing to bet in financialism's casino economy—using consumer credit—would reward everyone with yet more consumption became entrenched.[45] As a result, consumer debt rose rapidly from the start of the neoliberal era. In 1980, for example, consumer debt outstanding—excluding mortgage debt—was at 68.0 percent of disposable income.[46] In 2000, it reached 96.8 percent, and by 2005 it had increased to nearly 130 percent. No prior time in American history had seen a similar increase in consumer debt.

The economic crisis that started in 2007 provided a rude awakening from this debt-supported trajectory. It also exposed the underlying, long-term stagnation trend that had been a fundamental—but much ignored—feature

---

44. Debt securitization helped increase credit substantially. In 1964, for example, total credit issued in the American economy amounted to about $1 trillion—by 2010 it had risen to over $50 trillion; see Richard Duncan, *The New Depression: The Breakdown of the Paper Money Economy* (New York: Wiley, 2012); Justin O'Bryan, *Engineering a Financial Bloodbath: How Sub-Prime Securitization Destroyed the Legitimacy of Financial Capitalism* (London: Imperial College Press, 2009); Louis Hyman, *Borrow: The American Way of Debt* (New York: Vintage, 2012).

45. See Steve Fraser, *Every Man a Speculator: A History of Wall Street in American Life* (New York: HarperCollins, 2005); Long and Sievers, *Socioanalysis of Money*; Hyman, *Borrow*.

46. "Disposable income" defined as income after tax payments; consumer debt comprises credit card, automobile, and personal loans (home loans are excluded). See Board of Governors, Federal Reserve System, *Flow of Funds Accounts of the United States*, Historical Series and Flows (various years), http://www.bog.frb.fed.us/releases/z1/current/ and http://federalreserve.gov/releases/z1/current/ (accessed March 16, 2011); Foster and McChesney, "Endless Crisis"; Hyman, *Borrow*.

of the American economy.[47] That long-term stagnation trend—and the concealment of its effects through debt accumulation—becomes obvious when U.S. economic growth is weighed against outstanding debt. Estimating a ratio of GDP growth in dollars per additional dollar of debt, for example, reveals a $0.88 ratio in 1957 that declined to $0.75 by 1980, and sank farther down to $0.10 by 2010.[48] Thus, ninety cents out of every dollar of GDP growth generated in 2010 could be accounted for by debt outstanding—as opposed to only twelve cents in 1957. The disturbing observation to be drawn from this estimation, therefore, is that most U.S. economic growth achieved since the late 1950s seems to have been fueled by rising indebtedness. *A mountain of accumulating debt thus concealed the long stagnation trend that oligopoly capitalism spawned.*

Financialism was very much at the core of this phenomenon. In 1980, for example, financial activities' share of U.S. GDP amounted to 35 percent. By 1990, this proportion had risen to 50 percent—after a decade of deregulation and expanding speculation—further increasing to 59 percent by 2000, and reaching 65 percent of U.S. GDP in 2010—a substantial rise over the relatively short span of three decades.[49] This takeover of GDP by financial activities is all the more noteworthy when one considers the magnitude of the American economy. Also, financial activities' rising share of GDP did not generate a similar increase in employment, relative to production. Since 1990, for example, financial activities' share of employment—relative to goods production—stayed essentially level, at 22 percent.[50] Financial activ-

---

47. One that radical political economists Paul Sweezy and Paul Baran had long called attention to, despite the typically dismissive attitude of mainstream (neoclassical) economists; see Baran and Sweezy, *Monopoly Capital.* Their work conceptualized how an economic surplus is generated under oligopolistic conditions—and why it leads to long-term stagnation.

48. These estimates include all domestic nonfinancial debt, using three-year moving averages; see U.S. Bureau of Economic Analysis, *National Income and Product Accounts* (various years), http://www.bea.gov/ national/; Board of Governors, U.S. Federal Reserve System, *Flow of Funds* (Historical part, various years), http://www.bog. frb.fed.us/.

49. Financial sector estimates based on data for finance, insurance, and real estate; see U.S. Bureau of Economic Analysis, *National Income and Product Accounts,* National Income Without Capital Consumption Adjustment (various years), http://www.bea.gov/national/ nipaweb/; Foster and McChesney, "Endless Crisis," 16.

50. U.S. Bureau of Economic Analysis, *National Income and Product Accounts,* National Income Without Capital Consumption Adjustment (various years), http://www.bea.gov/ national/nipaweb/; Foster, Magdoff, and McChesney, "Stagnation of Employment"; Harry Magdoff and Paul M. Sweezy, *Stagnation and the Financial Explosion* (New York: Monthly Review Press, 1987), 23.

ities' rapidly rising share of GDP thus benefited a very small segment of the population—mostly the financial elites and those linked to the financial oligopolies.

For the vast majority of the population, the long-term stagnation trend meant rising economic insecurity. High indebtedness to sustain consumption and living standards only masked the negative effects temporarily. The offshoring and outsourcing of jobs and the decline of labor unions provided a growing reserve army of labor with no choice but to work for less. This panorama was compounded by a decline in domestic hiring by United States–based multinational oligopolies—compared with their operations abroad—even as their profits rose substantially.[51] The corporate oligopolies and their associated elites, however, were—and are—insulated from this panorama of distress, as their wealth kept on accumulating. Such insulation from the larger socioeconomic reality is another outcome of oligopolistic power, as profits increase even in difficult economic times.[52] Prices are thus largely immune to downward pressure even as aggregate demand stagnates or drops. At the same time, rising or sustained revenues and profits means that oligopolistic influence over public governance continues, since the resources are there to support lobbying, contributions, and other forms of political co-optation. *The influence of the oligopolies can therefore increase with stagnation, as a reserve army of unemployed labor grows, labor unions are further impaired, and the distress of the population all too often inspires*

---

51. In 2011, for example, American multinational corporations' employment in the United States was practically stagnant, while their worldwide hiring rose by 1.5 percent; see Sudeep Reddy, "Domestic-Based Multinationals Hiring Overseas," *Wall Street Journal,* April 19, 2013, A2. This was part of a long trajectory of expansion abroad that started in the 1950s, which contributed to underemployment and unemployment at home; see Magdoff and Magdoff, "Disposable Workers"; Denpankar Basu, "The Reserve Army of Labor in the Postwar US Economy," *Science and Society* 77 (2013): 179–201.

52. As a share of GDP, U.S. corporate profits were higher in 2011 (15 percent) than before the start of the economic crisis (13 percent in 2005)—despite the weak economic recovery that started in 2009 and the fact that this crisis was the deepest one since the Great Depression; see, for example, "Capital Gains," *The Economist,* July 21, 2012, 62. Although perhaps surprising to many mainstream economists, this outcome was long ago anticipated by scholars who understood the deeper structure of oligopolies and monopolies; see Edward H. Chamberlin, *The Theory of Monopolistic Competition* (Cambridge: Harvard University Press, 1933); Joan Robinson, *The Economics of Imperfect Competition* (London: Macmillan, 1933); Paul M. Sweezy, "Demand Under Conditions of Oligopoly," *Journal of Political Economy* 47 (1939): 568–73.

*political recipes—such as deregulation, more tax loopholes, or lower corporate
taxes—that favor oligopolistic power.*[53]

Since price competition is largely absent in oligopolistic sectors—and
concentration sustains revenues and profits—the accumulated surplus capital
must find uses. An important one is speculative finance. Financialism thus
comes into play in this panorama of overaccumulation, exacerbating it in
many ways. Very high executive compensation, along with rich payouts for
the privileged elites tied to the oligopolies, are common destinations for
part of the accumulated surplus. At the same time, the corporate oligopolies
build on the relations of power stacked in their favor by cutting employee
pensions, benefits, and employment—while outsourcing or offshoring production to further boost profits and raise share prices. After all, an executive
who does not do everything possible—and often also the impossible—to
boost the bottom line and raise share prices cannot be considered competent
in a time when increasing shareholder returns is the key to promotion. This
leads to yet more capital being accumulated. Capital for which there is a
dearth of productive investment outlets in the real economy—the one where
reproduction and commodification come apart and pose difficult dilemmas,
as noted in the previous chapter.

Sending the surplus capital abroad as investment can alleviate the
problem, but only temporarily, since any repatriated profits will eventually add to overaccumulation at home. Also, the incipient oligopolization
of the global economy means that the overaccumulation of capital could
soon become a global problem.[54] This prospect can be seen in the rapidly
increasing revenues of multinational oligopolies as a share of world income.
In 2004–08, for example, the total annual revenue of the five hundred
largest corporations in the world amounted to more than 40 percent of
world income.[55] This share—which is now larger than the gross economic

---

53. Especially when such recipes are sponsored or diffused by the corporate-controlled news
media; see Robert W. McChesney, *Corporate Media and the Threat to Democracy* (New York:
Seven Stories Press, 1997).

54. A problem anticipated long ago by radical political economists who researched mul-
tinational corporations; see Stephen H. Hymer, *The Multinational Corporation: A Radical
Approach* (New York: Cambridge University Press, 1979); Richard J. Barnet and Ronald E.
Müller, *Global Reach: The Power of the Multinational Corporations* (New York: Simon and
Schuster, 1974).

55. John Bellamy Foster, Robert W. McChesney, and R. Jamil Jonna, "Monopoly and
Competition in Twenty-First Century Capitalism," *Monthly Review*, April 2011, 12–13.

product of most nations—increased rapidly since the early 1990s, and is likely to increase to more than half of world income in the near future.[56] For American corporations, profits from operations abroad increased sharply since the 1970s—compounding the problem of overaccumulation at home, as vast sums were repatriated. Thus, while U.S. corporate profits from abroad averaged about 6 percent during the decade of the 1960s, by the 1990s they had increased to 15 percent—rising further to 21 percent during 2001–2010.[57]

It is perplexing that this global trend toward oligopolization has been largely ignored by mainstream economics—the rising power and spread of multinational oligopolies being presented instead as rising competition between nations, and also between their workers.[58] This masquerade made it possible to hide the fact that the corporate models showcased as "optimal" examples of "competitive" corporate organizations were all oligopolies.[59] Equally important, perhaps, is that the neoliberal strategies and policies recommended for nations to become "competitive" were actually the opposite of

56. The rising profile of multinational oligopolies in many nations is often accompanied by substantial increases in government debt. The opening of nations to greater multinational corporate influence, and neoliberal policies advocated by metanational organizations, seem to be part of this dynamic. See, for example, Eric Toussaint and Damien Millet, *Debt, the IMF, and the World Bank: Sixty Questions, Sixty Answers* (New York: Monthly Review Press, 2010); John Perkins, *Confessions of an Economic Hit Man* (San Francisco: Berrett-Koehler, 2004); Richard Peet, *Unholy Trinity: The IMF, World Bank, and WTO* (London: Zed, 2009).

57. Based on decades-long estimates of corporate profits (capital consumption adjustments excluded, inventory valuation adjustments included); U.S. Executive Office of the President, Council of Economic Advisers, *Economic Report of the President* (2012), "Corporate Profits by Industry, 1963–2011" (Table B-91), http://www.whitehouse.gov/administration/eop/cea/; Foster, McChesney, and Jonna, "Monopoly and Competition." Corporate profitability, supported by overseas operations, continued its rise during the crisis that started in 2007—reaching a seven-decades high (proportionate to GDP) in 2013; see "Margin for Error: American Corporate Profits Seem to Have Defied Gravity," *The Economist*, November 2, 2013, 78.

58. Among the best-known academic proponents of this distraction were business economists, who largely brushed off any concern about the rising global tide of oligopolies—while also often serving as their consultants. See, for example, Michael Porter, *The Competitive Advantage of Nations* (New York: Free Press, 1989). One exception among mainstream economists was Louis Galambos, "The Triumph of Oligopoly," in *American Economic Development in Historical Perspective*, ed. Thomas J. Weiss and Donald Schaefer (Stanford: Stanford University Press, 1994), 241–314.

59. One of the most successful oligopolistic corporate models presented (and admired) during the 1980s and '90s was the Japanese *keiretsu*. Certain authors actually recommended forming *keiretsu*-style American oligopolies to imitate their practices and gain more influence; see, for example, David N. Burt and Michael F. Doyle, *The American Keiretsu: A Strategic Weapon for Global Competitiveness* (Homewood, IL: Business One Irwin, 1993).

those followed by the advanced capitalist nations when they industrialized.[60] Rather than a competitive international market structure, what has actually occurred is a global oligopolistic effort to dominate production—targeting low-cost labor and exploiting wage differentials between nations—with fewer corporations in control over time, as mergers and acquisitions increase concentration.[61] The emphasis on low-cost labor in production, a key aspect of most poor countries, also reflects the growing complexity—and higher costs—introduced by the severance of reproduction from commodification in advanced capitalist nations. *This phenomenon works to the advantage of oligopolists targeting the lowest-cost nations, where greater internal control over reproduction and commodification in production can be maintained*—especially when local subcontractors are involved. More internal control also translates into greater exploitation, with deplorable labor conditions and a lack of workplace rights. This global oligopolistic effort to dominate production partly accounts for the vast amount of capital accumulated by some of the richest oligopolistic corporations of our time. Apple Computer, for example—largely because of its operations abroad—amassed $110 billion in capital by early 2011, for which it had no real productive use.[62] Offshoring

---

60. See Ha-Joon Chang, *Bad Samaritans: The Myth of Free Trade and the Secret History of Global Capitalism* (New York: Bloomsbury Press, 2008). Nations that gained early global supremacy in manufacturing actually adopted highly protectionist policies to industrialize, and did not start to promote the idea of "free trade" until after they had consolidated their industrial base—and established a powerful international projection.

61. One result is that labor's worldwide share of national income has declined rapidly since the late 1970s; see "Labour Pains: All around the World, Labour is Losing Out to Capital," *The Economist*, November 2, 2013, 77–78; Organization for Economic Cooperation and Development, *OECD.StatExtracts*, "Unit Labour Costs, Annual Indicators: Labour Income Share Ratios" (accessed December 8, 2013), http://stats.oecd.org/.

62. John Smith, "The GDP Illusion: Value Added versus Value Capture," *Monthly Review*, July-August 2012, 90; Carol J. Loomis, "Apple: What It's Like to Drown in Cash," *Fortune*, May 20, 2013, 164–72; "The World's Biggest Public Companies," *Forbes*, April 2012, http://www.forbes.com. Apple Computer was found to have paid no corporate income taxes to any national governments, on at least $74 billion in revenue during 2009–12—a practice that compounded the vast amounts of unutilized capital it held; see, for example, Danny Yadron, Kate Linebaugh, and Jessica E. Lessin, "Apple Avoided Tax on Overseas Billions," *Wall Street Journal*, May 21, 2013, A1. Because of their global reach, it is quite feasible for American oligopolies to avoid paying corporate income taxes in the nations where they operate—and also in the United States—by moving or keeping revenues in countries without such taxes. This strategy often involves the creation of offshore subsidiaries—which are not reported to U.S. regulators or tax authorities—a practice made possible by regulatory loopholes kept in place through lobbying and political influence; see Jessica Holzer, "The Incredible Vanishing Subsidiary: And Then There Were Two—in 2009, Google Disclosed over 100 Subsidiaries; in 2012, Two," *Wall Street Journal*, May 23, 2013, B1.

jobs only compounded Apple's overaccumulation, as its profits were boosted by the substantially lower labor costs it obtained. Thus, the total wage costs for its iPod-related production in China came to $19 million in 2006, while the wage costs of its U.S. operations for the same product, during the same year—employing a similarly skilled workforce and producing much the same output—was $719 million.[63] Apple's oligopolistic position, and the early start of some of its products—including the iPod—also provided it with control over pricing. Its emphasis on boosting profits by offshoring production thus added substantially to its vast amount of accumulated capital.

One consequence of the overaccumulation of capital is that almost every oligopolistic corporation today is involved with financialism. Since surplus capital cannot find enough productive investments, then it can be used to speculate in the casino economy by, for example, buying up a large number of the corporation's own outstanding shares to drive up the stock price artificially. Or, the surplus capital can be used to provide easy credit to customers and suppliers, driving up their indebtedness—and their obligations to the oligopolistic creditor. Or, it can be used to speculate against the stocks and bonds of a potential rival, to drive it into a merger or takeover—that can further increase oligopolistic concentration and the power of the suitor. Or, the surplus capital can be used to speculate in real estate, diversifying the oligopolistic corporation's assets to further boost its profits and capital. Or, it can be used to speculate in the emerging area of intellectual property futures, betting on patent rights that can be used to force others to purchase licenses. *Financialism thus seems to have reached into almost every corner of the real economy, compounding the problem of capital overaccumulation—as practically all the schemes employed lead to yet more accumulation.* The vast amounts of surplus capital—which can find little use in the real economy of production—virtually guarantee that this will occur.[64] At the same time, this dynamic also seems to guarantee that more crises—and stagnation, for the vast majority of the population—will be part of our future reality.

63. Smith, "GDP Illusion," 89; Greg Linden, Jason Dedrick, and Kenneth L. Kraemer, *Innovation and Job Creation in a Global Economy: The Case of Apple's iPod.* (Irvine: Personal Computing Industry Center, University of California, 2009).

64. American corporations held almost $2 trillion in cash in early 2010—an unprecedented amount that practically sat idle—reflecting the problem of overaccumulation; see, for example, Justin Lahart, "US Firms Build Up Record Cash Piles," *Wall Street Journal,* June 10, 2010, A1; John Bellamy Foster, "The Financialization of Accumulation," *Monthly Review,* October, 2010, 1–17.

If the government promotes indebtedness to boost aggregate demand, then it creates problems down the line—since debt cannot increase indefinitely to overcome stagnation without triggering a credit crisis. Government policies that create more public debt can nonetheless boost aggregate demand—and generate some growth and employment in the short term— but they are clearly not a solution for the long-term stagnation tendency of advanced capitalism.[65] Typically, those policies also end up favoring the oligopolies and the wealthy elites tied to them, by helping transfer their risk to the public sector—then bailing them out when crises occur. Such policies are, of course, nominally undertaken to stimulate growth and recovery for "all" of society—per the usual jargon and propaganda spins of corporatocratic politics—but the real beneficiaries are the powerful oligopolies, which end up acquiring more power and accumulating yet more capital.

Central bank monetary policies also exacerbate the problem of overaccumulation. This often starts by inducing (or requiring) banks and other financial institutions in the private sector to place some of their surplus capital in the central bank's custody. Such capital is then used by government to support its expenditures and cover its deficits—particularly when significant amounts of new monetary instruments have to be printed—in the form of money or Treasury Bonds, for example. In the end, this only compounds the problem of overaccumulation—as central banks eventually flood the financial system with liquidity. Such liquidity then translates into more capital for banks and financial institutions—as central banks try to stimulate growth by inducing them to issue more debt.[66] In the case of

---

65. The short-term dimension of such policies was implicit in Keynes's work; Keynes, *The General Theory of Employment, Interest, and Money*. During his time, government debt and deficits were quite limited—and even after the onset of the Great Depression they remained a relatively small percentage of governments' total operating budgets (and of national income). The size of contemporary governments' debt and deficits—particularly in advanced capitalist nations—would have most certainly astounded Keynes.

66. American banks held about $1.5 trillion in cash in their balance sheets as of mid-2012, in excess of their required reserves—an amount that was practically idle and reflects the problem of capital overaccumulation in the financial system (data from Allan H. Meltzer's "What's Wrong With the Federal Reserve?" *Wall Street Journal*, July 10, 2012, A13). In addition, banks' excess reserves—held by the Federal Reserve to cover their transactions and deposits—amounted to $2.5 trillion as of late 2013; see Alan S. Blinder, "The Fed Plan to Revive High-Powered Money," *Wall Street Journal*, December 11, 2013, A21. Private equity firms (hedge funds) were estimated to have $325 billion in cash at the start of 2013; see Cambridge Associates LLC, *US Private Equity Index and Selected Benchmark Statistics* (June 2013), http://www.cambridgeassociates.com/pdf/.

the United States, for example, the Federal Reserve augments the surplus capital it receives from banks with newly printed money.[67] And, to finance the government's deficit—*incurred partly through the transfer of risk from corporations to the public sector, a key aspect of corporatocracy*—what may be referred to as a *two-handed monetary scheme* was devised: the right hand of government (the Federal Reserve) prints vast amounts of money, and then uses it—along with whatever capital it receives from banks—to purchase bonds issued by the left hand of government (the U.S. Treasury).

One hand of government thereby provides credit to the other hand, by printing vast amounts of monetary instruments and by using some of the surplus capital it obtains from banks. And, true to the nature of corporatocracy, the U.S. Treasury Bonds so purchased help finance the government deficit incurred through the corporate bailouts, tax breaks, subsidies, and myriad programs—of corporate welfare—that benefit oligopolistic corporations and their privileged elites. Through these monetary gymnastics, the right hand of government (the Federal Reserve) bought almost two-thirds of all bonds issued by the left hand of government (the U.S. Treasury) during the 2011–12 fiscal year alone.[68] By mid-2012, the Federal Reserve and other government entities "owned" 41 percent of all U.S. Treasury bond debt outstanding ($6.6 trillion)—an unprecedented share that surpassed that of all other holder categories (domestic private and foreign) of such debt,

---

67. Massive money printing by the U.S. Federal Reserve without short-term negative consequences has been made possible mostly by the dollar's seven-decade status as the prime international currency. The scrapping of the Bretton Woods Agreement in 1971 (which had indexed the dollar's value to a specific quantity of gold), in particular, helped expand monetary supply rapidly. The end of this arrangement by the U.S. government has been considered an important step on the way to the globalization of neoliberal policies; see, for example, David Harvey, *A Brief History of Neoliberalism* (New York: Oxford University Press, 2005), 10. Almost any nation whose currency is not widely used for international exchange would find it catastrophic to print the vast amounts—and create the high levels of liquidity—that the Federal Reserve customarily does; see, for example, David Wessel, "Why Dollar Is King Despite US Woes," *Wall Street Journal*, December 5, 2013, A4. See also Maria N. Ivanova, "The Dollar as World Money," *Science and Society* 77 (2013): 44–71.

68. "Quantitative Easing," *New York Times, Times Topics,* July 24, 2012, http://topics.nytimes.com/. The Federal Reserve thus displaced all domestic private and foreign entities to become the main customer for U.S. Treasury Bonds. One highly experienced international financial specialist noted, on this and other measures, that "the Federal Reserve has become an enabler of the financial havoc it was designed to prevent"—John Phelan, "The Fed Celebrates its 100th Birthday: The Institution Created to End Bank Failures Has Morphed into an Engine of Financial and Economic Instability," *Wall Street Journal*, December 23, 2013, A15.

and that reflects the inbred nature of U.S. government debt financing.[69] *In order to support, in part, the massive transfer of risk from corporations to the public sector—a phenomenon that is a hallmark of corporatocracy—the federal government thus became its own prime financier.*

A vast amount of funds, near one trillion dollars altogether—newly printed money and capital received from banks—was deployed by the Federal Reserve in this manner during 2010–12 (a period spanning two fiscal years). The purpose was to finance the U.S. government's deficit by purchasing massive amounts of Treasury Bonds. The desired result was to depress yields (the interest rate to be paid by the U.S. Treasury to any bond purchasers) substantially—by vastly and artificially increasing demand for Treasury Bonds. The right hand of government (the Federal Reserve) thus artificially generated demand for the public debt that the left hand (the U.S. Treasury) was selling—to reduce the interest rate that the left hand would have to pay to purchasers.[70] In this way the immense, artificial demand

69. *TreasuryDirect,* "Debt Distribution" (August 2012), http://www.treasurydirect.gov/govt/charts/; Spencer Jakab, "Ahead of the Tape: Uncle Sam Needs Its Patient Investors," *Wall Street Journal,* September 17, 2012, C1.

70. The Federal Reserve's two-handed monetary gymnastics included, for example, the first so-called Quantitative Easing operation (QE1, fourth quarter 2008 to first quarter 2010), a second one (QE2, fourth quarter 2010 to first quarter 2011), and a third (QE3, fourth quarter 2012-on). The third one also involved the purchase of securitized mortgages for an unlimited period of time, to try to depress interest rates—by late 2013, such purchases had reached $40 billion per month, while monthly purchases of Treasury Bonds were at $45 billion; see Nick Timiraos, "Fed's Mortgage Role Expands: Central Bank's Asset Purchases Are Bigger Share of Market as It Begins to Taper," *Wall Street Journal,* December 20, 2013, C1. Inducing more borrowing and indebtedness to trigger some growth was the obvious goal. Inflating stock markets—as a way to generate growth and benefit all who depend on stock betting for income or wealth—also seemed to be part of the objective, although it was not officially stated. In addition, a time-sensitive bond swap (Operation Twist) was arranged in 2011–12, to exchange long-term Treasury bonds for shorter-term ones—also with the purpose of depressing interest rates as much as possible. By December 2013, the Federal Reserve had accumulated more than $4 trillion in Treasury Bonds, loans, mortgage-backed securities, and other assets—from less than $900 billion before the crisis (2007)—the largest amount ever; see Victoria McGrane, "Portfolio Reaches Past $4 Trillion," *Wall Street Journal,* December 20, 2013, A2. In general, the effects of these measures were considered by many specialists to be limited or even counterproductive; see, for example, Andrew Huszar, "Confessions of a Quantitative Easer: We Went on a Bond-Buying Spree that Was Supposed to Help Main Street—Instead, It Was a Feast for Wall Street," *Wall Street Journal,* November 12, 2013, A17; Meltzer, "What's Wrong"; Phil Gramm and Thomas R. Saving, "Janet Yellen's Greatest Challenge," *Wall Street Journal,* November 22, 2013, A15; U.S. Bureau of Economic Analysis, *Integrated Macroeconomic Accounts for the United States,* http://www.bea.gov/national/nipaweb/ (accessed September 10, 2012).

created by the Federal Reserve for Treasury Bonds made it easier for the government to finance its own deficits—and to spend more—since the interest it would have to pay on those bonds (and on its accumulating debt) was sharply reduced.[71] Because interest rates for other types of debt—mortgages, for example—are influenced by U.S. Treasury Bond rates, an ulterior motive was to *also* force those other rates lower—so as to induce everyone to incur more debt.[72] Massive debt creation thus became a major (but undeclared) Federal Reserve policy, in order to generate economic growth and overcome stagnation.

These efforts were buttressed by the Federal Reserve's earlier lowering of general interest rates—its most important policy tool—to negative real levels (positive but near zero in nominal terms).[73] This was a very unusual situation—starting in 2008—which tried to overcome fears of a financial meltdown by collapsing the cost of capital.[74] The setting of negative real interest rates meant that the Federal Reserve was practically giving money away—in the hope of concocting some growth by inducing everyone to take on more debt. At the same time, it potentially created a major future government debt crisis—since outstanding debt will almost certainly increase

---

71. It should not surprise, therefore, that starting in 2009 federal deficits reached an unprecedented sequence of high levels: $1.4 trillion in 2009, $1.3 trillion each in 2010 and 2011, and $1.2 trillion in 2012. This four-year period of federal borrowing alone amounted to $55,000 per U.S. household. Data obtained from George P. Shultz, Michael Boskin, John F. Cogan, Allan H. Meltzer, and John B. Taylor, "The Magnitude of the Mess We're In," *Wall Street Journal,* September 17, 2012, A19.

72. Partly because of this policy, individual indebtedness was not reduced much during and immediately after the crisis—thus, for example, U.S. consumer debt declined only about 15 percent from its 2008 peak, as of mid-2012; Board of Governors, U.S. Federal Reserve System, *Consumer Credit Historical Data* (various years), http://www.federalreserve.gov/releases/g19/ HIST/. Also, debt due to purchases of expensive consumer products—such as automobiles— increased rapidly; see, for example, Christina Rogers, "Car Sales Fuel Boom in Debt," *Wall Street Journal,* December 18, 2013, B2. Starting in 2012, student loan debt (at that time almost $1 trillion) was added to consumer debt—making the total outstanding in that year the same as in 2008; David Reilly, "Rising Student Debt Weakens Credit Story," *Wall Street Journal,* August 6, 2012, C1.

73. This action seems to have been influenced by the experience of Japan in the 1990s; see, for example, "The Global Crash: Japanese Lessons," *The Economist,* August 4, 2012, 63–65.

74. The setting of negative real interest rates was extremely unusual. A well-known financial journalist, for example, noted that "interest rates below zero used to be more economists' fantasy than reality. Few thought central banks would ever need, let alone be able, to cut rates below zero"; David Wessel, "Interesting Situation: When Rates Turn Negative," *Wall Street Journal,* August 9, 2012, A2.

rapidly when interest rates have to be raised. That prospect was diminished by federal officials, who prioritized the short-term over any critical long-term problems. An immediate effect of this interest rate policy was to severely disadvantage saving. Almost two hundred million Americans with savings accounts thus began to experience losses, relative to inflation.[75]

Those most negatively affected by the Federal Reserve's interest rate policy were working people and the middle class, who found their savings losing value over time. Pension funds—a fundamental support for the vast majority of the population in old age—were also very negatively affected, as negative real interest rates made it impossible for them to cover their obligations.[76] Most pension funds thus began to experience losses and engage in very risky speculation to try to boost returns by any means possible.[77] Those most favorably affected by the negative real interest rate policy, on the other hand, were the corporate oligopolies—as incurring debt became cheaper

---

75. Another major negative effect was to induce many individuals who depended on income from savings and interest rates to speculate in very risky assets—such as "junk" or high-risk corporate bonds—to try to cover their living expenses or sustain their retirement. High-risk corporate bond sales thus began to see record-breaking increases—of 100 percent or more—in the number of buyers over a short time; see, for example, Matt Wirz, "Low Rates Spur Record Debt Sales," *Wall Street Journal*, October 1, 2012, C9; "High-Yield Bonds: An Appetite for Junk," *The Economist*, October 19, 2013, 75–76. Sales of those bonds reached such high levels in May 2013 that yields plummeted to a historical low of 4.96 percent; see Katy Burne, "Yields on Junk Bonds Reach New Low: As Investors Fight for Returns, Payout on Debt from Weak Companies Takes Its First Dip Below 5%," *Wall Street Journal*, May 9, 2013, C1. At the same time, margin debt—the use of borrowed money to bet in the stock and bond markets—reached $379.5 billion by March, 2013—very close to the record $381.4 billion set in July 2007 (just before the start of the crisis); see Alexandra Scaggs and Steven Russolillo, "Investors Rediscovering Margin Debt," *Wall Street Journal*, May 10, 2013, C1. Beyond savings losses and the rise of risky speculation, life insurance policies—which are indexed to interest rates set by the Federal Reserve—also began to experience serious declines in estimated future benefits; see Leslie Scism, "Low-Rate Era Hits Insurance Policies," *Wall Street Journal*, November 4, 2013, C1.

76. See, for example, Vipal Monga, "Why the Pension Gap Is Soaring: Companies Struggle to Get Handle on Liabilities as Low Rates, Other Forces Inflate Funding Needs—$347B Gap Between What Pension Plans Say They Owe Retirees and What They Have to Pay Them," *Wall Street Journal*, February 26, 2013, B1.

77. See Michael Corkery, "Pensions Bet Big with Private Equity," *Wall Street Journal*, January 25, 2013, A1, and his "Pensions Increasing Their Ties: Public Pensions Increase Investments in Private-Equity Funds," *Wall Street Journal*, January 26, 2012, C1; Andrew G. Biggs, "The Hidden Danger in Public Pension Funds: Their Investments Expose Government Budgets and Taxpayers to 10 Times More Risk than in 1975," *Wall Street Journal*, December 16, 2013, A13.

than ever. Borrowing in the United States to invest or speculate abroad also became quite profitable for oligopolistic corporations and their associated elites—given the difference in rates set by the Federal Reserve and those of most other central banks. Higher rates abroad thus attracted much capital and generated speculative surpluses—contributing to overaccumulation in the United States and elsewhere. Households that could continue borrowing to sustain their consumption—and any financialist betting—also found it easier to accumulate more debt, and to ignore the reality of declining real incomes and wages.[78]

The substantial future risks and losses to be faced by the government—when U.S. interest rates rise again—were thus ignored in the frenzy to refloat financialism. In past times, the prospect of rising interest rates had little impact on the Federal Reserve's accounts, since its capital reserves were trivial. Once interest rates start rising, however, it will very likely have to sell a vast quantity of the Treasury Bonds it has accumulated—those purchased from the left hand of government—for much less than what it paid. The losses incurred could possibly be in the hundreds of billions, or perhaps more than a trillion dollars. Such losses will most certainly have to be shouldered by the vast majority of American taxpayers—most of all, working people, the middle class, and the poor—as benefits or services are cut and tax increases further erode incomes. Apparently to divert public attention from this possible future scenario, however, the Federal Reserve—and the U.S. government—orchestrated a publicity campaign to claim that "profits" of $89 billion (in 2012) were derived from its two-handed monetary trick, characterizing this scheme as a major "success."[79] Beyond the vast potential losses, specialists have estimated that the high debt and rising deficits to be incurred by the government during a likely future crisis may force the Federal Reserve to pursue highly inflationary policies—without correspond-

---

78. See, for example, Sean Fieler, "Easy Money is Punishing the Middle Class," *Wall Street Journal,* September 27, 2012, A19; Neil Shah, "Consumer Borrowing Picks Up," *Wall Street Journal,* November 15, 2013, A4; Jane Sterngold and Matt Wirz, "For Corporations and Investors, Debt Makes a Comeback," *Wall Street Journal,* September 6, 2013, A1. Michael Perelman, a critical political economist, linked the wage and debt panoramas to the Federal Reserve's monetary policies; see his "Sado-Monetarism: The Role of the Federal Reserve System in Keeping Wages Low," *Monthly Review,* April 2012 27–35, and *The Invisible Handcuffs of Capitalism: How Market Tyranny Stifles the Economy by Stunting Workers* (New York: Monthly Review Press, 2011).

79. See "The Fed's Profits: The Other Side of QE; What Happens When the Fed Starts Losing Money," *The Economist,* January 26, 2013, 68.

ingly higher interest rates.[80] Should such a scenario occur, a majority of the population would likely be driven into poverty on a scale and at a speed never experienced before.

The Federal Reserve's two-handed monetary scheme was also implemented to boost the stock market through asset price inflation—without adequate regard for the high risks involved.[81] From the Federal Reserve's perspective, refloating financialism depended on getting as many people as possible to speculate in stocks—massively, above and beyond the usual number of bettors. A major problem, however, was that this unwritten (and unacknowledged) policy caused stock prices to rise without a corresponding increase in profits—becoming what a well-known financial analyst referred to as a "sugar high"—an inflation of asset prices that is out of touch with profitability and does little or nothing for long-term growth.[82] Inflating the

---

80. David Greenlaw, James D. Hamilton, Peter Hooper, and Frederic Mishkin, "The Federal Reserve's 'Fiscal Crunch' Trap," *Wall Street Journal*, March 8, 2013, A13.

81. A highly experienced specialist and former hedge fund manager noted, for example, that "the [Federal Reserve's] justification for low interest rates is . . . to goose the stock market as an indirect way to create jobs." Andy Kessler, "When Interest Rates Rise, Watch Out," *Wall Street Journal*, February 22, 2013, A11. According to another specialist—chief executive of a financial firm managing $2 trillion—the "Fed and the other central banks cannot afford to see a massive decline in equity prices." Quoted in Tom Petruno, "Too Big to Fail?: The Fed's Efforts to Keep the US Economy Growing May Not Work Unless the Bull Market in Stocks Rolls On," *Los Angeles Times*, March 3, 2013, B8. In 2012, the Federal Reserve's asset price inflation scheme also began to affect housing, triggering concerns that a new speculative bubble might occur in this sector; see, for example, Edward Pinto, "Is the Fed Blowing a New Housing Bubble?," *Wall Street Journal*, April 10, 2013, A11.

82. Quoted in "Ben Buys, Bulls Buoyant: How Asset Prices React to Quantitative Easing," *The Economist*, September 22, 2012, 84. Speculation through highly complicated vehicles and deals reemerged quickly; see, for example, Matt Wirz, "Complex Deals Finding New Fans," *Wall Street Journal*, November 27, 2013, C1; Ryan Dezember, "Buyout Firms Throw Toggle: A Precrisis Debt-Financing Tool Resurfaces in Neiman Marcus Deal," *Wall Street Journal*, October 23, 2013, C4; Katy Burne, "One of Wall Street's Riskiest Bets Returns," *Wall Street Journal*, June 5, 2013, A1. Hedge funds also rushed to add debt to companies they owned, to fund payouts to themselves; see Ryan Dezember and Matt Wirz, "Private-Equity Payout Debt Surges: Companies Owned by Buyout Shops Rush to Loan, Bond Markets in Anticipation of Rate Increase," *Wall Street Journal*, August 6, 2013, C1. See also Holman W. Jenkins, "Rewriting the Lehman Postmortem: Asset Bubbles for the Rich and a Welfare Boom for the Rest Does Not a Recovery Make," *Wall Street Journal*, September 21, 2013, A13; Alexandra Scaggs, "Stocks Regain Broad Appeal: Mom-and-Pop Investors Are Back, but Some Say that Could Be Cause for Concern," *Wall Street Journal*, November 11, 2013, A1; Ryan Dezember, "Private Equity Enjoys a Record Year," *Wall Street Journal*, December 31, 2013, C1.

stock market thus became a tacit, prime objective of the Federal Reserve—despite the fact that it was neither part of its charter, nor was it ever authorized by Congress.[83] Since so many pension funds depend on the stock market to meet their obligations—and so many individual speculators rely on it for income—boosting this fundamental institution of financialism became very important for the Federal Reserve. *In this way, the alignment of the public interest with that of corporate power that is at the core of corporatocracy also ended up driving monetary policy.* The Federal Reserve hoped that any feelings of greater wealth derived from this artificial boosting of the stock market—no matter how unsustainable—would prompt more spending and also *more indebtedness*—to increase aggregate demand and help overcome stagnation. It is therefore not difficult to see how much that observation made earlier in this chapter—about indebtedness fueling growth—has come to explain the American economic dynamic.

The Federal Reserve's policies, and those of other central banks around the world, also made speculators more dependent on their monetary policies. Such policies became the prime guide for speculation—as refloating financialism developed into the top priority. The European Central Bank, for example, "loaned" $1.3 trillion to banks by the end of 2011, hoping that such a vast sum might be refinanced by private entities within three years—a highly unrealistic expectation.[84] With central banks as the real managers and sponsors of speculation, a single policy announcement could thus take stock markets up five or ten percentage points over a short period of time—upstaging the usual considerations of profitability, product market conditions, and basic indicators such as price-earnings ratios. A well-known financial specialist noted that a new measure had replaced the price-earnings ratio for stock market speculators—the "price-to-expectations ratio"—which placed expected Federal Reserve actions over any other consideration.[85] Thus, the inflation of asset prices—the "sugar high" noted before, concocted by the

83. Benn Steil and Dinah Walker, "Bernanke's 'Risk-On, Risk-Off' Monetary Policy: There Is Strong Evidence that for More than a Decade the Fed Has Been Using Interest Rates to Push Investors Toward or Away from Stocks and Other Assets," *Wall Street Journal,* September 19, 2012, A13.

84. "The Rise of the Financial-Political Complex," *The Economist,* May 26, 2012, 72.

85. Romain Hatchuel, "So Long Price-Earnings, Hello Price-Expectations," *Wall Street Journal,* October 11, 2012, A17. See also Walter Hamilton and Tiffany Hsu, "Stocks Soar on Hopes for Fed Support," *Los Angeles Times,* July 12, 2013, A1; Spencer Jakab, "Surging Stocks Don't Pass the Sniff Test," *Wall Street Journal,* November 29, 2013, C1.

Federal Reserve to promote a "wealth effect" and refloat financialism—created a notion of valuation that had no objective benchmark. The price-to-expectations ratio, in other words, could never get to be too high, since expectations can always be raised depending on expected Federal Reserve actions—already-inflated stock prices notwithstanding. This and the other frantic efforts to overcome recession and stagnation ultimately benefited the financial oligopolists that were a major cause of the crisis.

Enlisted in the all-out effort to overcome stagnation—and prevent a deeper recession—were the oligopolistic, too-big-to-fail banks at the core of financialism. They, more than any other corporate entity, became the Federal Reserve's closest associates in formulating the monetary policy scenario, because of their overwhelming power in finance—and over government. *True to the nature of corporatocracy, these most powerful elements of the economy became the guides, partners, and executors of financial policymaking.* The oligopolistic megabanks benefited immensely from the Federal Reserve's actions, and they also became vital for its monetary policy—as vehicles for the purchase and sale of U.S. Treasury Bonds—which were at the core of the two-handed monetary scheme noted before. The megabank oligopolies thus became the conduit for expanding or contracting the Federal Reserve's money supply. In addition, they had the official (and exclusive) privilege of securing short-term funding directly from the Federal Reserve, by means of its "discount window"—the vehicle used to secure vast amounts of funds at lower (or negative real) interest rates. This privileged access to the Federal Reserve's discount window allowed the megabank oligopolies to obtain vast amounts of capital—hundreds of billions of dollars—*practically for free, and without any risk at all.* Through negative real interest rates, the Federal Reserve was thus essentially giving away vast amounts of risk-free funds to the oligopolistic megabanks. *The same entities responsible for the crisis thus became the main beneficiaries of the government's rescue efforts.*

The megabank oligopolies, in turn, did not use the vast (and risk-free) "discount window" giveaway to loan to the distressed businesses, mortgage holders, and households who were so negatively affected by the crisis—the majority of the population. The vast (risk-free) funds the megabanks obtained were instead used, in part, to purchase (risk-free) U.S. Treasury Bonds—all of which paid higher rates than the vast amounts of practically free money they received through the Federal Reserve's discount window. The rest of the vast sums obtained through the discount window were sent abroad to speculate with, or place in accounts in nations that had higher interest rates than the United States.

Significant spreads (the difference) between U.S. interest rates and those prevailing in other nations made this speculative export of Federal Reserve–provided funds quite profitable, with practically no risk. Annual spreads of over 10 percent in some nations (such as Brazil), obtained many billions of dollars in profit for the megabanks within a relatively short time.[86] Such vast sums of funds flowing into those nations partly caused their inflation rates to rise, which in turn drove their interest rates even higher—thus making it all the more profitable for the megabank oligopolies to place their Federal Reserve–supported money there.[87] For the vast majority of those nations' populations, the cost of living went up rapidly, outstripping increases in income or wealth, and leading to further hardship for many. At the same time, the vast profits obtained by the oligopolistic megabanks compounded the problem of overaccumulation—generating a vicious cycle whereby greater profit, obtained through Federal Reserve policy and foreign speculation, leads to yet more capital being accumulated—and, eventually, to more speculation at home and abroad.

The Federal Reserve thus practically conducts its monetary policy through the too-big-to-fail bank oligopolies—using U.S. Treasury debt that is both cost-free and risk-free to them—in what is one of the more blatant examples of corporatocracy at work. Then, the Federal Reserve "regulates" those very same oligopolistic megabanks that it has turned into its partners. And, the megabank oligopolies in turn boost their own capital overaccumulation by failing to provide credit to struggling businesses, mortgage holders, and households—thus voiding the purpose of financial intermediation in a capitalist economy. From the perspective of the megabanks, it makes no sense to lend some of their surplus capital to that distressed population in order to boost aggregate demand—as some public officials might wish—since there are more profits to be made by speculating with derivatives, commodities, currencies, foreign interest rates, or by betting on government debt—the very government debt they purchase through the free, no-risk discount window the Federal Reserve provides.[88] Or, alternatively, by sending

---

86. "Free Exchange, Tide Barriers: Capital Controls Would Work Better if There Were Some International Norms," *The Economist*, October 6, 2012, 90.

87. A problem that reflects the global reach of American finance; see, for example, the articles in Leo Panitch and Martijn Konings, eds., *American Empire and the Political Economy of Global Finance* (New York: Palgrave Macmillan, 2008).

88. See Jim Puzzanghera, "Bank Profits Soar to a Record High: The 22.6% Increase Marked the 16th Straight Quarter of Year-Over-Year Gains," *Los Angeles Times*, August 30, 2013, B2. Immense and widespread speculation on derivatives by the megabanks also made it very difficult to account for their assets. The total asset value of one such megabank, for example,

some of their surplus capital abroad, to obtain yet more capital through other nations' higher interest rates. Herein lies part of the explanation for how government—through the Federal Reserve—compounds the problem of capital overaccumulation. And, at the same time, this dynamic makes it easier to notice how deeply entwined public governance has become with oligopolistic corporate power.

The takeover of public governance by oligopolistic financial corporations became the central theme of a book written by the Special Inspector General who oversaw the Troubled Asset Relief Program (TARP)—a federal agency created to provide bailouts and various forms of corporate welfare to oligopolistic corporations that were failing in 2008 and 2009. One major point was his realization that "the U.S. government had been captured by the banks, and that those running the bailout program . . . would come from the same institutions that had both helped cause the crisis, and then become the beneficiaries of the generous terms of their bailout," adding that—despite his previous extensive experience in the U.S. Department of Justice—"I couldn't have imagined the ugliness of the Washington that I'd experience as someone who went against the grain by challenging powerful government officials and the Wall Street powerhouses."[89] The views of another participant in the bailouts, the head of the Federal Deposit Insurance Corporation—a federal agency that guarantees bank deposits and many home mortgages—are also noteworthy. Even after the financial system stabilized, this official noted that "we continued generous bailout policies, instead of imposing discipline on profligate financial institutions by firing their managers and boards, and forcing them to sell their bad assets."[90] The main targets of these criticisms were both the U.S. Treasury Department and the Federal Reserve, institutions that were shown to be practically controlled—in their most important decisions—by the oligopolistic megabanks that caused the crisis. These two federal agencies had in fact allowed megabanks and financial corporations to shift much risk to the federal government for quite some time, without attracting much attention

can vary by as much as several trillion dollars—depending on the criteria used to value the derivatives it holds; see, for example, David Reilly, "Deriving the True Size of US Megabanks Is Far from Simple," *Wall Street Journal,* September 24, 2012, C10.

89. Barofsky, "Fraud 101," in *Bailout,* 1–19; see also, "The Lapdog, the Watchdog, and the Junkyard Dog," 39–63, and "By Wall Street for Wall Street," 121–37.

90. Sheila Bair, "The Big Bailout," *Fortune,* October 8, 2012, 87; see also her *Bull by the Horns: Fighting to Save Main Street from Wall Street and Wall Street from Itself* (New York: Free Press, 2012).

from the media or from public officials.[91] Beyond these assessments, and perhaps more problematic, were the global repercussions of this takeover of governance by the megabanks—given the impact of Federal Reserve policies on almost every kind of financial vehicle in existence.

According to the Bank for International Settlements, for example, more than three-quarters of the notional value of all outstanding derivatives in the world—almost two-thirds of a quadrillion dollars in 2011—is based on derivatives contracts linked to interest rates set by the Federal Reserve.[92] The influence of oligopolistic megabanks on the Federal Reserve thus reaches far beyond U.S. shores, to project itself over the globe's financial system. Recalling the "revolving door" vehicle of influence that links Wall Street's oligopolies to government and regulation, perhaps this should not come as a surprise.[93] *An alignment of the interests of regulators and politicians with those of oligopolistic corporate power thus seems to be at the core of monetary policy—complementing the three-decades-old neoliberal effort to align the public's interest with that of corporate power.* Monetary policy, far from being the neutral or value-free exercise assumed in monetary economists' models, is therefore deeply entwined with oligopolistic high finance.[94] *The megabank oligopolists are not only the main beneficiaries of monetary policy, but also drive the transfer of immense risk from corporate finance to the state.* Beyond the effects

---

91. See, for example, Damian Paletta, "Worried Bankers Seek to Shift Risk to Uncle Sam," *Wall Street Journal,* February 14, 2008, A2.

92. Bank for International Settlements, *Regular OTC Derivatives Market Statistics* (2011):http://www.bis.org/statistics/derstats.htm. With speculation spreading around the world, and the help of the Federal Reserve's (and other central banks') high liquidity policies, financial bubbles increased substantially during the past six decades—many ending in crashes or crises that required government (or international) bailouts. The global spread of derivatives, in particular, seems to have propelled this dynamic greatly in recent decades. During the 1950s, for example, approximately fifteen speculative bubbles were estimated to have occurred—the total rising to twenty-seven in the 1960s, forty-five in the 1970s, and sixty-two in the 2000s decade; see "Asset Prices: Not Fully Inflated," *The Economist,* December 7, 2013, 73–74. Based on data from GMO (Grantham Mayo van Otterloo), http://www.gmo.com/.

93. This also applies to central banks and powerful financial interests in most every advanced capitalist nation, which, often imitating U.S. practices, have helped set the global agenda on monetary policy; see Steven Solomon, *The Confidence Game: How Unelected Central Bankers Are Governing the Changed Global Economy* (New York: Simon and Schuster, 1995); Panitch and Konings, *American Empire.*

94. A condition that can be traced, in part, to the abrogation of the Bretton Woods Agreement in 1971—and that was ignored by those who, led by Milton Friedman, advocated its end. See Robert Leeson, *Ideology and the International Economy: The Decline and Fall of Bretton Woods* (New York: Palgrave Macmillan, 2003).

of monetary policy, these oligopolists then help compound the problem of capital overaccumulation that leads to stagnation—by using their power to increase concentration through mergers, acquisitions, entry-barrier formation, standards setting, political influence, and the closed loops of control they engineer for themselves. They, and the privileged elites tied to them, are the greatest beneficiaries of an unprecedented bonanza made possible by the corporatocratic state—paid for by the vast majority of the population.

Monetary policies, supported intellectually by neoclassical (mainstream) economics, largely overlook this panorama of distress. The vast influence of neoclassical economics on policymaking since the 1970s made this situation possible, by diverting attention from reality through reductionist recipes and models—which cannot take into account the problems of corporatocratic governance. The long-term stagnation trend, the problem of capital overaccumulation, and the oligopolistic domination of the economy and society have thus been ignored realities in neoclassical economics. Their neglect in public policymaking raises many troublesome questions, as dysfunctions deepen and socioeconomic stress increases. The most powerful elements in society—the corporate oligopolies and the privileged elites linked to them—would no doubt feel quite threatened if policymakers and the economics establishment questioned their power. For this reason, anyone who finds a voice to express what has been said in this book will likely be cast out of the mainstream—and tacitly barred from having any influence in the circles of power where policies are formulated. Powerful barriers have been built—analogous to the entry barriers that oligopolies erect—that effectively (but without formally decreeing censorship) maintain the status quo. So much historical memory has been erased that mainstream economists and policymakers seem unable to grasp the dysfunctions and pathologies that are now entrenched in our governance.[95]

95. The lack of historical perspective seems to have much to do with mainstream economics' neglect of oligopolistic power, corporatocracy, and stagnation. Its reductionist outlook has instead generated an obsession with productivity as the one and only vehicle to overcome stagnation—a view that has trickled into, and is widely promoted by, the media; see, for example, "Age Shall Weary Them: The Productivity Challenge of the Rich World's Demography," *The Economist*, May 11, 2013, 78. Although the deep crisis that started in 2007 attracted attention to some of its effects, few mainstream economists questioned the broader panorama of dysfunction that triggered it. For critical perspectives on the crisis and mainstream economics' neglect of its causes, see Foster and Magdoff, *The Great Financial Crisis*; Yanis Varoufakis, Joseph Halevi and Nicholas Theocaraki, *Modern Political Economics: Making Sense of the Post-2008 World* (New York: Routledge, 2011); David Orrell, *Economyths: Ten Ways That Economics Gets It Wrong* (London: Icon, 2010).

Mainstream economic theory has, for example, long assumed that growth and price competition are "normal" conditions of an economy— with oligopoly and stagnation being ignored or cast out as rare anomalies. Those assumptions—growth and perfect price competition—are at the core of neoclassical general equilibrium models, which rule economic theory and have served as the basis for numerous Nobel prizes. These models, which are the staple of mainstream—or neoclassical—economics, depend on those assumptions to work. An economy where perfect competition cannot be assumed to be the norm is an economy that cannot be modeled by the standard tools—or by any tool—of neoclassical economics. Similarly, an economy where growth does not occur is practically impossible to fathom, since that is the outcome expected by the models that assume perfect competition to be the norm. Without those models and their assumptions, most every economic textbook used today in every basic economics course—macro or micro—would be rendered useless. Models that have been the basis for so many Nobel prizes and high honors cannot be allowed to be seen as useless or irrelevant—or be discarded—by the insensitive act of taking reality into account—the reality of oligopoly capitalism and of stagnation. It is simply a lot easier and safer for mainstream economics to ignore reality and to exclude—or censor—work grounded in a critical vision of those models.

How did this state of affairs come to be? To try to explain it, one has to look at the evolution of mainstream economic theory and its failure to deal with oligopoly. Economic theory had, since its earliest days, taken up the assumption that price competition and growth are normal conditions of an economy. Adam Smith enthroned these assumptions in the theoretical edifice of classical economics, noting how "free competition" (meaning price competition) would always result in a lower price than any other condition.[96] Such competition was assumed to be possible only when numerous producers—preferably small—compete with each other in any sector of an economy—a logical and internally coherent deduction. Smith and other classical economists from the eighteenth and nineteenth centuries assumed that growth would be the natural result of competition among a large number of (preferably small) producers, and that the proper role of public governance should be to remove obstacles to their operation. Price competition and growth thus became central theoretical assumptions about

---

96. Adam Smith, *An Enquiry into the Nature and Causes of the Wealth of Nations* (New York: Modern Library, 1937), 61.

the workings of any economy.[97] Those assumptions, however, eventually took up the mantle of "truths"—so desirable and so obvious that a divergent or contrarian condition, no matter how well grounded in reality—could not be accepted.[98] *The confusion of mere theoretical assumptions with reality—and the false notion that those assumptions somehow represent truth—would plague economic theory from that time onward.*

An example of how blatantly mainstream economists confuse assumptions with truth can be found in the work of one of the most revered exponents of "free market" economics, Nobel laureate Friedrich von Hayek—one of the two most influential thinkers (Nobel laureate Milton Friedman being the other) on neoliberal dogma during the second half of the twentieth century. A key precept in Hayek's work was the assumption that producers (corporate businesses) cannot influence "wants" no matter how hard they try, simply because they are faced with competition from other producers trying to do the same.[99] What eluded Hayek's perception is that it is precisely such inability—as can be expected under competitive conditions—that leads a producer (or a set of producers) to form an oligopoly (or a monopoly, if the opportunity should present itself and regulators allow it). Or, that any regulations created to prevent oligopolies would be dismantled—as they were, curiously,

---

97. The assumption of growth as the normal condition of *any* economy was largely based on Jean-Baptiste Say's notion that supply creates its own demand; see Jean-Baptiste Say, *A Treatise on Political Economy* (Boston: Wells and Lilly, 1824). However, Say's notion (also known as Say's Law) was grounded on the assumption that competition among many small producers would also be the normal condition of an economy—and supply would only involve products that meet specific, or prespecified, needs (as opposed to superfluous ones). The supply of products that meet nonsuperfluous needs would necessarily require many small producers to operate in all sectors of an economy, since only when competition is absent can an enterprise produce or sell a superfluous product. Growth, in this sense, would require competition.

98. Some contemporary mainstream economists have gone so far as to consider growth to be one of the two top justifications for capitalism's existence (freedom being the other one); see Allan H. Meltzer, *Why Capitalism?* (New York: Oxford University Press, 2012). Any acknowledgment of stagnation as a normal feature of advanced economies would thus presumably make capitalism's existence unjustifiable. And, regarding freedom, prolonged stagnation in advanced capitalism seems to turn it into a mirage—as economic insecurity, downward mobility, and social injustice for the vast majority of the population become prominent features.

99. See Friedrich A. von Hayek, *The Pure Theory of Capital* (Chicago: University of Chicago Press, 1941) and his *Freedom and the Economic System* (Chicago: University of Chicago Press, 1939). Hayek's thoughts on this aspect became a fundamental component of neoliberal political dogma; see Daniel Stedman Jones, *Masters of the Universe: Hayek, Friedman, and the Birth of Neoliberal Politics* (Princeton: Princeton University Press, 2012).

by the same neoliberal ideologues who used Hayek's work to legitimize their ideas.[100] Or, that future oligopolies would press for such regulations to be dismantled, as they see the need to create artificial (superfluous) wants to boost their profit and power. Or, that powerful marketing would be mounted to see that artificial wants end up being perceived as "necessities" by the targeted populations—through clever propaganda and "branding" tactics.[101] Or, that the deliberate creation of wants—something Hayek assumed could not occur—would spawn a major industry—advertising—with immense influence to support the oligopolies and the politicians who serve their interests.

The confusion of assumptions with truth became all the more entrenched when general equilibrium models started to take over economic theory in the 1950s—becoming the cornerstone of neoclassical economics. And, the assumptions of perfect price competition and growth became essential for the models to work, as noted earlier, thus establishing a link that could not be dissolved without substantial cost to mainstream theory. At that point, *the assumptions of perfect competition and growth were mistaken for truth, mainly because they allowed the models to work—and thus validated the internal logic of the models—also making the utopia they embedded seem self-justifying.* The aesthetics of the mathematical gymnastics involved were attractive to many economists, and provided a sense of novelty at a time when mathematics was not much used in any of the other social science disciplines. The mathematical aesthetics also provided an illusion of perfection that made the utopian assumptions embedded in the models—perfect competition, perfect optimality, perfect foresight, perfect knowledge—take up an aura of truth. A reality or trend that did not meet the assumptions required by the models was typically ignored—or ended up regarded as a mere temporary way station on the road to utopia—the one embedded in the models' assumptions, and that made the models workable.[102]

---

100. Most notably in the financial sector—starting in 1980 with the Depository Institutions Deregulation and Monetary Control Act, and leading eventually to the abrogation of the Glass-Steagall Act in 1999; see Harvey, *Brief History of Neoliberalism*; Magdoff and Sweezy, *Stagnation and Financial Explosion*; U.S. Federal Reserve System, *History of Central Banking: From 1791 to the 21st Century*, http://www.phil.frb.org/ (accessed December 14, 2013).

101. Building a powerful brand through products that most people readily identify—and fear of not having one, even if not needed—is at the core of many marketing strategies. AT&T, for example, has sought to turn "nomophobia"—a fear of being unable to communicate for lack of a cell phone—into a vehicle for sales; see Geoff Colvin, "Building a Super-Brand—Superfast: What's the Secret of Survival These Days? Change Quickly, Says AT&T's Marketing Chief, Along with Your Customer," *Fortune*, September 3, 2012, 60–64.

102. *Innocent fraud* was the term used by one prominent economist to refer to mainstream economics' tendency to misinterpret reality; see John Kenneth Galbraith, *The Economics of Innocent Fraud* (Boston: Houghton Mifflin, 2004).

If mathematical models worked for physical science, how could they not work for neoclassical economics—when economists assumed their discipline to be a science? The very suspicion that the general equilibrium models used in economics could be counterproductive or even useless was untenable for neoclassical economists since they had assumed that their discipline should be considered a science—much like physical science.[103] The emergence of those models in the 1950s and their eventual domination of economic theory—along with their neglect of oligopoly and stagnation— thus allowed neoclassical economics to imitate physical science, and to take up an appearance of science to impress the public. This seemed vital in order to gain greater legitimacy for neoclassical economics, at a time when physics had just helped end a world war, establishing its prestige in the public's eye as immense and growing.

The notion that economic decision making, and the workings of an economy, could be reduced to a set of general equilibrium formulas—much as formulas in physics can be devised to predict the trajectory of a planet or molecule—thus became entrenched in neoclassical economics. One fundamental difference overlooked in neoclassical economics' masquerade of science, however, was the nature of human social relations and the importance of social behavior. In society or the economy, an idea can become self-fulfilling if enough people learn and decide to practice it. Thus, for example, discrimination can become reality if enough people decide to practice it, to make the social order conform to their beliefs. Similarly, a management concept can become self-fulfilling if it is widely practiced—as enough people learn and decide to implement it, as in the case of agency theory.[104] In physics, however, an idea about a planet's or a molecule's movement will

---

103. Curiously, even as the economic crisis that started in 2007 showed how inadequate economic forecasting models are, two Nobel laureates advocated permanent (and rising) federal funding for neoclassical economics as necessary for "formulating wise policy." In their arguments, they compared neoclassical economics to "physics, chemistry, biology and medicine." Also, despite their strong and long-standing advocacy for market solutions for most every problem, they noted that "we cannot expect the market alone to support basic economic research." Gary S. Becker and James J. Heckman, "Why the Dismal Science Deserves Federal Funding," *Wall Street Journal,* August 10, 2012, A11.

104. The learning of neoclassical economic theories and their application to management practice—along with their consequences—were addressed by one of the best-known management scholars of the late twentieth century; see Sumantra Ghoshal, "Bad Management Theories Are Destroying Good Management Practices," *Academy of Management Learning and Education* 4 (2005): 96–100. A major flaw regarding the application and practice of neoclassical economic precepts is their all too frequent moral blindness—on such aspects as fairness and conflict of interest. One case, for example, involved a prominent economist's advisory assistance to Russia in the early 1990s to create financial markets—with $30 million

not change its trajectory, no matter how many people decide to believe it. The workings of physical phenomena are not affected by our concepts, decisions, or beliefs about them, since—unlike concepts in economics—they are independent from human social behavior. This fundamental difference between economics and physical science was lost on neoclassical economics.

Even so, the fact that the standard neoclassical assumptions of perfect competition and growth have been taught to—and believed by—many generations of economists has not eliminated the reality of oligopoly and stagnation. They have, instead, caused a great deal of discrimination against those who have challenged the standard assumptions, as the relations of power within neoclassical economics made it possible for that to happen.[105] By casting out dissidents, neoclassical economists felt secure in the belief system they concocted—beliefs that were enthroned by the general equilibrium models that are the staple of their discipline. Those who adopted the belief system of neoclassical economics—confusing mere theoretical assumptions with truth, and discarding reality—gained the upper hand within the discipline. With so much invested in general equilibrium modeling it was not possible for it to be otherwise, lest all the Nobel prizes and the thousands of books and articles become discredited.[106] Unlike physical science, neoclassical economics' confusion of mere assumptions with truth turned the discipline into a belief system. Believing in the assumptions of general

in funding from the U.S. Agency for International Development (AID). After finding out that the said individual, an associate, and their spouses had personally invested and profited greatly through the project, AID suspended it—suing to recover some of the funds; see Carla Anne Robbins, "For Harvard Board, Professor's Woes Pose Big Dilemma: University Weighs Options After Shleifer Ruling on Russian Investments—Mr Summers Recuses Himself," *Wall Street Journal*, October 12, 2004, A1, and her "Harvard Settles Suit over Profit in Russian Aid," *Wall Street Journal*, August 4, 2005, B1.

105. Discrimination included the tacit elimination of dissent on the most important assumptions of neoclassical economics. Myths—a key component of a belief system—were thus created and passed along, that had no basis in reality. See, for example, Michael Perelman, *Railroading Economics: The Creation of the Free Market Mythology* (New York: Monthly Review Press, 2006); Galbraith, *Economics of Innocent Fraud*; Orrell, *Economyths*; Luis Suarez-Villa, "Review of *The Dismal Science: How Thinking Like an Economist Undermines Community* by Stephen Marglin," *Growth and Change* 40 (2009): 533–63.

106. Among the consequences of this masquerade were to rename capitalism "the market system" in the neoclassical economic literature, and to wipe away much historical information; see Galbraith, "The Renaming of the System," in *Innocent Fraud*, 3–10. In this sense, neoclassical economics—and its general equilibrium modeling apparatus—became nonhistorical, or in some ways antihistorical. History was therefore taken out of consideration, along with any critical perspective about the socioeconomic system we live in. Any notion about

equilibrium models—legitimized through Nobel prizes and thousands of publications—thus became paramount for building a career in mainstream economics.

It must, however, be noted that the seeds of economic theory's neglect of oligopoly and stagnation had been sown long before general equilibrium modeling took over economics. As noted earlier, the assumptions of perfect competition and growth had taken hold with classical economists in the nineteenth century, making it very difficult for the discipline to acknowledge the existence of oligopoly. One voice, however, raised questions about the trend toward oligopoly early on, as industrial capitalism deepened and began to project more influence over society. In the 1850s, Karl Marx—the most important critic of classical economics—had noted a tendency for capital to concentrate and centralize—a development that led to larger enterprises.[107] Capital accumulation—a most distinctive feature of capitalism—was at the core of this trend, relying on scale economies and greater pricing power to generate more capital—especially in industries that were expanding abroad. In the case of centralization, Marx noted that fewer enterprises were hiring more of the labor force, proportionately, and accounting for more of production. He attributed this trend toward concentration and centralization to finance, which allowed enterprises to grow larger through credit—and to efforts to reduce competition. Marx understood that, as competition intensified, enterprises tended to grow larger—to increase profits, reduce operating costs, and improve their chances of long-term survival. Thus, competition would lead to larger and more powerful enterprises—contrary to the static perspective of classical economists, who assumed it to be a constant feature of any economy. Marx's prescient observations were accompanied by insights on how the evolution from a competitive to an oligopolistic condition might occur.[108]

---

the relations of power or the dominance of corporations—as in the case of oligopolies—was also taken out of consideration. Part of this dynamic was to make the market system seem "neutral"—much as conditions in a physics laboratory are arranged to make the laboratory environment neutral. Neither stagnation nor crises could therefore be taken into account, since they were not supposed to happen—except when the "market system" was interfered with. The "system" was thus absolved of any responsibility for crises or stagnation, since it was assumed that it could never create or trigger them.

107. Karl Marx, *Capital: A Critique of Political Economy*, Vol. 1: *A Critical Analysis of Capitalist Production*, ed. F. Engels (New York: International Publishers, 1974; orig. Hamburg: Verlag von Otto Meissner, 1867), Part VI: "The Accumulation of Capital."

108. Something that escaped Friedrich von Hayek's attention when he wrote his most important works—almost one full century after Marx made these observations; see Hayek, *Pure Theory of Capital*, and his *Freedom and Economic System*.

Marx's observations were disregarded by classical economists, who preferred to hold on to their assumptions and ignore the transformation of capitalism that was occurring all around them. By the last quarter of the nineteenth century, oligopolies and monopolies had become noticeable in the most industrialized nations of the time—yet they continued to be ignored by mainstream economists.[109] This perplexing neglect can be explained by the confusion of assumptions with reality that prevailed in economic theory. However, also important in this panorama of neglect were the relations of power that prevailed within the field of economics—and the powerful economic interests, among them the elites in control of oligopolies and monopolies, who influenced the most important individuals in the discipline. The links of these individuals with major corporate interests of that time—the corporate elites and those in control of oligopolies and monopolies—can be found through a thorough examination of biographies, social class status, professional activities, and individual political outlook.[110]

Then, during the first decade of the twentieth century, the rising importance of oligopolies and monopolies was noticed by Rudolf Hilferding, who associated this phenomenon with the growth of finance. The increasing integration of finance with powerful industrial and mercantile interests was behind this trend—one that Hilferding referred to as "finance capital"—to differentiate it from productive capital.[111] Oligopolies and monopolies required substantial financial support, because their capital requirements

---

109. In the United States, oligopolies and monopolies are understood to have begun their emergence after the 1850s—the period 1860–1920 being considered the early stage of monopoly-oligopoly formation; see John R. Munkirs, *The Transformation of American Capitalism: From Competitive Market Structures to Centralized Private Sector Planning* (London: Sharpe, 1985). The first nationwide monopoly was Western Union—a telegraph service provider; see Joshua D. Wolff, *Western Union and the Creation of the American Corporate Order, 1845–1893* (New York: Cambridge University Press, 2013). In 1888, a duopoly between Western Union and the Postal Telegraph and Cable Co. emerged, setting prices and dividing up the market—until their merger in 1931. See also Foster and McChesney, "Endless Crisis," 20; Robinson, *Economics of Imperfect Competition*; Sweezy, "Demand under Conditions of Oligopoly."

110. Not an easy task, given the glorification of prominent economists of that time by many historians. Information on individual class status, subservience to powerful economic interests—to the politicians who served those interests—personal wealth, and other indicators can nonetheless be gleaned from some texts; see, for example, Robert L. Heilbroner's *The Great Economists: Their Lives and Their Conceptions of the World* (London: Eyre and Spottiswoode, 1955); Nicholas Giraldi, *John Stuart Mill: A Biography* (Cambridge: Cambridge University Press, 2004). Mills's association with the East India Company—one of the largest monopolies of his time—and his political service on behalf of interests closely associated with monopolies and oligopolies, is just one of many examples.

111. Rudolf Hilferding, *Finance Capital: A Study of the Latest Phase of Capitalist Development* (London: Routledge and Kegan Paul, 1981), translated from his *Das Finanzkapital: eine Studie über die jüngste Entwicklung des Kapitalismus* (Vienna: Brand, 1910).

were greater and more complex than those of small or medium-size enterprises. Also, because of their large scale and complexity, oligopolies and monopolies undertook more diverse kinds of financial operations—issuing shares, bonds, seeking credit for acquisitions and mergers, arranging for financial intermediaries abroad, or securing insurance for their operations, for example. This meant that banks or stock markets that served oligopolies and monopolies became larger, to provide the necessary range and depth of services. An important strategy of banks—directly related to oligopoly formation—was to finance the merger of industrial companies, hoping to inflate the value of outstanding shares and obtain vast profits quickly. This strategy depended on the personal relations of bankers with industrial capitalists, and on privileged internal information. Hilferding also noted how the growing economic power of finance, and of oligopolies and monopolies, led to efforts to manipulate government such that it could be made to systematically support their interests. This early understanding of how the most powerful corporate interests strive to manipulate government is, in some respects, a precursor of what is referred to as corporatocracy in this book.

One way to have economic theory take oligopoly and stagnation into account was to focus critically on competition. Thus, the first attempt to do so sought to establish that price competition under oligopolistic conditions is less than perfect. This is how Edward Chamberlin and Joan Robinson, and later Paul Sweezy, approached the problem in the late 1920s and the 1930s.[112] *Imperfect competition* was the term used to refer to oligopolistic conditions—to try to establish this phenomenon in mainstream economic theory. The reduction of new investment possibilities—a condition associated with stagnation—was also assumed to accompany imperfect competition.[113]

---

112. Chamberlin, *Theory of Monopolistic Competition*; Robinson, *Economics of Imperfect Competition*; Sweezy, "Demand Under Conditions of Oligopoly."

113. In the mid-1930s, reduction (or insufficiency) of new investment possibilities was considered to be a cause of stagnation by Alvin Hansen—the most important follower of Keynes's ideas in the United States at that time; see Alvin H. Hansen, *Full Recovery or Stagnation?* (New York: Norton, 1938). The advent of World War II, the creation of a planned wartime economy, and the rapid boost in government spending ended the Depression-era debate on stagnation. Curiously, in the aftermath of the financial crisis that started in 2007, some neoclassical economists argued that the global economy might be suffering from what they refer to as a "secular stagnation"—attributing it to central banks' efforts to inflate speculative bubbles in order to generate growth; see "Stagnant Thinking: An Old Explanation for Economic Drift Gains a New Following," *The Economist*, December 7, 2013, 80; Lawrence Summers, "On Secular Stagnation," *Reuters*, December 16, 2013, http://blogs.reuters.com/; Paul Krugman, "The Conscience of a Liberal: Secular Stagnation, Coalmines, Bubbles, and Larry Summers," *New York Times*, November 16, 2013, http://krugman.blogs.nytimes.com/. Lost in the debate was the fundamental role of oligopolies—and, because of the lack of historical perspective, Hansen's work on this topic more than seven decades before was largely ignored.

This term thus became synonymous with oligopolistic (and monopolistic) control over pricing—a situation that often results in excess productive capacity.[114] This treatment of competition met with much resistance from mainstream economists, however, who saw in it a serious threat to their cherished assumptions. In a broader way, they also saw it as a menace to the entire theoretical apparatus they had built around competition. Thus, the immediate reaction was to marginalize this effort. Oligopolistic and monopolistic conditions were therefore cast out of economic theory—to be regarded as extraneous to the "normal" condition of perfect competition, at most. Devious terms—such as *workable competition*—were coined to avoid using "imperfect competition"—in what became a semantic masquerade to convey the notion that price competition typically does occur under oligopolistic conditions.[115]

At the same time, economists who felt threatened by any theoretical recognition that competition may be less than perfect—as Chamberlin's, Robinson's, and Sweezy's work had shown—tried to refocus attention away from pricing. Their main argument was that oligopolies engage in competition in areas other than price. The meaning of the term *imperfect competition* was also distorted—interpreting it to mean cases where enterprises simply gain an advantage through geographical location—or because they differentiate some products sufficiently to make them unique.[116] Both of these cases were assumed to be only temporary, however, since in the end a freely competitive situation would always prevail. This distortion of Chamberlin's original formulation of product differentiation was rather amusing. A few large auto manufacturers that, for example, tacitly colluded to sustain prices in their sector were not to be considered oligopolies. According to the distorted rationale, they could only be considered to engage in "imperfect

---

114. Oligopolies and monopolies typically cut back on output—rather than prices—when faced with lower demand. The result is excess capacity while stagnation sets in. See Chamberlin, *Theory of Monopolistic Competition*, 109, and the discussion in Foster and McChesney, "Endless Crisis," 21.

115. Among the various prominent economists spearheading this effort was John Maurice Clark; see, for example, his *Social Control of Business* (New York: McGraw-Hill, 1939) and *Competition as a Dynamic Process* (Washington, DC: Brookings Institution, 1961). See also Foster and McChesney, "Endless Crisis," 22.

116. The idea of "product differentiation," introduced by Chamberlin, was thus used to draw attention away from the case of oligopolies and monopolies—applying it instead to small or medium-size enterprises that differentiated some products to gain some advantage on pricing; see Foster and McChesney, "Endless Crisis," 22.

competition" when one of them differentiated a product enough such that it had no rival in its market niche—as, for example, in the case of an amphibious automobile that had no competing product. However, when the product in question generated enough of a market, it was thought that rival products would invariably be created—thus, control over pricing was assumed to be rather temporary. In this manner, any serious consideration of oligopoly—and, implicitly, of stagnation—was dismissed by mainstream economics, to preserve the theoretical apparatus in which it was invested.

The notion that oligopolies routinely engage in product price competition was then bolstered by Joseph Schumpeter's work on economic change. His idea that "gales of creative destruction"—mainly triggered by innovations—would wipe away any enterprises unable to come up with breakthroughs that can increase productivity, reduce costs, or create new products helped many mainstream economists justify their position.[117] This idea had been partly honed by Schumpeter's personal experience in business, during the turmoil of the 1920s in central Europe, when established enterprises collapsed as high inflation and economic contraction took their toll. His idea was also partly influenced by Nikolai Kondratieff's concept of "long waves," which envisioned long-term economic change as a cyclical series of periods of growth—each usually lasting about twenty-five years—followed by periods of decline of about the same duration.[118] Schumpeter's "gales of creative destruction" generally corresponded with periods of decline in the long wave concept, when many established enterprises would be expected to collapse while new ones were assumed to emerge—creating new sectors, products, and technologies. Missing from this romanticized vision of economic cataclysm, however, were the barriers to entry that oligopolies and monopolies typically erect, their power to manipulate government regulation to their advantage, their ability to set exclusionary standards, and the extreme difficulties that new enterprises—which are typically small—experience during such periods. To many mainstream economists, however, the effects of Schumpeter's idea were analogous to what they had assumed

---

117. Joseph A. Schumpeter, *The Theory of Economic Development* (Cambridge: Harvard University Press, 1934), and his *Capitalism, Socialism and Democracy*.

118. Kondratieff's work on long waves was initially published in the early 1920s, and was essentially an empirical exploration using selected historical data. One important omission in this exploratory work was its failure to account for oligopolies and monopolies in the data he considered. See Nikolai D. Kondratieff, *The Long Waves in Economic Life* (New York: Foundation for the Study of Cycles, 1944).

competitive conditions might do. The hypothetical effects of Schumpeter's concept thus fit their preestablished assumptions on competition. Mostly for this reason, his work did not experience the immediate rejection (and distortion) that met Chamberlin's, Robinson's, and Sweezy's work. Also, for business economists Schumpeter's idea was appealing, since it allowed them to reconcile the assumption of perfect competition with the evolving nature of business enterprise.

Schumpeter, however, had toyed with the idea that monopolies and oligopolies might be best placed to unleash the "gales of creative destruction." Oligopolies and monopolies, in his view, might have the resources to dedicate to innovation—unlike enterprises mired in competition, for which achieving profitability is a daily struggle that limits their possibilities. This consideration reflected Schumpeter's personal experience with the difficulties faced by new enterprises during periods of economic crisis. He also assumed that oligopolists operate in "co-respective" ways—as opposed to the sort of competition assumed by mainstream theory—meaning that they collude on various aspects, such as influencing government and setting standards—even though they might compete with each other in some areas, such as innovation and operational efficiency.[119] Schumpeter thought that co-respectiveness was essential for oligopolists to protect their common interest—most of all, to prevent downward price swings for their products. These views contrasted sharply, however, with the blanket assumption of competition assumed by mainstream economic models.

The fact that Schumpeter—who was not fond of, nor ever engaged in, general equilibrium modeling—would acknowledge the existence of oligopolies and monopolies disturbed many mainstream economists, however. He eventually paid a price for this daring admission as his work became almost completely neglected—except by some historians—when general equilibrium modeling took over economic theory. By the 1960s, Schumpeter—later to be considered one of the two most important economists of the twentieth century—was an unknown figure among economics students, and his work went typically unmentioned in economics textbooks and curricula.[120] The revival of Schumpeter's work in the 1990s—as neolib-

---

119. Schumpeter, *Capitalism, Socialism and Democracy,* 87–106. See also Foster, McChesney, and Jonna, "Monopoly and Competition."

120. Much the same fate awaited others who challenged the fundamental precepts of neoclassical economics and its models. The work of Herbert Simon, a 1978 Nobel laureate in economics, for example, challenged the notion of perfect rationality—a fundamental assumption of general equilibrium models that is absolutely necessary to operationalize another key

eralism gained momentum—mainly occurred in business schools, due to a growing interest in innovation that sought some historical grounding. This interest was also partly motivated by the fact that general equilibrium modeling is woefully incapable of dealing with innovation—given the overarching role that risk, uncertainty, and trial-and-error luck play in it. These qualities cannot be handled by the models, given their complete dependence on perfect foresight, total certainty, and perfect knowledge—assumptions that are vitally necessary for optimization to be operationalized in the models.

Despite the obvious reality of oligopoly and stagnation, mainstream economics nonetheless held on to its belief in perfect competition and growth as normal conditions of any economy. The spread of general equilibrium models since the 1950s, and their takeover of economic theory, made it all the more necessary to keep these assumptions entrenched in mainstream economics. For theoretical purposes, the terms *workable competition* and *creative destruction* were interpreted to be synonymous with perfect competition—a convenient ruse meant to marginalize and ignore any treatment of oligopolies and monopolies.[121] *In this way, stagnation was*

---

premise—optimization. Without optimization as the overarching objective, general equilibrium models—the staple of economic theory making and teaching—simply will not work. Because it showed that humans typically seek satisfactory outcomes rather than optimality—a central point of Simon's work—due to limited knowledge, and their behavior is all too often less than perfectly rational, this approach became unacceptable. Simon's contributions thus ended up being ignored in economics curricula and in almost every economics text. See Herbert A. Simon, *Models of Bounded Rationality* (Cambridge: MIT Press, 1982), and his *Models of Man: Social and Rational* (New York: Wiley, 1957). A fairly similar situation awaited the work of two other prominent scholars who challenged mainstream economics' assumptions on behavior—Daniel Kahneman (Nobel Prize in economics, 2002) and Amos Tversky. Their work showed that a wide range of heuristics and biases—grounded in incomplete knowledge, cultural influences, past experiences, and less than rational outlooks—is typically very important in how humans make economic decisions. Their vast empirical documentation and realistic findings, however, attracted little interest or support from the mainstream economics establishment and its entrenched general equilibrium modeling elite. See the articles in Daniel Kahneman, Paul Slovic, and Amos Tversky, eds., *Judgment Under Uncertainty: Heuristics and Biases* (New York: Cambridge University Press, 1982), and Kahneman and Tversky, eds., *Choices, Values, and Frames* (Cambridge: Cambridge University Press, 2000).

121. A scheme in which the Chicago School of economics—the most important beacon of neoliberal ideology—played an important role. See Rob Van Horn, "Reinventing Monopoly and the Role of Corporations: The Roots of Chicago Law and Economics," in *The Road from Mont Pelerin: The Making of the Neoliberal Thought Collective,* ed. Philip Mirowski and Dieter Plehwe (Cambridge: Harvard University Press, 2009), 204–37, and the articles in Robert Van Horn, Philip Mirowski, and Thomas A. Stapleford, eds., *Building Chicago Economics: New Perspectives on the History of America's Most Powerful Economics Program* (New York: Cambridge University Press, 2011).

also cast out of the theoretical framework of neoclassical economics—for, to take stagnation into account, it was necessary to acknowledge and understand the existence of oligopolies. Acknowledging the long-term trend toward stagnation in advanced capitalism also required a critical assessment of corporate power—without which it is impossible to grasp the phenomenon of oligopoly. Attempting to understand this phenomenon without taking into account the relations of power that allow it to occur—and how they make it possible to influence public governance—is about as effective as trying to navigate with a rudderless sailboat and no sails.

While mainstream economics rejected any treatment of oligopoly and stagnation, radical political economists continued to work on these topics. In the 1940s and 1950s, Josef Steindl and Michał Kalecki advanced the discourse on oligopolies and monopolies—and stagnation. Steindl, in particular, devoted considerable attention to the problem of stagnation in mature capitalism and the question of enterprise scale—a key aspect of oligopoly formation.[122] Kalecki's contributions on cyclical and long-term economic dynamics addressed key questions about investment, profit, and income distribution—helping subsequent work on oligopolies, especially their conceptualization.[123] Their work was followed in the mid-1950s by Paul Baran's effort to conceptualize the importance of growth in advanced capitalism, and the challenge posed by stagnation.[124] In the mid-1960s, Baran and Paul Sweezy then linked stagnation directly to the role of oligopolies and monopolies in advanced capitalism—referring to this reality as *monopoly capitalism.*[125] Drawing from Steindl's and Kalecki's work—and

---

122. Josef Steindl, *Small and Big Business: Economic Problems of the Size of Firms* (Oxford: Blackwell, 1945), and his *Maturity and Stagnation in American Capitalism* (Oxford: Blackwell, 1952).

123. Michał Kalecki, *Theory of Economic Dynamics: An Essay on Cyclical and Long-Run Changes in Capitalist Economy* (London: Allen and Unwin, 1956).

124. Paul Baran, *The Political Economy of Growth* (New York: Monthly Review Press, 1957).

125. Baran and Sweezy, *Monopoly Capital.* It is unclear why they preferred the term *monopoly* instead of *oligopoly.* Since the enactment of antitrust laws in the United States in the early twentieth century, a shift occurred from monopolies to oligopolies—as some of the largest corporations with monopolistic power were broken up. The newly split companies nonetheless retained substantial control over pricing. And, since the word *monopoly* had long been used in the literature—with oligopolies continuing to control pricing—it was likely more convenient to retain the term. Also, most oligopolies essentially operated like a collective monopoly—through tacit price collusion—over the sectors they controlled. Sweezy had nonetheless started exploring oligopolies in the mid-1930s, adopting this term in a 1939 article that attracted considerable attention; see Sweezy, "Demand Under Conditions of Oligopoly."

from Chamberlin's and Robinson's contributions in the 1920s and 1930s—Baran and Sweezy considered that the oligopolization of a mature capitalist economy would result in stagnation, mainly because of the problem of surplus capital.

Surplus capital due to overaccumulation—which Baran and Sweezy considered to be the main source of stagnation—stems from oligopolistic control over pricing. Exchange thereby becomes subsidiary to oligopolistic control, as prices follow the trajectory that oligopolists—as a group—tacitly decide. Price wars, although beneficial to everyone who must exchange money for goods, are ruinous for oligopolists. For this reason alone, corporations that exercise oligopolistic control over a sector can be expected to sustain their collective control over pricing, by all means possible. Revisiting the fundamental dynamic of capitalism considered previously in this book—$M \rightarrow C \rightarrow C' \rightarrow M^N$, where $M^N = M + \Delta m + \Delta N$—a stagnation or reduction of aggregate demand does not influence the oligopolistic price paid for C' (new commodities) when exchange occurs ($C' \rightarrow M^N$). Stagnation does not therefore lead to a reduction in price—although it will most likely lead to reductions in the supply of the product or service—such that the oligopolist can sustain its surplus. At the same time, costs would likely be reduced—by, for example, cutting labor through layoffs, outsourcing, or offshoring jobs and production. Or, alternatively, costs could be reduced through automation or the adoption of newer production technologies.

Such reductions in product supply and costs would, combined with control over pricing, either sustain or increase the oligopolistic surplus (ΔN), thereby contributing to capital overaccumulation. Increasing that surplus—or at least sustaining it—is what executives, shareholders, and investment fund managers are after, with short-term performance being paramount to their interests. The oligopolistic surplus thus becomes the main vehicle of overaccumulation, making it possible for new money-capital (M^N) to exceed the initial money-capital (M) invested in production—$M^N > M$—over the long term. Comparing this scenario to a competitive one, ΔN also makes it possible for M^N to exceed any new-money capital (M') derived under competition—$M^N > M'$—over the long term. However, increasing the oligopolistic surplus in the face of long-term stagnation can be a difficult proposition—especially when possibilities for cost cutting are limited. How, then, do oligopolies manage to increase them under such conditions? The answer is all around us, if we care to look—consumer capitalism provides innumerable examples. Creating a product or service that has a *contrived value*—an artificial (or superfluous) want, one that is not truly needed—is the most common way. Such products or services are not really needed by humans or society (or nature) and are therefore primarily created to serve a prime need of the oligopolist—an increase of its surplus. Increasing the oligopolistic surplus through contrived use value is an important strategy in advanced capitalism—one in which marketing, advertising, and increasingly R&D (research and development) play key roles.

Contrived value—the oligopolistic concoction of wants—in advanced capitalism is typically accomplished through intangibles. Design, branding, and frivolous innovations are very important in this phenomenon, as almost any observer of consumer products and services can attest to. For example, an automobile whose brand, appearance, and "feel" (when driven) induce feelings of personal gratification involving social status (making the user seem richer or more influential)—yet cannot reduce travel time (given speed limits) and may even attract theft. Or, the shape of a toothbrush that has some ergonomic qualities and seems to allow a firmer grip, when in fact a tight grip on a toothbrush is not necessary at all. Or, the shape of a vacuum cleaner that does not actually work better than any other, but whose form evokes erotic feelings or a sense of power in users.[126] In these and many other cases of contrived value, the container (packaging or exterior design) often becomes more important than the actual function, usage, or performance of the product.[127]

Contrived value can also be time sensitive, when users are forced to repurchase products after a given period—for no real reason other than to increase an oligopolist's surplus. In this case, an oligopolistic corporation controls not only price but also timing. This dual control over usage time and pricing can be most profitable. An example is the case of software that expires periodically and requires repurchase—even though the replacement may represent little or no improvement. Another one is vaccines that must be repurchased (and readministered) after a certain period of time to

---

126. An advertisement for a cordless vacuum cleaner published in *Wired* (October 2012), 57, for example, showed images of a model named "Slim Jim," with an unusual design that makes it resemble a gun with a fairly long cannon. The advertisement emphasized "no loss of suction" as the prime quality of the product—a term that could be interpreted to have multiple meanings.

127. Contrived values often depend on triggering acquisitive impulses on the part of those targeted—which can be less than rational. Such impulses have been associated with the political emergence of the "autonomous individual"—a feature that seems to be at the core of consumer capitalism. Crawford B. Macpherson's *The Political Theory of Possessive Individualism: Hobbes to Locke* (Oxford: Clarendon, 1962) related this feature to historical currents in political philosophy, which helped shape notions of governance under capitalism.

continue providing protection, when a one-time administration would be effective enough. Built-in (programmed) obsolescence of parts and components is another case—a major source of surplus for many oligopolistic manufacturers in almost every industrial sector. Boosting the surplus through time-sensitive, contrived value can be a formidable profit engine, even when aggregate demand is stagnant—all the more so when the oligopolist claims it will serve a need which in fact it does not. Clever advertising is typically used in such cases, appealing to fears, egos, intelligence, or vanity. These profit engines can contribute significantly to the problem of overaccumulation, especially when they help fence in market niches.

A major problem, however, is that with stagnant aggregate demand any expansion of the oligopolistic surplus will likely end up being supported through debt—accumulated by consumers. Debt accumulation is thereby linked to increases in the oligopolistic surplus, with the credit system serving as the lubricant of consumption. Credit thus becomes an ally of oligopoly power through the financial system, an aspect understood and exposed by Hilferding more than a century ago.[128] Given the obvious limitations of debt accumulation, are there other possible sources of growth that can help overcome stagnation? Baran and Sweezy assumed (in the mid-1960s) that one potential source, though unsustainable over the long term, would be to boost government spending—for the military, or as stimuli to support aggregate demand.[129] This was the Keynesian prescription for stimulus that had become standard policy since the Great Depression. Another potential source of growth might be new markets abroad, though Baran and Sweezy considered that the United States, being a net importer of capital (in their time), would not find in them a solution to stagnation. The flow of capital finding its way to the United States could not be offset by outflows large enough to make much difference, they concluded. And later on, even when the United States began to experience major (and continuous) trade deficits along with capital outflows, the problems of overaccumulation and stagnation were not ameliorated (as noted earlier in this chapter).

Baran and Sweezy thought that new technologies and the markets they established could be a potential source of growth, albeit a temporary one, but assumed that the rate of substitution of existing technolo-

128. See Hilferding, "Money as a Means of Payment: Credit Money," in *Finance Capital*, ch. 3, and "The Banks and Industrial Credit," ch. 5.

129. See Baran and Sweezy, "The Problem of Surplus Absorption: Government Spending" and "The Problem of Surplus Absorption: Militarism and Imperialism," in *Monopoly Capital*.

gies would be slower under oligopolistic conditions. Also, they considered that new technologies would not necessarily increase much the quantum of new investment outlets, mainly because oligopolies would likely sever that link—by fencing in the new markets that emerged. This actually occurred twenty years later (in the 1980s) in the case of high tech, when existing oligopolies such as IBM, or new ones such as Apple and Microsoft, fenced in their respective sectors by acquiring other companies or merging. Also, it is significant to note that the emergence and growth of new high tech sectors was unable to reverse the long-term stagnation trend. In this regard, as in the general case of stagnation, Baran and Sweezy's views proved to be prescient.

In general, Baran and Sweezy assumed that the panorama of oligopolization would lead to a *stagnation trap*, since whatever aggregate demand could be generated—and any productive investment—would be insufficient to absorb much of the surplus capital accumulated.[130] Output would then fall or increase very slowly—with no built-in, automatic way to generate significant growth over the long term. They also assumed that rising productivity would accompany long-term stagnation—an effect of steady technological progress. Stagnation therefore did not necessarily mean economic contraction, depression, or deep downturns—though these might nonetheless occur at some point—but slow growth over the long term. *The notion that stagnation is the actual, "normal" state of an advanced capitalist economy—with robust growth being only a temporary exception—thus turned upside down a fundamental assumption of neoclassical economics.* Tacitly, the perception that stagnation was *not* a cyclical phenomenon—in the sense of Hyman Misky's short-term business cycles or Kondratieff's long waves, for example—and that any cyclical change would neither stop nor reverse the overall long-term trajectory of stagnation was part of this vision. Baran and Sweezy therefore implicitly assumed that stagnation was more deeply systemic to advanced capitalism than any cyclical phenomena—short or long-term—and that the tendency toward stagnation would prevail because of its structural character.

In the early 1970s, James O'Connor provided perspectives that are very relevant to stagnation and oligopolies, and that were grounded in the

---

130. Paul A. Baran and Paul M. Sweezy, "Some Theoretical Implications," *Monthly Review,* July-August 2012, 24–59; John Bellamy Foster, "A Missing Chapter of *Monopoly Capital*: *Introduction to Baran and Sweezy's 'Some Theoretical Implications,'" Monthly Review,* July-August 2012, 3–23.

reality of the postwar decades. Those perspectives are also relevant to contemporary capitalism and to corporatocracy. O'Connor primarily addressed the fiscal crisis of the state in advanced capitalism at that time—mainly its inability to continue increasing spending as expenses surpassed revenues.[131] This aspect tied in with Baran and Sweezy's work from the 1960s, their vision of oligopoly capitalism, and their expectation that increasing government spending to try to overcome stagnation would be unsustainable. In O'Connor's view, the fact that the state was made to favor dominant economic entities—oligopolies and monopolies—and a dominant social class—capitalists and the wealthy—at the expense of everyone else, was considered to be the prime cause of the fiscal crisis.

The fiscal crisis was therefore a systemic problem of advanced capitalism, and could be best understood in terms of two contradictory functions—the state's obligation to support and provide the conditions that make private capital accumulation possible *and* its need to legitimize itself by redistributing resources to preserve some social harmony.[132] Contrary to neoliberal dogma—which believes that the state expands at the expense of the private sector—O'Connor posited that *the capitalist state has to expand primarily because it is obliged to provide the conditions that support private (corporate) capital accumulation.* The expansion of state spending, he noted, was not coordinated by the market—by any market—and was a result of political influence, pure and simple. That expansion—necessary to fulfill the first function of the capitalist state—was the prime reason why government expenses outstrip revenues. Thus, *the key to the fiscal crisis of the state was to be found in government's obligation to serve the private sector. The fiscal crisis, in turn, contributed to economic stagnation, as cutbacks in state support ended up affecting the vast majority of the population—thus reducing aggregate demand and consumption.* At the same time, cutbacks in government spending reduced its capacity to provide stimuli during recessions, thereby compounding stagnation. The state's first function—support for private

---

131. James O'Connor, *The Fiscal Crisis of the State* (New York: St. Martin's Press, 1973). This pathbreaking analysis of fiscal political economy was grounded in American postwar reality. The area of fiscal politics—a branch of political economy—owes much to Rudolf Goldscheid, who laid the foundation for critical fiscal analyses (O'Connor's contribution included). See Rudolf Goldscheid, *Sozialisierung der Wirtschaft oder Staatsbankerott: ein Sanierungsprogramm* (Leipzig: Anzengruber-Verlag Brüder Suschitzky, 1919), and his *Das Verhältnis der äussern Politik zur innern: ein Beitrag zur Soziologie des Weltkrieges und Weltfriedens* (Vienna: Anzengruber, 1915).

132. O'Connor, *Fiscal Crisis*, 6.

capital accumulation—also contributed to the problem of overaccumulation discussed earlier, as it relieved corporations from having to spend their own capital to provide to themselves what the state did for them.[133] Related to corporatocracy and our current reality, these aspects are part of *the massive shift of risk from corporations to the state* that we have witnessed during the past three decades. In this sense, at least, O'Connor's early 1970s work was prescient about the larger panorama we now witness.

The ongoing, massive shift of risk from corporations to the state can therefore be related to the long-term stagnation trend. Such immense shifting of risk translates into rapid increases in the growth of state spending— or in government liabilities meant to cover oligopolistic corporate failures when they occur. One such liability, for example, involves the vast growth in government-guaranteed debt that ultimately benefits corporations. In subsequent work during the mid-1970s, O'Connor went on to relate the fiscal crisis of the state in advanced capitalism to major aspects of corporate power—production, surplus value, economic policy, international corporate expansion, imperialism—which are also relevant to a consideration of stagnation.[134] All of these aspects were dealt with from the perspective that *it is the priorities of corporate power, above those of the population, that govern the allocation of resources in the advanced capitalist state*. Thus, changing fiscal policy without radically altering the priorities of the capitalist state would result in a withdrawal of public resources from the social classes with the least political power. And, because of the fiscal crisis of the state—expenses surpassing revenues—policies that cut government spending would deepen stagnation by reducing incomes and aggregate demand. O'Connor's work provided a basis for understanding both fiscal crises and the deeper roots of stagnation—related to fiscal allocation, policymaking, and the role of the state in advanced capitalism.

Stagnation during the decade of the 1970s—with high inflation during much of the second half—greatly alarmed the corporate and political elites in the United States and other advanced capitalist nations. It seemed that advanced capitalism had encountered a serious roadblock, one that

---

133. An aspect very relevant to our time—if the vast array of corporate tax loopholes, subsidies, bailouts, and corporate welfare is taken into account; see, for example, Foster and Magdoff, *Great Financial Crisis*; Perelman, *Invisible Handcuffs*; Barofsky, *Bailout*; Matt Taibbi, *Griftopia: Bubble Machines, Vampire Squids, and the Long Con that is Breaking America* (New York: Spiegel and Grau, 2010).

134. See O'Connor, *The Corporations and the State*.

could not be overcome without major changes in regulation and fiscal policy.[135] Those changes, however, would not alter the priorities of the state. O'Connor's early 1970s vision of how changes in fiscal policy would withdraw resources from the majority of the population—to serve the interests of corporate power and the wealthy—seemed prescient for the rest of that decade and the ones that followed. What occurred during the following four decades was a massive redistribution of resources and wealth *from* the vast majority of the population *to* benefit oligopolistic corporate power and the elites tied to it. Neoliberal dogma thus came to dominate policy formulation, offering recipes that set the stage for rising inequality and greater oligopolistic influence over government.

Many of those "recipes" had been tried out earliest in Chile, starting in the mid-1970s, with the advice and support of Chicago School economists (the most neoliberal group of mainstream economists at that time)—after the military coup brought Augusto Pinochet and his generals to power. The ideas of Milton Friedman, Friedrich von Hayek, and other conservative, "free market" economists thus found an appropriate trial ground in one of the most brutal regimes in Latin American history (one installed with U.S. government and corporate support).[136] This is a fact that neoliberals and many mainstream economists have typically brushed aside or simply ignored—much as they have brushed aside and ignored the reality of oligopolies for a century and a half—or that of stagnation for more than six decades. The Pinochet neoliberal experiment in Chile was followed by that of Margaret Thatcher's conservative government in Britain starting in 1979, and by Ronald Reagan's administration in the United States starting in 1981. The Chilean neoliberal policy experience was valuable for the Thatcher and Reagan governments, since they were advised by many of

---

135. The relative prosperity of the postwar decades thus seemed to have come to an end. This panorama was captured by two radical political economists who had earlier understood (and foreseen) the long-term stagnation trend of the American economy; see Harry Magdoff and Paul M. Sweezy, *The End of Prosperity: The American Economy in the 1970s* (New York: Monthly Review Press, 1977).

136. See Karin Fischer, "The Influence of Neoliberals in Chile Before, During, and After Pinochet," in *Road from Mont Pelerin*, ed. Mirowski and Plehwe, 305–46; Peter Winn, *Victims of the Chilean Miracle: Workers and Neoliberalism in the Pinochet Era, 1972–2002* (Durham: Duke University Press, 2004). Despite the Pinochet regime's bloody legacy of tyranny, oppression, and injustice, some neoliberal pundits still fervently defend Milton Friedman's and the Chicago School's role; see, for example, Brett Stephens, "How Milton Friedman Saved Chile," *Wall Street Journal*, March 1, 2010, A11.

the same economists that had assisted the Pinochet regime—the Chicago School and its ideas retaining a dominant position in policy formulation.[137]

Parallel to the Chicago School's influence at the time was the effort by some business school academics to justify the existence and power of very large organizations. The overarching criterion of these efforts was efficiency—that very large organizations made sense because they were supposedly more effective, through greater economies of scale and scope.[138] Consolidation and expansion—through mergers, takeovers, and new operations—was thus justified, while ignoring the relations of power that typically accompany oligopolistic control, and their effects on governance and society. In this way, Adam Smith's "invisible hand" of markets—and its presumed drive for greater efficiency—was assumed to be complemented by the "visible hand" of corporate management—and its drive for efficiency through large size. This justification—and tacit apology—for oligopolistic consolidation would be readily accepted in business schools, at a time when neoliberal dogma and neoclassical economics were making deep inroads in their curricula and faculties. A related effort considered efficiency in terms of transaction costs, positing their minimization to be the prime justification for large-scale corporate organizations.[139] Larger corporations were thus assumed to be more efficient than markets since they could more effectively enforce covenants that are important for exchange. Thus, the larger and more powerful a corporate organization, the better placed it would be to ensure that contractual obligations—involving labor, supply chains, marketing, for example—would

---

137. See Rob Van Horn and Philip Mirowski, "The Rise of the Chicago School of Economics and the Birth of Neoliberalism," in *Road from Mont Pelerin*, ed. Mirowski and Plehwe, 139–80; Harvey, "The Neoliberal State," in *Brief History*, 64–86. The Mont Pelerin Society, a secretive group that comprises some of the most influential corporate executives and political leaders in the planet—founded by Friedrich von Hayek—has long promoted neoliberal ideology and dogma in policymaking. This group has derived much of its intellectual inspiration from Chicago School economists; see Philip Plickert, *Wandlungen des Neoliberalismus: eine Studie zu Entwicklung und Ausstrahlung der "Mont Pèlerin Society"* (Stuttgart: Lucius and Lucius, 2008), and the articles in Mirowski and Plehwe, eds., *Road from Mont Pelerin*. Milton Friedman is credited with the introduction of the term *neoliberal* in economics; see Milton Friedman, "Neoliberalism and Its Prospects," *Farmand*, February 17, 1951, 89–93.

138. Alfred D. Chandler, *The Visible Hand: The Managerial Revolution in American Business* (Cambridge, MA: Belknap, 1977).

139. Oliver E. Williamson, *Markets and Hierarchies, Analysis and Antitrust Implications: A Study in the Economics of Internal Organization* (New York: Free Press, 1975). For a discussion of the link between Williamson's and Chandler's contributions from a critical political economy perspective, see Rahul Varman, "The Neoclassical Apology for Monopoly Capital," *Monthly Review*, November 2012, 29–47.

be met. Contract enforcement (and its efficiency) thus took precedence over all other considerations, as a justifier of oligopolistic power. These efforts helped make very large corporations—oligopolies, most of all—acceptable to policymakers and neoliberal ideologues, who viewed antitrust laws as a major obstacle to deregulation.

Starting in the early 1980s, neoliberal deregulation would open the door to an immense shift of risk from oligopolistic corporations to the state—along with a massive redistribution of wealth and power from the vast majority of the people to corporations and their elites. Such deregulation also made it possible for financialism and its casino economy to emerge. At the time, political economists—among them Sweezy—saw this large-scale deregulation effort, the rapid concentration in banking it triggered, and the proliferation of myriad financial corporations, as a desperate attempt to try to overcome long-term stagnation—a largely unsustainable one, in their view.[140] Deregulation and the massive shift of risk to the state was accompanied by a consolidation of the American political system behind corporatocracy in the 1990s, as the Democratic Party reoriented itself to serve finance and the Wall Street interests that benefited most from deregulation—and that also contributed most to political campaigns.[141] Up to that point, labor unions had largely struggled to raise wages based on productivity, but they would now find themselves increasingly powerless—more and more at the mercy of corporate power. The link between higher wages and greater productivity that unions had implemented over the years was severed, as higher productivity *with* lower wages (and benefits) became the norm. Corporate power—most of all, oligopolies—thus started to unilaterally reduce wages and benefits using the threat of layoffs, jobs offshoring, outsourcing, or automation. This development contributed to the long-term stagnation trend by further constraining aggregate demand, while boosting corporate capital accumulation through lower costs and greater profitability.

The Democratic Party's shift in the 1990s meant that *a two-party political system essentially became a one-party system, insofar as the subservi-*

---

140. See Magdoff and Sweezy, *Stagnation and the Financial Explosion*. This work, written in the early and mid-1980s, when financial deregulation had barely started, was prescient about finance's takeover of the American economy.

141. Wall Street thus practically gained veto power over President Clinton's economic policies; see, for example, John Bellamy Foster and Hannah Holleman, "The Financial Power Elite," *Monthly Review*, May 2010, 1–19; James Surowiecki, "Bonds and Domination," *New York Magazine* (accessed September 11, 2012), http://nymag.com/; Lance Selfa, *The Democrats: A Critical History* (Chicago: Haymarket, 2012).

ence of the state to corporate power—most of all, oligopolies—was concerned.
O'Connor's early 1970s observation about the state being at the service of
corporate power became all too obvious and real, as the Democratic Party
practically aligned itself with Wall Street and with oligopolistic power, not
only in finance but in almost every area of the economy. Some of the
party's longstanding rhetoric and propaganda remained—especially during
campaigns—but words became increasingly meaningless as actions, decisions, and money made it all too clear that corporate power was largely in
control. This made it plain that, politically, there was only one road ahead
to follow—the road set by oligopolistic corporate power. Any awareness of
stagnation as a long-term tendency, or of oligopoly, was practically discarded
as neoclassical economists monopolized government policy—most of all,
in economic and monetary matters. Dissident economists, especially radi-
cals, were practically expelled from economics departments in the United
States, as academic discourse became dominated by neoclassical economic
precepts.[142]

The deregulation of finance during the 1980s and 1990s made neoliberal dogma predominant, giving the false impression to many people—
including mainstream economists—that a magic policy formula to concoct
long-term growth in mature capitalism had been found. Because they had
never recognized the problem of long-term stagnation—or oligopolies—
mainstream economists interpreted the growth of finance—and eventually
financialism itself—as a result of the United States' "comparative advantages"
in that sector. The true character of financialism, its distortions, injustices,
and its crisis-prone and unsustainable nature—along with its real raison
d'être: overcoming long-term stagnation—was thus lost on them. Perhaps,
then, it should not surprise that mainstream economists could not fore-
see the crisis that started in 2007—the most severe one since the Great
Depression.[143] None of the neoclassical general equilibrium models at the

---

142. For aspects relevant to this trend see Perelman, *Railroading Economics*. Part of it also
involved casting out critical political economy from mainstream economics, and a distanc-
ing of economic theory from those who practice it in their everyday decisions—see David
Laibman, *Political Economy After Economics: Scientific Method and Radical Imagination* (New
York: Routledge, 2012).

143. A point inconveniently taken up by the British queen during a meeting with main-
stream economists in November 2008; see Heather Stewart, "This Is How We Let the Credit
Crunch Happen, Ma'am . . . ," *The Guardian*, July 25, 2009, http://www.guardian.co.uk/.
See also Paul R. Krugman, *The Return of Depression Economics and the Crisis of 2008* (New
York: Norton, 2009).

core of mainstream economics could predict it, much less understand it, since such a crisis was never supposed to happen in the first place.

The growth generated through deregulation, especially in finance, thus came at a heavy price to the vast majority of the population. An acceleration of oligopoly formation—in banking and finance as well as other sectors—was one of the consequences. The oligopolization dynamic in turn planted the seeds for more stagnation down the line, as capital accumulated in unprecedented ways. A fiscal crisis eventually developed, because of the massive shift of risk to the state that occurred during three decades of neoliberal policies, and the state's inability to meet its obligations. The tension between the first and second fiscal functions of the state in advanced capitalism, posited by O'Connor four decades before, thus became more difficult and strident. The vast amount of federal government debt accumulated, and the limited prospects for financing greater deficits, led to an unprecedented credit rating downgrade. Credit downgrades for many local and state governments made it more difficult and costly to obtain financing—while numerous local governments around the United States filed for bankruptcy. Neoliberal ideologues then opened a front against "entitlements"—an aggressive campaign against the social programs that had long tried to maintain some level of social harmony—and keep a large segment of the population above poverty or destitution. O'Connor's second function of the capitalist state—redistribution of resources to the needy—thus came under increasing attack.[144] The neoliberal era that started three decades earlier had long been bringing about a redistribution of wealth and power *from* the vast majority of the population *to* the corporate elites and the wealthy—a dynamic that had become established as the norm. Now, however, during the deepest crisis since the Great Depression neoliberal ideologues sought to accelerate this dynamic of dispossession—advocating the withdrawal of more resources from the second function of the state in order to enhance the first one—its subservience to and support for oligopolistic power.

---

144. Neoliberal think tanks were at the vanguard of this effort, receiving wide support and space in pro-corporate (and corporate-controlled) media. Subterfuge and distractions from the causes of the crisis became common. See, for example, Ben J. Wattenberg's "What's Really Behind the Entitlement Crisis?" *Wall Street Journal,* July 13, 2012, A11, which blames birthrates for the government's inability to meet its social obligations—the final sentence admonishing that "the real danger for the future is too few births." Nonetheless, troubling data showing substantial increases in the population living in poverty motivated some journalists to take a fresh look at programs that had long served the needy; see, for example, Galston, "Defense of Food Stamps."

Withdrawing resources from the second function of the state, in any case, contributes to stagnation by further reducing aggregate demand. This fine point—and linkage—did not seem to be understood by neoliberal ideologues. Being firm believers in neoclassical economic precepts, they—like the economists they take advice from—could not acknowledge or understand advanced capitalism's tendency toward stagnation. In this way, at least, their "solution" to the fiscal crisis of the state is self-defeating—besides being socially unjust. Far from achieving growth, as they claim they want to do, neoliberal ideologues plant the seeds of greater crises down the line by compounding the problem of stagnation. As for oligopolies, neoliberal ideologues typically believe that their power and dominance is a product of "comparative advantages"—and, true to their faith in "free markets" and market-based solutions, typically oppose any intervention to reduce such power. International "competitiveness" is also often drawn into the neoliberal discourse, applied to the case of nations and their oligopolies, to oppose any intervention.[145] The problem of oligopolistic overaccumulation, and its linkage to stagnation, is thus missed completely.

Another neoliberal attack on the second function of the state, beyond that on "entitlements," has involved the privatization of public resources. This corporatization of the commons is by no means new since it has been a standard component of neoliberal dogma and policy for more than three decades, but it gained more prominence after 2007.[146] It includes not only public resources, but also any function of government that can be made to turn a profit for corporate power. The results of this "solution" to the fiscal crisis of the state typically involve a curtailment of access to the public—especially the neediest segments of the population. Pricing effectively becomes a mechanism for segregation against those who cannot pay—an essential prerequisite for turning a profit by the corporate entities that take over. The commons are thus no longer "commons"—they become private

---

145. A view that usually draws its substance from Porter's *Competitive Advantage*. The possibility that oligopolies may help make a nation "competitive" (in a global economy dominated by oligopolistic corporations) but at the same time lead it into long-term stagnation, was completely lost on neoliberal advocates of this point (as it was on Porter).

146. Early neoliberal experiences with privatization of public resources occurred in Chile during the Pinochet regime (mid and late 1970s), and in Britain under the Thatcher government (early 1980s). See, for example, Silvia Borzutzky, "From Chicago to Santiago: Neoliberalism and Social Security Privatization in Chile," *Governance* 18 (2005): 655–74; and the articles in Thomas Clarke and Christos Pitelis, eds., *The Political Economy of Privatization* (London: Routledge, 1993). These experiences provided templates that would later guide privatization efforts in other countries. As with so much related to neoliberal ideology, practices, and policy, the Chicago School of economics had much influence in this area.

and corporate, if they do not come under oligopolistic control altogether. Greater inequality is another result of this "solution," as those who cannot pay end up being left farther behind. Equally disturbing, greater "efficiency"—the prime justification for privatizing a public resource—usually ends up contributing to stagnation as it speeds up accumulation by the corporate entity that takes over—all the more so when it happens to be an oligopoly. Neoliberal ideologues also miss this link between privatization and stagnation, mainly because their neoclassical economics grounding prevents them from recognizing it. The neoclassical economics albatross they hang around the neck of their ideology thus keeps them from understanding a most important phenomenon of our time.

Neoliberal ideologues and corporate power also favor immigration of highly skilled individuals—the brain-gain free ride that most advanced capitalist nations encourage—as a way to save the state's fiscal resources. Such savings occur by reducing expenditures on the second function of the state—specifically, the obligation to provide education and training. Immigration rule changes that favor highly skilled individuals can also be considered to be part of the first fiscal function of government—subservience to and support for corporate power—since the skills gained usually benefit corporate profits and accumulation most of all.[147] At the same time, such changes help the second function, by increasing the pool of the population that contributes to old-age programs involving pensions, Social Security, and Medicare. In all these respects, therefore, adjusting immigration laws to stimulate brain-gain immigration can find broad support from corporate interests.[148] Even though

---

147. Arguments in favor of looser—brain-gain oriented—immigration rules typically focus on "competitiveness." Although corporate interests, especially oligopolistic ones, are not usually mentioned, the substance of the arguments is highly beneficial to them; see, for example, Darrell M. West, *Brain Gain: Rethinking US Immigration Policy* (Washington, DC: Brookings Institution, 2010).

148. In a Brookings Institution conference on immigration, for example, Microsoft proposed loosening up visa requirements for highly skilled individuals, in return for employer payments to the U.S. government of as much as $15,000 per permanent residence permit and $10,000 per immigrant visa—a total of $25,000 per individual; see Brookings Institution, *Building and Unlocking Immigrant Skills Event,* September 20, 2012, http://www.brookings.edu/events/; L. Gordon Crovitz, "Washington's New Twist on Human Sacrifice," *Wall Street Journal,* October 1, 2012, A13. A high-level Microsoft executive noted that American universities would graduate forty thousand students with bachelor's degrees in computer science in 2012, but 120,000 jobs would be created that require such a degree—thus leaving a deficit of eighty thousand (unfilled) positions. The executive also noted that out of about thirty thousand public and twelve thousand private high schools in the United States, only 2,100 offer advanced placement courses in computer science (an important prerequisite for entry into university-level computer science programs). See Brad Smith, "How to Reduce America's Talent Deficit," *Wall Street Journal,* October 19, 2012, A13.

such immigration might save the state some resources, it can nonetheless contribute to overaccumulation through higher corporate profitability.

Although there is little evidence on the long-term fiscal effects of brain-gain immigration, its benefits might end up cancelling themselves if they help capital overaccumulation. For the United States, long the world's greatest recipient of such immigration, this phenomenon seems to have had little or no effect in moderating the long-term stagnation trend. It must, however, be noted that this consideration typically does not enter at all in the calculus of corporate power, or of politicians and government officials, who tend to see only immediate benefits. The nations that expended resources to educate, provide health care, and other support used by highly skilled individuals who emigrate are shortchanged, of course, but this matters little or not at all to the oligopolistic corporations—or the nations—at the receiving end. The current global relations of power prevent any compensatory mechanism for the countries that lose their most talented individuals, in this large-scale game of free riding by the wealthiest nations of the planet.[149]

The case of new technologies as a potential means to overcome stagnation also drew attention after 2007. Although new technologies can potentially generate some short-term growth, their impact on long-term stagnation in advanced capitalism seems, at best, to be very limited. The emergence of high tech sectors in the 1980s and 1990s, initially grounded in the invention of microprocessors, followed by personal computers, software, and eventually the Internet, the Web, along with new waves of computing, telecommunications, and software—a formidable lot of new technologies that made up the "IT revolution"—did not reverse or even stop the long-term stagnation trend. Pioneering companies such as Microsoft, Hewlett-Packard, or Apple grew large and became oligopolies, fencing in almost every sector they had helped create. Preexisting oligopolists that survived, such as IBM, retained or increased their power. Financialism also extended its reach over the new sectors, as megabanks and hedge funds supported consolidation in all the new sectors—while feverish speculation led to the tech crash of 2000 and the liquidation of thousands of small companies. *Oligopolistic control over the new technology sectors seems to be the answer to why their emergence and myriad effects failed to stop the long stagnation trend.* And the greater surplus, productivity, and profits the new

---

149. See Luis Suarez-Villa, "Brain Drain Conquest," in *Globalization and Technocapitalism: The Political Economy of Corporate Power and Technological Domination* (London: Ashgate, 2012), 164–67, and 195–97.

technologies generated for the oligopolies that took them over—and for all the other oligopolistic sectors in the economy—further compounded the problem of overaccumulation.[150]

New technologies poised to become symbolic of the twenty-first century—part of a phenomenon I have referred to in other books as technocapitalism—seem to have little prospect of stopping or reversing long-term stagnation.[151] *They—like the important high tech sectors of the late twentieth century—are already, or are rapidly coming, under oligopolistic control.* Startup tech companies are typically not under oligopolistic control, but have become more risky because of the entry barriers set up by oligopolists. One symptom of this problem is that only one-quarter of venture capital firms—those that supply the capital needed by startups—have been profitable in recent times.[152] As venture capital financing becomes more risky, it inhibits investment and reduces investment possibilities—contributing to capital overaccumulation. Specialists in venture capital financing have also noted that, to have any chance of success, a new tech startup must necessarily be global *from the start*—a most difficult proposition, but one that has become essential to have any chance of overcoming the entry barriers set up by oligopolists in the new sectors.[153] These difficulties seem to be lost on those who make future predictions about the effects of new

---

150. Neoclassical economic treatments of technological innovation's failure to overcome stagnation missed the oligopolization of new sectors. See, for example, Robert J. Gordon, *Is US Economic Growth Over? Faltering Innovation Confronts the Six Headwinds*, NBER Working Paper 18315 (Cambridge: National Bureau of Economic Research, 2012); Tyler Cowen, *The Great Stagnation* (New York: Dutton, 2011); "Has the Ideas Machine Broken Down?" *The Economist,* January 12, 2013, 22.

151. See Suarez-Villa, *Technocapitalism* and *Globalization and Technocapitalism.*

152. Henry Kressel and Thomas V. Lento, *Entrepreneurship in the Global Economy: Engine for Economic Growth* (Cambridge: Cambridge University Press, 2012). To try to attract venture capital, startup companies are increasingly using "ratchet" provisions—guaranteeing that the value of shares when they begin to be traded in stock markets through an IPO (initial public offering) will be much higher than their estimated value when a venture capital investment is made. If this does not occur, then the startup company must provide its venture capital investor a larger quantity of shares to make up the difference—a very risky proposition that some specialists refer to as "a crapshoot"—see Telis Demos and Douglas MacMillan, "Startups Boosting the Risk," *Wall Street Journal,* December 26, 2013, C1.

153. Kressel and Lento, *Entrepreneurship.* The authors, however—in keeping with neoliberal dogma—fail to attribute this problem to oligopolistic control, blaming "government planning" instead.

technologies—especially the neoliberal assumption that they will generate a "golden era" of growth.[154]

In biotechnology, for example, pharmaceutical and agro-chemical oligopolies have been taking over almost any promising company that emerges—through purchases, strategic alliances that lead to acquisition, or by providing capital to gain control. This is very much the case for new biotech companies that own patents with potentially profitable uses. Oligopolists taking over such companies are aided by the high costs, risk, and uncertainty of biotech research—and the need for capital to support it. Having a pharmaceutical oligopolist as "partner," no matter how asymmetrical the relationship may be, is therefore unavoidable for most biotech companies. Clinical trials with failure rates as high as 8,000:1 for a successful compound, for example, means that companies must experiment continuously to have any chance of success.[155] Those trials can take as many as five to ten years from start to approval, assuming they are successful. Expensive research expertise from diverse fields, such as genetics, bioinformatics, proteomics, medicine, chemistry, microbiology, pharmacology—in addition to legal counsel on intellectual property—are usually required to come up with any products. The high risk, uncertainty, cost, and extensive time required for testing and approval mean that biotech companies can only undertake a very narrow set of activities—typically, those closely related to their research program. For oligopolists that invest in a biotech company, it makes sense to take it over to prevent failure—and safeguard its intangibles, the patents it owns, and any projects in progress. Such takeovers take away potential investment targets, however, adding to the overaccumulation problem.

Another problem with biotech is that most products tend to be unprofitable after they are marketed. Partly, this is because of the high cost of treatments and applications, which, in the area of human health, insurance companies are often unwilling to cover. Many biotech products often do not work as expected, even after undergoing years of testing, due to their complexity and unexpected effects. High complexity is reflected in molecular weights—a biotech therapy product's, such as Epogen, can be as much as 8,500 percent greater than that of a commonly used pharmaceutical one, such as Zantac.[156] These aspects add to cost and can create substantial

---

154. See, for example, Michael S. Malone, "The Sources of the Next American Boom," *Wall Street Journal*, July 6, 2012, A13.

155. See Suarez-Villa, *Globalization and Technocapitalism*, 56.

156. See, for example, James C. Mullen, "Gene Therapy," *Wall Street Journal*, April 27, 2007, A17; Suarez-Villa, *Globalization and Technocapitalism*, 103.

problems during and after clinical testing. Many biotech companies therefore become dependent on a very narrow range of successful products—to make any profit or even recover their research costs. To cover such costs, they must often license their patents to oligopolists—who end up capturing most of the profits (if any are made) and become de facto owners of the licensed inventions. In other cases, covering research costs means having to be subcontracted by a pharmaceutical or agro-chemical oligopolist—becoming subservient to its priorities. Also, many biotech companies do not have the marketing clout or distribution networks to sell their products and must depend on their oligopolistic patron to do so.

Some biotech corporate pioneers also became oligopolists in their own right. These companies typically fenced in market niches that were new, and which none of the pharmaceutical or agro-chemical oligopolists were ready to exploit. They thus used their knowledge and research capabilities to fence in their areas of expertise—much as Microsoft did early on with desktop computer software. However, biotech corporations that build up oligopolistic positions tend to merge or be taken over eventually by pharmaceutical or agro-chemical oligopolies. Genentech, for example, a pioneering company thought to have founded the biotech sector, was eventually acquired by the multinational pharmaceutical oligopolist Hoffmann-La Roche.[157] Genentech built an early oligopolistic position by focusing on a few areas—mainly immunology, oncology, neuroscience, tissue repair—fencing them in by using its research capabilities.[158] Despite its successes in this narrow range, becoming part of a larger, multinational oligopolist became attractive—because of the wider marketing and distribution possibilities and the need to offset the high risk, costs, and uncertainty of research. Another biotech oligopolist—Amgen—built its position in biopharmacology by elaborating a fairly narrow range of products based mostly on its genomics and proteomics research. It has bet its future on the expectation that a new kind of medical care, targeting each patient's specific genetic makeup, will eventually replace conventional medicine. Amgen thus hopes that biomedicine—and the biopharmacology it owns (or will fence in)—will replace the pills and potions that pharmaceutical companies have traditionally manufactured.[159]

---

157. See Sally Smith Hughes, *Genentech: The Beginnings of Biotech* (Chicago: University of Chicago Press, 2011).

158. See, for example, Marilyn Chase, "How Genentech Wins at Blockbuster Drugs," *Wall Street Journal*, June 5, 2007, B1; Hughes, *Genentech*.

159. Formation of corporate oligopolies targeting biomedicine seems to be underway, as genomics companies merge; see, for example, "Getting Personal: A Genomics Merger Highlights the Potential for Personalized Medicine," *The Economist*, June 21, 2008, 76.

Although it is tempting to think that this may occur on a large scale someday, its timing is still very uncertain given the high costs and risks involved.[160] These conditions will most likely induce further oligopolization of biotechnology—compounding capital overaccumulation.

The agro-biotech sector is already highly oligopolistic, with global agro-chemical corporations such as Monsanto and DuPont controlling most of the genetically engineered seeds and plants used in farming. These and other corporations are also expanding into related areas involving food production and nutrition, among others.[161] An important objective for agro-biotech oligopolies is to create genetic engineering platforms that can support horizontally and vertically integrated production structures—allowing them to branch into and seek oligopolistic control over almost any area that can be related to them. A disturbing aspect is that oligopolistic corporate power in agro-biotech is intimately bound up with science—in a way that biomedical and biopharmacological oligopolists would someday want to be.[162] *Science has thus been manipulated to support corporate power in agro-biotech, by "engineering" the oligopolistic surplus (ΔN)—and the resulting profits—into products.* Thus, for example, farmers who use genetically engineered seeds are typically forced to stay with them, and to continue purchasing or paying royalties forever—thus boosting the oligopolistic surplus perpetually since they cannot switch back to natural seeds.[163] A designed lifetime window of one crop for each genetically engineered seed means that farmers must

---

160. The path to biomedicine seems populated with numerous obstacles, even for a powerful oligopolistic corporation such as Amgen; see, for example, Daniel Costello, "Amgen Needs Mojo Working: A Series of Missteps and Problems with Its Top Sellers Put the Drug Maker on Its Heels," *Los Angeles Times,* March 12, 2008, C1.

161. See Marie-Monique Robin, *The World According to Monsanto: Pollution, Corruption, and the Control of the World's Food Supply* (New York: New Press, 2010) and her documentary, "The World According to Monsanto" (Ottawa: National Film Board of Canada, 2008); Dominic Clover, *Monsanto and Smallholder Farmers: A Case Study on Government Accountability*, IDS Working Paper (Brighton, UK: Institute for Development Studies, University of Sussex, 2007).

162. See, for example, Suarez-Villa, *Globalization and Technocapitalism,* 149–53.

163. Winds, water and soil erosion often carry genetically engineered seeds away from the farms that purchased them—mixing them with crops in nearby areas where natural seeds are used. To protect its market power, aggressive lawsuits against farmers whose crops have incorporated its genetically engineered seeds—unwillingly—have been pursued by Monsanto; see Michael Perelman, *Steal this Idea: Intellectual Property Rights and the Corporate Confiscation of Creativity* (New York: Palgrave Macmillan, 2004), 123; Robin, "The Iron Law of the Patenting of Life," in *World According to Monsanto,* 201–24.

repurchase seeds for every crop—unlike the natural ones, which provide new seeds to plant the next crop. Special fertilizers needed to allow engineered seeds to work typically modify or destroy ecologies that would support natural seeds—making it practically impossible for farmers to switch back.[164] Farmers who cannot afford the cost of engineered seeds for every crop then end up bankrupt and often have to sell their land to the agribusiness oligopolists. The sales allow those oligopolists—which in turn are highly dependent on the engineered seeds supplied by the agro-biotech oligopolies—to assemble vast areas and take over entire crop territories.[165] The agribusiness oligopolies are not only better customers for the agro-biotech oligopolists but also have mutually well-aligned interests—for lobbying and political contributions, for example.[166] *One oligopolist thus feeds on the other, compounding overaccumulation through their vast combined surplus and market power, while also expanding their influence over politicians and regulators.*

Intellectual property regimes for agro-biotech also hold little promise for redressing overaccumulation. They actually help support oligopolistic power by granting monopoly rights over ideas, life, and nature that last twenty years for every patent. Well before a patent for a genetically engineered seed or plant expires, a new one for an improved version is often filed for—to keep the oligopolistic surplus machine running.[167] The improvements may be marginal but nonetheless patentable—something that R&D departments can do well and have turned into an art, assisted by clever patent attorneys. The new, improved seed may therefore not provide much benefit over the one it replaces, but will nonetheless likely be billed as "cutting edge"—to justify a higher price. Usage of the marginally improved, newly patented seed may thus gain an aura of "best practice" for anyone purchasing it. And which producer—agribusiness oligopolists, most of all—

164. Robin, "One of the Great Polluters in Industrial History," 9–130, and "Roundup: A Massive Brainwashing Operation," 69–88, and chs. 2 and 3 on Dioxin, and ch. 4, in *World According to Monsanto*; Kurt Eichenwald, *The Informant: A True Story* (New York: Broadway Books, 2000).

165. Robin, "How Multinational Corporations Control the World's Food," in *World According to Monsanto*, 307–17; Marianne Kaplan's documentary, "Deconstructing Supper" (Oley, PA: Bullfrog Films, 2002); Clover, *Monsanto*.

166. See James B. Lieber, *Rats in the Grain: The Dirty Tricks and Trials of Archer Daniels Midland* (New York: Four Walls Eight Windows, 2000).

167. See Robin, "Monsanto Weaves Its Web, 1995–1999," in *World According to Monsanto*, 178–200; Suarez-Villa, *Globalization and Technocapitalism*, 149–53.

would ever want to be tagged as doing anything other than "best practice"? Also, by the time a genetically engineered seed's patent expires, the natural seed it replaced will probably be a historical memory, and may only be found in some museum exhibit or farming history text—with no chance of returning to cultivation. In any case, the destruction of the ecologies that sustained the natural seed will likely make its cultivation impossible, even when it is available for use. In agro-biotech, as in other biotech sectors, the channels that lead to overaccumulation are therefore well protected through intellectual property rights.

Nanotechnology, another promising new technology that is bound to become symbolic of the twenty-first century, is also being taken over by oligopolies. In computing and microprocessors, for example, existing oligopolists such as Intel and AMD (Advanced Micro Devices)—which together practically dominate the entire CPU (central processor) sector—are poised to control nanotech-based processing. Such nanotech processors will be at the core of quantum computing, and will likely be as important to electronics and computing as integrated circuitry and silicon were in the 1970s—or as vacuum tubes were for televisions and radios earlier in the twentieth century. This new form of computing will be essential for the production of extremely small and very powerful supercomputers—the new frontier of miniaturization in computing—with vast applications across the entire spectrum of human activities. Chemical oligopolists are also taking over nanotech for industrial, transportation, household, and textile uses—especially the production of graphene, a carbon allotrope that will be at the core of a vast range of uses, from solar cells to antibacterial filters and ballistic transistors. In medical technology, nanotech is a target for biotech and pharmaceutical oligopolists, as it will allow the super-miniaturization of sensors and transmitters—to be implanted in and monitor almost any physiological function in any living organism (human, animal, or plant), for example. Ultraminiaturized, nanotech-based sensors and transmitters are also likely to be targeted by the oligopolistic corporations that now supply the military, intelligence, and surveillance sectors.[168] Among the many uses of nanotech already being targeted by corporate oligopolies in various sectors is three-dimensional industrial printing—a new technology that can create prototypes, and perhaps eventually disengage production from scale economies—for such products as tools, machine parts, weapons, or furni-

---

168. See Suarez-Villa, "Fast Militarism," in *Globalization and Technocapitalism*, 167–71.

ture.[169] Through all these diverse applications and sectors, the oligopolistic takeover of nanotechnology will likely compound overaccumulation, even as efficiency gains temporarily create some growth in certain activities.

Advanced software is also practically under oligopolistic control. Bioinformatics, an emerging sector that is essential for genomics, biopharmacology, proteomics, biomedicine, synthetic bioengineering, and agro-biotech, is being targeted by software and computing oligopolies. Similarly, "cloud computing" is practically under the control of a few oligopolists—such as Google, Amazon, Microsoft—which are using their vast networks and computing capabilities as an entry barrier. This means that computing for both individual *and* mass usage of information—as opposed to just computing for individual usage *of* mass information—will be completely under their control. "Big data" capabilities obtained through "cloud computing" allow the oligopolists in control to track billions of sensors that can monitor almost anything—from individual health to shopping habits, vehicle performance, location, weather, animals, and espionage targets, among many other possibilities.[170] The oligopolistic corporations in charge will therefore be able to own and mine vast amounts of personal and mass information, linking them, and gaining the capability to intrude in our lives as no government has ever done before—with more precision. These corporations may possibly take over government functions involving surveillance and data mining—and their oligopolistic power will also likely compound overaccumulation.

Oligopolists in this sector will therefore be able to track every step we take, every action or activity we undertake, along with our health, finances, vices, social relations, psychological tendencies, not to mention our most mundane or intimate daily habits. In the United States, for example, some corporations are already engaged in the daily act of using automatic cameras and software, that record all license plates of vehicles circulating on the

---

169. Treatments of this new technology ignore the oligopolistic dimension, and its larger implications for overaccumulation. The emphasis seems to be on communicating the impression that it can usher in a new era of growth—business journalists being the most enthusiastic advocates of this view. See, for example, Peter Marsh, *The New Industrial Revolution: Consumers, Globalization, and the End of Mass Production* (New Haven: Yale University Press, 2012); Malone, "Sources."

170. See, for example, Viktor Mayer-Schönberger and Kenneth Cukier, *Big Data: A Revolution that Will Transform How We Live, Work, and Think* (London: Murray, 2013).

roads or parked.[171] The routine compilation of that information now yields private databases with hundreds of millions of vehicle owners' names and addresses, that can be augmented through other sources to include income and financial information, health data, judicial and property records, traffic violations or accidents, and many other items.[172] Such data are then sold to other corporations or to government agencies, so that they can locate the individuals they seek—or pinpoint those most likely to purchase their products and services. This immense wealth of personal and mass information—extrapolated to entire communities and nations—means that the oligopolists in charge will amass an immense, global wealth of intelligence that can be used for targeting and marketing of all sorts—including political, consumer, health, police, military and almost any other purpose. At the same time, their political power—and the nature of our corporatocratic governance—may allow them to more freely influence politicians, regulators, and almost any state function that can limit them.

Other promising new technologies are also coming under oligopolistic control, or are very likely to—through waves of mergers and acquisitions similar to those that occurred in computing and software in the 1990s and 2000s. Companies involved in developing fuel cell technology for road vehicles, for example, are likely to be targeted by the oil oligopolists. The immense amounts of capital that these oligopolists have accumulated might thus be used to fence in a new technology that will likely replace oil in vehicle transportation. The largest automotive oligopolies may also target fuel cell technology, much as they took over oil-dependent combustion engine technology in the early twentieth century. Fuel cell technology may also eventually allow buildings to disengage completely from the electric grid—a possibility that will likely attract interest from utility and energy generation oligopolists. Oil and electric utility oligopolists may also likely target solar power—another promising technology that may also allow buildings to disengage from the grid. Oligopolists have often targeted new technologies that are likely to replace those they have long exploited—to retain or augment their power.

---

171. Julia Angwin and Jennifer Valentino-DeVries, "New Tracking Frontier: Your License Plates," *Wall Street Journal,* September 29, 2012, A1—the authors state that "data about a typical American is collected in more than 20 different ways during everyday activities," adding that "storing and studying people's everyday activities, even the seemingly mundane, has become the default rather than the exception."

172. Ibid., A13.

For the oligopolists who control these new technologies and sectors, patenting is a most helpful support. Granting monopoly rights over an invention boosts such control by creating a formidable entry barrier. A sector or market niche under oligopoly control can therefore be kept fenced in. The recent adoption of a first-to-file rule in U.S. invention patenting, moreover, stacks the deck in favor of oligopolies—since they typically have the resources and research capabilities to speed up R&D operations. Also, the systematized research regimes that are at the core of contemporary R&D tend to be more effectively controlled by oligopolists, because of their vast resources.[173] Being upstaged in filing for a patent is usually very damaging to small and medium-size companies, given the high costs of research. In many such cases, the upstaged companies have little choice but to offer themselves to be acquired—by the oligopolist that filed first. Years of research and vast resources may thus be wasted when a company cannot be the first to file— even if it came up with the invention before anyone else. This situation can create serious difficulties for any company, but an oligopolist will always be in a better position to overcome them. And, although over 90 percent of all patents are never put to any use, they can nonetheless be turned into powerful barriers to support oligopolistic power.[174] Accumulating a vast number of patents that will never be used has thereby become an important component of oligopolistic strategy. *Thus, an overaccumulation of patents—which supports oligopolistic power in emerging technologies—now accompanies the overaccumulation of capital at the core of long-term stagnation.*

In sum, long-term stagnation in advanced capitalism is part of the larger panorama of oligopolistic corporate power—and of corporatocracy. Slow growth, greater inequality and social injustice, downward mobility for the vast majority, multidimensional crises, and a state that is increasingly disengaged from the needs of the people, are some of the symptoms of this phenomenon. Although the removal of oligopolistic hegemony seems to be a major prerequisite for overcoming stagnation, there are powerful obstacles. A very important one involves *the incipient alignment of the public interest with that of oligopolistic corporate power.* This is a structural problem of corporatocracy and oligopolistic power in mature capitalism that is quite

---

173. See Suarez-Villa, "Systematized Research Regimes," in *Technocapitalism*, 124–35.

174. An aspect being used to justify the securitization of invention patents. The first step in this direction was taken with the creation of the Intellectual Property Exchange International in 2011; see IPX International, *IPXI Market Rulebook*, Working Edition 1.0 (Chicago: IPX International, 2012), http://www.ipxi.com/.

intractable. Oligopolies' influence over governance, their market power, vast accumulated capital, and stock market weight tend to preserve the status quo. To many speculators, those features convey an impression of safety—despite the fact that they are a root cause of crises. The illusion of safety is further enhanced by their too-big-to-fail status—feeding the expectation that they will be bailed out by the corporatocratic state whenever their existence is threatened. A disarticulation of the alignment of the public interest with oligopolistic power, necessary as it is, therefore seems unlikely to occur on its own. Such disarticulation may be expected, however, in the context of a systemic breakdown of capitalism—accompanied by the insolvency of the state, greater downward mobility and economic insecurity for the majority, market failure, and the unsustainability of financialism.

A systemic overhaul that ends oligopolistic hegemony would necessarily have to be accompanied by a restructuring of the relations of power in society—public governance being a most important vehicle. Only through a systemic overhaul can there be any hope of overcoming stagnation, and of reorienting the state to serve the needs of the vast majority of the population. Any restructuring that does not radically change the priorities of the state would thus be incomplete and most likely doomed to fail. Such restructuring would run up against another powerful obstacle—*the alignment of the interests of politicians with those of oligopolistic corporate power.* This alignment is very important to the previously mentioned one, mainly because the subservience of politicians to oligopolistic power (and corporate power in general) is of paramount importance to corporatocracy. Without it, the corporatocratic ship of state founders—particularly when fiscal insolvency impedes its navigation, and the ill winds of downward mobility, economic insecurity, and financialist collapse make themselves felt in full force.

A third powerful obstacle involves *the massive transfer of risk from oligopolistic corporations to the state.* This phenomenon contributes to long-term stagnation by impairing the state's resources, and is a major vehicle for fiscal crises. It is a product of oligopolistic influence over public governance that helps perpetuate corporatocracy, and a vital support for financialism and its casino economy—which contribute to overaccumulation. Through this risk transfer, stagnation feeds inequality by shortchanging a major function of the state in advanced capitalism—the obligation to serve the people, and sustain the sort of redistribution that is at the core of socially responsible governance. The transfer of risk also makes it more difficult for the state to support the intangibles—education, knowledge, creativity—needed to sustain the workforce and that are essential to improve living standards. Such support is also at the core of the social function of the state—a vital one for public governance to retain any semblance of legitimacy.

Neo-Oligarchy

It would be remiss in a consideration of oligopolies and the state in advanced capitalism to ignore the privileged few who have the most influence on governance. That small but very powerful element can be considered an oligarchy in the general sense of the term—de facto manipulation of public governance and society by a relatively small group. Such control may be at odds with certain documents—constitutions or charters—that prescribe how governance should occur, but we know that social reality is often far removed from the letter and spirit of such declarations. The fact that their spirit—if not also the letter—is all too often contradicted has, after all, been a key ingredient of social and political upheavals throughout human history.

The conventional meaning of oligarchy will be modified in this chapter to take into account the peculiar nature of corporatocracy—and the new reality it creates. Because of the novel character of this reality, that small privileged elite in command of corporatocracy—and the oligopolistic power that sustains it—will be referred to as the *neo-oligarchy*. Although the conventional meaning of oligarchy is not vacated, the treatment of this key component will qualify and adapt it to the reality of advanced capitalism. The term *neo-oligarchy* will thus help differentiate the privileged group associated with corporatocratic power from all other forms of oligarchy, past or present.[1] Related to its definition, this chapter will also address the most distinctive characteristics of the neo-oligarchy, relating them to the major phenomena discussed previously.

The neo-oligarchy associated with oligopolistic power and corporatocratic governance is by no means monolithic. The neo-oligarchy does not speak

---

1. C. Wright Mills, in his *The Power Elite* (New York: Oxford University Press, 1956), tended to see the corporate, political, and military elites as equally important partners. The treatment of neo-oligarchy offered in this book diverges greatly from that conceptualization of elite power.

with one voice, and elements or individuals within it often compete among themselves for greater power or influence. In many ways, the neo-oligarchy's power may seem fragmented, even abstract, and subject to circumstantial factors—working through an apparatus of control that is pretty much out of the grasp of the average citizen. The vast majority of the public may thus be about as removed from any awareness of the neo-oligarchy's power as underground water is from clouds. Its real power is, moreover, all too often camouflaged by media reports of how some members pulled themselves out of poverty, how they struggled against all odds in life or business, how their religious beliefs made them attain the impossible, or how personal accomplishments through financial or managerial talent justify their vast influence. Such reports may even adopt a critical tone, to avoid an impression of partiality—even when their general thrust is quite partial to their interests. The corporate-owned media has many ways of generating subtle spins, narrative arcs, and other artifices to build up the image of those it favors. And, the interests of the oligopolistic, corporate-owned media are typically very close to those of the neo-oligarchy. Despite any appearances to the contrary, the corporate-owned media is in many ways an appendage of the neo-oligarchy, for it cannot do well without its favor.

What remains of noncorporate media, such as those run by nonprofit organizations or governments, is in no position to challenge its oligopolistic, corporate-owned counterpart—or the power of the neo-oligarchy, for that matter. The reporting and diffusion of news is now globally in the hands of a few oligopolistic corporate-run networks—all of them tied in many ways to the neo-oligarchy. Similarly, multidimensional media oligopolies—such as News Corp., AOL-Time Warner, and Disney—now provide most of the content that people watch, read, and listen to in the United States and many other nations around the world.[2] An internationally well-known media specialist has, for example, noted that "the single-most-alarming fact about global communications today—given the immensity of its reach, power and effect—is how few global corporations control it. The concentration of global media ownership rivals that of the global oil industry, but the difference between oil and media is that the former deals with tangible things, while the latter deals with consciousness."[3]

---

2. See Robert W. McChesney, *Rich Media, Poor Democracy: Communication Politics in Dubious Times* (Urbana: University of Illinois Press, 1999), and his *The Political Economy of Media: Enduring Issues, Emerging Dilemmas* (New York: Monthly Review Press, 2008).

3. Jerry Mander, "Privatization of Consciousness," *Monthly Review*, October 2012, 34.

In the United States, noncorporate media typically do not have enough resources to report on their own on most events, and so must depend greatly on what the corporate-owned media oligopolies provide. In many nations, even government-owned media with significant resources now depend on what the global corporate-owned media oligopolies interpret and diffuse. It should not surprise, therefore, that much news and many features today end up being reported in a fairly similar way—expressing much the same key points, even when the facts can lead to different interpretations. The oligopolistic media corporations thus wield immense power over diffusion, and can "orient" the public's attention toward certain news, features, or opinions that receive more weight than others—and can make a stronger collective impression. Among the most prominent examples of vehicles that carry out such orientation is the Rupert Murdoch–owned *Wall Street Journal*—part of his global News Corp. oligopoly—and its opinion-editorial offensive to dismiss inequality as a criterion of social well-being.[4] Another example is the same newspaper's propaganda drive against what neoliberal pundits refer to as "entitlements"—the rights and benefits that in the past allowed the vast majority of the population to count on a minimal social net of support in times of crisis or individual distress.[5] Reporting that disparages disability programs as an obstacle to economic growth, and a drain on fiscal resources, has also been part of that newspaper's contribution to the anti-entitlement offensive—providing views that play well with pro-corporate interests and those of the neo-oligarchy.[6]

---

4. In an article authored by two pro-corporate think tank members, for example, inequality was referred to as a "myth." The authors, attempting to show that consumption should replace any consideration of inequality, failed to consider that increases in consumption—which they lauded as the benchmark of social well-being—have occurred through immense, unsustainable increases in consumer debt. See Kevin A. Hassett and Aparna Mathur, "Consumption and the Myths of Inequality," *Wall Street Journal*, October 25, 2012, A17.

5. See, for example, Nicholas Eberstadt, "Yes, Mr. President, We Are a Nation of Takers," *Wall Street Journal*, January 25, 2013, A13—this article notes that "entitlement transfers have grown twice as fast as personal income" while ignoring the immense (and much more rapid) growth of disparities in income, wealth, and most every indicator that occurred during the cited period of time. Another article disputes well-known (and proven) facts on the erosion of the middle class, attributing this phenomenon to an artificial overestimation of inflation by the CPI (consumer price index) and a disregard of nontaxable "fringe benefits" in take-home pay. See Donald J. Boudreaux and Mark J. Perry, "The Myth of a Stagnant Middle Class," *Wall Street Journal*, January 24, 2013, A17.

6. Leslie Scism and Jon Hilsenrath, "Workers Stuck in Disability Stunt Economic Recovery," *Wall Street Journal*, April 8, 2013, A1.

The neo-oligarchy's and the corporate-owned media's offensive against "entitlements" took an opportunistic turn when it seized the debate on U.S. federal deficits in 2012.[7] Members of the neo-oligarchy and their acolytes in the media essentially declared everyone except themselves—and their oligopolies—to be wasteful, apparently forgetting the unprecedented sums lost in Wall Street because of their reckless bets and power games. Or the vast amount of public funds the federal government had to spend to bail out the financial system and keep it from melting down because of their deeds—in addition to other corporate bailouts and the myriad forms of corporate welfare that are now institutionalized. Or, all the wasteful and unfair drain of public resources that the wealthy enjoy through targeted tax breaks. This is something that many people realized for the first time, when the Republican presidential candidate in 2012 (himself a member of the neo-oligarchy) was found to have paid a 13.9 percent federal income tax rate (on income of $21.6 million, 2010)—far below the proportion paid by the vast majority of taxpayers.[8] Partly because of all the tax exemptions, loopholes, deductions, and other benefits accumulated over time, it was found out that this candidate had amassed a fortune of approximately $250 million (net worth estimate)—making him the wealthiest presidential contender ever.[9] Tax loopholes and benefits for the wealthy and for corporations—and the massive transfer of risk from oligopolies to the state—were estimated to account for much of the federal government's $16 trillion debt at the end of 2012, a figure that increased sixteenfold during the previous three decades.[10] While ignoring or covering up all these facts, the neo-oligarchy and their acolytes also spun their propaganda offensive to target such topics as reducing inflation adjustments for federal social programs—a measure that would eventually cause many Americans to slide into poverty in old age.

Overlooked in the corporate-owned media's propaganda offensive is the fact that their usage of the term *entitlement* is misleading, since they present

---

7. Among the few critical newspaper articles that drew attention to this offensive were Michael Hiltzik's "Deficit Debate Driven by the Wealthy," *Los Angeles Times,* July 29, 2012, B1.

8. Jeffrey Sparshott, "GOP Assails Harry Reid on Romney Tax Charge," *Wall Street Journal,* August 6, 2012, A4.

9. Kim Geiger, "Mitt Romney Worth Up to $250 Million, Election Filings Show," *Los Angeles Times,* August 13, 2011, AA1; Robin Abcarian, "On a Trail of Her Own: Ann Romney's Testimony in a Lawsuit Over a Prized Horse Opens a Rare Window into Her Private World," *Los Angeles Times,* May 22, 2012, A1.

10. See, for example, Jim Puzzanghera, "Average Americans Feel US Debt's Pain," *Los Angeles Times,* February 25, 2013, A1.

it to mean *unearned* benefits that people receive—a false presumption in the case of Social Security and Medicare, for which beneficiaries pay during their working lives. Additionally, ruses applied to estimates of social programs' costs often inflate them artificially—to try to impress the public. Among the most prominent is the so-called infinite horizon projection, which involves an estimation of funding costs extrapolated out to an unlimited future, with the estimate then subsequently converted to current value—while, on the other hand, revenues are not similarly projected out to infinity. Estimates that use this imbalanced approach show immense shortfalls. Yet, when the revenue side is projected out in the same manner a funding surplus for those programs is shown to be substantial.[11] Another tactic involves the argument that younger workers are being "impoverished" today to pay for Social Security, while current beneficiaries receive too much—or more than what they contributed to this program.[12] But analysts who researched this question based on lifetime employee and employer contributions to Social Security, showed the opposite is actually the case.[13]

Corporate-owned media oligopolies usually provide ample coverage to advocates of "entitlement" cutting or elimination—all of whom tend to be members of the neo-oligarchy, their acolytes, or politicians who receive contributions from them. Curiously, one of the great advocates of ending "entitlements" is Lloyd Blankfein, chief executive of Goldman Sachs—the megabank that received a $12.9 billion government bailout in 2009—to cover losses from its bets on insurance oligopolist AIG (American International

---

11. Michael Hiltzik, "Five Biggest Lies about Entitlement Programs," *Los Angeles Times*, March 10, 2013, B1; American Academy of Actuaries, *An Actuarial Perspective on the Social Security Trustees Report* (Washington, DC: AAA, 2003 and subsequent years), http://www. actuary.org/pdf/socialsecurity/.

12. See, for example, Geoffrey Canada, Stanley Druckenmiller, and Kevin Warsh, "Generational Theft Needs to Be Arrested," *Wall Street Journal*, February 14, 2013, A17. The so-called INFORM (Intergenerational Financial Obligations Reform) Act—introduced in Congress in 2013—was one of the products of the anti-entitlement offensive, receiving support from many mainstream economists (including fifteen Nobel laureates), neoliberal pundits and government officials; see Michael Hiltzik, "The Skinny on the Inform Act: It's Likely to Misinform," *Los Angeles Times*, September 18, 2013, B1, and his "Five Biggest Lies"; John Thune, "Thune, Kaine Introduce Bill to Better Project Long-Term Impacts of Current Fiscal, Economic Policy," Press Release, July 24, 2013, http://www.thune.senate.gov/.

13. C. Eugene Steurle and Stephanie Rennane, *Social Security and Medicare Taxes and Benefits Over a Lifetime* (Washington, DC: Urban Institute, 2011); Hiltzik, "Five Biggest Lies." Disinformation has also been exposed with regard to other federal social programs—Food Stamps, for example; see, William A. Galston, "In Defense of Food Stamps," *Wall Street Journal*, November 6, 2013, A13.

Group).[14] Also a prominent advocate of cutting "entitlements" is billionaire Peter Peterson—former chairman and chief executive of another Wall Street megabank—founder of the Concord Coalition, an advocacy organization that contributes vast amounts to influence the media and politicians.[15] Another organization he founded—the Peter G. Peterson Foundation, also part of his anti-entitlement offensive—has built a web of partnerships, focus organizations, and commissions that promote his views to politicians and the public. This foundation—and the numerous organizations it supports—have become models for other efforts to advance political interests aligned with those of the neo-oligarchy.

The most important sources of "entitlements" targeted are the kinds of programs that have provided old age, medical, welfare, and unemployment support to hundreds of millions of Americans during the past seven decades—Social Security, Medicare, Food Stamps, and Medicaid, for example. Possibly the most important strategic ploy in their offensive has been to try to pit the younger generation against the old—an effort that some authors refer to as "generational warfare." Foremost in this front has been the Peterson Foundation and the constellation of organizations it created or funded—such as Fix the Debt and The Can Kicks Back—which attract much coverage from the media oligopolies. Two of the more visible acolytes associated with this foundation and the organizations it supports are a board member of oligopolistic megabank Morgan Stanley—who served as White House Chief of Staff during the Clinton Administration—and a former U.S. Senator, both very wealthy individuals.[16]

At the core of the generational warfare effort is the argument that the federal government spends far more on the elderly than it does on the young. However, the fact that the vast majority of government spending on the young occurs at the local or state level is conveniently ignored. When such outlays are tabulated, spending on the young is actually eight times

14. Michael Hiltzik, "Haste Is Waste in 'Fiscal Cliff' Fix," *Los Angeles Times*, December 2, 2012, B9; Paritosh Bansal, "Goldman's Share of AIG Bailout Money Draws Fire," *Reuters*, March 18, 2009, http://www.reuters.com/article/2009/03/18/.

15. Michael Hiltzik, "Middle Class Loses in This Kind of 'Reform,'" *Los Angeles Times*, October 3, 2012, B1; Thomas Frank, "Avoiding the Austerity Trap," *Wall Street Journal*, June 30, 2010, A19; Concord Coalition Web site, http://www.concordcoalition.org/about-us.

16. See Michael Hiltzik, "Seniors vs. Kids Claim is a Sham," *Los Angeles Times*, February 27, 2013, B1, and his "Skinny on the Inform Act"; Canada, Druckenmiller, and Warsh, "Generational Theft."

greater (8:1) than on the old, on a per capita basis.[17] And, the fact that federal outlays for Social Security and Medicare for the older generation have been paid for by the beneficiaries themselves, over their working lives, is also conveniently ignored. Individuals such as Peterson and others also seem to ignore the fact that a most blatant and wasteful "entitlement" has involved tax cuts for the wealthiest—benefiting the neo-oligarchy above all. Tax cuts for the wealthiest Americans have been estimated to have been close to one trillion dollars during the 2000–09 decade alone.[18] The corporate-owned media oligopolies, however, typically evade this argument—or the fact that if total tax cuts for the wealthy were tabulated for the past four decades they would amount to a substantial share of the accumulated federal debt.

Among other individuals who influence and orient the corporate-owned media oligopolies are extremely wealthy individuals—all of whom can also be considered members of the neo-oligarchy. They contribute vast amounts to politicians and think tanks that favor their views—in what has become a game of loaded patronage, involving unprecedented amounts of money. The think tanks, in particular, tend to be little more than propaganda machines, which provide arguments to support the neo-oligarchy's privileges. Billionaire Wall Street speculator Paul Elliott Singer, owner of Elliott Capital Management—a hedge fund specializing in "distressed" debt acquisitions (a type known as a "vulture fund")—for example, chairs and funds the Manhattan Institute for Policy Research, a think tank engaged in influencing the media, setting the political agenda of conservative candidates, providing intellectual support for their views, and attracting funding to their campaigns. According to a report in one of the best-known American financial magazines, Singer "shows little sympathy for the plight of the 99 percent" and commands "a large network of rich donors ready to follow his lead."[19] Curiously, Singer's hedge fund benefited greatly from the $1.3 billion federal bailout of Delphi Automotive—a parts supplier (previously known as Delco) rescued by the government along with General Motors in 2009—an instance of corporate welfare that never seems to show up

17. Hiltzik, "Seniors vs. Kids," B4.

18. Donald L. Bartlett and James B. Steele, *The Betrayal of the American Dream* (New York: PublicAffairs, 2012). See also William A. Galston, "A Decade of Decline in the American Dream," *Wall Street Journal*, December 18, 2013, A15.

19. Michelle Celarier, "Mitt Romney's Hedge Fund Kingmaker: Elite Money Manager Paul Singer Is a Passionate Defender of the 1% and a Rising Republican Power Broker," *Fortune*, April 9, 2012, 104 and 102.

in Singer's (or the Manhattan Institute's) media orientation campaigns.[20] One consequence of Singer's hedge fund involvement with Delphi—and the small syndicate of Wall Street funds that also participated—was to be rid of all the 25,200 union workers Delphi employed, and to close all but four of the company's twenty-nine American plants.[21] Delphi's pension and health care obligations were also eliminated, with the federal government taking over what could be covered by federal programs—thus making the bailout extremely profitable for Singer and his hedge fund.

Allied with Singer are Charles and David Koch—two of the wealthiest individuals in the United States—owners of the energy conglomerate Koch Industries, the second-largest privately held corporation in the world. The billionaire Koch brothers, as they are known in financial circles, have long executed an orientation agenda to influence American politics at every level. Koch Industries has consistently been the top donor in the oil and gas sector to federal election candidates—one populated by some of the largest and richest oligopolies in the world.[22] The Koch brothers' status within the neo-oligarchy, and their vast wealth, provide immense clout to influence the corporate-owned media oligopolies. They also help funnel vast amounts to political action committees and think tanks that support their agenda to reduce government, deregulate the economy, and eliminate "entitlements." Somehow, however, the fact that Koch Industries is a major beneficiary of corporate welfare—in the form of tax credits, loopholes, subsidies, and other vehicles that depend on American taxpayers—seems to be lost on the media oligopolies that they engage and orient.[23]

---

20. Greg Palast, "Mr Singer and Mr Romney," *The Nation,* November 5, 2012, and his "Mitt Romney's Bailout Bonanza," *The Nation,* November 5, 2012, http://www.thenation.com/.

21. See Greg Palast and Ted Rall, *Billionaires and Ballot Bandits: How to Steal an Election in 9 Easy Steps* (New York: Seven Stories, 2012); Palast, "Mitt Romney's Bailout Bonanza."

22. Matea Gold and Joseph Tanfani, "Silent Money Speaks Volumes: More than $55 Million for the Conservative Agenda, but Where Did It All Come From?" *Los Angeles Times,* May 28, 2012, A1. Revenues from the Koch brothers' diversified investments amounted to $115 billion in 2012—compared to the $162 billion of Warren Buffet's Berkshire Hathaway—as they extended their reach into numerous sectors and activities across the American economy; see, for example, James R. Hagerty, "Billionaire Brothers Put Irons in Fire: Known for Politics More than Its Brands, Koch Industries Says It Can Do Big Deals Like Buffett," *Wall Street Journal,* July 3, 2013, B1.

23. See Tom Hamburger, Kathleen Hennessey, and Neela Banerjee, "Conservative Duo Reach Seat of Power," *Los Angeles Times,* February 6, 2011, A11; Palast, *Billionaires and Ballot Bandits.* The Koch brothers founded the Cato Institute in 1974—a very influential think tank

There seems to be no shortage of members of the neo-oligarchy who seek to orient the media, set the political agenda, and deepen American corporatocracy. Billionaire Joe Ricketts, who made his fortune as the founder of TD Ameritrade—the corporation that helped attract tens of millions of individuals to Wall Street betting and financialism—has contributed substantial amounts to political candidates who conform to his vision of governance.[24] A crusader for business deregulation, fiscal austerity, and government spending cuts—the kind that would hit hard the vast majority of the population—he founded and provided vast amounts to the Ending Spending Action Fund—a "super PAC" that attempts to set the political agenda, get favored politicians elected, and defeat those who do not cooperate.[25] Previously, Ricketts had founded and funded Taxpayers Against Earmarks, an organization that employed aggressive tactics to target elected politicians who did not conform with his views on spending. Learning how to set the agenda for the media became easier when he founded his own media corporation in 2009—DNAinfo.com—a business that seems destined to build a locally rooted media empire. Lost to the media that support or acquiesce to his crusade is the fact that Ricketts's ownership of a major league baseball team—the Chicago Cubs—"offloads business costs on the public," as stated by a report in one of the best-known American business magazines.[26]

Cyberspace has also facilitated these crusaders' orientation campaigns, by providing greater and faster diffusion and more space—for the kinds of news and features they favor—in the oligopolistic, corporate-owned media. The Web has made this homologation of news content, feature reports, and diffusion easier—allowing the few global oligopolistic media networks that interpret the news and diffuse content to get all the attention. Any other media—the noncorporate or non-oligopolistic one—thus tend to land far out on the Web's skewed (and very long) connectivity "tail"—that vast

---

on economic and public policies; see John C. Samples, *The Struggle to Limit Government: A Modern Political History* (Washington, DC: Cato Institute, 2010). In 2013, they considered acquiring a media-newspaper company—Tribune Co., owner of the Chicago *Tribune* and Los Angeles *Times,* among other media and news businesses; see James R. Hagerty and William Launder, "Koch Declares His Interest in Newspapers Is All Business," *Wall Street Journal,* June 6, 2013, B1.

24. Jennifer Reingold and Doris Burke, "The New Billionaire Political Activist," *Fortune,* October 8, 2012, 100–107.

25. See Jim Ruttenberg and Jeff Zeleny, "Magnate Steps into 2012 Fray on Wild Pitch," *New York Times,* May 17, 2012, A1; Reingold and Burke, "New Billionaire."

26. Reingold and Burke, "New Billionaire," 102.

wasteland of Web sites that never show up on any search engine's first page. And, as noted in the chapter on oligopolies, the Web is itself coming under oligopolistic control in multiple ways—turning itself into a major vehicle to build such power. In many respects, the oligopolistic global media corporations have already seized the Web as their main vehicle for diffusing and interpreting news—launching "orientation" strategies that ostensibly frame debates and set reporting agendas around the world. The Web, long regarded as a potential vehicle for democracy is—much like conventional media— thus becoming more closely tied to the interests of the neo-oligarchy. The negation of its potential to be a vehicle for democracy is disastrous, for all who believed it would usher in a new era of political accountability.[27] The strengthening link between the Web and financialism—evidenced by Wall Street's growing influence over social networks, for example—seems to guarantee that this trajectory will deepen.

The rising power of the neo-oligarchy and the inequality that accompanies it manifests itself clearly in the top 1 percent's rising share of income gains and wealth. During the decade of the 1990s, for example, this minuscule segment of the population took 45 percent of all gains in disposable household income, on average. By contrast, during the 2000–09 decade the share of the top 1 percent increased to 73 percent of all income gains.[28] This 28 percent increase from one decade to the next is astounding, and it is the highest since data on household income change started to be recorded. By 2010, in the aftermath of the worst economic crisis since the Great Depression, the 1 percent at the top of the pyramid took 93 percent of all income gains in the United States—indicating a rising trend that is very likely to continue. These increases do not include income from capital gains, which typically go to the wealthiest segment of the population—and overwhelmingly so to the top 1 percent. Also, nonwage income—the kind obtained from dividends, interest, rent, and profits from unincorporated businesses, for example—tends to be underrepresented in these data.[29] Such

---

27. See, for example, Robert W. McChesney's *Digital Disconnect: How Capitalism Is Turning the Internet against Democracy* (New York: New Press, 2013), esp. chs. 3, 4, and 5.

28. William K. Tabb, "The Crisis: A View from Occupied America," *Monthly Review*, September 2012, 15–21. See also Michael D. Yates, "The Great Inequality," *Monthly Review*, March 2012, 1–18; Andrew G. Berg and Jonathan D. Ostry, *Inequality and Unsustainable Growth: Two Sides of the Same Coin?* IMF Research Department (Washington, DC: International Monetary Fund, 2009), http://www.imf.org/.

29. See U.S. Bureau of the Census, *Income Main* (accessed October 25, 2012), http://www. census.gov/.hhes/www/income/; Yates, "Great Inequality." Census Bureau data on household income are based on surveys that do not include capital gains income—and are considered to underreport income from nonwage sources.

income also tends to benefit the top 1 percent greatly. Thus, the share of income gains for the top 1 percent would likely be significantly greater if those components were included.

The top 1 percent now has more private net household wealth, or net worth—the value of all assets possessed, after taxes—than the bottom 90 percent of the population, a situation that is almost unprecedented in the United States. Only in periods preceding major crises, such as the 1920s, or in socially distressed nations—the kind usually thought to be ruled by oligarchies—can similar statistics be found. Compared to the median net wealth of all U.S. households, the top 1 percent's net wealth was about 225 times greater in 2009—the highest ratio observed since data on net worth started to be recorded—while in 1983, by comparison, it was 131 times. In contrast, the share of American households with zero or negative net worth increased by 60 percent between 1983 and 2009.[30] Within that privileged 1 percent of the population, those in control of the largest Wall Street financial oligopolies—and of the largest global oligopolistic corporations—possess the greatest wealth. This means that inequality can also be found within the top 1 percent—as those most closely associated with the largest oligopolies accumulate wealth faster. According to *Forbes* magazine's "Forbes 400" listing of the wealthiest individuals in the United States, for example, the wealth of the top individual in its list was fourteen times greater than the average for all four hundred individuals in 2011.[31] By comparison, this ratio was 8.6 in 1982—a rise that reflects how increases in wealth inequality also occurred within the wealthiest segment. As the neo-oligarchy grows in power and wealth, therefore, inequality also occurs within its ranks.

International research based on the Gini coefficient—a common measure of inequality—has shown the United States' overall trajectory on income to be much worse than that of every advanced capitalist nation during the past three decades.[32] Similarly, comparisons on child poverty among twenty-one rich nations found the United States to be worst, reflecting how

---

30. Sylvia A. Allegretto, *The State of Working America's Wealth, 2011: Through Volatily and Turmoil, the Gap Widens* (Washington, DC: Economic Policy Institute, 2011), http://www. epi.org/publication/; Yates, "Great Inequality."

31. *Forbes* magazine, *The Richest People in America* (accessed October 26, 2012), http://www. forbes. com; Yates, "Great Inequality."

32. See Carmen DeNavas-Walt, Bernadette D. Proctor, and Jessica C. Smith, *Income, Poverty, and Health Insurance Coverage in the United States: 2010*, Current Population Reports P60-239 (Washington, DC: U.S. Government Printing Office, 2011), http://www.census.gov/prod/2011pubs/ p60-239.pdf.

306 / Corporate Power, Oligopolies, and the Crisis of State

growing inequality jeopardizes the well-being of children.[33] The worsening of inequality can be associated with the neoliberal era since its beginning three decades ago—a phenomenon that is considered to have had wide-ranging impacts on American society.[34] Perhaps it should not surprise that, according to the CIA's own World Factbook, the United States—long considered the top advanced capitalist nation—ranks worse than Cameroon and the Ivory Coast on income inequality, and is only slightly less unequal than Uganda—all of them nations that are often portrayed as examples of injustice or underdevelopment.[35] From a global perspective, the United States—thought by many to be the richest nation on the planet—therefore now ranks with some of the poorest and most unjust societies in most indicators of inequality. Most such societies are, moreover, considered to be ruled by oligarchies—an aspect that is thought to be closely associated with great disparities. An article published in a very well-known American magazine noted that income inequality is "more severe in the United States than it is in nearly all of West Africa, North Africa, Europe and Asia. We are on par with some of the world's most troubled countries, and not far from the perpetual conflict zones of Latin America and Sub-Saharan Africa."[36] In many ways, therefore, the situation in the United States today has much in common with those of distressed societies, where the wealthiest have privileges that allow them to perpetuate their wealth, while the poor suffer disadvantages that tend to perpetuate their poverty.[37]

Beyond the effects of greater wealth concentration, and influence over media and politics, which then are the most distinctive characteristics of the neo-oligarchy? Four characteristics set this phenomenon of advanced capitalism apart from prior modes of oligarchic control. Not one of them, but *all four acting in combination* make the neo-oligarchy a distinctive feature of

33. United Nations Children's Fund, *Child Poverty in Perspective: An Overview of Child Well-Being in Rich Countries* (Florence: UNICEF Innocenti Research Centre, 2007), http://www.unicef-irc.org/; Arlie Russell Hochschild, "Free Markets vs. Family Values," *Los Angeles Times*, June 3, 2012, A27.

34. See Richard Wilkinson and Kate Pickett, *The Spirit Level: Why Greater Equality Makes Societies Stronger* (New York: Bloomsbury, 2010).

35. Central Intelligence Agency, *CIA World Factbook* (Washington, DC: CIA, 2009).

36. Max Fisher, "Map: US Ranks Near Bottom on Income Inequality," *The Atlantic*, September 19, 2011, http://www.theatlantic.com/international/.

37. An aspect that has been taken up in Eric Schutz's *Inequality and Power: The Economics of Class* (London: Routledge, 2011).

contemporary advanced capitalism. The *first* characteristic is *the neo-oligar-chy's intimate association with oligopolistic corporate capital*. Although it may be argued that in prior times oligarchies were associated with oligopolies, never before has its control been as hegemonic as it is today—given the breadth and depth of oligopolistic corporate power, and the magnitude of advanced capitalist economies. These aspects are magnified by the global reach of oligopolistic corporate power. Never has oligopoly capitalism been as global or far-reaching as it is today. No nation, culture, region, group, or community in the world can consider itself out of reach of oligopoly capitalism—or the economic and political influence of the neo-oligarchy.

The neo-oligarchy's association with oligopolistic corporate power has also been the most important element in the emergence of corporatocracy, a related phenomenon that is now part and parcel of advanced capitalism. Without neo-oligarchic control over oligopolistic corporate power, corpora-tocratic governance would find it very difficult to exist. The power of the corporatocratic state, and its subservience to oligopolistic corporate power, thus depends greatly on the neo-oligarchy's capacity to sustain and augment its wealth. *Shifting risk to the state—and eventually to taxpayers—is, in part, how the neo-oligarchy's wealth and privilege is sustained and increased.* For this to happen, *aligning the interests of politicians with those of oligopolistic corpo-rate power* became essential. Such alignment occurs through the three vehi-cles of influence discussed previously in this book—political contributions, lobbying, and the "revolving door" mechanism—and the vast amount of wealth accumulated. Without this apparatus of risk-transfer and alignment of interests, the neo-oligarchy would find it very difficult to retain its power.

The *second* characteristic is *the neo-oligarchy's association with finan-cialism*. The most powerful and wealthiest group within the neo-oligarchy derives its status from the financial sector's takeover of advanced capitalism.[38] The rise of oligopolistic corporate finance provided the platform for this development—one that in the United States can be traced to the start of financial deregulation in the 1980s.[39] Many members of the neo-oligarchy

---

38. See Matthew Miller and Duncan Greenburg, "The Richest People in America," *Forbes*, September 30, 2009, http://www.forbes.com/2009/09/30/; John Bellamy Foster and Hannah Holleman, "The Financial Power Elite," *Monthly Review*, May 2010, 1–19.

39. Financial deregulation, among other important initiatives in the neoliberal agenda, was presented as part of a "moral" crusade for freedom in the 1980s; see Jeff Madrick, *Age of Greed: The Triumph of Finance and the Decline of America, 1970 to the Present* (New York: Knopf, 2011).

wax nostalgic about that decade and the following one, when speculation drove the stock market to one historical high after another. Between August 1982 and January 2000, for example, the S&P 500 index—comprising the largest five hundred stock market–traded corporations in the United States, the vast majority oligopolies in their sectors—rose by 1,194 percent.[40] A major consequence of that prolonged period of unfettered speculation was the severance of finance from production—a phenomenon discussed earlier that is a source of crises and threatens the very essence of capitalism as an economic system. One fundamentally important support for the neo-oligarchy's financial power, which arose from that prolonged period of speculation, was the *alignment of the public's interest with that of oligopolistic finance*—a project to expand and deepen financialism that depends greatly on corporatocratic governance. The spread of unfettered speculation, targeting almost anything and everything that has a probabilistic dimension, is at the heart of this alignment. The casino economy of financialism thereby becomes a major support for the neo-oligarchy and its privileged power.

The neo-oligarchy's association with financialism negates the bourgeoisie's historic grounding on tangible property. *This is a major aspect that sets the neo-oligarchy apart not only from the bourgeoisie but also from previous oligarchic modes.* To be successful, financialist speculation usually requires betting with or selling what one does not own. The ownership of tangible property—land, buildings, jewelry, machinery, factories, materials—thus becomes largely secondary, when it is not vacated altogether, in the context of financialism and neo-oligarchic power. In previous times, the bourgeoisie—and prior forms of oligarchy—rose to power and wealth through their ownership of such property. Owning them was not only the vehicle to obtain power and wealth in society, but also to sustain and increase them. One example of how this longstanding element of bourgeois power has been vacated involves financialist gambling on almost *anything that has a probabilistic dimension*—weather, elections, sports, debt, harvests, life, death, illness, romance, for example—no matter how absurd or abstract, so long as there are others who put up money that can be bet against. Such betting usually has little or nothing to do with ownership—not even of capital, especially when it is done with borrowed money. Another example involves the "vulture funds"—hedge funds that use debt that has been defaulted on (commonly known as "distressed" debt).[41] Such funds never really "own" the

40. S&P 500 Historical data, http://www.standardandpoors.com/indices/sp-500/en/us/; Rich Karlgaard, "The Stock Rally That Isn't," *Wall Street Journal*, February 6, 2013, A11.

41. See, for example, Celarier, "Romney's Hedge Fund Kingmaker."

debt obligations, in the sense that they never actually purchased them from those who issued them—be they governments, corporations, or institutions. The intent of the vulture funds is *to merely use those debt obligations to pressure or intimidate* the original issuers—through litigation and seizures—to pay up more than what the majority of the original holders of the debt agreed to be paid—after default became inevitable.[42] The vulture funds' takeover of those debt obligations simply becomes part of *a game to extract money*, that has very little to do with ownership—of the taken-over debt claims or any assets attached to them. Property is simply not important in such cases, certainly not in the way it was to the bourgeoisie and to prior modes of oligarchy.

The bourgeoisie (or what remains of it) is therefore upstaged or even vacated in the new reality set by neo-oligarchic power. At best, members of what once was—or would have been—the bourgeoisie can hope to be acolytes of the neo-oligarchy, by becoming part of the managerial elites needed to run the oligopolies.[43] The severance of reproduction from commodification adds to this situation—as complex intangibles become more important in production. Such intangibles require more specialized and skilled management—a technocratic elite of sorts that expects to be richly compensated and to whom employees (and their talents) are merely commodities. This makes management both more difficult and more technical, with the consequence that the neo-oligarchy becomes farther removed from the workings of production—the real economy—not to mention its day-to-day operation. *Speculation is, after all, a lot easier to do than production,* and betting schemes can also be potentially more profitable (even if only on paper). *The neo-oligarchy thereby ends up being the owner of capital, period—of financialist capital, overwhelmingly.* In finance, the managerial elites similarly perform the role of acolytes—as advisors and executors—for

---

42. Agustino Fontevecchia, "Billionaire's Hedge Fund Rebuffs NY Fed in Argentina Case: No Risk to $2.6T Payments System," *Forbes*, November 26, 2012, http://www.forbes.com/; Celarier, "Romney's Hedge Fund Kingmaker."

43. The managerial elites that served American multinational oligopolies during the 1950s and '60s can, in some ways, be considered predecessors of the acolytes that serve the neo-oligarchy and their oligopolies. Analyses of the earlier corporate elites can show some of the similarities; see, for example, S. M. Menshikov, *Millionaires and Managers* (Moscow: Progress, 1969); Richard J. Barnett and Ronald E. Müller, *Global Reach: The Power of the Multinational Corporations* (New York: Simon and Schuster, 1974); Stephen Hymer, *The International Operations of National Firms: A Study of Direct Foreign Investment* (Cambridge: MIT Press, 1976).

the speculative strategies that benefit the neo-oligarchy. Given the spread of automatic betting schemes, and of financialist expertise, such acolytes also tend to become more disposable—if their short-term performance does not generate the returns expected by those they serve.

In this regard, therefore, *the alignment of the interests of the managerial acolytes with those of the neo-oligarchy becomes very important.* It can be argued that the scope of agency theory, discussed in previous chapters, ends up being distorted in this new panorama of neo-oligarchic power—as the interests of shareholders, generally speaking, end up being upstaged by the interests of the neo-oligarchs. They typically amass more shares or have greater voting privileges than common shareholders—because of their founder status, prior ownership rights, or vast holdings. Such individuals may, for example, control the vast majority of voting rights in a corporation, even when they actually own a minority of shares—a privilege that founders and past owners often enjoy and deploy to their personal advantage.[44] At the same time, *the transfer of risk to the state becomes an important priority for the acolyte managerial elite, to lighten their own burden, especially when crises strike—or to enhance their own performance when they do not.* In this regard, the vehicles of influence that seek to align the interests of politicians with those of oligopolistic corporate power—political contributions, lobbying, and the "revolving door" mechanism—gain much importance.

The neo-oligarchy's association with financialism also negates the function of socially productive work in capitalism—partly a byproduct of the severance of finance from production discussed earlier in this book. The financialist neo-oligarchy thus provides a role model for society based in the amassment of paper profits through speculation.[45] Time is also part of this dynamic, taking up a role that requires practically no effort once a scheme is set and executed. *Speculation and time, rather than socially productive work, become the keys to "success" in the financialist culture that benefits the*

---

44. See Michael Hiltzik, "Like It or Not, He'll Get His Way," *Los Angeles Times,* May 20, 2012, B1; James Wallace and Jim Erickson, *Hard Drive: Bill Gates and the Making of the Microsoft Empire* (New York: Wiley, 1992); Mike Wilson, *The Difference Between God and Larry Ellison: Inside Oracle Corporation* (New York: Morrow, 1997); David Kirkpatrick, *The Facebook Effect: The Inside Story of the Company that is Connecting the World* (New York: Simon and Schuster, 2010).

45. See, for example, Simon Lack, *The Hedge Fund Mirage: The Illusion of Big Money and Why It's Too Good to Be True* (New York: Wiley, 2012); Satyajit Das, *Extreme Money: Masters of the Universe and the Cult of Risk* (New York: McGraw-Hill, 2012).

neo-oligarchy. Such speculation typically involves betting, as noted earlier, and often includes efforts to try to make others believe that something has more value than it actually has, or to otherwise place others in situations from which they cannot extricate themselves without having to pay to do so. Tricks and ruses (legal or not) are thus also at the heart of the new culture of betting and greed set by the financialist neo-oligarchy—an example that spreads throughout the social fabric as it is enhanced or otherwise presented as a desirable model by the corporate media oligopolies.

The *third* characteristic is *the neo-oligarchy's rootlessness.* As an economic group or class, the neo-oligarchy is much less rooted than the bourgeoisie— or any prior oligarchic form—ever was. Its reach and scope are mobile and global, in the sense that it tends not to have a deeply localized identity, and is therefore not much identified with any particular place—as the bourgeoisie tended to be. The neo-oligarchy's capital is therefore not really bound up with any specific locale, but to many locales—or to none in particular. In this sense, it tends toward anonymity, making it possible for its members to be from nowhere—if they so wish—or from anywhere—a contradiction in terms, but one that reflects the *opportunistic mobility and flexibility* of neo-oligarchic power. The neo-oligarchy's anonymity—partly derived from its rootlessness—also extends to national identity. Its members need not necessarily be bound up with any particular nation, but can be connected to several or many—or none—in the sense that they need not have any symbolic national economic identification—if they so wish. This is all in contrast with the most important capitalist elites of bygone eras, in which such individuals as Henry Ford, John Pierpont Morgan, Thomas Mellon, Armand Peugeot, Gottlieb Daimler, and practically all others—were greatly identified with specific nations and locales, unavoidably so.[46] National and local roots were thus extremely important to such individuals and to the bourgeoisie in general, since a visibly rooted identity was essential to sustain their power and wealth.

Financialism contributes greatly to the neo-oligarchy's rootlessness, as speculation has by and large become rootless. Speculative schemes can be carried out from almost anywhere today. The probabilistic dimension at the core of such schemes also makes the mobility and flexibility granted

---

46. See Carol W. Gelderman, *Henry Ford: The Wayward Capitalist* (New York: Dial, 1981); Cass Canfield, *Outrageous Fortunes: The Story of the Medicis, the Rothschilds, and J. Pierpont Morgan* (New York: Harcourt Brace Jovanovich, 1981); John Rowland and Martin Henley, *The Rolls-Royce Men: The Story of C. S. Rolls and Henry Royce* (New York: Roy, 1969).

by rootlessness more attractive. The possibility of being flexible and mobile makes financialist schemes more adaptable and more capable of rapid adjustment. At the same time information technology and globalization have enhanced the neo-oligarchy's rootlessness. Being rootless makes it easier to trespass cultural barriers, co-opt government officials and regulatory systems in multiple nations, bypass longstanding prejudices against certain national identities, and create new spaces of economic power. Perhaps for such reasons, residing physically—without being rooted—in wealthy, small-nation tax havens has become attractive to some members of the neo-oligarchy.[47] Holding citizenship or residency documents in such locales can help bypass barriers—cultural, economic, or political—that stand in the way of speculative schemes.

The *fourth* distinctive characteristic is *the neo-oligarchy's pervasive influence on the political system, and on major functions of governance.* Such influence is more systematic and in many ways deeper than what any bourgeoisie in advanced capitalist societies could ever achieve—despite the neo-oligarchy's seemingly fragmented and amorphous character. *Oligopolistic corporate power and corporatocracy are the platform and means that support the neo-oligarchy's political influence.* The spread and depth of oligopolistic corporations in almost every key sector, the apparatus of corporatocratic governance, and the neo-oligarchy's fundamental association with both, are at the core of this fourth characteristic. The main vehicles for the neo-oligarchy's vast political influence are the same three vehicles that serve oligopolistic corporate power—political contributions involving vast amounts of money, legislative and regulatory lobbying, and the high-level "revolving door" mechanism. In addition, the corporate-owned media provides an important vehicle of influence over politics and governance.

The neo-oligarchy's political influence is also *systemic,* in the sense that it is entwined with the institutions of advanced capitalism in myriad ways. One example involves the apparatus of philanthropy. Vast contributions to philanthropy by the neo-oligarchy convey an impression of altruism—whereas the real purpose is usually to strengthen institutions that cater to their interests, promote personal (or family) power, or to benefit from tax breaks.[48] Such deductions and breaks are in various ways engineered by the

---

47. By one estimate, such locales now hold more than $10 trillion in bank accounts, and process over one-half of world trade—as well as most international lending; see Nicholas Shaxson, *Treasure Islands* (London: Vintage, 2012).

48. See, for example, Teresa J. Odendahl, *Charity Begins at Home: Generosity and Self-Interest among the Philanthropic Elite* (New York: Basic Books, 1990).

political system at the service of the neo-oligarchy—through legislation and tax rules that provide very favorable terms. Often, however, a combination of those factors rather than simply tax breaks is the motivator of their philanthropy. The neo-oligarchy's philanthropic pursuits also support, directly and indirectly, its apparatus of political control—and, through the media, its influence over society and governance. Media reports on how this or that philanthropy will help fight some prevalent disease, for example, often result from strategies aimed at neutralizing public concern over their vast political power. Such reports also help conceal how oligopolistic corporate power—the neo-oligarchy's most important source of wealth—harms the public interest. In many ways, those reports help divert attention from the negation of democracy that corporatocracy entails—especially the redistribution of wealth and power that favors the neo-oligarchy, and the economic insecurity that accompanies it.

The main vehicles of neo-oligarchic political and governmental influence—contributions, lobbying, and "revolving door" control schemes—require many acolytes, beyond those managing the oligopolistic corporate domain. What remains of the bourgeoisie may thus be employed to run these vehicles of political influence. The acolytes put in charge of these vehicles are typically found among the upper middle class in contemporary advanced capitalism. Among those in this stratum are the attorneys, the managers in charge of "super PACs" and similar political organizations, lobbyists of assorted professional backgrounds, spinmasters and damage control wizards, and diverse public relations specialists—all of whom help lubricate the neo-oligarchy's political machinery. These acolytes tend to be very well compensated and many of them are even multimillionaires—a status they owe to their service. Some may even get a chance to become part of the neo-oligarchy—if performance, influence, and luck generate upward mobility into their ranks. Some of these acolytes may be descendants of the bourgeoisie who once owned small or medium-size businesses that either failed or were taken over by oligopolies.[49] Mobility from the acolyte class to the neo-oligarchy may thus benefit some elements of the bourgeoisie at the service of neo-oligarchic power.

The most expedient way for individuals to ascend from the acolyte class to the neo-oligarchy, however, is through service as chief executives of oligopolistic

---

49. The low survival rates of small enterprises may be a significant source of acolytes, especially during and after crisis periods. In 2007–2010, for example, only 57 percent of small enterprises (those with annual revenues of less than $10 million) survived in the United States; see "The Mighty Middle," *The Economist*, October 20, 2012, 59.

corporations. The super-compensation that such service entails usually provides a financial platform to enter roles that influence the political system.[50] Average annual compensation for a corporate chief executive in the United States in 2010, for example, was almost $12 million, according to a major research firm.[51] The total combined compensation of chief executives for the six largest megabanks in the United States—all of them oligopolists—was $88.8 million in 2012, and involved raises that ranged between 15 and 75 percent from the previous year for the three highest-paid executives.[52] In 2009–2011, the highest-paid executive in this group received $60.2 million in compensation—a sum that reflects the overwhelming importance of finance, and of financialism, for the neo-oligarchy and its acolytes.[53] "Golden farewell" packages for chief executives who retire or go into politics has often amounted to very substantial sums. In one case, for example, the chief executive of an oligopolistic pharmaceutical corporation—affected by quality problems and major recalls of various medicines during his tenure—received $143.5 million in pension benefits and deferred compensation.[54] Accumulated regular compensation—excluding "golden farewells"—can amount to hundreds of millions of dollars over time, as in the case of the chief executive of an oil oligopolist who received more than $850 million.[55]

Politically, American business schools served as great training and contact centers of the acolyte class—if not for the neo-oligarchy itself. *They spawned or embedded the social relationships and networks needed by the aco-*

50. Vast sums accumulated by chief executives can help fund expensive political campaigns of their own when they decide to enter politics; see, for example, Evan Halper and Jack Dolan, "Whitman's Words Put Spotlight on Her Deeds," *Los Angeles Times,* May 12, 2010, A1; Michael Hiltzik, "She Has Her Own Ethics Code," *Los Angeles Times,* April 25, 2010, B1.

51. Governance Metrics International, *GMI Ratings, Key Metrics Series: Combined CEO/Chair* (various years), http://www3.gmiratings.com (accessed March 12, 2013); "Pay Up: Overpaid Bosses Are Back," *The Economist,* June 18, 2011, 74.

52. E. Scott Reckard, "Wells' CEO Is Top-Paid Banker: John Stumpf Earned $22.87 Million in 2012; Goldman's Lloyd Blankfein was No. 2," *Los Angeles Times,* March 15, 2013, B4.

53. Ibid., B1.

54. Peter Loftus, "J&J Chief to Receive $143 Million Farewell," *Wall Street Journal,* March 15, 2012, B1.

55. Michael Hiltzik, "Irani's Pay: It's Even Worse than I Thought," *Los Angeles Times,* October 20, 2010, B1. See also Kathy M. Kristof, "Executive Pay Report: Fat Raises, Hints of Limits," *Los Angeles Times,* May 29, 2011, B1—on chief executive compensation in California's largest one hundred stock market–traded corporations. The vast majority of those receiving annual compensation of $10 million or more were in oligopolistic corporations.

lyte class to influence politics—while providing the necessary training needed to run the large corporations associated with the neo-oligarchy. The takeover of American business schools by neoclassical economics dogma, starting in the 1970s, set the stage for indoctrinating generations of management students—among them future acolytes—with the precepts of profit maximization, aggressive strategic deployment, and the widespread "kill-or-be-killed" mentality that now pervades corporate decision making.[56] A largely amoral mindset thus entrenched itself in the corporate domain—mirroring the amoral outlook of neoclassical economic precepts taught in business schools—pretending to be "scientific" to claim legitimacy. Perhaps this should not surprise, if one takes into account the trajectory of mainstream (neoclassical) economics since the 1940s, discussed in the previous chapter. Ideas grounded in neoclassical economic precepts thus came to be implanted in business school curricula, and were eventually adapted and diffused as "best practice" recipes to practitioners.[57] One of the much-lauded concepts, for example, was agency theory. Its neglect of that most important element of enterprise—employees and their welfare—in favor of shareholders' interests and profit maximization above all else, became deeply entrenched in corporate managerial practice.[58]

As business schools fulfilled their indoctrinatory mission, it is not difficult to see why they also became the ideological training centers of neoliberalism and of its political influence. All the amoral precepts of neoclassical economics (and of the "new" business education) were quite compatible with—and in many ways supportive of—neoliberal ideology. At the same time, the incipient split of reproduction from commodification in manufacturing and service production—and the no less important severance of

---

56. Cutthroat strategies and schemes, even those that were ethically dubious or downright dishonest, became standard recipes, dispensed by even the best-known management consultants; see, for example, Stalk Jr., Lachenauer, and Butman, *Are You Playing to Play or Playing to Win?* and Stalk and Lachenauer's "Hardball," 62–71.

57. Recipes based on those precepts came to dominate business school training—fierce advocates of neoclassical economics becoming the most influential professors; see, for example, Geoff Colvin, "There's No Quit in Michael Porter: He Has Influenced More Executives—and More Nations—Than Any Other Business Professor on Earth," *Fortune,* October 29, 2012, 162–66.

58. A critic of agency theory, and the import of neoclassical economic theories into business school curricula, was Sumantra Goshal—see, for example, his "Bad Management Theories Are Destroying Good Management Practices," *Academy of Management Learning and Education* 4 (2005): 75–91.

finance from production—required more technically trained management professionals. Although the contradictions posed by these splits were never explicitly addressed in business schools—given the exclusion of critical political economy from their curricula—their managerial pathologies have elicited innumerable recipes and tactical schemes over the years. Many of those "recipes" helped some management consultants build a reputation and become quite wealthy in the process—achieving the celebrity-like status of "gurus" in popular business culture.[59] And, some of those recipes even gained academic status when they were incorporated in business school curricula—usually as part of narrow, problem-solving templates. Despite their indoctrinatory biases and narrow scope, business schools nonetheless came to fulfil a necessary acolyte-training role—also becoming neoliberal ideological training nodes.[60] While fulfilling these roles, their influence on government policymaking—particularly on finance and deregulation—grew immensely, thus becoming indispensable to the neo-oligarchy and to oligopolistic power.[61]

Ideologically linked to business schools, drawing from their pools of graduates, and garnering massive contributions from the neo-oligarchy and its oligopolies, are the richly endowed neoliberal think tanks that greatly influence politics and government. Among the more prominent ones, for example, are the American Enterprise Institute, Hudson Institute, Heritage Foundation, Hoover Institution, and the Manhattan Institute for Policy Research.[62] In some cases, these think tanks have provided the deans who

59. Many of them owe their visibility and wealth to those recipes; see, for example, Erin White, "New Breed of Business Gurus Rises," *Wall Street Journal,* May 5, 2008, B1; James Hoopes, *False Prophets: The Gurus Who Created Modern Management and Why Their Ideas Are Bad for Business* (Cambridge, MA: Perseus, 2003).

60. American conservatism also benefited, as neoliberal values practically took over the neoconservative movement—eventually spreading to corporate boardrooms; see, for example, Kim Phillips-Fein, *Invisible Hands: The Making of the Conservative Movement from the New Deal to Reagan* (New York: Norton, 2009); Michael Perelman, *The Confiscation of American Prosperity* (New York: Palgrave Macmillan, 2012).

61. The prominence of the acolyte class in policymaking and government was partly responsible for the tendency to preserve the status quo during (and after) the crisis that started in 2007; see, for example, Thomas Frank, "The Economic Crisis: Lessons Unlearned," *Wall Street Journal,* August 11, 2010, A13; Barofsky, *Bailout*; Damian Paletta, "Worried Bankers Seek to Shift Risk to Uncle Sam," *Wall Street Journal,* February 14, 2008, A2.

62. The Hoover Institution's affiliation with Stanford University, in particular, has provided this neoliberal think tank with much legitimacy over the years; see "Hoover Institution," Institute for Policy Studies, IPS Right Web, http://www.rightweb.irc-online.org/profile/hoover_institution (accessed February 23, 2013). Another key player in the neoliberal agenda is the Heritage Foundation—a richly funded organization that became a major source of

run American business schools and take up strategic roles to serve the neo-oligarchy's agenda—such as the anti-entitlement offensive noted earlier.[63] Individuals affiliated with these and other neoliberal think tanks typically (and easily) gain access to the networks of the corporate-owned media oligopolies—such as the *Wall Street Journal* (a major outlet of the Rupert Murdoch–owned News Corp. global empire).[64] Among the more prominent objectives of neoliberal think tank research has been to corporatize public governance—advocating the privatization of government functions, or at least making them more corporate-like.[65] Pro-corporate propaganda and cleverly biased analyses are thus disseminated to the public by the respective think tanks—in league with the editors who run the corporate-owned media oligopolies. In this manner, a neoliberal *corporate-propaganda-media complex* developed during the past three decades, run by the neo-oligarchy's acolytes—closely linked to the think tanks. The political, ideological, and intellectual agendas of these organizations, and of the acolytes running them, coalesced as never before to support the political interests of the neo-oligarchy.

The three main vehicles of political influence—contributions, lobbying, and "revolving door" control—along with rising oligopolistic power in the media, the richly funded think tanks, and an aggressive acolyte class, created momentum for an important political milestone in the 1990s. What in the United States had long been a two-party political system became prac-

---

ideas and inspiration for the Reagan administration, and for right-wing politicians and acolytes thereafter; see Lee Edwards, *Leading the Way: The Story of Ed Feulner and the Heritage Foundation* (New York: Crown Forum, 2013). The lobbying arm of this think tank—Heritage Action for America (founded in 2010)—claimed to have 61,000 donors in 2012 and more than five thousand local activists (known as "sentinels") who monitor and rank each member of Congress on their votes—pressuring them to vote for or against targeted legislation, and channelling campaign funding to those who closely follow its directives; see Patrick O'Connor, "Think Tank Becomes a Handful for GOP," *Wall Street Journal*, July 23, 2013, A4.

63. See, for example, Glenn Hubbard, "Thought Leaders: Still on the Cliff; To Really Fix Our Deficit We Must Critically Address Overspending," *Fortune*, March 18, 2013, 34—by the dean of Columbia University's business school, a former chair of the Council of Economic Advisers during the George W. Bush administration.

64. One article, for example, involved six prominent neoliberal academics affiliated with the Hoover Institution, who targeted cuts in "entitlements" as the top priority for any solution of the federal government's debt problem; see George P. Shultz, Gary S. Becker, Michael J. Boskin, John F. Cogan, Allan H. Meltzer, and John B. Taylor, "A Better Strategy for Faster Growth," *Wall Street Journal*, March 25, 2013, A17.

65. See, for example, "Fixing Common Affairs: Some Ideas for Making Government More Businesslike," *The Economist*, February 2, 2013, 58; Edwards, *Leading the Way*.

tically a one-party system, insofar as its subservience to oligopolistic corporate power is concerned.[66] Financialism's rising importance and its intimate
connection with oligopolistic power was an important catalyst for this development—one that would make corporatocracy more feasible and important.
Notwithstanding its official rhetoric and propaganda, the Democratic Party
came to act much as the Republican Party did—so far as oligopolies and
corporate power were concerned.[67] *Both parties thus came to compete strongly
with each other to be most favored by the corporate oligopolies—and indirectly
by the neo-oligarchy—as money became more important than ever in politics.*[68]
The corporate oligopolies—and the rising neo-oligarchy that controlled or
owned them—clearly had much money to give, much more than anyone
else. This state of affairs gathered more momentum during the first decade of
the twenty-first century. By 2008, for example, a new movement seeking to
change some aspects of governance—the Tea Party—largely became a front
for the neo-oligarchy's and the oligopolies' interests—as vast amounts of
money were channelled to support (and elect) its candidates.[69] Other efforts
aimed at changing governance, which did not have the monetary support
of the neo-oligarchy and its oligopolies, fell apart quickly.[70] Unions, whose
favor the Democratic Party had cultivated for many decades, were in decline
as deregulation, globalization, and deindustrialization took their toll. The

---

66. This can be considered an important milestone in the trend toward corporatocracy in
American public governance; see Sheldon Wolin, *Democracy Incorporated: Managed Democracy
and the Specter of Inverted Totalitarianism* (Princeton: Princeton University Press, 2010).

67. Lance Selfa, *The Democrats: A Critical History* (Chicago: Haymarket, 2012); Foster and
Holleman, "Financial Power Elite"; Wolin, *Democracy Incorporated.*

68. One result—unexpected and unnoticed by many—was the elimination of reforms enacted
in the 1970s, which sought to make high-level officials more accountable; see, for example,
Carol J. Williams, "Reforms Are Rolled Back: Forty Years after Watergate, Many Changes
Prompted by the Scandal Are Gone," *Los Angeles Times,* June 17, 2012, A14.

69. See Anthony DiMaggio, *The Rise of the Tea Party: Political Discontent and Corporate
Media in the Age of Obama* (New York: Monthly Review, 2011); Nick Gillespie and Matt
Welch, *The Declaration of Independents: How Libertarian Politics Can Fix What's Wrong with
America* (New York: PublicAffairs, 2012). Libertarians, whose ideas influenced many Tea
Party advocates, also received support—despite differences with some of the neo-oligarchy's
political interests. Mainly, however, it seems that the ultimate objective was to co-opt and
align both the Tea Party and libertarian movements with the interests of the neo-oligarchy
and of oligopolistic power.

70. See, for example, Doyle McManus, "A Party No One Attended: Americans Elect Had a
Grand Vision for Breaking Washington's Partisan Gridlock; Then Reality Set In," *Los Angeles
Times,* May 17, 2012, A19.

ongoing redistribution of wealth and power from the vast majority toward the wealthiest segment of the population compounded this trend—giving many politicians the impression that the easiest way to win was to side with the interests of the oligopolies and the neo-oligarchy.[71]

As both parties tacitly coalesced, political campaigns became more like electioneering contests—turning almost any run for political office into a personality competition—through which voters decided whom to vote for much as they chose which soap or mouthwash to consume.[72] Elections became more like an electoral game, with campaign organizations' capacity for gaming gaining paramount importance. Debates between candidates began to seem more superficial, with body language and involuntary reactions—such as twitching, blinking, sweating, or a change in voice tone, for example—becoming important and in some cases even decisive in influencing voters' decisions. Superficialities aside, debates between candidates also began to be compared to sports matches, but with much less entertainment value.[73] Voters thus became less interested in politics and voting—as the treadmill of economic insecurity and debt consumed more of their attention and time. After all, if both political parties espoused much the same ideas, or in the final analysis acted much the same way, the voting process began to seem more like an irrelevant waste of time.

Absenteeism therefore became an expeditious way to save time and effort in the United States, with less than half of the eligible population bothering to vote in most elections.[74] American politicians are thus typically

---

71. A trend whose start can be traced to the early 1980s—when corporate lobbyists and conservative thinking became more influential in Washington; see Jacob S. Hacker and Paul Pierson, *Winner-Take-All Politics: How Washington Made the Rich Richer—and Turned Its Back on the Middle Class* (New York: Simon and Schuster, 2010).

72. See Robert W. McChesney and John Nichols, "The Bull Market: Political Advertising," *Monthly Review*, April 2012, 1–26; Joe McGinniss, *The Selling of the President: The Classic Account of the Packaging of a Candidate* (New York: Penguin, 1988).

73. Robert C. Bordone and Heather Scheiwe Kulp, "A Political Timeout: Presidential Debates Should Be Dialogues, Not Football Games," *Los Angeles Times*, October 25, 2012, A21.

74. Less than 40 percent of the eligible population voted in interim elections during 1974–2010—for presidential elections, less than 60 percent voted during 1976–2008 in all but two years: 1992 (61 percent), 2004 (62 percent). See International Institute for Democracy and Electoral Assistance, *Voter Turnout* (Stockholm: International IDEA, various years), http://www.idea.int/vt/ (accessed March 30, 2012). See also Thomas E. Patterson, *The Vanishing Voter: Public Involvement in an Age of Uncertainty* (New York: Knopf, 2002); McChesney and Nichols, "Bull Market."

elected by a majority of those who bother to vote, *not* by a majority of the electorate. Among those who do vote, the wealthiest quintile of the population has been heavily represented—by a ratio of 1.6 to 1 (1996–2008) compared to the poorest quintile—reflecting the importance of politics to the wealthy.[75] Obstacles to voting and to voter registration also contributed to absenteeism among the poor and working people, adding frustration to the perceived futility of elections.[76] Meanwhile, the all-important (but unannounced) neoliberal effort to align the interests of the voting public with those of the corporate oligopolies began to show results, as many voters seemed to forget their own interests altogether. Many middle-class and working people thus began to vote as if they fantasized themselves to be part of the neo-oligarchy or its acolyte class—much as consumers often identify with the manufacturer of a product and lose track of their own welfare.[77] This phenomenon played right into the hands of the neo-oligarchy, as money increasingly became *the* decisive factor in American politics.[78]

Just before the 2012 presidential election, for example, a total of $2 billion—an unprecedented amount in the history of American and world politics—was raised by the two main candidates combined, with the vast majority of the funds coming from political organizations supported by large corporations and very wealthy individuals.[79] Behind the seemingly respecta-

---

75. See Robert W. McChesney, "This Isn't What Democracy Looks Like," *Monthly Review,* November 2012, 1–28; John Kenneth Galbraith, *The Culture of Contentment* (Boston: Houghton Mifflin, 1992), 10.

76. See, for example, Michael Cooper, "New State Rules Raising Hurdles at Voting Booth," *New York Times,* October 2, 2011, http://www.nytimes.com/2011/10/03/; Frances Fox Piven and Richard A. Cloward, *Why Americans Still Don't Vote: And Why Politicians Want It That Way* (Boston: Beacon, 2000); McChesney, "This Isn't What Democracy Looks Like," 24–25.

77. See, for example, Thomas Frank, *What's the Matter with Kansas? How Conservatives Won the Heart of America* (New York: Metropolitan Books, 2004); Maria Elizabeth Grabe and Erik Page Bucy, *Image Bite Politics: News and the Visual Framing of Elections* (New York: Oxford University Press, 2010); Robert Spero, *The Duping of the American Voter: Dishonesty and Deception in Presidential Television Advertising* (New York: Lippincott and Crowell, 1980).

78. Beyond contributions, politicians' own personal ties to corporate power—as owners, board members, or consultants, for example—must be taken into account. By one estimate, sixty-eight members of the U.S. Congress took in $28 million in outside income in 2010; see Danny Yadron and Brody Mullins, "Side Jobs Bolster Some Lawmakers' Paychecks," *Wall Street Journal,* September 19, 2011, A5.

79. Nicholas Confessore and Jo Craven McGinty, "Obama, Romney, and their Parties on Track to raise $2 Billion," *New York Times,* October 25, 2012, http://www.nytimes.com/. See also Gold and Tanfani, "Silent Money Speaks"; Celarier, "Romney's Hedge Fund Kingmaker"; Hiltzik, "Like It or Not."

ble facade of American "representative democracy," corporatocracy was thus becoming more noticeable, as politics and political campaigning came to depend more than ever on corporate largesse—and the vast wealth of the neo-oligarchy. Gaming the electoral game—a prime function of political campaigns—became more a matter of securing the money and support of the neo-oligarchy and of their corporate oligopolies.[80] It also became clearer that the machinery for aligning the interests of politicians with those of the neo-oligarchy—via the corporate oligopolies—is lubricated by the vast amounts "invested" in political organizations set up to fund campaigns.[81]

Much related to this dynamic was the neo-oligarchy's—and oligopolistic corporations'—rising influence over the American judicial system. A prime example was the U.S. Supreme Court's political institutionalization of what may be called the "corporate persona" in 2010. Through that decision, the law practically became blind to corporate influence on politics, and corporations came to have the same legal rights as individual human beings—insofar as political contributions are concerned.[82] The Supreme Court thereby allowed corporate entities to provide unlimited amounts of money to political organizations—and, indirectly, to candidates.[83] The only restraint was to disallow corporate donors from "coordinating" funding and activities with individual campaign organizations—a largely meaningless restriction since "super-PACs" and similar political organizations in many ways serve as campaign organizations, often more effectively so. Their flexibility, their influence with the corporate-owned media, their visibility, and the vast sums of money they marshal in fact make them the ideal campaign organization. The only difference is that—in contrast with individual campaign organizations—they are oriented to serve ideas and agendas, and usually help elect more than a single candidate. By and large, political organizations such

---

80. A reality that has led some scholars to consider the American system of governance a "dollarocracy"; see McChesney, "This Isn't What Democracy Looks Like."

81. This can be considered part of the "money-and-media election complex," a term introduced in McChesney and Nichols, "Bull Market."

82. Although it has been argued that, through the Supreme Court's decision, corporations actually came to have more rights than people; see Jeffrey D. Clements, *Corporations Are Not People: Why They Have More Rights than You Do and What You Can Do about It* (San Francisco: Berrett-Koehler, 2012).

83. A majority of states had long allowed unlimited spending by corporations on state-level elections and campaigns; see David Savage, "Supreme Court Oks Unlimited Spending on Elections," *Los Angeles Times*, January 22, 2010, http://articles.latimes.com/. The Supreme Court's decision thus affirmed what was already the norm in many states.

as the super-PACs are the main channels used by the neo-oligarchy for their "investment" in political campaigns.[84] The anonymity they can provide allows a comfortable distance between neo-oligarchs and a candidate, in the public's eye—a "distance" that is actually imaginary, since candidates easily get to know who provides the money while the public generally does not.[85]

The levels of oligopolistic corporate money to be "invested" in future political campaigns—as a result of the Supreme Court's 2010 decision—will most likely dwarf the unprecedented amounts cited previously.[86] For almost any oligopolistic corporation, dedicating even a minute fraction of its annual profit to political contributions will most likely amount to several times the $2 billion in donations that both presidential candidates garnered in 2012.[87] Thus, for example, an energy sector oligopolist that donates, say, 3 percent of its annual profit to politics could provide as much as $6 billion or even more in contributions—all by a single corporation. No other competing interests, such as labor unions or public interest groups, will ever be able to match corporate political contributions in this new scenario created by the Supreme Court. All the more so if or when the sum of such contributions reaches, say, the quarter-trillion dollar mark for a single presidential election—a plausible scenario even if corporate contributions amount to as little as 5 percent of the average annual profit of the one hundred largest oligopolies.[88] Clearly, the future of American politics seems to be heavily stacked in favor of the neo-oligarchy and oligopolistic corporate power.

---

84. The terms *investment* or *investor* are often used by donors to political organizations and by recipients; see, for example, Seema Mehta and Matea Gold, "Top Romney Donors Are Rewarded at Leader Retreat: They Spend Three Days at Posh Utah Resort Mingling with Other Republicans," *Los Angeles Times,* June 24, 2012, A19.

85. See, for example, Patrick O'Connor, "Campaigns Drop Clues to PACs: Barred from Direct Planning with Groups, Candidates Send Signals to Keep Them on Message," *Wall Street Journal,* July 7, 2012, A4; Michael Hiltzik, "Artfully Dodging Donor Scrutiny," *Los Angeles Times,* March 4, 2012, B1. Corporate donors also usually maintain secrecy; see Noam N. Levey and Kim Geiger, "Big Business Keeps Spending to Itself: Few Major Financial, Energy and Healthcare Companies Disclose All the Cash They Lay Out, a Times Review Finds," *Los Angeles Times,* April 24, 2011, A15.

86. See, for example, Tom Hamburger and Melanie Mason, " 'Super PACs' Show Power: The Committees Outspend Candidates in the First Presidential Contest Since Donation Limits Were Ended," *Los Angeles Times,* January 1, 2012, A1; Matea Gold, Tom Hamburger, and Maloy Moore, "The 'Super PAC' Millionaires' Club," *Los Angeles Times,* February 2, 2012, A6.

87. See Doug Kendall, "Elections for Sale? If the Supreme Court Lifts Restrictions on Corporate Campaign Contributions, Watch Out," *Los Angeles Times,* September 8, 2009, A21.

88. Based on average annual profitability for the top 100 corporations in the Fortune 500 list during 2000–2011—see "Fortune 500," *Fortune,* http://www.fortune.com/.

Any notion that "representative democracy" can exist under such conditions becomes a fantasy.

In many respects, the "corporate persona," which the U.S. Supreme Court created and empowered through its 2010 decision, has become a very useful front for the neo-oligarchy. *Oligopolistic corporations can now more effectively serve as tools of—and be proxies for—the neo-oligarchy in politics, to deploy immense political influence, supported by unlimited amounts of money—that no other element in society will ever be able to match.* Also, corporate oligopolies, having been empowered to contribute unlimited amounts to political organizations, can help the neo-oligarchy maintain some appearance of detachment from politics. The public's attention can thus be more easily channelled—with the help of the corporate-owned media oligopolies—into ignoring the reality of *whose interests* politicians actually serve. The nature of corporatocratic governance can thereby also be more easily hidden from the public eye. Beyond its importance to the neo-oligarchy, this state of affairs is essential to the relations of power of advanced capitalism, if one takes into account a statement by the world's best-known economics magazine: "[T]he legal conceit that companies are natural persons is vital to capitalism."[89] Perhaps, then, the Supreme Court's decision should lift any doubts on the question of whose interests are actually being served.[90]

The proliferation of pro-corporate rulings at all levels of the judicial system—with corporate oligopolies and the neo-oligarchy as the most important beneficiaries—have become so common during the past three decades that they now tend to be accepted as natural. Limits on consumer—and employee—class action suits against corporations are among the most important rulings.[91]

---

89. "Peculiar People: How Far Should One Push the Idea That Companies Have the Same Rights as Ordinary People?" *The Economist*, March 26, 2011, 78.

90. See, for example, Brent Kendall, "High Court Comes to Defense of Business," *Wall Street Journal*, June 24, 2013, A1. Related to this point are the alleged conflicts of interest of some Supreme Court judges on the 2010 decision; see, for example, Tom Hamburger, "Justices' Impartiality Doubted in Campaign Spending Case," *Los Angeles Times*, January 21, 2011, A24; Common Cause, *The Supreme Court's Deafening Silence*, http://www.commoncause.org/ (accessed February 26, 2013).

91. See David G. Savage, "Ruling Limits Consumer Class Actions," *Los Angeles Times*, April 28, 2011, B1; David Segal, "A Rising Tide against Class-Action Suits" *New York Times*, May 5, 2012, http:// www.nytimes.com/2012/05/06/; Brent Kendall, "Supreme Court Further Limits Generic-Drug Lawsuits," *Wall Street Journal*, June 25, 2013, B8. The Supreme Court ruling on class action suits was based, in part, on a 1925 law that governs maritime transactions; see Legal Information Institute, Cornell University Law School, *9USC§2-Validity, Irrevocability, and Enforcement of Agreements to Arbitrate*, http://www.law.cornell.edu/uscode/text/9/2 (accessed March 3, 2013).

Through the limits imposed on such litigation by the U.S. Supreme Court, for example, oligopolistic corporations are now protected from any class action suits from their customers and from their own employees. Oligopolies—and all other corporations—are thus practically exempt from the reach of the civil justice system, and can act with greater impunity than ever on matters that affect their customers and employees (discrimination and wage issues included). As a result of the ruling, most any individual who purchases a good or service, or accepts employment from a corporation, automatically agrees to let any dispute go to arbitration—and gives up all rights to seek litigation against the offender. The ruling, moreover, requires customers and employees to bring up their arbitration claims on their own, individually, rather than as a group.[92] For cases involving discrimination, the ruling requires affected employees to show that their employer has an explicit, or written, policy to discriminate—thereby casting out any consideration of the role of internal managerial culture on this problem. Because arbitration panels, which make final decisions on any claim, are often staffed by individuals selected by the corporation against which the claim is made—or by an industry group with which the corporation is associated—individuals who file any complaints are less likely to win their claim. Also, arbitration judges tend to have an interest in being called upon to serve in other cases, and are unlikely to displease those who compensate them for their service.[93]

The vast spectrum of pro-corporate judicial rulings also involves the common practice of allowing corporate bankruptcy (Chapter 11) filings to become a means to reduce or eliminate employee pension obligations and health care benefits, vacate collective bargaining agreements, lower wages, and damage unions—as courts typically place creditors' interests above those of employees.[94] Any balancing of employees' interests with those creditors in corporate bankruptcy filings has thus practically vanished from bankruptcy court rulings and proceedings—a practice that benefits greatly the

---

92. David G. Savage, "Wal-Mart Bias Case Blocked by High Court," *Los Angeles Times,* April 28, 2011, B1. See also Melanie Trottman and Lauren Weber, "Bar is Raised in Worker Bias Cases," *Wall Street Journal,* June 25, 2013, B1.

93. See David Lazarus, "Giving Up Your Right to Sue," *Los Angeles Times,* May 3, 2009, B1, and his "Aiming to Restore Our Right to Sue," *Los Angeles Times,* October 18, 2011, B1; Searle Civil Justice Institute, *Consumer Arbitration before the American Arbitration Association* (Chicago: Northwestern University School of Law, March 2009). Corporations tend to win the vast majority of arbitration cases filed against them.

94. See, for example, Sharon Terlep, "GM Cuts Benefits for Salaried Staff," *Wall Street Journal,* February 16, 2012, B3.

oligopolistic megabanks that are often creditors, and members of the neo-oligarchy linked with them.[95] Part of this troubling dynamic is that pension obligations tend to be loaded on the federal government's pension guarantee program—with much reduction in benefits to employees.[96] Obligations—and risk—are thus transferred from the corporate domain to the state—adding to the fiscal strain, and to public debt and deficit problems over time. At the same time, while bankruptcy proceedings are underway, the bankrupt corporations are all too often allowed by the courts to continue compensating their executives lavishly—under the justification that such compensation is indispensable to keep their leadership and continued service. This usually occurs even when such executives contributed to the bankruptcy in the first place, by making risky or unwise decisions or by allowing the enterprise to be loaded up with substantial debt—through takeovers by hedge funds, for example (from which they may have also profited handsomely).

The pro-corporate spectrum of judicial system rulings also comprises a long history of leniency for wrongdoing involving chief executives.[97] Such rulings have benefited corporate oligopolies greatly over the years and, indirectly, favored the interests of the neo-oligarchy. By reducing the chance of prosecution—or the possibility of facing prison sentences if convicted—the judicial decisions created precedents and expectations that likely compounded executive wrongdoing over the years. After all, if hiring powerful attorneys to present cases to sympathetic judges (and juries) can produce lenient judgments, if not exoneration, the value obtained through wrongdoing may more than offset whatever costs and penalties are incurred. Perhaps the spirit of pro-corporate rulings on executive wrongdoing throughout the American judicial system is best summarized in a statement by two federal prosecutors,

---

95. See, for example, Phil Milford, Mary Schlangenstein, and David McLaughlin, "American Airlines Parent AMR Files for Bankruptcy as Horton Is Named CEO," *Bloomberg,* November 29, 2011, http://www.bloomberg.com/news/2011-11-29/; CNN Wire Staff, "American Airlines Union: Company's Letter, Threats, Further Enrage Pilots," *CNN,* September 28, 2012, http://edition.cnn.com.

96. See, for example, Sharon Terlep, "GM Acts to Pare Pension Liability," *Wall Street Journal,* June 2, 2012, B3; Jerry White, "Detroit Bankruptcy Ruling Triggers Calls for Pension Cuts across the US," *World Socialist Web Site,* December 6, 2013, https://www.wsws.org/en/articles/.

97. See, for example, Henry N. Pontell and Gilbert Geis, *International Handbook of White-Collar and Corporate Crime* (New York: Springer, 2007); Stephen M. Rosoff, Henry N. Pontell, and Robert Tillman, *Profit Without Honor: White-Collar Crime and the Looting of America* (New York: Prentice-Hall, 1988); Glenn Greenwald, *With Liberty and Justice for Some: How the Law Is Used to Destroy Equality and Protect the Powerful* (New York: Picador, 2011).

who refer to a "two-tiered system of justice, one for well-connected CEOs who can break the rules, secretly inflate their compensation and lie about it with virtual impunity, while ordinary citizens . . . will face far more severe penal consequences."[98]

The Supreme Court in 2010 helped greatly the tendency toward leniency for corporate executive wrongdoing, by overturning the concept of "honest services" embedded in many judicial rulings since the 1940s—in particular, the federal Honest Services Law of 1988.[99] This concept—and the 1988 law—were based on a series of decisions that applied fraud statutes to cover corporate and political corruption—affecting primarily corporate executives or politicians who placed their interest above those of shareholders or taxpayers. The Supreme Court ruling's impact will likely be substantial over time, since it discourages prosecutors from pursuing charges against corporate chief executives. An immediate effect was to make it very difficult for federal prosecutors to pursue executives of the oligopolistic Wall Street megabanks involved in the financial crisis—which may account for the lack of prosecutions related to that crisis, as noted earlier in this book.[100] Another immediate effect of the Supreme Court's ruling was to favor three chief executives of oligopolistic corporations in the energy, media, and health care sectors—who had previously been convicted for fraud.[101] The ruling also set the stage for future "re-sentencing agreements" to occur between the U.S. Department of Justice and incarcerated corporate executives—which

---

98. Federal prosecutors Paul Stern and Harvinder Anand, quoted in Stuart Pfeifer and Nathan Olivares-Giles, "Karatz May Avoid Trip to Prison," *Los Angeles Times,* October 16, 2010, B1.

99. See Legal Information Institute, Cornell University Law School, *18 USC§1346—Definition of "Scheme or Artifice to Defraud,"* http://www.law.cornell.edu/uscode/text/18/1346 (accessed March 5, 2013).

100. See, for example, Shan Li, "Banks May Be Too Big to Prosecute, US Says," *Los Angeles Times,* March 8, 2013, B2; Thomas Catan and Kara Scannell, "Convictions from Crisis Hard: Settlement with Goldman Shows Difficulty in Holding Bankers Accountable," *Wall Street Journal,* July 17, 2010, B2; Jean Eaglesham, "Missing: Stats on Crisis Convictions," *Wall Street Journal,* May 14, 2012; Michael Hiltzik, "Execs Off the Hook at S&P," *Los Angeles Times,* February 10, 2013, B1.

101. "Not Guilty? The Supreme Court Favours Three Jailed Bosses in a Crop of Pro-Business Rulings," *The Economist,* July 3, 2010, 62. See also Jess Bravin, "Court Backs Skilling Appeal: Justices Narrow Reach of Fraud Statute Used in Several High-Profile Convictions," *Wall Street Journal,* June 25, 2010, A1; Michael Rothfeld, "Enron Ruling Dims Prosecution Picture," *Wall Street Journal,* June 25, 2010, A6; Michael Hiltzik, "Skilling Doesn't Deserve a Break," *Los Angeles Times,* May 19, 2013, B1.

can lead to release or substantially reduced terms—a favor that practically no other kinds of prisoners can hope to gain.[102]

Beyond these examples of judicial favor toward corporate power is the character and reach of the American prison system—and its importance for preserving the status quo. The United States today has the largest number of prisoners of any nation in the world—in both absolute and per capita terms.[103] From the start of the neoliberal era, incarceration rates per 100,000 population grew from 221 (1980) to 762 (2008).[104] By 2008, this figure was six times higher than those of China or Britain. More than 90 percent of American prisoners are from the ranks of the poor or the working class—and the vast majority are from disadvantaged minorities—reflecting the longstanding association of incarceration with social class background and race.[105] Also, a significant proportion of prisoners are, or become, mentally ill during their terms—prompting an official to note that "jails have become de facto mental institutions."[106] A survey of twenty-three states, for example, found that one-half or more of all prisoners in two states—and

102. See, for example, Shan Li, "Enron Figure May Be Resentenced," *Los Angeles Times*, April 5, 2013, B2; *The Economist*, "Not Guilty?"

103. With less than 5 percent of the world's population, the United States has about 25 percent of all prisoners in the world; see "A Nation of Jailbirds: Far Too Many Americans Are Behind Bars," *The Economist*, April 4, 2009, 40; Hannah Holleman, Robert W. McChesney, John Bellamy Foster, and R. Jamil Jonna, "The Penal State in an Age of Crisis," *Monthly Review*, June 2009, 1–17.

104. Stephen F. Eisenman, "The Resistible Rise and Predictable Fall of the US Supermax," *Monthly Review*, November 2009, 31–45; Bureau of Justice Statistics, U.S. Department of Justice, http://bjs.ojp.usdoj.gov/ (accessed March 6, 2010); International Centre for Prison Studies, *World Prison Population List*, 8th edition (London: ICPS, 2009). U.S. per capita incarceration data excluded individuals held in juvenile detention centers, prisons in native American territories, military prisons, U.S. territorial prisons, U.S. Immigration and Customs Enforcement detention centers, and those on probation or parole.

105. See Loïc J. D. Wacquant, *Prisons of Poverty* (Minneapolis: University of Minnesota Press, 2009), and his *Punishing the Poor: The Neoliberal Government of Social Insecurity* (Durham: Duke University Press, 2009); Becky Pettit and Bruce Western, "Mass Imprisonment and the Life Course: Race and Class in US Incarceration," *American Sociological Review* 69 (2004): 151–69; "The New Debtors' Prisons: If You Are Poor, Don't Get Caught Speeding," *The Economist*, November 16, 2013, 32. The U.S. War on Drugs and the lack of drug rehabilitation programs has also affected the poor greatly; see Jimmy Carter, "Call Off the Global Drug War," *New York Times*, June 16, 2011, http://www.nytimes.com/.

106. Esteban Gonzalez, president of the American Jail Association (an organization of prison employees), quoted in Gary Fields and Erica E. Phillips, "The New Asylums: Jails Swell with Mentally Ill," *Wall Street Journal*, September 26, 2013, A1.

one-third or more in three other states—were so classified, while in six states the proportion was between one-fifth and one-third of the total.[107] Because prisoners are typically cast out of the political system, a segment of the population—which would likely reduce the power of the neo-oligarchy's favored politicians in elections—becomes *politically invisible*. Also, the world's highest incarceration rate is compounded by very high recidivism.[108] The United States' high recidivist rate can be attributed to a lack of effective rehabilitation programs, and the very limited resources devoted to reinserting ex-prisoners in society. Although it is difficult to establish a connection, it seems that the most important enemies of reform in this area are those who receive the largest political contributions from the oligopolies and the neo-oligarchy. Those politicians would likely have a more difficult time in elections if recidivism declined and the prison population became politically visible. In these respects, at least, the trajectory of the prison system—and the judicial apparatus that sustains it—seems oriented to support the power of the neo-oligarchy, although not in very direct or obvious ways.[109]

Related to this dimension is the privatization of prisons, as corporate power increasingly takes over incarceration. It has been estimated that more than three-quarters of all states in the United States now use prison corporations in one form or another—even though private prisons seem to offer little in the way of savings to the public treasury.[110] These corporations' shares are traded in stock markets, offering another opportunity for speculation in the vast repertory of financialism. The prison corporations are potential future oligopolists in this sector, and their takeover of a previously unconquered area of public governance is another symptom of the

---

107. In almost half of the states, therefore, the percentage of prisoners classified as mentally ill was one-fifth or more. See Fields and Phillips, "New Asylums"—all U.S. states were contacted (twenty-three responded). Generally, the definition of mental illness included prisoners who required medication for serious problems—such as major depression, bipolar disorder, or schizophrenia—an overnight stay at a mental hospital, or those who showed serious impairment.

108. See, for example, Loïc Wacquant and Glenn C. Loury, *Race, Incarceration, and American Values* (Cambridge: MIT Press, 2008); Pettit and Western, "Mass Imprisonment and the Life Course."

109. The historical association of prisons with the power of elites—as a sociopolitical control mechanism—can be related to this point. However, the establishment of prison systems initially had a reformist perspective, oriented toward the eventual reinsertion of individuals in society; see, for example, Michel Foucault, *Discipline and Punish: The Birth of the Prison* (New York: Random House, 1977); Francis C. Gray, *Prison Discipline in America* (Boston: Little and Brown, 1847).

110. Richard A. Oppel Jr., "Private Prisons Found to Offer Little in Savings," *New York Times*, May 18, 2011, http://www.nytimes.com/; Holleman, McChesney, Foster, and Jonna, "Penal State."

advancing reach of corporatocracy. A major benefit they enjoy is access to very low-cost labor, as prisoners are typically engaged in production routines that generate revenues.[111] Prison factories have a very long history, but their connection with corporate power has never been as intimate as it is in the United States today—with corporate power becoming more deeply entwined with the judicial and penal systems.[112] Helping this dynamic are the very long prison sentences customarily imposed—including life imprisonment without parole on nonviolent offenders—a product of mandatory sentencing laws in the American criminal justice system.[113] Such laws seem, in many ways, to have been systemically tailored to benefit the corporatization of prisons. Another benefit the prison corporations enjoy is the constant stream of taxpayer-funded support to sustain operations and profitability—provided by the flow of "clients" secured through judicial sentencing practices, high recidivism, and a proliferation of new laws that penalize acts that were previously outside the scope of criminal sanctions.[114]

Part of the expanding scope of criminal prosecution is what some legal experts refer to as the "school-to-prison pipeline," which is increasingly incar-

---

111. See Donna Selman, *Punishment for Sale: Private Prisons, Big Business, and the Incarceration Binge* (Lanham, MD: Rowman and Littlefield, 2009); Vicky Pelaez, *The Prison Industry in the United States: Big Business or a New Form of Slavery?* Centre for Research on Globalisation, March 2008, http://www.globalresearch.ca/; Sherwood Ross, *The Incarceration Business: America's Private Prisons,* Centre for Research on Globalisation, November 2011, http://www.globalresearch.ca/.

112. See, for example, Dario Melossi and Massimo Pavarini, *The Prison and the Factory: Origins of the Penitentiary System* (Totowa, NJ: Barnes and Noble, 1981). The emergence of "private-probation" companies also seems to be part of the corporatization of the penal system. One such company—Judicial Correction Services—for example, manages ex-prisoners on probation for more than two hundred courts throughout the southeast. Individuals on probation are charged a $45 monthly service fee and, if they fall behind on payments, incur higher fees and are threatened with prison if they do not pay; see "The New Debtors' Prisons: If You Are Poor, Don't Get Caught Driving," *The Economist*, November 16, 2013, 32.

113. "American Oubliette: Life without Parole is an Outrageous Sentence for Non-Violent Criminals," *The Economist,* November 16, 2013, 16–17. An estimated 83 percent of sentences involving life imprisonment without parole for nonviolent offenders were imposed through the mandatory sentencing requirement; see *The Economist,* "New Debtors' Prisons," and "Throwing Away the Key: A Shocking Number of Non-Violent Americans Will Die in Prison," November 16, 2013, 31–32.

114. See Gary Fields and John R. Emshwiller, "As Criminal Laws Proliferate, More Ensnared," *Wall Street Journal,* July 23, 2011, A1; *The Economist,* "New Debtors' Prisons." The criminalization of many activities—not so previously classified and not subject to civil action—has been a boon for prison corporations, with poverty and race becoming major factors; see, for example, Michael A. Hallett, *Private Prisons in America: A Critical Race Perspective* (Urbana: University of Illinois Press, 2006); Selman, *Punishment for Sale*; Wacquant, *Prisons of Poverty*.

cerating minors for problems that never incurred prison time in the past.[115] Teenagers have thus become a new market target for prison corporations. Corporate contributions to local and state judges' election campaigns—and bribes—seem to be opening up this profitable market. In one case, for example, two judges were found to have received $2.6 million in kickbacks from a prison corporation that operates a juvenile prison.[116] One of the judges had a practice of issuing verdicts within a one-and-a-half to three-minute time span to speed up the flow of convicts—and tried a large number of cases in which the accused juveniles had no attorney.[117] For juveniles, having a prison record is quite unfortunate, especially in regard to employment, since their record will be with them during the rest of their lives—more so than at any prior time, given the digitization of such records and their instantaneous availability. And, the lack of programs to reinsert juvenile ex-convicts in society practically ensures that they will land in prison again as adults, if not earlier.

Compounding the rising incarceration rate in this and other prisoner categories is the fact that many federal and state statutes implemented during the past two decades do not require prosecutors to prove criminal intent—a fundamental principle of American law in the past—thus making prosecution and incarceration much easier.[118] Also, many problems that were previously only considered in civil lawsuits ended up being sanctioned as criminal. The scope of civil legal action was thus vacated in favor of criminal ones, adding to incarceration—and the prison corporations' "clientele." Beyond these aspects is the expanded use of plea bargain agreements, in which the accused plead guilty to charges in order to avoid court trials—which can be quite expensive, lengthy, and involve much uncertainty regarding outcomes. At the same time, such agreements make it easier and faster to send the accused to prison. Guilty pleas extracted through plea bargaining, for example, amounted to 97 percent of all federal cases that reached conclusion in 2011—up from 84 percent in 1990—indicating how common this practice has become.[119] During that two-decade span, the

---

115. Associated Press, "A 'School-to-Prison Pipeline' is Alleged," *Los Angeles Times,* August 12, 2012, A11; Office of Public Affairs, U.S. Department of Justice, "Justice Department Releases Investigative Findings Showing Constitutional Rights of Children in Mississippi Being Violated," August 10, 2012, http://www.justice.gov/opa/.

116. Thomas Frank, "Lock 'Em Up," *Wall Street Journal,* April 1, 2009, A21.

117. Ibid.

118. Fields and Emshwiller, "Criminal Laws," A10.

119. Gary Fields and John R. Emshwiller, "Federal Guilty Pleas Soar as Bargains Trump Trials," *Wall Street Journal,* September 24, 2012, A1. Plea bargaining often relies on criminals who have something to gain by testifying against the accused; see, for example, Harvey

number of defendants involved in plea bargaining almost doubled, while federal cases undergoing court trials dropped by almost two-thirds. As with so many other aspects of the judicial system, plea bargaining affects working people and the poor more than any other segment of society. Some researchers have observed that many accused who plead guilty in bargaining agreements are very likely innocent of the charges brought against them, but decide to declare guilt in order to avoid the uncertainty, time, and cost of submitting to court trials.[120] Through these examples it is possible to see a judicial system in dysfunction—one that increasingly caters to interests that are not those of the public or of society at large.

These cases and examples are symptomatic of an incipient *alignment of the interests of the judicial system with those of neo-oligarchic power*, as the scope of criminal law is expanded while oligopolistic corporations—and corporate power in general—receive privileged treatment. At the same time, judicial decisions and incarceration tacitly end up targeting the social classes who would most likely oppose the interests of the neo-oligarchy—if they could exercise their voting power or pursue their collective interest. The corporatization of prisons has also created what may very likely become future oligopolies in the incarceration sector—much as has already occurred with most every sector of the economy. The time may not be far off when those oligopolies-in-the-making will expand globally, to help corporatize prison systems in many nations, as has already occurred with water supply or electricity provision.[121] Such corporatization will most likely require, if the experience of the United States is any indication, increases in the flow of "clients"—supported by the co-optation of judicial systems.

Silverglate, "Using Killers to Win a Killer's Conviction: In the Whitey Bulger Case, Testimony Came from Men Who 'Sang' to Save their Own Lives—That's an Odd Kind of Justice," *Wall Street Journal*, August 26, 2013, A19.

120. See, for example, John Emshwiller and Gary Fields, "Academic Study Shows Innocent Plead Guilty at High Rate," *Wall Street Journal*, September 24, 2012, A20; Lucian E. Dervan and Vanessa Edkins, "The Innocent Defendant's Dilemma: An Innovative Empirical Study of Plea Bargaining's Innocence Problem," *Journal of Criminal Law and Criminology* 103 (2012): 1–47; Harvey Silverglate, *Three Felonies a Day: How the Feds Target the Innocent* (New York: Encounter, 2011).

121. The corporatization of water supply, for example, drove up rates substantially in many nations—as much as 100 percent in some cases; see the documentary by Philippe Diaz, "La Fin de la Pauvretè?" (2009), http://www.lafindelapauvrete.com/. In the case of prisons, their corporatization would likely lead to a rise of incarcerations, with the public paying the cost—which can be considered analogous to rate increases for water supply—although incarceration costs per inmate would likely rise as well.

The incipient alignment of the interests of the judicial system with those of the neo-oligarchy thus seems destined to follow the alignment of the interests of politicians with those of neo-oligarchic—and oligopolistic—power. These multifaceted alignments support the ongoing redistribution of wealth and power from the vast majority of the population toward the neo-oligarchy and its acolytes—a major feature of corporatocratic governance. The fact that these alignments could so blatantly occur in a society that claims to be democratic only goes to show how deeply the power of the neo-oligarchy—and its oligopolies—has managed to impose itself on our governance. The fact that these alignments are underlain by a fundamental negation of the interests of the public seems to have escaped our awareness as few other phenomena in modern times managed to do.

A fuller understanding of the social injustices and pathologies addressed in this chapter must take into account the fundamental distinction between the interest of the public—in its political, judicial, and general governance dimensions—and that of the neo-oligarchy. This distinction is parallel to, and can draw upon, the differentiation between public wealth and private riches introduced by James Maitland in the early nineteenth century, which eventually became known as the Lauderdale Paradox.[122] In his classic contribution, Maitland posited that there is an inverse relationship between public wealth and private riches, such that an increase in the latter often results in a reduction of the former. At a conceptual level this relationship has been examined innumerable times—as it provided an idea that has been at the core of debates on jurisprudence, politics, and governance for more than two centuries. Maitland used the term *wealth* to refer to resources or goods that are essential for human well-being—those that rightfully belong to the public or to all of society. The term *riches* he used to denote goods or resources that come under private control and therefore benefit solely or mostly their owner. This differentiation between public and private benefit has been a major element of policymaking in capitalist societies, and has also been embedded—explicitly or implicitly—in many national charters and constitutions.

Maitland posited these ideas at a time—early nineteenth century—when industrial capitalism was in its infancy—mercantile capitalism having

---

122. James Maitland, *An Inquiry into the Nature and Origin of Public Wealth, and Into the Means and Causes of its Increase, by the Earl of Lauderdale* (Edinburgh: Constable, 1804). His conceptualization expanded upon, and in some respects was critical of, Adam Smith's observations on private riches in *An Inquiry into the Nature and Causes of the Wealth of Nations*, Vols. 1 and 2 (London: Strahan and Cadell, 1776).

then reached maturity after two centuries, powered by global empires built on commodity extraction.[123] In his time, a new elite was emerging—the industrial bourgeoisie—which would be quite influential in manufacturing and finance, and later also in politics.[124] That elite was largely emerging out of the mercantile bourgeoisie that had accumulated great riches and thus had the means to finance the industrial workshops of that time. Maitland's work therefore addressed a problem that was becoming very obvious—the great inequalities that emerged as the poor migrated from the countryside, to work in the factories that were becoming the source of great riches for the elites. It was impossible not to see that the riches of the new industrial bourgeoisie were being accumulated at the expense of great misery for working people—who toiled endless hours in the factories of that time, under deplorable conditions while earning subsistence wages.[125] Child labor in factories was also quite common, and became a source of early mortality and abuse. Observing this panorama of great inequality and injustice, Maitland came to formulate the contradiction between private riches and public wealth that is at the core of his Lauderdale Paradox. After his time, capitalism would undergo a major qualitative transformation—a wave of consolidation that generated the first industrial oligopolies and monopolies—during the second half of the nineteenth century.[126] Other transformations of capitalism came about in the twentieth century, as oligopolies expanded, the nature of production changed, and services gained more importance. In our time, the emergence of the neo-oligarchy—and of corporatocracy—can be associated with major changes in advanced capitalism, marked by the overwhelming importance of finance and of intangibles. These are changes that—as

---

123. See, for example, Eric Hobsbawm, *Industry and Empire: An Economic History of Britain* (London: Weidenfeld and Nicolson, 1968), and his *Industry and Empire: From 1750 to the Present Day* (London: Penguin, 1999); Michel Beaud, *A History of Capitalism, 1500–2000*, trans. T. Dickman and A. Lefebvre (New York: Monthly Review Press, 2001).

124. The new bourgeois elite came to dominate political power in both England and France after 1830—an observation attributed to Marx; see Paul A. Baran and Paul M. Sweezy, "Some Theoretical Implications," *Monthly Review*, July-August 2012, 25; Karl Marx, *Capital: A Critique of Political Economy*, vol. 1: *A Critical Analysis of Capitalist Production*, ed. F. Engels (New York: International Publishers, 1974; orig. Hamburg: Verlag von Otto Meissner, 1867), "Preface to the First German edition."

125. See, for example, Eric Hobsbawm, *Labouring Men: Studies in the History of Labour* (London: Weidenfeld and Nicolson, 1964).

126. See Eric Hobsbawm, *The Age of Empire, 1875–1914* (London: Weidenfeld and Nicolson, 1987).

in Maitland's time—point to a fundamental contradiction between public wealth and private riches.

Public wealth, as defined by Maitland, included all value obtained through *usage* by society at large—the public—of any resources or goods (tangible or intangible) needed to sustain human well-being. So long as their usage remains accessible to all, those goods or resources are considered to provide *use value*.[127] Such value is obtained simply because the resource or good is available to all, and is not subjected to market exchange. In this sense, such resources or goods do not have a market value, yet they are essential for supporting human well-being and that of society at large. Whenever exchange—or market—value is attached to those goods or resources, however, Maitland concluded that private gain (or riches) can only be obtained by making them less available to society at large. Those who come to control the provision (or supply) of those resources or goods thus ration them through the market price mechanism—to extract their private gain. Making scarce those goods or resources needed by the public is therefore the key to private riches, in Maitland's view—as rationing through the price mechanism ensures that the public will have less access to them. Even if the increase in private riches translates into a rise in national economic product, public wealth will nonetheless be reduced.

Following Maitland's conceptualization, it is possible to argue that an increase in neo-oligarchic riches and power translates into a diminishment of social justice and fair public governance for society at large. This inverse relationship is at the core of the social dysfunctions and pathologies associated with the emergence of the neo-oligarchy, and of its power over governance and society. Maitland's inverse relationship is thus applicable to new understandings and definitions of public wealth. *Public wealth, broadly understood, can therefore encompass fairness in governance—and social justice for society at large.* This understanding of public wealth is at odds with the takeover of public governance by the neo-oligarchy and its acolytes that is at the core of corporatocracy. This interpretation of public wealth is also quite useful for pointing out that the alignment of the interests of the judicial system, and of politicians, with neo-oligarchic—and oligopolistic—power is contrary to the public interest.

---

127. Use value is analogous to the notion of *intrinsic value* posited by John Locke—one of the most influential philosophers of the Enlightenment—in his *Two Treatises of Government* (London: Awnsham Churchill, 1689).

Maitland's differentiation, and his understanding of public wealth—and the public interest—later provided the basis for many debates on use value. This definition of value is therefore the key to public wealth, and is intrinsically different from market (or exchange) value.[128] This point would later be used by other nineteenth-century economists and social theorists, such as Karl Marx, to try to understand the nature and contradictions of capitalism.[129] Use value was, however, cast out of consideration completely by neoclassical economics in the twentieth century.[130] In so doing, neoclassical economics considered value obtained through exchange—or markets—to be the *only* form of value. This unjustified exclusion would become very convenient for neoliberalism, and eventually for the interests of the neo-oligarchy, as it made it easy to dispense with any consideration of public wealth—and the public interest. And, similarly, with any notion of goods and resources that are not obtained through markets. Whatever happened to be obtained through market exchange thus became "legitimate" in an ideological and political sense—a notion that has validated the neo-oligarchy's accumulation of riches and power—even when it is detrimental to, or obtained at the expense of, the public interest. And whatever resource or good was not already submitted to market exchange—but had potential for private gain—would thus become a target for placement under market exchange. Incarceration, and the prison corporations' rising profile in Wall Street, is one such example.

---

128. David Ricardo, possibly the best known of nineteenth-century classical political economists, supported Maitland's views on the inverse relationship between private riches and use value—see his *On the Principles of Political Economy and Taxation* (London: Murray, 1817). See also Piero Sraffa, ed., *The Works and Correspondence of David Ricardo* (Cambridge: Cambridge University Press, 1951).

129. See Karl Marx, *The Poverty of Philosophy* (New York: International Publishers, 1973). Marx's support of Maitland's conceptualization was explicit in this work—and became a noteworthy response to philosopher Pierre-Joseph Proudhon's *System of Economical Contradictions: Or, the Philosophy of Poverty* (Boston: Tucker, 1888; orig. publ. 1847).

130. Largely based on Say's nineteenth-century objection to Maitland's conceptualization, and the treatment of use value as a separate category of value—apart from market value. See Jean-Baptiste Say, *Letters to Mr Malthus, on Several Subjects of Political Economy*, ed. Thomas R. Malthus and John Richter (London: Sherwood, Neely, and Jones, 1821). Say's objection would later be supported by another influential nineteenth-century classical economist, John Stuart Mill, in his *Principles of Political Economy: With Some of Their Applications to Social Philosophy*, Vols. 1 and 2 (London: Parker, 1878).

For neoclassical economics—the intellectual wellhead of neoliberal-ism—market value thus became the only source of value for any goods or resources. Those that had no such value—or could not be submitted to market exchange—became practically invisible in economic terms.[131] This blindness meant that almost any form of public wealth—or any goods or resources associated with it—would be largely ignored by neoclassical eco-nomic theory and policymaking. Generations of economics students have thus been kept ignorant about use value and its importance for the public interest—after neoclassical dogma monopolized economics teaching.[132] Such neglect was made necessary, in part, by the takeover of neoclassical theory by general equilibrium modeling during the second half of the twentieth century. Those models fundamentally had to have market prices—the only representation of value accepted—to be able to apply the optimality precepts upon which they were founded (and without which they could not work). This neglect of a most important aspect of society and economic life—public wealth—is now so dominant that it has come to be accepted as normal—a dysfunction that plays right into the hands and power of the neo-oligarchy.

The entwinement *of* the political and judicial systems, finance, neo-liberal ideology, and the intellectual domain of neoclassical economics *with* neo-oligarchic power has been establishing an apparatus of societal control that is amorphous, fragmented, and difficult to grasp in its totality. Its multifaceted nature and many contradictions make it difficult to synthe-size—especially because those facets and contradictions often provide an appearance of randomness, even chaos, which perplexes observers. Yet, such features are precisely what make neo-oligarchic power strong—to the extent that they allow it to escape public attention, even from the most learned quarters of society. All prior elites and forms of oligarchic power seem undeveloped, or even infantile when the many subtle facets, features, and levers of influence linked to the neo-oligarchy are taken into account.

---

131. This bias is now at the core of advanced capitalism—and of financialism—as selling and money gained overwhelmingly importance; see, for example, Michael Sandel, *What Money Can't Buy: The Moral Limits of Markets* (New York: Farrar, Straus, and Giroux, 2012); "Money and the Markets: Insatiable Longing," *The Economist,* July 21, 2012, 70.

132. A situation that has been denounced by some economists, at some risk to their careers; see, for example, Michael Perelman, *Railroading Economics: The Creation of the Free Market Mythology* (New York: Monthly Review Press, 2006); David Laibman, *Political Economy after Economics: Scientific Method and Radical Imagination* (New York: Routledge, 2012); Moshe Adler, *Economics for the Rest of Us: Debunking the Science that Makes Life Dismal* (New York: New Press, 2009).

The combined influence of the neo-oligarchy and oligopolistic power over governance, politics, the judicial system, media, finance, production, and other domains practically ensure that social justice and fairness end up diminished. As more facets of society come under the control of the neo-oligarchy and the oligopolies, it can be expected that public well-being and fair governance will be further shortchanged. *Corporatocracy provides the platform to achieve this unfortunate result, binding together the elements that are at the core of the crisis of the state.* Without it, the emergence of the neo-oligarchy as the dominant group in society, the hegemony of oligopolistic power, the spread of financialism—and the crucial alignments of the interests of the political and judicial systems with those of the neo-oligarchy and the oligopolies—could not be part of our contemporary reality.

Governance Derailed

At the core of the discussions in this book is the idea that the corpora-tocratic state, and the oligopolistic corporate apparatus that supports it, negate fair governance. Those discussions, moreover, sustain the view that a society ruled by corporate oligopolies and their privileged elites can be considered neither just nor democratic. These two considerations are at the core of the crisis of the state that we are witnessing, in the United States and in other advanced capitalist societies.

The influence of oligopolistic corporate power is everywhere around us. From cradle to grave, oligopolistic corporations have immense influence not only over our governance, but also over how we live and work, what we eat, how we sustain our health, the way we are educated, how our consciousness is shaped, where we live, how we move around, and how we deal with each other and with nature. Such influence is fragmented and often difficult to grasp, but it is authoritarian in character and spirit—hiding behind a veneer of propaganda, publicity spins, and clever talk about choices and freedoms that do not actually exist or can never materialize. At the same time, governance seems more subservient than ever to oligopolistic power, providing bailouts, guarantees, tax breaks, loopholes, subsidies, and diverse forms of corporate welfare—while some of the most basic needs of the population are neglected. *This subservience of public governance to oligopolistic corporate power is a central feature of the crisis of the state.*

The contemporary crisis of the state involves a derailment of pub-lic governance that has virtually no precedent in modern history. Three *alignments of interests* discussed in this book have contributed much to this crisis, and to the emergence of corporatocratic governance. They helped create new realities, which are prejudicial to social justice and subvert just governance in ways that are multifaceted and systemic. These alignments can now be found in virtually all advanced capitalist nations—in various forms and intensities—and they seem poised to become more pervasive as the twenty-first century advances. The realities they create have turned into major sources of social pathology and dysfunction that threaten our well-being and affect almost every aspect of life. The lack of significant public awareness about the existence of these alignments, their nature and effects, shows the success of corporate oligopolies and their privileged elite in establishing their power over society.

The alignment of the interests of politicians—and government officials—with the interests of oligopolistic corporate power negates just governance. This alignment promotes a loss of public trust in government that is part of the crisis of the state. Its effects violate a major function of government in advanced capitalist societies—to provide for the disadvantaged, such that a level of societal well-being commensurate with fairness and social justice can be maintained. This alignment has made it possible for oligopolistic corporate power to spread its influence over almost every sector of society, creating an apparatus of control that fences in activities, sets up closed loops of influence, and co-opts politicians by means that are now institutionalized. This alignment cuts across mainstream political party loyalties and affiliations, as the political system essentially becomes an appendage of oligopolistic power and its privileged elite. In this sense, the alignment of the interests of politicians with those of oligopolistic corporate power becomes a systemic problem of corporatocracy, created by the need to make public governance—if not society itself—"safe" for oligopolistic power. The banishment of this alignment—fundamental for fair governance—would thus likely create an existential crisis for oligopolistic power.

Yet, it seems that just governance would require government to be fundamentally disengaged from oligopolistic corporate power. Such a trajectory would also require breaking up oligopolies and creating new rules that prevent their formation—along with new modes of conduct for politicians and government officials. These changes would, needless to say, take up a revolutionary character within the existing parameters of advanced capitalism and its governance. They would most likely put an end to corporatocracy—a necessary prerequisite for public governance to serve society. Precisely for these reasons, this trajectory—and the existential threat it poses to oligopolistic corporate power and its privileged elite—is likely to be vehemently opposed, if not ruthlessly fought against, with every means possible. History has shown, repeatedly, how viciously the powerful can fight off attempts to reduce their privileges and pursue justice. At the same time, history has shown that a return to the past is not only unrealistic, insofar as the evolution of human society is concerned, but would most certainly also be prejudicial to our well-being. New forms of social, economic, and political organization that go beyond the framework of capitalism must therefore be found if any of these remedial possibilities are to have staying power. Advocating a return to pre-oligopolistic and pre-corporatocratic times therefore seems as unreal and ill-advised as turning the hands of a clock back to try to reexperience yesterday's events.

The alignment of the interests of the public with the interests of oligopolistic corporate power through financialism is a means for the oligopolies—and their associated elites—to impose their control over governance and society. This alignment has been a major, tacit objective of the neoliberal agenda since the early 1980s. Financial deregulation provided the initial impetus for what became a long process of redistribution of wealth and political power, to benefit oligopolies and the wealthiest segment of society. Financialism became the means to implement this alignment, by turning the financial sector's dominance—and its intimate association with oligopolistic corporate power—into a cultural phenomenon that has reached into almost every aspect of our existence. Thus, any human activity—or any aspect of life or nature—with a probabilistic dimension became a target for speculation in the casino society of financialism. In part, the continuation of this alignment depends on the public's confusion over its own interests and welfare. This is a confusion that has been nurtured by corporate propaganda, the fallacy that anyone can gain great wealth through betting in the financialist economy, and easy access to greater indebtedness.

The credit system and corporatocratic policies aimed at sustaining financialism by increasing monetary liquidity at any cost are also important aspects of this alignment. The accumulation of vast amounts of debt became a reality, to support corporate takeovers, sustain consumption, and speculate. Oligopolistic finance became more dependent than ever on government guarantees, subsidies, tax loopholes, diverse forms of corporate welfare, and the bailouts provided when crises occur. For the state, all the guarantees and obligations eventually translate into a vast accumulation of debt, credit rating downgrades, and cuts in services and benefits that severely affect the vast majority of the population—while the wealthiest segment of society increases its riches and power. In this way, the expansion of debt derails a crucial function of the state in advanced capitalism—its obligation to provide for the social well-being of the population, such that fairness and social justice are not impaired. This alignment therefore contributes to the crisis of the state in two dimensions—its fiscal functioning, and its existential mission as the guarantor of societal well-being.

Just governance that serves the public interest and ends this alignment would also require an end to financialism, and to financial oligopolies' corporatocratic influence over the economy, public governance, and society. Speculation and the culture of betting on most any aspect of life or nature would have to give way to productive work in the real economy. Financial oligopolies would need to be broken up as well, possibly reconfiguring financial corporations along distinct functional and geographical dimensions. Debt accumulation and government guarantees for corporate finance would have to be limited as well, to allow the state to sustain its fiscal responsibilities to society. In this regard, *the state's function as ultimate guarantor of societal well-being would take priority over its mission as lender of last resort and bailer of oligopolies.* As with the previous alignment, this reordering of priorities would undoubtedly elicit fierce opposition from those whose interests are grounded in financialism and on corporatocratic hegemony. Putting an end to financialism would thus likely take on a revolutionary character, given the existing relations of power in advanced capitalist societies. These remedial possibilities notwithstanding, it is important to think about an evolution of human society that can transcend financialism—along with capitalism itself. Returning to a pre-financialist past is not an option, any more than returning to precapitalist times would be. New relations of power and economic modes have to be envisioned to create a society that can advance human well-being, without delving into utopias.

The alignment of the interests of the judicial system with the interests of oligopolistic corporate power damages the integrity of the state, precluding fairness. This alignment also contributes to the lack of confidence in governance associated with corporatocracy and the crisis of the state. Fundamentally, it violates the imperative for social justice, as the interests of oligopolistic corporate power and its privileged elite are favored over those of the vast majority of the population. This alignment thus results in a negation of social justice that takes many forms and guises, such as the systematic social class orientation of incarceration, very high recidivism, the lack of rehabilitation, favoritism in prosecution and sentencing of corporate executives, and the institutionalization of corporate "personhood" in the legal system. Or the denial of labor rights in corporate bankruptcies, the rising incarceration of minors, the corporatization of prisons, and imprisonment rules that destroy the voting rights of working people and the poor. The United States, with the highest absolute and per capita incarceration rates in the world, provides one of the best examples today of how much this alignment can negate fairness. In various ways, the American judicial system has turned into an incarceration machine that is increasingly at the service of the most powerful interests in society.

Just governance would require the disengagement of the judicial system from oligopolistic corporate power—and its privileged elite. The legal artifact of corporate personhood would have to end, along with favoritism toward the corporate elite. Provision of voting rights for prisoners and the strengthening of employee rights in workplaces would be vital elements of just governance. The reinsertion in society of previously incarcerated individuals would have to be given great priority, through rehabilitation programs, to eliminate recidivism. At the same time, just governance would necessarily enlist the judicial system to redress the wrongs created by inequalities and the vast asymmetries in power that accompany corporatocracy. The judicial system would need to be enlisted to support a fundamental function of the state in advanced capitalism—providing social well-being for the disadvantaged commensurate with fairness and social justice. As with the other alignments, it can be expected that any attempt to change our current reality would face formidable opposition—not only from those within the system who seek to sustain it, but also from oligopolistic power and its privileged elite. Any remedial possibilities must also take the nature of capitalism into account. Remedies that are not accompanied by systemic changes within capitalism are unlikely to last. Returning to pre-corporatocratic, or pre-oligopolistic, times is no more realistic in regard to this alignment than the others. New forms of political, economic, and social organization must therefore be found that transcend capitalism, if an evolution toward greater justice is to occur.

Three *redistributive phenomena* at the core of the crisis of the state result from—and also sustain—the alignments discussed previously. They contribute greatly to the derailment of public governance that we witness, and their continuing dynamic poses an immense obstacle to just governance. All of these phenomena—addressed in various parts of this book—help define corporatocracy as a system that negates social justice. They involve dynamic processes that benefit the most powerful elements at the expense of the vast majority of the population, contributing greatly to the crisis of the state. These redistributive phenomena are therefore regressive, and represent a reversal of efforts to reduce social injustices within the framework of advanced capitalism.

The massive, long-term transfer of risk from oligopolistic corporations to the state damages its fiscal capacity and its obligation to ensure society's well-being. This phenomenon is a major contributor to crises, as it compromises the state's financial resources to benefit oligopolistic corporate power and its privileged elite—at the expense of the vast majority of the population. When crises occur, the people are forced to pay for damages inflicted by the risks transferred to the state—through cuts in services and benefits, greater economic insecurity, higher taxes, and an eroded standard of living. The state also has to incur greater long-term debt in such situations to cover its deficits, thus setting the stage for more crises down the line. This dynamic contradicts a fundamental neoliberal assumption, which posits that the state grows at the expense of the corporate sector. In corporatocracy, however, *the state grows in order to shoulder the risks that oligopolies transfer to it, and to support corporate power in general.*

This phenomenon is not mediated by any market. It is, rather, a result of the raw political power of corporate oligopolies, and in this sense it is outside the scope of market mechanisms. Markets, moreover, cannot rescue the state from the accumulation of risks and debt incurred to support oligopolistic power and its privileged elite. Much the opposite actually occurs, as markets severely punish the state—in the form of higher interest to be paid on its debt, credit rating downgrades, and a withdrawal of confidence when another crisis occurs. Most distressing is the fact that the financial and other corporate oligopolies that transfer much risk to the state are the greatest beneficiaries when crises strike—through the higher interest they charge the state to finance its debt and their speculative betting on that debt—which often increases the interest to be paid, along with the bailouts they receive. Thus, oligopolistic corporate power wins both ways, whether a fiscal crisis ensues or not. In the absence of a crisis, it wins by loading much risk on the state; when a crisis strikes, it wins by extracting greater obligations from the state. These obligations then place a greater burden on the state—in the form of guarantees, higher interest payments, greater debt, and deficits—along with the ever-present forms of corporate welfare, tax loopholes and other subsidies that benefit corporate power.

The long-term redistribution of wealth and power from the vast majority of the people toward oligopolistic corporate power—and its privileged elites— is a form of dispossession that negates the state's role as guarantor of societal well-being. The dispossession dynamic embedded in this phenomenon is a key aspect—and consequence—of corporatocratic governance. It contributes greatly to the crisis of the state in advanced capitalist societies, as both dispossession of the people and subservience to oligopolistic corporate power become purposes of governance. This phenomenon thus negates any notion of governance as a progressive vehicle to benefit society—depending greatly on a passive citizenry that is ignorant of its interests and unable to defend its social well-being. In this context, the public's lack of awareness is sustained through corporate propaganda, corporate-controlled media that exhorts everyone to hyper-consume and take up greater debt—while personal data is mined to pitch yet more advertisements and propaganda. The electioneering game of corporatocracy also supports this state of affairs, by overwhelming the public with political propaganda, and by channeling votes to politicians who either perpetuate the status quo or expand oligopolistic power. Public service that serves the public interest tends to be disparaged as a career possibility, and often ends up being characterized as a wasteful endeavor, fiscally and professionally—unless, of course, such service ends up switching to benefit corporate power.

The sustenance of this phenomenon—and of its corporatocratic under-pinnings—requires a state that neither provides the public with the means necessary to develop alternatives nor protects it against the deeper inequalities that result. In this regard, corporatocracy becomes authoritarian in charac-ter—fragmented and amorphous, but nonetheless authoritarian in deed and spirit. As the public's disengagement from governance deepens, the collective consciousness that makes people aware of their interests as social beings—and as a class or group—evaporates. Crises and the greater misery they bring might make some people aware of this panorama, but the possibilities of undertaking any effective action tend to be far-fetched and usually preserve the status quo. In the case of the United States, for example, the two-party political arrangement that in effect operates as a one-party system—in its sub-servience to oligopolistic power—has become practically impossible to change under existing laws. This de facto one-party arrangement is very important for oligopolistic power, as it makes it very easy to co-opt politicians (legally, of course)—compared to, say, other systems where coalitions of different political parties are needed to form governments. In those systems, co-opting or buying politicians (assuming legality) becomes more of a hedging game for corporate power—a complicated one, often—since there is some uncertainty in knowing a priori which parties would join a government, or the positions that some of their members would take up on corporate privileges.

The rise of a neo-oligarchy from the elites associated with oligopolistic power reflects the unjust and regressive nature of corporatocracy, as wealth and power become greatly concentrated. The emergence of the neo-oligarchy results largely from the previous two phenomena, and from the state's neglect of its function as guarantor of fairness and societal well-being. As it retreats from this fundamental role and becomes ever more subservient to oligopo-listic power, the stage is set for the enthronement of a minuscule—but extremely wealthy and powerful—elite. No class or groups within society may be able to stop this dynamic within the current context of advanced capitalism. Corporatocracy thus achieves one of its most important (and unjust) effects—the immense concentration of power and wealth among those who are ultimately in charge of its apparatus. The greater inequity associated with this phenomenon is also a negation of just governance that reflects the authoritarian character of corporatocracy—a character that is fragmented, multifaceted, difficult to grasp, and often even contradictory, but which shapes new realities.

Only a reconfiguration of the state to serve societal well-being may redress the effects of these redistributive phenomena. At the same time, efforts that can transcend the systemic reality imposed by capitalism must be considered. Ending the transfer of risk to the state is an urgent matter, which must work in concert with the breakup of corporate oligopolies noted earlier. The social function of the state must be redesigned, such that the interests of the public can be served and inequalities reduced. Efforts to address these phenomena would necessarily be multifaceted and involve major changes to government guarantees on debt that support corporate power, the tax system, and corporate welfare in all its numerous forms and guises, for example. Health care would also need to be part of any reconstitution of the state, to change the apparatus that perpetuates corporate control over this sector—one that typically places profits and market share, rather than health, as the uppermost priority. Education at all levels would have to be part of a move toward just governance, to recover it as a societal resource and place learning over profits. Just governance would also need to address employment, uphold employee rights, and enhance living standards for the vast majority—to reduce inequalities and reestablish a level of social justice.

Beyond the alignments and the redistributive phenomena, there are three major structural problems intrinsic to advanced capitalism, which also contribute greatly to the crisis of the state. These problems are part of the flawed nature of capitalist accumulation, but they are also associated with—and made worse by—the alignments and phenomena addressed previously. These structural problems may be more difficult to overcome than the alignments and the redistributive phenomena, since they are part of the very nature of capitalist accumulation. They must, nonetheless, be taken into account in any effort to understand the crisis of the state, and to transcend the systemic reality set by capitalism. Returning to precapitalist (or pre-oligopolistic) times to address these structural problems is also out of the question, as with the alignments and phenomena considered previously. Rather, a postcapitalist future must be envisioned—without utopian constructs—that can resolve their contradictions and pathologies.

The disengagement of finance from production negates a most important structural feature of capitalism and jeopardizes the fair functioning of the state. The linkage between production and finance has been a fundamental aspect of accumulation since capitalism's earliest days. This disengagement is a major source of dysfunction that has led to more frequent and deeper crises. As a defining characteristic of financialism, it has served as the foundation of the casino economy, with its unfettered speculation and the all-consuming obsession with paper profits—also setting the stage for the emergence of the neo-oligarchy. This disengagement—and its dysfunctions—contribute to the crisis of the state by increasing debt and deficits, promoting risk transfer from oligopolistic power, inducing greater guarantees and corporate welfare, and shortchanging fiscal resources.

The deregulation of finance, starting in the 1980s, turned this structural problem into a major dysfunction of contemporary advanced capitalism. Thereby, what had so far been a flaw of capitalist accumulation, kept under control through regulation, became a systemic problem—with almost unlimited potential to damage the state's fiscal functioning. Financial deregulation also helped open the gates to the oligopolization of most every sector, introducing new relations of power in society and governance. And it set the stage for the neoliberal offensive to align the interests of the public with those of oligopolistic corporate power—using financialism's plethora of speculative vehicles, unfettered betting, and boundless appetite for debt. This offensive, in turn, made it feasible for corporate power to disown its obligations to provide pensions, health care, and other employee benefits—contributing greatly to the economic insecurity of the vast majority of the population. An outcome of this dynamic was a deeper, long-term increase in inequality, as the state abandoned its obligation to sustain social justice.

The disengagement of reproduction from commodification in manufacturing and services production induces greater oligopolistic influence over the state and society. The linkage between reproduction and commodification has been fundamental to capitalism since its earliest days. This problem contradicts an essential feature of capitalist production—much as the disengagement of finance from production negates a fundamental aspect of accumulation. At the core of this structural problem is the overwhelming importance of intangibles in contemporary advanced capitalism. As discussed earlier, the reproduction of intangibles necessarily becomes more social—requiring societal mediation, which is largely outside corporate control—while commodification remains anchored within the corporate domain. The loss of internal control that this disengagement, or split, entails induces oligopolistic power to seek greater influence over public governance—as a way to safeguard its influence, reduce uncertainty, and sustain its surplus. From a broader perspective, this is also part of its omnipresent objective to make—and keep—public governance "safe" for oligopolistic power.

This structural problem contributes to the crisis of the state by making oligopolistic power more intrusive in the affairs of governance—increasing its subservience to its interests, while also shortchanging the state's fiscal obligations to society. Corporatocracy is a product of such influence. As a result, the state responds to the disengagement of reproduction from commodification *not* by providing the additional resources needed to educate or train the workforce—to bolster creativity and new knowledge—*or* by supporting employee rights and generating economic security, or by raising wages and creating employment to sustain the standard of living and reduce inequality. The corporatocratic state instead responds by creating tax loopholes and subsidies that mostly benefit oligopolistic control, by making debt easier to incur—while deregulating key aspects of the economy such that oligopolies become easier to form. Rather than helping those who provide the intangibles that are vital to production, the state instead favors oligopolistic power and its associated neo-oligarchy. As a consequence, production—the heart of the real economy—becomes more difficult to sustain. Financialist speculation, by contrast, becomes much easier to engage in—a situation that deepens the previously noted structural problem, finance becoming more disengaged from production.

The severance of reproduction from commodification also promotes the alignment of politicians' interests with those of oligopolistic power. Greater intrusion by oligopolies in the state's affairs furthers that alignment, as greater influence over governance serves to offset the loss of corporate control over reproduction. Such influence also furthers the alignment of the judicial system's interests with those of oligopolistic power. Leniency and favoritism in cases of corporate wrongdoing—along with selective enforcement or the scrapping of laws that protect employee rights—result in part from this structural problem. This combination of a systemic structural problem with alignments of interests that are detrimental to society compounds the crisis of the state and makes it all the more difficult to move toward just governance.

The oligopolistic overaccumulation of capital shortchanges growth and compounds the crisis of the state by promoting stagnation. Long-term stagnation—a product of overaccumulation—is largely grounded in oligopolistic control. As oligopolies grow and consolidate their power—eliminating price competition, throttling output, and creating entry barriers—productive investment possibilities decline. This dynamic helps set the stage for overaccumulation. Financialism compounded this structural problem as capital became easier to accumulate through speculation—central banks' monetary policies providing vast liquidity. The severance of finance from production—and of reproduction from commodification—helped as well, making speculation easier to engage in than production. The globalization of oligopolies also contributed—repatriated profits adding to overaccumulation. Corporatocratic governance deepened this structural problem by providing subsidies and diverse forms of corporate welfare, which fed overaccumulation through greater profitability. For the majority of the population, however, economic insecurity, downward mobility, high indebtedness, and an erosion of living standards generated greater distress. At the same time, the state found itself less capable of sustaining societal well-being. Thus, while capital overaccumulates—most of all, in the hands of the oligopolies—the state's fiscal resources diminish, as guarantees, tax loopholes, subsidies, bailouts, and diverse forms of corporate welfare are dedicated to support corporate power.

The transfer of risk from oligopolies to the state also contributed to its fiscal shortfall while promoting overaccumulation. Risk transfer made it easier for oligopolies to engage in risky schemes that generate more capital—and higher executive compensation—in the certainty that bailouts and corporate welfare would be forthcoming when crises arise. During periods of crisis the corporatocratic state, moreover, supports oligopolistic power—ensuring that overaccumulation can continue. At the same time, it cuts back its obligation to support the population and society at large. This unfortunate contrast became all too obvious during the economic crisis, as oligopolistic finance—and other favored oligopolies—received unprecedented amounts in government bailouts, while small and medium-size businesses were liquidated, unemployment rose, and the most disadvantaged saw their benefits cut or permanently dropped out of the labor force. Politicians, in turn, were rewarded by the oligopolies with unprecedented sums of money for their campaigns—as some of the vast hoards of capital were put to use—with the blessings of the judicial system. The alignment of the interests of politicians with those of oligopolistic corporate power made such actions easier to execute, thus joining the political system to the overaccumulation dynamic.

The political system's entwinement with this structural problem poses a formidable obstacle to any attempt to break up oligopolies. Policy measures that would be so targeted stand to be preempted, and are most certain to be rejected in a political system subservient to oligopolistic power. Yet it seems that only by breaking up the oligopolies might there be a chance of resolving overaccumulation—and the problem of stagnation. Breaking up the oligopolies—and their control over pricing and output, along with the entry barriers they create—however, would almost certainly diminish the paper profits generated by the betting economy of financialism. This would pose major difficulties to all entities that depend on speculation to survive.

So deeply has financialism reached into our institutions and daily lives that few areas are likely to be spared the impacts of an end to oligopolies. Yet, such an end seems inevitable and essential if we are to resolve the problem of overaccumulation and achieve a trajectory toward just governance. Transcending the systemic relations of power that accompany capitalism must also be given due consideration in this difficult panorama—as returning to pre-oligopolistic times seems deeply unrealistic, and would in any case fail to resolve the dynamic that allowed oligopolies to emerge.

This book has provided a critical overview of some of the most disturbing social phenomena of our time. At no prior time in history has corporate power—oligopolistic power, in particular—been as intrusive or influential as it is today. Never before has our governance been as subservient to oligopolistic corporate power as it is now. The fact that so few seem to be aware of what has been exposed here makes it all the more urgent to mobilize the public's attention on the need for change. Such awareness must necessarily start with a critical understanding of the phenomena involved, the dysfunctions and social pathologies they have created, and their systemic character. As the twenty-first century advances, these phenomena, their dysfunctions and pathologies, may deepen and pose a greater threat to our social well-being. The threat they already pose is around us, not only in the social alienation we experience in our daily lives, but also in their effects on nature, our health, our attitudes toward each other and society, and the way we perceive public governance. Systemic, rather than isolated, piecemeal solutions seem necessary if we are to overcome and redress their effects. Hopefully, this book will encourage us to view our reality critically, as we try to chart a trajectory toward greater justice in governance.

Index

academia, 6. *See also* higher education; neoclassical economics; neoliberal influence
academic journal publishing, 37–38. *See also* book publishing; oligopolies
accumulation. *See* capital over-accumulation; capitalist accumulation
acolyte class, 313–17. *See also* neo-oligarchy
Advanced Micro Devices, 290–91
advertising, 272–73. *See also* contrived demand
Affinion Group, 132–33. *See also* Citibank
agency theory, 204–205, 232–33, 310. *See also* alignment of interests
aggregate demand, 93, 224, 237, 245, 282. *See also* contrived demand; debt
agribusiness, 59–60. *See also* agro-biotech; food distribution; food production; oligopolies
agriculture. *See* agribusiness; food distribution; food production; oligopolies
agro-biotech: ecological impacts of oligopolies in, 60–61; intellectual property and oligopoly in, 289–90; oligopolistic power in, 59–61, 288–89. *See also* agribusiness; food distribution; food production; new technologies; oligopolies

AIG. *See* American International Group
air transportation: alliances and oligopolistic power in, 55–56; bankruptcy laws and, 57; geo-oligopolies and, 54–55; oligopolization of, 53–54; profits and oligopolistic power in, 57–58; working conditions and wages in, 56–57. *See also* oligopolies
aircraft. *See* commercial aircraft
airlines. *See* air transportation
alignment of interests: agency theory applications and, 204–205, 310; corporatocracy and, 205, 251–52, 293–94, 340–41; democratic governance and, 205; financialism and, 96–97, 119, 341–42; judicial system and, 331, 342–43, 348; neo-oligarchy and, 307–10, 331; politicians and, 204, 294, 332, 340–41; public interest and, 123–24, 203–204, 251–52, 293–94, 307–308, 332–35, 339–41; risk transfer to the state and, 310. *See also* oligopolies; political contributions; political influence; public interest; revolving door influence
Allergan, 24–26
alternative litigation funding, 116–17. *See also* casino culture; financialism
American Crossroads. *See* Crossroads GPS

organizations as, 75; super-PAC
organizations as, 65–68, 71–72, 303,
313, 321–22; trade associations as,
68–69, 85–86. *See also* alignment of
interests; corporatocracy; neoliberal
influence; political action committees; political contributions; political
influence; political insider intelligence; political lobbying; politicians;
revolving door influence
political power. *See* political influence
politicians, 3, 65–79, 80. *See also*
alignment of interests; corporatocracy; neoliberal influence; political
action committees; political contributions; political influence; political
insider intelligence; political lobbying; political organizations; revolving
door influence
price competition. *See* pricing power
price leadership. *See* pricing power
price-to-expectations ratio, 252–53. *See
also* Federal Reserve; financialism;
monetary policy
pricing power, 84–85, 258–68. *See also*
oligopolies
prisons: corporatization of, 329–31;
incarceration rates and, 327–28;
prison system and, 327–30; privatization of, 328–30; school-to-prison
pipeline, 329–30; sentencing and,
330–31. *See also* judicial system;
social justice
private equity. *See* hedge funds
privatization. *See* corporatocracy; neoliberal influence
production: accumulation and,
141–45, 188–202; commodification
and, 175–78, 188–95, 201–202;
disengagement and, 4, 138, 141–45,
180–81, 185–88, 346–47; finance
and, 4, 114, 141–43; financialism and, 103, 114, 138, 140–46;
offshoring of, 226–27; oligopolis-

tic surplus and, 142–44, 193–94;
reproduction and, 175–76, 180–81,
186–87, 189–202; severance of
finance from 4, 138, 141–45, 346–
47; speculation and, 103, 114, 138,
140–46; stagnation of industrial,
225–27. *See also* capitalist accumulation; commodification; disengagement; oligopolies; reproduction;
severance of finance from production; severance of reproduction from
commodification
public awareness, 3. *See also* news
media; social behavior; social class;
social identity
public governance. *See* alignment of
interests; corporatocracy; government
debt; government deficit; government regulation; judicial system;
neoliberal influence; political influence; public interest; risk transfer;
social justice
public interest: Federal Reserve and
the, 251–52; government debt and
the, 130–31; Lauderdale Paradox
and the, 332–35; Medicare and
the, 126–28; monetary policy and
the, 251–52; neo-oligarchy and the,
332, 336–37, 345–46; oligopolistic
power and the, 203–204, 251–52,
279–80, 293–94, 307–308, 340–42;
pensions and the, 123–25; risk
transfer and the, 128–30, 294,
343–44, 349–50; social justice and
the, 339–45; Social Security and
the, 125–26. *See also* alignment of
interests; corporatocracy; government
regulation; judicial system; neoliberal
influence; political influence; risk
transfer
public wealth, 334–36. *See also* Lauderdale Paradox
publishing. *See* academic journal publishing; media; news media

1

social justice *(continued)*
inequality and, 159–62, 172–74, 305, 334. *See also* corporatocracy; inequality; neoliberal influence; neo-oligarchy; social class; risk transfer; taxes
social legitimation, 199–200. *See also* reproduction; social mediation
social mediation, 176–77, 181–82, 184–85, 220–21. *See also* intangibles; networks; reproduction; severance of reproduction from commodification
Social Security, 125–26, 128, 298–301. *See also* entitlements; Medicare; pensions; social justice
software, 46–51, 272–73, 291–92. *See also* internet-based corporations; new technologies
speculation. *See* financial speculation
stagnation: agency theory and, 232–33; capital over-accumulation and, 4–5, 223–33, 244, 271–74, 284–86, 348–49; contrived demand and, 271–73; corporatocracy and, 223–24, 245–47, 264–65, 274–75, 293–94, 348–49; crises and, 87–88, 238, 274–77, 281–82; debt and 237–38, 245, 273, 281; demand and, 271–73, 282; disarticulation and, 226–27; economic insecurity and, 239–40; employment and, 226–27, 235; Federal Reserve and, 245–57; financialism and, 237–39, 244, 250–53, 280–81, 284–85, 348–49; fiscal crises and, 274–77; globalization and, 241–44, 256–57; gross domestic product and, 225; hedge funds and, 230; immigration and, 283–84; inequality and, 233–37, 249–50, 281; intangibles and, 272; investment and, 225–26, 228–33; Japan's, 225–26; labor costs

and, 224, 242–44; manufacturing and, 225–27; megabanks and, 253–56; middle class and, 235–37, 249–50; monetary policy and, 245–57; neoclassical economics and, 258–71; neoliberal influence and, 235, 276–84; new technologies and, 226–29, 273–74, 284–93; offshoring and, 226–27; oligopolies and, 4–5, 223–24, 239–41, 253–56, 269–70, 274, 281, 284–94; production and, 225–27; risk transfer and, 276; severance of finance from production and, 238–39, 247–48, 271; severance of reproduction from commodification and, 233, 238–39, 247–48, 271; short-term emphasis and, 230–33; social class and, 235–37, 249–50; taxes and, 227–28; United States's, 225–29; wages and, 227–28, 233–37; Western Europe's, 225–26. *See also* capital over-accumulation; Federal Reserve; financialism; inequality; social justice
stagnation trap, 274. *See also* Baran; Sweezy
Standard and Poor. *See* credit rating
Steindl, Josef, 270–71
stock market, 251–53. *See also* casino culture; financialism
strategies. *See* corporate strategies
structuring. *See* commodification
student debt. *See* debt
subprime lending. *See* debt
sugar, 62. *See also* agribusiness; oligopolies
super-PACs. *See* political action committees
Supreme Court. *See* U.S. Supreme Court
surplus capital. *See* capital over-accumulation
Sweezy, Paul, 80, 265–68, 270–71, 273–74, 279

systematization. *See* commodification
systemic risk, 3–4, 81–83, 129–30.
　See also financialism; oligopolies; risk
　transfer; too-big-to-fail corporations

takeovers. *See* hedge funds
tangible resources, 180–81, 189,
　190–91, 195–96. *See also* commodi-
　fication; production
TARP. *See* Troubled Asset Relief Pro-
　gram
tax breaks. *See* corporate tax breaks;
　taxes
taxes: capital over-accumulation
　and, 227–28; corporate, 73–75,
　101–102, 166–69, 227–28; debt
　and, 101–102; elites and, 74–75,
　101–102, 166–68, 298; executive
　compensation and, 74–75, 166–68;
　financialism and, 101–102, 166–69;
　inequality and, 74–75, 166–68,
　298; lobbying and, 73–75; loop-
　holes in, 74–75, 101–102, 298;
　neo-oligarchy and, 298; oligopolies
　and, 73–75, 101–102, 166–69,
　227–28; social justice and, 74–75,
　101–102, 166–69, 298; stagnation
　and, 227–28; subsidies in, 73–75,
　101–102, 298. *See also* corporate tax
　breaks; corporate welfare; corporato-
　cracy; inequality
Taxpayers Against Earmarks, 303
Taylor, Frederick, 180–81
teardown schemes. *See* reverse engi-
　neering
technology. *See* corporate research; new
　technologies
telecommunications. *See* internet ser-
　vice; oligopolies; telephone service;
　wireless telecommunications
telephone service, 39–43. *See also*
　internet service; oligopolies
television. *See* cable television

theft. *See* corporate espionage; intel-
　lectual property; reverse engineering;
　second-mover schemes
think-tanks, 301–302, 316–19. *See also*
　neoliberal influence; neo-oligarchy
3G Capital, 135–36. *See also* hedge
　funds
too-big-to-fail corporations: bailouts
　and, 86, 152, 154, 255–56; Dodd-
　Frank legislation and, 149–55;
　executive compensation in, 164–67;
　Federal Reserve and, 152–53,
　254–55; financialism and, 109–10,
　148–49; Glass-Steagall Act repeal
　and, 76–77; government debt
　guarantees and, 69–76; megabanks
　as, 12, 76–77, 149–52; oligopolies
　as, 76–77, 86, 109–10, 148–49;
　risk transfer and, 147–55. *See also*
　antitrust regulation; financial deregu-
　lation; financialism; government
　regulation; megabanks; risk transfer;
　oligopolies; systemic risk
Treasury Department. *See* U.S.
　Treasury Department
Tribune Co., 33–34. *See also* news
　media
Troubled Asset Relief Program, 255–56

U.S. Chamber of Commerce, 75
U.S. Congress, 43, 69–73, 100–101,
　118. *See also* political influence;
　political lobbying
U.S. Department of Health and
　Human Services, 23–24
U.S. Federal Reserve Bank. *See* Federal
　Reserve
U.S. Securities and Exchange Com-
　mission. *See* Securities and Exchange
　Commission
U.S. Senate Banking Committee,
　100–101. *See also* political influence;
　U.S. Congress